Dynamic Strategic Thinking for Improved Competitiveness and Performance

Georgette Andraz
CEFAGE, University of Algarve, Portugal

Helder Carrasqueira
University of Algarve, Portugal & CiTUR, Portugal

Rosaria Pereira
CiTUR, Portugal & University of Algarve, Portugal

Rita Baleiro
University of Algarve, Portugal & CiTUR, Portugal

A volume in the Advances in Business Strategy and Competitive Advantage (ABSCA) Book Series

IGI Global
PUBLISHER of TIMELY KNOWLEDGE

Published in the United States of America by
IGI Global
Business Science Reference (an imprint of IGI Global)
701 E. Chocolate Avenue
Hershey PA, USA 17033
Tel: 717-533-8845
Fax: 717-533-8661
E-mail: cust@igi-global.com
Web site: http://www.igi-global.com

Library of Congress Cataloging-in-Publication Data

Names: Andraz, Georgette, 1962- editor. | Carrasqueira, Helder, 1963- editor. | Pereira, Rosaria, 1970- editor.
Title: Dynamic strategic thinking for improved competitiveness and performance / Georgette Andraz, Helder Carrasqueira, Rosaria Pereira, and Rita Baleiro, editors.
Description: Hershey : Business Science Reference, 2020. | Includes bibliographical references and index. | Summary: "This book explores innovative methods organizations have implemented in order to improve their overall effectiveness. This book analyzes novel strategies companies are using to adjust and respond to modern challenges including globalization and digitization"-- Provided by publisher.
Identifiers: LCCN 2020000250 (print) | LCCN 2020000251 (ebook) | ISBN 9781799845522 (hardcover) | ISBN 9781799852346 (paperback) | ISBN 9781799845539 (ebook)
Subjects: LCSH: Strategic planning. | Business enterprises--Communication systems--Management. | Information technology--Management. | Organizational effectiveness.
Classification: LCC HD30.28 .D928 2020 (print) | LCC HD30.28 (ebook) | DDC 658.4/012--dc23
LC record available at https://lccn.loc.gov/2020000250
LC ebook record available at https://lccn.loc.gov/2020000251

This book is published in the IGI Global book series Advances in Business Strategy and Competitive Advantage (ABSCA) (ISSN: 2327-3429; eISSN: 2327-3437)

British Cataloguing in Publication Data
A Cataloguing in Publication record for this book is available from the British Library.

For electronic access to this publication, please contact: eresources@igi-global.com.

Advances in Business Strategy and Competitive Advantage (ABSCA) Book Series

ISSN:2327-3429
EISSN:2327-3437

Editor-in-Chief: *Patricia Ordóñez de Pablos* Universidad de Oviedo, Spain

MISSION

Business entities are constantly seeking new ways through which to gain advantage over their competitors and strengthen their position within the business environment. With competition at an all-time high due to technological advancements allowing for competition on a global scale, firms continue to seek new ways through which to improve and strengthen their business processes, procedures, and profitability.

The **Advances in Business Strategy and Competitive Advantage (ABSCA) Book Series** is a timely series responding to the high demand for state-of-the-art research on how business strategies are created, implemented and re-designed to meet the demands of globalized competitive markets. With a focus on local and global challenges, business opportunities and the needs of society, the **ABSCA** encourages scientific discourse on doing business and managing information technologies for the creation of sustainable competitive advantage.

COVERAGE

- Innovation Strategy
- Core Competencies
- International Business Strategy
- Globalization
- Small and Medium Enterprises
- Adaptive Enterprise
- Economies of Scale
- Strategic Management
- Value Creation
- Value Chain

IGI Global is currently accepting manuscripts for publication within this series. To submit a proposal for a volume in this series, please contact our Acquisition Editors at Acquisitions@igi-global.com or visit: http://www.igi-global.com/publish/.

The Advances in Business Strategy and Competitive Advantage (ABSCA) Book Series (ISSN 2327-3429) is published by IGI Global, 701 E. Chocolate Avenue, Hershey, PA 17033-1240, USA, www.igi-global.com. This series is composed of titles available for purchase individually; each title is edited to be contextually exclusive from any other title within the series. For pricing and ordering information please visit http://www.igi-global.com/book-series/advances-business-strategy-competitive-advantage/73672. Postmaster: Send all address changes to above address.

Titles in this Series

For a list of additional titles in this series, please visit:
http://www.igi-global.com/book-series/advances-business-strategy-competitive-advantage/73672

Transformation of Strategic Alliances in Emerging Markets
Desalegn Abraha Gebrekidan (University of Skove, Sweden) and Akmal S. Hyder (University of Gavle, Sweden)
Business Science Reference • © 2020 • 315pp • H/C (ISBN: 9781799826606) • US $195.00

Qualitative Exploration of Grounded Theory in Organizational Research
Maryam Ebrahimi (Independent Researcher, Germany)
Business Science Reference • © 2020 • 251pp • H/C (ISBN: 9781799842521) • US $195.00

Principles and Practices of Small-Scale Sport Event Management
Anestis Fotiadis (Zayed University, UAE) and Chris Vassiliadis (University of Macedonia, Greece)
Business Science Reference • © 2020 • 335pp • H/C (ISBN: 9781799847571) • US $215.00

Entrepreneurial Innovation for Securing Long-Term Growth in a Short-Term Economy
Jorge Gamez-Gutierrez (Universitaria Agustiniana, Colombia) and Jose Manuel Saiz-Alvarez (Tecnologico de Monterrey, Spain)
Business Science Reference • © 2020 • 300pp • H/C (ISBN: 9781799835684) • US $215.00

Handbook of Research on Transmedia Storytelling, Audience Engagement, and Business Strategies
Víctor Hernández-Santaolalla (University of Seville, Spain) and Mónica Barrientos-Bueno (University of Seville, Spain)
Business Science Reference • © 2020 • 457pp • H/C (ISBN: 9781799831198) • US $265.00

Developing Creative Economy Through Disruptive Leadership Emerging Research and Opportunities
Kristin Joyce Tardif (University of Arkansas – Fort Smith, USA)
Business Science Reference • © 2020 • 226pp • H/C (ISBN: 9781799834168) • US $185.00

For an entire list of titles in this series, please visit:
http://www.igi-global.com/book-series/advances-business-strategy-competitive-advantage/73672

IGI Global
PUBLISHER of TIMELY KNOWLEDGE

701 East Chocolate Avenue, Hershey, PA 17033, USA
Tel: 717-533-8845 x100 • Fax: 717-533-8661
E-Mail: cust@igi-global.com • www.igi-global.com

Editorial Advisory Board

Table of Contents

Detailed Table of Contents

To survive and remain competitive in a constantly changing environment, companies need to develop adaptive capabilities, that is, to become more resilient. Some authors argue that including young employees in the company's decision-making process contributes to enhance their organizational resilience. The present study aims to further investigate this assumption through a case study approach. To this end, 18 Generation Z Business Administration students form several European countries were familiarized with the processes of a luxury goods company and requested to propose solutions to five real challenges that affect the segment. In the presented solutions, they showed potential to enhance each of the dimensions of resilience according to the main conceptualizations of the subject. The findings suggest that companies should invest in attracting, training, and empowering young talents to make decisions in order to enhance their resilience capacity. Future studies should further investigate the topic through explanatory approaches in order to reach a more reliable understanding.

The purpose of this chapter is to identify and analyze the main organizational and technological factors that play a relevant role in a transformational strategic change inherent in changing the business model supported on the internet. An analysis was made of the different business models, as well as their connection to strategic management and how this is accomplished in the organizational and technological plan. This empirical study, based on the qualitative methodology, focuses on a single case study on a Portuguese company that recently changed its business model. The findings allowed the authors to assess the advantages and challenges posed by the transformation of an initial business based on a website that performs a comparison of prices for an integrated model based on a marketplace, in which customers can make their purchases and access all products, from different stores, in one place.

Financial technology companies (fintechs) have gained tremendous importance in the last decade and particularly in the last four years. They have contributed with disruptive technological solutions and provided not only complementary but also substitute products to the traditional banking sector. New incumbents have been challenging banks already established and forced them to innovate in order to remain competitive. Indeed, banks have a heavy burden of slow processes, costly business models, and few innovative solutions. The authors collected 100 articles from Scopus related with the fintech and bank topics. This study adopted a hybrid design comprising a systematic qualitative review methods and narrative, supplemented by semantic network analysis. Based on the results of the systematic literature review, the authors explored the impacts that fintechs have had on traditional banking sector.

This chapter presents a competitive framework suggesting a circular perspective in analyzing and managing competitive wars in a hyper-competitive and hyper-connected world. The author uses the expression "competitive cycles" to represent a typical journey of a competitive arena. The journey starts with the status quo, characterized by a direct confrontation on specific success factors (War of Position); eventually, this scenario is disrupted by the game-changing strategy of an insurgent (War of Movement). This leads to the next stage of the journey, the War of Imitation, ending up when the new game finally becomes the new status quo, that is, back to the War of Position. Then everything flows, until a new cycle, with its new rules, will start again. The digital tsunami is adding momentum and clock-speed to competitive cycles. In every moment of a firm's life, then, it is vitally important to be fully aware of its different wars. In fact, behind each of them lies distinctive rationales and dynamics, which call for specific strategic approaches.

We live on a finite planet with scarce resources, which entails major challenges such as the depletion of natural resources, the ecological footprint, and climate change. However, in the continued growth of global economy, the majority of companies' strategies and business models move away from sustainability while facing a big paradox: on one side, companies focus on economic development encouraging consumption, but on the other side, companies could play a key role in environmental issues, enhancing more sustainable consumption patterns. In this context, some companies have adopted marketing strategies that focus on turning garbage into value, as a way to tackle one of the major environmental issues. In this chapter, some of these companies and their marketing strategies are examined through a multiple case analysis. The main purpose of this chapter is to show that some companies are addressing one major environmental issue by turning garbage into value.

The concept of digital transformation (DT) has reached a heightened demand level on the executives' agenda, especially when it is related to elements that influence the development and activities of contemporary firms being prevalent in discussions about industrial and social changes. This theme leads the authors to reflect on the key strategic drivers used by firms to carry out the qualitative process (prior experience) of digital business transformation. It reinforces the purpose of understanding the key strategic drivers used by firms in recent years to guide the digital business transformation process. The systematic literature review was performed in the "WoS database," according to Boolean logic, aiming to capture the essential properties of the logical operators and sets of statements about the theme presented to compose the study. The results indicate a higher frequency for the big data and digitization drivers, followed by the innovation driver within the analyzed period.

Grounding in the socioemotional wealth approach, this chapter explores the effect of family influence on long-term performance. Moreover, this study also examines the moderating role of the bargaining power of vertical parties, namely supplier (SBP) and customer (CBP) bargaining power, on the preceding relationship. By utilising a panel dataset of 3,118 observations of Spanish private manufacturing firms in the 2007–2016 period, the chapter finds that family influence negatively impacts long-term performance. The findings also reveal that CBP mitigates the negative effect of family influence on long-term performance. In this light, CBP is found to be a potential environmental factor that enables family influenced firms enhancing their long-term performance.

The globalization of the economy, the evolution of technology, and the increasing level of competition have imposed constant change to companies, namely on the continuous improvement of their functioning and organization, in the permanent updating of their products, and in the attitude towards the satisfaction of their customers. This pressure for change has led to the emergence of new approaches and management methods. One of these new approaches, called value management, is based on the concept of value, which translates a relationship between the satisfaction of a product or service and the resources necessary for its execution. This study presents the main tools for monitoring performance, highlighting the most expressive indicators of business performance. Before, however, brief reflection will be made on management oriented towards value creation.

Preface

In times of change, of rapid technological transformation and new business models, it is crucial to count on the work of researchers to help understand the emergent corporate challenges. Therefore, the purpose of this book is to share knowledge, perspectives, and strategic guidelines, with a view to contributing to the improvement of companies' strategic positioning in this ever-changing market.

Our aim was to gather academic research from several parts of the world, with different objects of analysis and approaches. In the end, and after going through the different stages of reviewing and editing, we selected these eleven chapters. Before moving on to presenting them, we will briefly consider the context that led us into this editorial project.

The main purpose of strategic management is to develop a business model that allows the organization to ensure its existence and its competitive development. Until the mid-1970s, this role was rather predictable, because, although a new cycle was starting, there were still many business decisions based on the historical knowledge of society and on the post-war electro-mechanical and analogical technology (a cycle of about 30/35 years). However, the seed of the great transformation that marks current socio-economic developments was already underway: the information and communication technologies.

In the 1980s, the change to a digital model of organization was ongoing, with the implementation of the 2G network. The era of information management based on personal computer and mobile phone communication advanced, paving the way for remote connection and control. In the same decade, there was an increase in flexible production, often involving other companies through *outsourcing* and accelerating logistics processes of *just in time* supply, aiming to ensure in real time the current stocks for each operation. The worker was then asked to process information, and automation was increasing. Meanwhile, the so-called generation Y or millennial was being born, and the level of consumer demand was increasing.

For the decision-maker, who must ponder strategic positioning to maintain competitiveness in the market and add value to *the stakeholders,* the puzzle became more complex. However, the best part was still to come, at the beginning of the

90s, with three remarkable events: a political - the fall of the Berlin Wall - and two technological - the invention of the Internet and the implementation of the 3G network. Since then, there has been an unparalleled transformation, with new actors in the business scenario and a refocus of the protagonists of the new economy.

Globalization involves an open economy on a global scale, with free movement of people, goods, companies, and capital in almost all countries. The Internet connects everything to everyone, enabling a homogenization of consumers, their tastes, and customs. Increased productivity and reduced costs lead to a relocation of industrial capacity to Asian countries, benefiting from the global supply chain. Physical work is performed by machines, with increasing robotization; mental work is shifted to the computer and for human beings, the imperative is to be creative and to constantly innovate. International means of payment are implemented and there is more security within the travel industry, because of *yield management* techniques, that enhanced the emergence of low-cost airlines. The services/tourism sector increases together with a growing productive specialization of the European countries. The entertainment industry, including the digital games, proliferates. Consumers are increasingly more informed, environmentally concerned, and active participants in critical product evaluation, who are eager to spin on consumption. It becomes clear that the phases of the product life cycle are shortening.

If at the beginning of the 1980s the puzzle of the strategic decision maker had 1000 pieces, in the 1990s it had 5000 pieces, and the multiplication of the analysis factors stood out, with the consequent complexity and positioning decision (adaptation or rupture). The business world ceased to be a crossroad, in which companies had to choose one of the paths, and it became a roundabout, with multiple exits, where information and communication technologies stood in the center. At this stage, a cycle of 20/25 years (between 1980 and 2005) was close to an end, exhausting the potential of the technology in force at the time. From the year 2000, a generation of digital natives was born: the so-called generation Z.

By 2006 the seeds of the new impulse had already been sown and soon two digital icons would become a reality: platform companies and smartphones. In between, a black swan – the financial economic crisis of 2007 –, a global event resulting from the low interest rates that sought to keep an unviable post-war business model. The genesis of this crisis was the exploration of financing models (credit) only possible in a digital environment. As a result, there were massive interventions by central banks and the consequent increase in global indebtedness, closure of multiple companies that failed to adapt to the new economy (discontinuity) or companies that were acquired by Asian capital, given the financial strength of the "factory of the world".

During this time, platform companies and smartphones lacked a technological breakthrough to expand their full potential, that would only occur with the 4G network in 2011. Platform companies operate in *cloud computing,* and process huge amounts of data. As a rule, they do not have physical assets or tangible products of their own; they promote a multilateral value chain in which producers and consumers interact in the search for the optimal decision to buy/sell. Everything is amplified by the fact that consumers and other *stakeholders* are permanently connected via smartphones, which has an impact on relationships and forms of consumption. The consumers' evaluation feedback generates value for both parties and the price is dynamic and guided by artificial intelligence, which adapts products to meet the needs. Platform companies eliminate intermediaries, promote efficiency, and part-time and mobile jobs. They are disruptive.

As if all this was not fascinating enough to elevate the philosophical spirit or to scare the ordinary citizens who have to keep their jobs, pay for their houses, and raise their children, a new business mindset is placed on the table: the sharing economy. This proposal meets the behaviour and lifestyle of the millennial generation (and it will be continued by generation z), which does not favor the ownership of the product, but the experience of that product. Therefore, they ask themselves: why should I buy a car if I can share one with other users? Why should I pay for standard, expensive accommodation in a given city if I only wish to spend the night in a clean room? Why should I buy garden appliances if I just need them for 20 days in a year? In this context, several companies can, through platforms, connect the product holder to potential users. The paradigm changed from selling products to selling services.

Other examples could be presented here, however, the above already describes how disruptive platform organizations and the sharing economy are. We consider that this is a cycle that extended from 2006 up to 2019 (thirteen years), which proves the decrease in the duration of cycles led by the dynamics of the digital environment and innovation based on the information and communication technologies.

At this stage, regarding the strategic decision-maker's positioning, words become hard to find. The puzzle will now have 10000 pieces and the roundabout of decisions is now full of traffic seeking to find digital exits. In this tumultuous environment, what is the way out? Our suggestion is to look at the analyses offered by the researchers whose work is published in this book.

- **Young Ideas to Improve Organizational Resilience in Turbulent and Changing Environments:** The authors seek to investigate whether including young employees in the company's decision-making process contributes to increasing their organizational resilience. In fact, in an ever-changing environment, companies are challenged to adapt their products/services to the needs and preferences of new generation of customers. Following a similar Problem Based Learning methodology, 18 generation Z business administration students analyzed issues and offered solutions to four real challenges affecting the luxury goods segment. The solutions presented have shown that companies should invest in attracting, training and empowering young talents to make decisions in order to enhance their resilience capacity.

- **Exploring the Organizational and Technological Implications on Strategic Business Model Change – A Case Study of One Electronic Marketplace:** this chapter summarizes and compares different concepts and definitions of business models. The study investigates how these models, namely those online, relate to strategic management and how they are explored at the organizational and technological level. The chapter further analyses the transformation of a company that adopted an integrated business model supported on the Internet, namely the dimensions of context, diagnosis, evaluation and strategy. The authors also identify the critical success factors and the path taken in the digital arena for the current positioning.
- **Digital Business Transformation in the Banking Sector:** The rapid evolution of the so-called fintech companies (mostly startups that work with the objective of innovating and improving the financial system), developed on the digital model, challenge the traditional relationship between banks and their customers. In this context, the authors seek to answer the question: What insights does the current literature offer regarding the impact of fintechs in the banking sector? The investigation concluded that fintechs are clearly reshaping the traditional market of financial services by offering digital solutions and customer centric products. Traditional institutions are adapting to this new reality and are adopting technological solutions to remain competitive. This is an ongoing duel, and, in the future, we will see if the adaptation of traditional banking will prevail or if there will be disruptions in the relationship between customers and banks, through technological channels.
- **Competitive Cycles in a Hyper-Connected World – Everything Flows:** A competitive cycle originates from an industry's *status quo*, which is characterized by a direct confrontation over specific success factors: these are the winning weapons at any given time. Later, however, the status quo will be disrupted by a game-changing strategy by an insurgent (innovative) company that may be an existing player or an outsider. If the Movement is successful, then the industry will move on to the third phase of a competitive cycle (imitation). Eventually, the company's circular journey will be completed when the new disruptive game becomes the new status quo: everything flows, until a new cycle, with its new rules, will resume. The author offers an analysis of competitive cycles and forms of positioning, discussing the evolution of the digital tsunami and its impact on business.

- **Creating Value From Garbage – A Marketing and Circular Economy Strategy for Sustainability:** We live on a finite planet with scarce resources, which entails major challenges such as the depletion of natural resources, the ecological footprint or climate change. However, in the ongoing growth of the global economy, most business strategies and models of companies move away from sustainability, facing a great paradox: on the one hand, companies focus on economic development by encouraging consumption; but, on the other hand, companies can play a key role in environmental issues by enhancing more sustainable consumption patterns. In this context, some companies adopt marketing strategies that focus on transforming waste into value, as to address one of the main environmental issues. This chapter brings forward examples of companies that are taking this approach.
- **Key Strategic Drivers for Business Digital Transformation – Systematic Literature Review:** The authors seek to answer the question "what are the key strategic drivers used by firms to carry out the qualitative process (prior experience) of digital business transformation?" by conducting a systematic literature review on the topics of business, digital transformation, and strategic drivers. They concluded that digitization and big data drivers, as well as innovation, are the most frequently used in the digital transformation process. The qualitative process as well as previous experiences underlying the digital business transformation are performed in two different stages. The first is the technological approach, and it includes processes and technologies for gathering data, information analysis and business decision making. The second includes a behavioral approach based on organizational values and social and corporate responsibility.
- **Does the Bargaining Power of Vertical Parties Improve or Worsen the Effect of Family Influence on Long-Term Performance? A Socioemotional Wealth View:** With this study on the interaction between family influence and company performance, the authors make three major contributions. First, they fill a gap in the literature by exploring the interaction between family influence and long-term performance, providing a better understanding of this relationship. Second, they examine the moderating effect of the bargaining power of suppliers, and customers, which are contingent variables that help clarify the interaction of the family with the company's performance. Third, they investigate private companies, which are underrepresented in previous research, despite prevailing and playing a significant role in economies worldwide. This chapter offers a timely analysis and reflection, if we consider the large number of family businesses and the strategic management challenges that they often.

- **Business Performance Valuation and Value Creation:** Value management is based on the concept of value, which translates a relationship between the satisfaction of a product or service and the resources needed for its performance. Currently, this relationship is a key factor and of the utmost importance for the survival of companies, their monitoring and permanent control. The context in which the measurement of business performance is carried out is changing as well as the approaches used for its evaluation, which try to overcome the limitations of more traditional approaches, focused essentially on accounting indicators or financial results. Given the complexity of the business reality, the authors present several performance measurements instruments and report that flexibility and the use of performance and efficiency evaluation models based on multiple factors are necessary.
- **Business Policy – A Systems Approach to Corporate Governing:** The purpose of this chapter is to explore improvements in existing corporate governing practices that are currently being implemented through methods that lag behind most of the recent developments in computer science. The authors suggest taking on board systems modeling by adopting a computer-assisted policy design based on system dynamics simulators. Implementing a system thinking approach to business organizations allows the designing of virtuous strategies by simulating organizational behavior. Besides, this approach may also help to mitigate unintended consequences, like risks and outcomes which may surprise the firms, particularly from the perspective of the management board. This study brings together recent developments in the fields of business policy, systems thinking and computer-assisted policy design.
- **Systematic Literature Review on Global Strategy – Mapping Trends and Gaps:** The global economy changed the way products and services are exchanged and it also reminded organizations' managers of the need to find new ways to achieve competitive advantage and define strategies to operate in the global market. Thus, this chapter aims to perform a systematic literature review to identify the main theoretical topics of global strategy over the past 43 years using bibliometric analysis. The results allow to identify and cluster five main trends: cluster 1 (firm performance in the global market); cluster 2 (power and market share development); cluster 3 (government regulation, government and regulation); cluster 4 (economic cycles); and cluster 5 (societal changes). Findings also revealed eventual gaps in global strategy regarding the topics of entrepreneurship, competitive strategy, capitalism, transitions, climate change, law, portfolio, financial performance, global sourcing, and global value chain.

- **Improved Global Competitiveness on the Basis of New Business Models Influenced by Dynamic Strategic Thinking:** The key task of strategic management is to create a business model that consists of a unique combination of programs, sales conditions, distribution channels, and market communication, in order to create value (benefit) for target customers in a competitive environment. This will allow the company to achieve its fundamental goal and, indirectly, the goals of the organization's participants. Innovation, based on dynamic strategic thinking, is aimed at looking for organizational forms and features. Business models are necessary to maintain or increase existing competitive advantages in today's global market, and they can be modified through revolutionary or evolutionary methods based on digital transformation and knowledge management. Various studies about companies in trouble suggest that there is still a gap between the declared need to introduce and improve existing business models and the actual change in business practice.

These texts provide several lessons, from practical and theoretical points of view. Lessons which are valuable in a time of vertiginous change, when we are confronted by a surprising capacity for innovation and advancement of knowledge, on the one hand, and expectation for the future, on the other hand, both as business decision-makers and as citizens.

To sum it up, this preface is being written during the coronavirus pandemic: an extraordinary and unique event (we hope), that fits the profile of a "black swan", taking into account that in the Western world production has almost come to a stop. What will its impact be? What will the economy be like in the post-pandemic stage? We do not know, and we do not dare to guess. However, regardless of what the future will bring, the 5G communication network cycle is well on the way, and we believe the ICT and the digital will continue to be in the center of the roundabout, both in the corporate world and in our lives. Just as we believe that environmental sustainability is the new energy paradigm and an increasingly relevant factor in the strategic matrix of companies.

We hope you enjoy this book.

Helder Carrasqueira
University of Algarve, Portugal & CiTUR, Portugal
Translation by Rita Baleiro & Rosária Pereira (coeditors)

Chapter 1
Young Ideas to Improve Organizational Resilience in Turbulent and Changing Environments

Diego R. Toubes
https://orcid.org/0000-0001-7017-6659
University of Vigo, Spain

Noelia Araújo-Vila
https://orcid.org/0000-0002-3395-8536
University of Vigo, Spain

Arthur Filipe de Araújo
Lusófona do Porto University, Portugal

ABSTRACT

To survive and remain competitive in a constantly changing environment, companies need to develop adaptive capabilities, that is, to become more resilient. Some authors argue that including young employees in the company's decision-making process contributes to enhance their organizational resilience. The present study aims to further investigate this assumption through a case study approach. To this end, 18 Generation Z Business Administration students form several European countries were familiarized with the processes of a luxury goods company and requested to propose solutions to five real challenges that affect the segment. In the presented solutions, they showed potential to enhance each of the dimensions of resilience according to the main conceptualizations of the subject. The findings suggest that

DOI: 10.4018/978-1-7998-4552-2.ch001

companies should invest in attracting, training, and empowering young talents to make decisions in order to enhance their resilience capacity. Future studies should further investigate the topic through explanatory approaches in order to reach a more reliable understanding.

INTRODUCTION

Change is the defining element of current business reality. Organizations operate in increasingly dynamic global markets, and their interconnected nature leads to inequalities and risky spatial dynamics (Fischbacher-Smith & Smith, 2015). In these turbulent periods, organizations experience disruptions that present several threats to their long-term survival (Burnard & Bhamra, 2011). In this context, traditional strategic planning models, characterized by market predictability, which were perfectly adequate in a not so distant past, are no longer effective. Instead, companies must continually strive to adapt their strategies to different requirements, intense competition and rapid changes in consumers' tastes. Therefore, flexibility and continuous adaptation are the key elements for successfully achieving organizational objectives (Hamel & Välikangas, 2003), that is, to survive and prosper in a changing and unpredictable environment.

Lengnick-Hall and Beck (2016) argue that resilience capacity favors companies' agility and ability to recognize the need for adapting to changing environmental conditions. In the context of engineering, for instance, a system's resilience can be enhanced by increasing its ability to quickly adapt to new situations that might arise (Dalziell & McManus, 2004). Under disruptive conditions and drastic changes, resilient organizations manage to maintain positive adjustments (Dahles & Susilowati, 2015; Sutcliffe & Vogus, 2003), which in turn, enable them to survive and achieve their objectives. However, developing agile business models that can adapt quickly in dynamic environments is a challenging task. On many occasions, companies' formal structures and their employees' refusal to change make them inflexible and unable to the take decisions on time (Smith, Binns, & Tushman, 2010). In these instances, companies are more likely to carry out poor strategies that are disconnected from reality, leading to equally poor results, which can potentially force them out of business.

The addressed contributions show that organizational resilience is essential to respond to the inevitable and continuous changes that characterize current business environments. In this context, it is important to know what make companies more resilient, so that managers can cultivate these traits in order to make their organizations more adaptable and competitive. Although the subject of resilience has received increasing academic attention since the early 2000's (Hamel & Välikangas, 2003; Jamrog et al., 2006), the concept is normally seen as an outcome, which emerges when individuals and organizations perform well and manage to bounce back from disruptive situations (Duchek, 2014). Meanwhile, the process of organizational resilience – and most of all, the factors that contribute to it – are still largely unexplored. Several authors believe that resilience capacity is favored by having young employees in executive positions and including them in the company's decision-making process. Boschma and Groen (2010), for instance, believe that the so-called neo-digital natives, or Generation Z, are not "programmed" to follow traditional managing methods, and therefore, are more open to changes and new ways of planning and executing strategies. In this context, empowering them to make strategic decisions may favor the adoption of counter-intuitive or unconventional measures, which in turn, might help develop the company's resilience capacity. These arguments are in line with those from Hamel and Välikangas (2003) and Stoltz (2004), and imply that younger generations are better suited to provide intuitive solutions that are adequate to the current the business reality.

The present chapter addresses this assumption through a case study in a luxury goods company, as according to Deloitte (2019), these companies are increasingly interested in the younger segments of the population. Moreover, the incorporation of the new generation as part of their target has led to a series of challenges, mostly due to the world view of this public, which in some instances, is in conflict with some of the essential characteristics of the industry. In this vein, we through it would be interesting to verify how luxury goods company might deal with challenges brought about by their expansion to the Generation Z market by adopting ideas from employees of this same segment. To this end, a group of 18 Generation Z international Business Administration students from a varied set of European countries was familiarized with the company's strategy and processes through a visit to its headquarters and meetings with department managers. Then, they were requested to present solutions to four key-challenges that currently affect companies in the luxury goods market. The solutions proposed by the students reflect some of the literature regarding the dimensions and capabilities of resilient organizations, showing that they do have the potential to make companies more resilient.

The present chapter includes five sections. The next two sections present a literature review on the main topics related to the study: environmental change, organizational resilience and the potential contribution of young ideas to the latter. Then, in the methodology section, the case study is addressed in detail. In the following section, the main results are described and some of the segments of students' responses that best illustrate the addressed topic are reproduced. Next, these results are examined in light of the extant literature on the topic, especially of two conceptualizations that were adopted as the main frameworks for the analysis. Finally, in the conclusion, the relevance of the results for the literature and for practitioners is highlighted, the limitations are pointed out and suggestions for future studies are made.

ENVIRONMENTAL CHANGE AND ORGANIZATIONAL RESILIENCE

Organizations are open systems, that is, they interact with their surroundings in multiple ways (Scott, 2003). Companies' surroundings provide resources and opportunities, but also impose restrictions and situations to which they must adapt (Ferreira, Serra & Reis, 2011). For example, many studies have described the challenges involved in making business in emerging markets (Hoskisson, Eden, Lau, & Wright, 2000; Landau, Karna & Sailer, 2016; Xu & Meyer, 2013). Khana and Palepu (2010), for instance, observe that consumers' needs and behaviors in emerging markets are different from those in developed ones. In this context, these markets present risks that challenge the effectiveness of business models originally designed to be applied in developed countries. This forces companies to innovate and adapt (Landau et al., 2016) in order to achieve results that are compatible with those they achieve in their original markets.

In addition to different business environments, companies also need to adapt to sudden changes in the environments in which they operate (Miller, 1992; Weick & Sutcliffe, 2001). Changes caused by sudden variations in demand, strikes or economic crises, for instance, tend to lead to interruptions in the company's activities. Therefore, organizations need to develop adaptation mechanisms (Kovoor-Misra, Zammuto & Mitroff, 2000) such as business model innovations (Baden-Fuller & Haefliger, 2013; Chesbrough, 2010), which are defined as "the search for new logics of the firm and new ways to create and capture value for its stakeholders" (Casadesus-Masanell & Zhu, 2013 p. 464). In this context, the concept of business model is employed in a dynamic and transformative way, which requires integration with the external environment, as well as with clients and partners (Zott & Amit, 2010). In the current complex global business environment, companies are increasingly employing these and other strategies to enhance their capacity to adapt to changes.

An organization's ability to adapt to environmental changes has been conceptualized as organizational resilience. In this context, a resilient organization has the ability to anticipate threats, cope with unexpected events, and learn from them (Duchek, 2014). The term "resilience" comes from material sciences, where it is defined as a material's ability to absorb energy when elastically deformed and release that energy upon unloading. When applied to the business world, it refers to organizations that are both stable and flexible (Kaz, 2019). As observed back in the late 90's by Mallak (1998), these adaptive capacities are what allow companies to differentiate from competition.

Resilience allows companies not only to effectively handle crises, adapting to incremental changes and sudden disruptions in order to survive and prosper (Kaz, 2019), but to potentially come out better off from them, and even develop competitive advantages as a result of experiencing them (Harland, Harrison, Jones, & Reiter-Palmon, 2005). In this vein, Lengnick-Hall & Beck (2016) differentiate the concepts of recovery and robust transformation. The former, which is normally the result of modest levels of resilience capacity, refers to coming back from environmental disruptions and continuing to achieve previous levels of performance. Robust transformation, on the other hand, applies when a company capitalizes on environmental disruptions in ways that create new options and capabilities.

Although the subject of resilience has received increasing academic attention, the concept is normally seen as an outcome, which emerges when individuals and organizations perform well and manage to bounce back from disruptive situations (Duchek, 2014). Several recent studies have attempted to understand the nature of organizational resilience (Herbane, 2019) and the relationship between different types of resilience (Prayag, Spector, Orchiston, & Chowdhury, 2019). However, the process of organizational resilience – and most importantly, the factors that contribute to it – are still largely unexplored. As addressed in the introduction, the present study aims to test the assumption that having young employees is one of these factors, as they are supposedly better suited to offer innovative solutions to help companies bounce back and achieve robust transformation upon experiencing disruptive events. The rationale behind this assumption is addressed in more detail in the next section.

YOUNG PERSONNEL AND ORGANIZATIONAL RESILIENCE

The assumption investigated in the present work is based upon the consideration of several contributions from previous studies. Some authors directly argue that having young employees in executive positions and including them in the company's decision-making process tends make the company more resilient. This is because senior managers have a psychological and sociological inclination to avoid conflict and adopt linear and rational thinking. Therefore, communicating an overarching vision, managing conflict and adopting integrative thinking are clear challenges to them (Smith et al., 2010). In this context, Boschma and Groen (2010), argues that as the called neo-digital natives, or Generation Z, are not "programmed" to follow traditional methods, they become more open to changes and to develop new strategies. Therefore, empowering them to make strategic decisions potentially favors the adoption of counter-intuitive or unconventional measures, which in turn, might enhance the company's resilience capacity. In this context, the younger generations are arguably better suited to provide intuitive solutions that are adequate to the current business reality and the firm's strategy. Reinforcing such argument, Hamel & Välikangas (2003) state that having young personnel and including them in the company's strategic decision-making process is essential to increasing corporate resilience, as it favors the emergence of innovative strategies and fresh ideas, instead of blocking young talents' contributions in favor of conventional practices. In the same vein, Stoltz (2004) advises senior managers to stimulate organizational flexibility by rewarding those who are willing to face the future and take risks.

In the current study, these assumptions are discussed in light of two reference conceptualizations of organizational resilience: Lengnick-Hall & Beck's (2016) dimensions of resilience capacity and Duchek's (2014) capabilities of organizational resilience. Those conceptualizations are adopted as the main theoretical frameworks for the discussion because their authors are amongst the few that adopt a process perspective to resilience, rather than treating it as a feature. As first addressed by Lengnick-Hall, Beck, & Lengnick-Hall (2011), and elaborated on Lengnick-Hall & Beck's (2016), an organization's resilience capacity is created from interactions among specific cognitive, behavioral and contextual factors. Therefore, the three dimensions of resilience capacity are cognitive resilience, behavioral resilience and contextual resilience. Duchek (2014), in turn, address resilience as a desirable capacity of organizations that is favored by three capabilities: anticipating, coping and learning.

The first dimension, cognitive resilience, is the company's ability to notice changes, make sense of unfamiliar situations and decide on the best way to respond to disruptive, uncertain and surprising conditions (Lengnick-Hall & Beck, 2016). This is similar to what Duchek (2014) describes as the anticipation capability, which means the ability to identify crucial developments and adapt proactively. Cognitive resilience is useful for refining persistent, repetitive dynamic capabilities and for creating fluid, emerging agility routines (Lengnick-Hall & Beck, 2016). The ability to achieve competitive advantage through dynamic capabilities emphasizes two key aspects: the "dynamic" element, or the ability to renew competencies through innovative responses to achieve adaptation to a changing business environment; and the "capabilities", which emphasizes the key role of strategic management in properly integrating resources and internal and external organizational skills (Teece, Pisano & Shuen, 1997). Young people can arguably favor this dimension (or capability) of resilience, since, as argued by Boschma and Groen (2010), they are not bound by traditional ways of dealing with situations, and therefore, are more inclined to implementing new solutions. Besides, they are more risk-taking, which furthers increases their likeliness to implement new solutions.

As also stated by Lengnick-Hall & Beck (2016), besides a solid grasp on reality, cognitive resilience requires a relentless desire to question fundamental assumptions that may no longer apply. This is often a characteristic of young people, particularly the current generation entering the work market, the neo-digital natives, as they were born and raised within the information era, and therefore, are accustomed to autonomously acquire knowledge that allows them to question procedures that may no longer be the most efficient solution to the problems or situations they were designed to tackle. Once more, not being "programmed" to deal with problems in traditional ways favors young thinkers' potential to enhance organizational resilience.

The second dimension of resilience capacity, behavioral resilience, refers to routines and activities that are developed through a combination of practiced resourcefulness and counterintuitive action juxtaposed with useful habits and behavioral preparedness (Lengnick-Hall & Beck, 2016). The components of behavioral resilience have a strong influence on the fluid dynamic capabilities needed for innovation and radical improvisation to respond to emerging requirements (Lengnick-Hall & Beck, 2016). Therefore, it is the result of a dynamic tension between behaviors that favor creativity and unconventional actions, and familiar and well-rehearsed routines. The concept resembles what Duchek (2014) describes as coping, the second capability of organizational resilience, which includes the ability to accept a problem and the capability to search and implement a solution. In this context, searching a solution is a combination of sensemaking and action, where the first is favored by what Weick (1993) describes as bricolage: the capability to improvise and solve problems with creativity. Accordingly, implementing a solution is favored by Weick's (1993) notion of virtual role systems, a state in which an organization maintains a shared vision among its constituents, so that each member cognitively reproduces the organization.

Considering the above addressed concepts, it can be argued that, while experienced professionals who work in the company for a long time are probably more inclined to stick to well-rehearsed routines – or reproduce the company through its virtual role system –, young personnel members are more likely to adopt creative and unconventional actions – search solutions through bricolage – in face of changing conditions. In other words, they are more likely to "follow a dramatically different course of action from that which is the norm for the organization" (Lengnick-Hall & Beck, 2016, p. 11), providing the necessary contrast for fostering behavioral resilience. A clear example of lack of this capability is provided by Weick's (1993) analysis of Mann Gulch fire disaster, in which the crew refused to escape form the fire by stepping into another one intentionally set, in what the author describes as the climax of sensemaking erosion.

Finally, contextual resilience, the third dimension, is the combination of interpersonal connections, resource stocks and supply lines that allow for quick actions in response to disruptive, uncertain and surprising conditions (Lengnick-Hall & Beck, 2016). One of the three factors that favor it is deference to expertise, which is typical of non-hierarchical, or holographic, organizations. Such enterprises tend to favor self-organization, disperse influence, and individual and group accountability, in opposition to relying on hierarchical positions. As rigid hierarchies are typical of more traditional organizations, it could be argued that having younger and more "free-thinking" personnel favor the cultivation of holographic organizations' characteristics, and consequently, the company's contextual resilience. Moreover, resilient organizations tend to share decision-making (Mallak, 1998). Therefore, including young personnel in the decision-making process, as suggested by Hamel and Välikangas (2003) is also likely to favor a company's resilience capacity.

The dimension also relates to another of Duchek's (2014) resilience capabilities: adaptation, which refers to incorporating the experience gained from the crisis to the existing knowledge base. Naturally, by applying the knowledge gained from the experiences of previous crises, companies enhance their expertise in dealing with disruptive situations. Such capability is arguably favored by the same flexibility characteristics of holographic organizations, which tend to make the company more inclined to accepting new approaches. Reinforcing the connection between learning from crises and resilience building, Caniëls and Baaten's (2019) results show that employer resilience mediates the relationship between a learning-oriented organizational environment and proactive work behaviors. Once again, it is argued that Generation Z personnel members favor this capability as they are more open to new ways of working and adapting to new scenarios.

In sum, literature provides plenty of indications that having young people in the organization and empowering them to participate on the decision-making process can potentially contribute to enhance each dimension (i.e., cognitive, behavioral and contextual) and each capability (i.e., anticipation, coping and adaptation) of organizational resilience. Such assumption has been further explored through the case study. In this vein, the study also sheds light on the linkages, suggested by Teece (2012), between management actions affecting individuals or small groups and the dynamic capabilities and firm performance. For the study setting, a luxury fashion items was selected, due to its interesting relationship with Generation Z. In this context, the next section addressed this relationship and the challenges it brings about to the industry.

CURRENT CHALLENGES FACED BY THE LUXURY INDUSTRY

The concept of luxury depends, to a great extent, on personal appreciation and experience (Nia & Zaichhkowsky, 2000). In this vein, the perception of luxury varies according to age and other socio-demographic variables (Gardyn, 2002), which explains the lack of consensus in its definition. Literature suggests that an important characteristic of luxury products is their scarcity (Catry, 2003). A good example of this is Supreme's artificial scarcity business model, which allows the company to sell the most varied products with huge profit margins. In this context, luxury products can be classified according to their level of exclusivity into the following categories: unique pieces, limited editions, limited-diffusion products, and expanded-diffusion products (Heine, 2012). Fashion products usually fall into the two last categories. Limited-diffusion fashion items' rarity is normally a consequence of the complexity of their manufacturing process, which typically requires a high degree of craftsmanship. Expanded-diffusion fashion products, on the other hand, have a more massified manufacturing process (Sicard, 2003), and therefore, are less rare. However, they are still marketed as a luxury product due to aspects such as cost of materials, premium quality or exclusive design.

We could expect that a scarce luxury product would fit in with a corporate social responsibility approach, as this scarcity of product can help convey the idea that luxury brands encourage more responsible consumption and help protect natural resources. However, according to Janssen et al. (2014) this expectation does not apply to all types of luxury products. Ephemeral luxury products are unlikely to trigger a perception of social responsibility in consumers. By definition, fashion items are considered ephemeral products, as they have a short life cycles and the designs and materials are renewed every season. This approach of lack of durability can be perceived as not being very much in line with sustainable approaches (Berthon et al., 2009). In this context, fashion brands, both budget and luxury, face many difficulties conveying credible CSR messages.

Luxury companies' effort to become and appear more socially responsible has been fueled by another recent trend, characterized by the democratization of luxury products, with the incorporation of new segments and generations. Changes in society are leading to an increasing number of middle market consumers moving to higher levels of quality and price (Silverstein & Fiske, 2003). This democratization of luxury has led to the concept of "masstige", or accessible luxury. In this context, new segments have been incorporated into the set of accessible luxury companies' target market. One of the most relevant of these segments is the Generation Z. According to most definitions, this generation includes people born between the mid 1990's and early 2010's. In this context, it comes right after Generation Y, also known and Millennials, consisting of people born between the early 1980's and the mid 1990's. Although they share some common background, they are two distinct groups. As generally accepted, the main difference is that, while millennials witnessed the technological advances of the digital revolution while growing up, Generation Z members were born in the digital area. Naturally, there is not clear line separating them, as even the so-called digital revolution was not a punctual event, and technology is constantly evolving. However, the differences in shared experiences are between the two groups are still significant. While early millennials saw the emergence of the e-mail already as teenagers, late Gen-Z members played with tablets before they could speak, which has huge implications for their view of the world and their behavior as consumers.

Traditionally, young people had not been the focus of luxury good items, as they typically lacked the discretionary income to afford such items. This has changed. Due to different lifestyle choices of the new generations, such as having children later, or not having children at all, Millennials and Generation Z members are more likely to have fewer financial responsibilities, and consequently, more discretionary income than previous generations (Chu and Kamal, 2011). Likewise, Generation Z members are highly fashion conscious and demands high-end luxury goods, especially apparels (Jain, Vatsa, & Jagani, 2014). Another important new segment for the luxury fashion segment, is the HENRYs (High-Earners-Not–Rich-Yet) (Deloitte, 2019), which is, to a great extent, also composed by millennials and generation Z members. Tully and Caplin (2008) coined the term in the United States as the spearhead of the professional and business class that drives the economy. They are hardworking, still young, with incomes over $250,000 and have worked hard to build their careers and move forward.

To approach these new markets, luxury brands' positioning strategies often combine a high perceived prestige with reasonable price premiums in order to attract middle-class (and HENRYs) consumers (Truong et al., 2008). With this growing luxury market, new challenges arise for luxury brands, particularly regarding the increased perception of the social and environmental impact of their products by the younger generation (Hill & Lee, 2012). In this context, Hill and Lee (2012) observe that the younger generation believes that actions should be taken to achieve sustainability in the apparel industry, as they are skeptical of the industry's performance in this area (Kanchanapibul et al., 2014). For instance, aspects of luxury fashion items that traditionally enhanced the perception of sophistication and exclusivity of these products – e.g., the use genuine fur or leather, especially from exotic animals – no longer offer the same prestige. Quite the contrary, they are now being criticized, not only by pure environmentalists and ONG members, but by their own target market, as within the new generation, environmental awareness is no longer an exclusivity environmental scientists and alternative community members.

In sum, the incorporation of a broader target market creates an environment of change, and consequently challenges, to the luxury fashion industry, of which the pressure to rethink materials in light of a now mainstream sustainability-oriented mentality is but one. The very idea of broadening the market shakes up some of the essential characteristics of the industry and its products, including the idea of exclusivity. Accordingly, the different tastes and cultural background of this new market further adds to the challenge of pleasing a bigger and more varied audience without losing the essence that keeps the industry alive. The study reported in the following sections contributes to the discussion on how the luxury industry has been responding to those challenges. More specifically, the study analyses how the incorporation of members of this new target market (namely, generation Z) as employees might allow luxury items companies to come up with ideas to thrive in this changing environment. The specific procedures carried out during the study are addressed in the next section.

METHODOLOGY

To further investigate the addressed assumption, a case study was carried out in a luxury goods company. The choice for a company of this segment was due to luxury goods companies' increasing interest in the younger segments of the population, namely Millennials and Generation Z (Deloitte, 2019). The chosen company design, produces and markets clothing and accessories for women, men and children, and integrate Deloitte's Global Powers of Luxury Goods 2019's top 100. The company operates in over 40 countries, with around 700 shops, and international expansion is currently a key element in its business strategy. The organization is licensed to produce goods of brands advertised as luxurious but accessible, discrete, elegant and refined, as they are targeted to the stylish and modern consumer. The level of craftsmanship and labor employed in production is very high.

For four months, at the end of 2019, a group of 18 Business Administration undergraduate students from five countries – five from Germany, four from France, four from Spain, two from Belgium and two from Turkey – discussed possible solutions and strategies to deal with challenges brought about by a changing environment that affected luxury goods companies. The participants, ten males and eight females, were born between 1994 and 1999, and therefore, fit into the post-millennial generation, or Generation Z (APA, 2018). The students were divided into five groups, whereas only one was formed by individuals from the same country (German). The other four groups were multi-national. The study, however, did not aim to carry out a cross-cultural analysis of the strategies planned by the groups, that is, examine the differences in responses according to the country of origin of each group or individual. The composition of the groups merely aimed to provide a multicultural scenario, so that within each group, opinions could be shared and discussion, like in social networks.

All participants were first trained in concepts of Strategic Management applied to organizations, and then familiarized with the company's strategic context through in-plant meetings with directors of different departments. During a visit to the company, they experienced the logistic processes of input, production and output. At the same instance, they had meetings with the production and human resources managers.

Four Environmental Challenges and Relevant Factors

After being familiarized with the company and its processes, the students were presented to four current key challenges in luxury goods companies' relationships with the environment and their customers, which had been previously identified by Deloitte (2019) and Luxury Institute (2019). For each challenge, participants were requested to suggest solutions by answering a specific question. The question were designed to allow them think of innovative approaches based on anticipating relevant changes, coping with them and adapting to them (Duchek, 2014) in order to maintain satisfactory results and potentially improve from the experience, that is, achieve robust transformation. More specifically, students were expected to demonstrate the abilities to make sense of unfamiliar situations and decide on the best way to respond; propose creative and unconventional approaches that are dramatically different from the company's norms; and think for themselves and take responsibility for their proposals (Lengnick-Hall & Beck, 2016). In sum, the procedures aimed to verify whether respondents demonstrated potential to increase the company's resilience capabilities and contribute to its resilience dimensions, as described on the literature review. The pairs of challenges and questions are described below:

- A new consumer class currently rising and is going to become increasingly relevant in the future: the HENRYs (High-Earners-Not–Rich-Yet) (Deloitte, 2019: 6). Including this costumer segment to luxury brands' product portfolio can help them build a relationship with future affluent consumers.

Q1. H*ow could the company engage this customer segment and build a long-term loyalty relationship?*

- The integration between physical and online sales is a priority, but online sales in the luxury goods sector could damage brand value. Simultaneously, the rapid digitalization and ease of use of the digitalized platforms have led consumers, especially the youngest ones, to increasingly use social media tools to express their brand preferences.

Q2. *How to use social media platforms to engage with young consumers, while trying to keep brand value intact?*

- Aspects of Corporate Social Responsibility (CSR), such as environmental care, animal welfare, labor practices and sustainability in general, are likely to influence purchasing decisions in the luxury goods sector as well.

Q3. *What steps or actions would you propose to allow the company to evolve towards new models of ethical and sustainable luxury?*

- When making purchasing decisions, millennials rank attributes of luxury brands, such as quality, customer service, design, craftsmanship, and product exclusivity (Luxury Institute's, 2019).

Q4. *Do you think that introducing radical redesigns and mixing the company's two brands with others that are more popular with young generations could be a good strategy? For example, would collaborating with streetwear companies or adding new brands to their portfolio be good ideas?*

The groups worked independently, that is, after the contact with the company's managers, there were no more occasions in which they gathered. Therefore, they did not exchange impressions, and their suggestions were developed independently. In the end, the way each group dealt with the challenges was evaluated from both the academic and the corporate perspective. The results incorporate the thinking of each group into the formulation of corporate strategies. The set of answers provided by each group is presented in next section.

RESULTS

The proposals of the different groups were arranged in tables and subjected to a content analysis. Then, the answers were classified within each question. For a better understanding and to simplify the presentation of results, the main themes were grouped together. For reasons of confidentiality, the name of the company is not mentioned. Hereafter, it is referred to as XYZ.

Summary of Responses

Q1. *How could XYZ engage this customer (the HENRYs) segment and build a long-term loyalty relationship?*

Several proposals address the importance of digital marketing tools, such as social media, to increase product accessibility, spread the image of the brand and adapt strategies to current demands. The following quote illustrates this point:

It's crucial to attend to the way how new generations consume fashion and the characteristics of the segment (…) since brands are usually used by new generations for exhibiting high standing status on social media, brand recognition becomes an influent purchase factor. (Team 5)

The proposals coincide in pointing out that customer experience and satisfaction are essential to achieve long-term loyalty. To this end, team 2 recommends "to build a strong relation based on trust and the will to growth mutuality: Integrate the customer in the future of the firm" and "to create a wow effect throughout the purchase trip of the customer" (Team 2). To stimulate that eagerness for the next product, team 1 proposes to "offer private sales to its customers, a feeling of exclusivity settles in and encourages consumption".

Teams views converge concerning the need to have information about customers. This requires "collecting information on customers such as their purchase history (…) and create a customer database to ensure follow-up" (Team 1). This idea is further elaborated on the quote below:

The company must understand not only the HENRYs needs, also their preferences, way of thinking, shopping habits and favorite brands. Those habits and preferences are continued into their later stages of life, in which they will probably have higher incomes. The organization should know as much about them as possible. (Team 4).

Regarding after-sale services, "in the luxury sector, this part is even more important than elsewhere due to the demand, which is touchier" (Team 2). The groups also propose that this strategy should not be based exclusively on discounts, but also include gifts, that is, rewards that are given to customers through loyalty programs, as the following quote illustrates: "It is important to follow up on these clients, and not only offer them discounts but even gifts to make them feel special and in some way committed to the company." (Team 4).

Respondents also showed to be aware that only certain companies are fully capable to serve different segments, as pointed out by some of the teams, e.g., "Only large companies can afford to divide their customers into segments because generally styles differ according to brands and each company already has its own customer base that corresponds to a certain category." (Team 1).

Q2. *How to use social media platforms to engage with young consumers, while trying to keep brand value intact?*

The company must adapt the strategies to current demands. For all teams, social networks are the appropriate way to reach young people, as the following quote illustrates:

The content that Millennials and Generation Z create on social media is valuable feedback for luxury firms to anticipate and better meet the needs of a challenging market. If such companies keep the value and guarantee of their products, the brand perception doesn't have to worsen." (…) "Luxury likes to be based on strong heritage, longevity and conservatism. However, social networks are synonymous with ephemerality, which contradicts their values. To combine the two would then be to use its social pages to tell the brand's story and accentuate its aura. XYZ could then showcase its unique know-how while retaining some mystery. The aim is to make a storytelling in which the trade secrets, the backstage, the craftsmen, are partially revealed. (Team 5)

Participants argue that regular posts cultivate customers' trust, as shown by the following quote: "The most important fact for social media is consistency. XYZ should post on a regular basis, minimum every second, third day, and the content should always be high-quality photography of their clothes and bags." (Team 3). All five teams agree that Instagram is the ideal social network for promotion. Only two teams also mention Twitter in second position. There is also unanimity in pointing out the importance of employing celebrities and influencers who share the brand's values to engage with young consumers. This idea is summarized in the following quote:

Influencers would be a good way to appeal to young costumers and to gain status, and though it is not very common to partner with influencers in the luxury fashion industry, XYZ could take advantage of the presence that social media applications like Instagram have in every day's life of young people, in order to reach the target market. (Team 5)

The teams propose concrete ideas for the company to engage with young consumers through social media, such as organizing customers' photos competitions and awarding winners with one of the company's products, promoting advertisements and using filtering tools, minimizing any hassle or steps that might dissuade people from making an online purchase, and even adopting the same "pop stitching" approach employed by other successful fashion companies that target young audiences.

Despite the obvious benefits of using social media, participants also point out risks. For instance, the dynamic and uncontrolled nature of information flows, which can lead to unfavorable messages that harm brand perception and trust. In this context, one of the teams states that "the primary goal in communicating on the networks will not be to sell to a target or reach a large mass of potential customers, but on the contrary to work on its image and reputation with demanding consumers who want to listen to a prestigious advertiser who also knows how to show respect" (Team 3).

Q3. *What steps or actions would you propose to allow the company to evolve towards new models of ethical and sustainable luxury?*

Four teams expressly mention the use of natural leather in the manufacturing process and that the company should replace real leather, skin and fur with synthetic products or recycled raw materials. They believe that the use of natural skins is unethical for many customers, and that there has been a change of mentality on the younger generations. One of the teams proposes: "use false fur and leather by developing and using the 3D fur and leather printing (…) and partnerships with companies that using bio-printed clothes such as the organic Bio-printed tissues" (Team 1).

It is also striking how young people judge the situation more by facts than by statements, without taking anything for granted. This is illustrated in the following quotes:

We can assume that XYZ tries to achieve their goals in regard of corporate social responsibility by what we've been told, but we do not have any closer background information how sustainable the actions really are. (Team 4).

On the official website of XYZ reading through their Corporate responsibility statement makes a first great impression. But looking more closely, the statement does not imply any strategy at all. (…) They never explain, how exactly they fulfil these goals. (Team 3)

Other teams proposed a combination of actions with more detailed communication of the changes the company made in response to the increasing concern on climate change and other social issues. For instance, one of the groups proposed improvements in the work environment, as "we notice a significant difference between the people working in the sales and marketing department and the people working in the factory" (Team 5).

Q4. *Do you think that introducing radical redesigns and mixing the company's two brands with others that are more popular with young generations could be a good strategy? For example, would collaborating with streetwear companies or adding new brands to their portfolio be good ideas?*

Teams' views converge regarding the idea that targeting the young generation market would be a good investment for the company. However, there are disagreements regarding whether mixing the company's brands with others that are more popular with young generations is a good strategy. Only one team thinks the strategy is highly risky and could lead to dramatic problems, since "the style of the products they sell are for people who love elegance and prestige while people who are wearing streetwear aren't looking automatically for elegance and prestige but more for comfort." (Team 5).

The remaining teams think it could be a good strategy. One team observes that both fashion styles have one thing in common: the search for exclusivity. "The spirit of core streetwear customers is to create exclusivity tied to authenticity instead of money. So a streetwear item, should first be exclusive, special, limited, before being expensive" (Team 4). With due caution, positive synergies can be observed in the collaboration with firms of a different fashion style, as illustrated in the following quotation:

For long established "deadlocked" companies a collaboration with a start-up or another successful brand can be lifesaving sometimes. Even though we´re far away from this situation at XYZ, thinking about a collaboration with a popular brand could be a thing to keep your brand in mind and reaching new people with your products (…). Due to the fact that brands of XYZ strive for expansion on the American market, leading their focus to the younger generation could be a key factor. There is a number of collaborations in the recent past that show how successful this strategy can be (Louis Vitton with Supreme, Fila with Fendi, and Versace with H&M). (Team 3).

Partnership seems to be one of the best ways to attract customers and develop a permanent (fashion) collection in order to build loyalty among this new clientele (Team 1). However, it is important to choose the right partner and set the new product at the right price (Team 3), as well as to be careful not to change too much because, as otherwise, long-term customers could feel alienated (Team 1).

DISCUSSION

The solutions proposed by the Generation Z students provide some clear contribution for the XYZ to tackle the presented challenges in creative and, in some cases, unconventional ways, demonstrating their potential to enhance the company's resilience capacity. Suggestions like engaging with HENRYs now through social media and providing them with satisfactory experiences through every interaction irrespective of their current purchasing behavior (which might not yet be particularly profitable for the company), demonstrate these young "managers'" focus on the long run, as well as their capacity to adapt proactively. In this sense, they clearly illustrate their contributions to Duchek's (2014) anticipation capability: the ability to identify crucial developments and adapt proactively; through what Lengnick-Hall and Beck (2016) refer to as cognitive resilience: the ability to notice changes, make sense of unfamiliar situations and decide on the best way to respond.

Some of the answers demonstrate a critical view towards the company and the whole industry in which it operates. This is particularly visible on answers to question three, where participants address issues of sustainability and business ethics. Those responses must be understood considering the limitations in respondents' knowledge on the company's production and operations. Nevertheless, the suggestions do illustrate another condition for cognitive resilience: a solid grasp on reality paired with a relentless desire to question fundamental assumptions that may no longer apply (Lengnick-Hall & Beck, 2016). A clear example of these assumptions is the use of genuine leather and fur, students identified a change in young customers' attitudes towards items that involve the use of animals and proposed alternative solutions.

The solutions to items of animal origin, such as synthetic and 3D printed materials that resemble leather and fur, also illustrate another resilience capability: coping, that is, the ability to accept a problem and the capability to search and implement a solution (Duchek, 2014). This is achieved through what Weick (1993) describes as bricolage: the ability to improvise and solve problems creatively. More specifically, it demonstrates the capacity of following a dramatically different course of action from that which is the norm in the organization, or in this case, in the entire industry. To Lengnick-Hall and Beck (2016), this characteristic must be combined with well-rehearsed routines in order to provide the necessary contrast to foster behavioral resilience. In other words, it must be combined with what Weick (1993) conceptualizes as the company's virtual role system.

The well-rehearsed routines could be understood as the company's production know-how, which must be combined with these new materials that are more adequate with new and future customers' values, and consequently with their preferences. In this sense, as argued in the literature review, this dimension of organizational resilience can be achieved by including these young decision makers – who demonstrate to have plenty of bricolage, and thus, are capable to creatively solve problems – along with more senior employees – which are more prone to stick with the well-rehearsed routines, that is, to cognitively reproduce the company through its virtual role system –, in the decision making-process, in order to create the necessary juxtaposition for cultivating behavioral resilience.

Participants' propositions for how to engage with Millennial and Generation Z customers through social media while maintaining brand image, in turn, illustrate the capability referred to by Duchek (2014) as adaptation, that is, incorporating the experience gained from the crisis into the existing knowledge base. Suggestions for the second challenge do illustrate the capacity to adapt, as group 5, for instance, clearly suggests capitalizing on the valuable feedback Millennials and Generation Z consumers provide via social media in order to better meet their needs. Accordingly, the same group suggests using this knowledge in the same medium to strengthen the image of heritage and mystery, rather than jeopardizing them by simply interacting on social media without considering these aspects.

At last, participants' suggestions in general illustrate Lengnick-Hall and Beck's (2016) final dimension of resilience capacity: contextual resilience. Such dimension is favored by deference to expertise, which involves self-organization, disperse influence, and individual and group accountability, in opposition to relying on hierarchical positions. As argued in the literature review, having younger and more "free-thinking" personnel favor the cultivation these characteristics, and consequently, the company's contextual resilience. This is clearly demonstrated by the case study, as empowering the students with decision making power, by requesting them to suggest solutions to real challenges, resulted in the proposition of creative and counter-intuitive strategies, which, as demonstrated throughout this discussion, do have a potential to enhance the company's resilience capacity. In this sense, the case study also reinforces Mallak's (1998) statement that resilient organizations tend to share decision making.

In sum, the studied case illustrates all the aspects addressed in the literature review: strategic change, innovation in business models, organizational resilience and the potential contribution of young ideas to the latter, and consequently to enhancing organizational strategies. The contribution of young ideas demonstrates their potential to contribute to all the capabilities required to foster each of the dimensions of resilience capacity. In this sense, the suggestions allow the company not only to respond to environmental conditions and changes in demand, but also to anticipate such changes and propose innovative solutions.

CONCLUSION

The present work aimed to further explore the assumption that resilience capacity is favored by having young employees in executive positions and including them in the company's decision-making process, which had been suggested by several previous studies (Boschma & Groen, 2010; Hamel & Välikangas, 2003; Stoltz, 2004). To this end, a case study was carried out in a luxury goods company. The study involved familiarizing Generation Z Business Administration students from several European countries with the company through a visit and meetings with managers, and finally asking them to propose solutions to four real challenges that currently affect players in this segment.

The results are in line with the mentioned authors' view about the potential of young thinkers to enhance organizational resilience. The students did demonstrate that, as argued by Boschma and Groen (2010), since they are not "programmed" to follow traditional managing methods, and therefore, are more open to changes, empowering them to make strategic decisions favors the adoption of counter-intuitive or unconventional measures. More specifically, the suggestions offered by participants show young thinkers' potential to foster each of Duchek's (2014) capabilities of organizational resilience (anticipating, coping and adapting) and enhance each of Lengnick-Hall and Beck's (2016) dimensions of resilient capacity (cognitive, behavioral and contextual).

Participants demonstrated potential to anticipate and enhance cognitive resilience, which requires anticipating changes and acting accordingly, by suggesting proactive actions to deal with segments that will be more important in the future. They showed potential for enhancing behavioral resilience, which requires a relentless desire to question fundamental assumptions that may no longer apply, by pointing out practices that are no longer in line with modern consumers' values and preferences (the use of animal origin materials) and suggesting unconventional and creative solutions – bricolage – to cope with these changes. They demonstrated capacity of adaptation by suggesting several ways in which the company could collect information and capitalize on them to better serve consumers' needs and generate purposeful interactions. Finally, the whole experiment illustrates young thinkers' potential to enhance contextual resilience, as empowering them to take decision has led to innovative and counter-intuitive solutions to the proposed challenges.

The present work explores a novelty proposition, which incorporates young thinkers into the formulation of corporate strategies. In this context, it offers a new insight on the discussion on young minds and their fresh ideas' potential to enhance companies' resilience capacity, and consequently, to help them survive in changing environments. Additionally, the work sheds light on what Hamel and Välikangas (2003) describes as the paradox between the tireless effort to achieve efficiency and the systematic search for new strategic options in highly dynamic environments. In sum, the study reinforces the assumption that having Generation Z employees and empowering them to participate in the decision-making process has a significant potential to enhance the company's organizational resilience. This also brings about a clear managerial implication, as companies should invest on attracting and training young talents, as well including them in the company's decision-making process, in order to enhance their organizational resilience and increase their chances to adapt and prosper in the current business environment.

Despite its contribution, the present study does have some limitations, which in turn, point to fertile avenues for future research. First, being a single case study, the collected data is restricted to a single company of a specific industry. Further studies on different industries, and potentially adopting multiple case studies, should increase the comprehensiveness of the conclusions. The main limitation, however, regards the exploratory, qualitative nature of the study, which leads to results that have a high level of validity, but a low level of reliability. In this context, in order to achieve a reliable understanding on the role of young ideas to organizational resilience, explanatory studies need to be carried out. Naturally, the execution of this type of study is currently limited by the state of the art in organizational resilience research, as there are no validated scales to measure the dimensions used here to illustrate the effect of young ideas, for instance. In this context, future studies could propose a list of items to operationalize these dimensions, and once they have been validated, quantitatively test the effects of young ideas in each one of them.

REFERENCES

APA. (2018). *APA stress in America™ survey: Generation Z stressed about issues in the news but least likely to vote*. Retrieved from https://www.apa.org/news/press/releases/2018/10/generation-z-stressed

Baden-Fuller, C., & Haefliger, S. (2013). Business models and technological innovation. *Long Range Planning*, *46*(6), 419–426. doi:10.1016/j.lrp.2013.08.023

Berthon, P., Pitt, L., Parent, M., & Berthon, J.-P. (2009). Aesthetics and ephemerality: Observing and preserving the luxury brand. *California Management Review*, *55*(1), 45–66. doi:10.1525/cmr.2009.52.1.45

Boschma, J., & Groen, I. (2010). *Generatie Einstein*. AW Bruna Uitgevers.

Burnard, K., & Bhamra, R. (2011). Organisational resilience: Development of a conceptual framework for organisational responses. *International Journal of Production Research*, *49*(18), 5581–5599. doi:10.1080/00207543.2011.563827

Caniëls, M. C. J., & Baaten, S. M. J. (2019). How a learning-oriented organizational climate is linked to different proactive behaviors: The role of employee resilience. *Social Indicators Research, 143*(2), 561–577. doi:10.100711205-018-1996-y

Casadesus-Masanell, R., & Zhu, F. (2013). Business model innovation and competitive imitation: The case of sponsor-based business models. *Strategic Management Journal, 34*(4), 464–482. doi:10.1002mj.2022

Catry, B. (2003). The great pretenders: The magic of luxury goods. *Business Strategy Review, 14*(3), 10–17. doi:10.1111/1467-8616.00267

Chesbrough, H. (2010). Business model innovation: Opportunities and barriers. *Long Range Planning, 43*(2-3), 354–363. doi:10.1016/j.lrp.2009.07.010

Chu, S. C., & Kamal, S. (2011). An investigation of social media usage, brand consciousness, and purchase intention towards luxury products among Millennials. In S. Okazaki (Ed.), *Advances in advertising research* (Vol. 2, pp. 179–190). Gabler. doi:10.1007/978-3-8349-6854-8_12

Dahles, H., & Susilowati, T. P. (2015). Business resilience in times of growth and crisis. *Annals of Tourism Research, 51*, 34–50. doi:10.1016/j.annals.2015.01.002

Dalziell, E. P., & McManus, S. T. (2004). *Resilience, vulnerability, and adaptive Capacity: Implications for system performance.* Paper presented at the International Forum for Engineering Decision Making (IFED), Stoos, Switzerland.

Deloitte. (2019). *Global powers of luxury goods 2019. Bridging the gap between the old and the new.* Retrieved from https://www2.deloitte.com/global/en/pages/consumer-business/articles/gx-cb-global-powers-of-luxury-goods.html

Duchek, S. (2014). Growth in the face of crisis: the role of organizational resilience capabilities. In *Academy of management proceedings* (Vol. 1, p. 13487). Academy of Management. doi:10.5465/ambpp.2014.225

Eisenhardt, K. M., & Martin, J. A. (2000). Dynamic capabilities: What are they? *Strategic Management Journal, 21*(10-11), 1105–1121. doi:10.1002/1097-0266(200010/11)21:10/11<1105::AID-SMJ133>3.0.CO;2-E

Ferreira, M. P., Serra, F. A. R., & Reis, N. R. (2011). On the adaptation of the firm's strategies to the international business environment: A knowledge-based and evolutionary perspective. *European Journal of International Management, 5*(6), 633–655. doi:10.1504/EJIM.2011.042735

Fischbacher-Smith, D., & Smith, L. (2015). Navigating the 'dark waters of globalisation': Global markets, inequalities and the spatial dynamics of risk. *Risk Management*, *17*(3), 179–203. doi:10.1057/rm.2015.12

Gardyn, R. (2002). Defining luxury: Oh, the good life. *American Demographics*. Retrieved from http://findarticles.com/p/articles/mi_m4021/is_2002_Nov_1/ai_93089467/?tag=content;col1

Hamel, G., & Välikangas, L. (2003). The quest for resilience. *Harvard Business Review*, *81*(9), 52–63. PMID:12964393

Harland, L., Harrison, W., Jones, J. R., & Reiter-Palmon, R. (2005). Leadership behaviors and subordinate resilience. *Journal of Leadership & Organizational Studies*, *11*(2), 2–14. doi:10.1177/107179190501100202

Heine, K. (2012). The concept of luxury brands. *Luxury Brand Management*, *1*, 2193–1208.

Herbane, B. (2019). Rethinking organizational resilience and strategic renewal in SMEs. *Entrepreneurship and Regional Development*, *31*(5–6), 476–495. doi:10.1080/08985626.2018.1541594

Hill, J., & Lee, H. (2012). Young Generation Y consumers' perceptions of sustainability in the apparel industry. *Journal of Fashion Marketing and Management*, *16*(4), 477–491. doi:10.1108/13612021211265863

Hoskisson, R. E., Eden, L., Lau, C. M., & Wright, M. (2000). Strategy in emerging economies. *Academy of Management Journal*, *43*(3), 249–267.

Jain, V., Vatsa, R., & Jagani, K. (2014). Exploring generation Z's purchase behavior towards luxury apparel: A conceptual framework. *Romanian Journal of Marketing*, *2*(Apr-Jun), 18–29.

Jamrog, J. J., McCann, J. E. III, Lee, J. M., Morrison, C. L., Selsky, J. W., & Vickers, M. (2006). *Agility and resilience in the face of continuous change: A global study of current trends and future possibilities 2006-2016*. American Management Association.

Janssen, C., Vanhamme, J., Lindgreen, A., & Lefebvre, C. (2014). The Catch-22 of responsible luxury: Effects of luxury product characteristics on consumers' perception of fit with corporate social responsibility. *Journal of Business Ethics*, *119*(1), 45–57. doi:10.100710551-013-1621-6

Kanchanapibul, M., Lacka, E., Wang, X., & Chan, H. K. (2014). An empirical investigation of green purchase behaviour among the young generation. *Journal of Cleaner Production*, *66*, 528–536. doi:10.1016/j.jclepro.2013.10.062

Kaz, K. (2019). Building resilience into the organization. In R. Schmidpeter, N. Capaldi, S. Idowu, & A. Stürenberg Herrera (Eds.), *International dimensions of sustainable management. CSR, sustainability, ethics & governance: Latest perspectives from corporate governance, responsible finance and CSR* (pp. 69–85). Springer. doi:10.1007/978-3-030-04819-8_5

Khanna, T., & Palepu, K. G. (2010). *Winning in emerging markets: A road map for strategy and execution*. Harvard Business Press.

Kovoor-Misra, S., Zammuto, R. F., & Mitroff, I. I. (2000). Crisis preparation in organizations: Prescription versus reality. *Technological Forecasting and Social Change*, *63*(1), 43–62. doi:10.1016/S0040-1625(99)00049-9

Landau, C., Karna, A., & Sailer, M. (2016). Business model adaptation for emerging markets: A case study of a German automobile manufacturer in India. *R & D Management*, *46*(3), 480–503. doi:10.1111/radm.12201

Lengnick-Hall, C. A., & Beck, T. E. (2016). Resilience capacity and strategic agility: Prerequisites for thriving in a dynamic environment. In Ch. P. Nemeth, E. Hollnagel, & S. Dekker (Eds.), Resilience engineering perspectives, Vol. 2: Preparation and restoration (pp. 39-69). Surrey, UK: Ashgate Publishing Limited.

Lengnick-Hall, C. A., Beck, T. E., & Lengnick-Hall, M. L. (2011). Developing a capacity for organizational resilience through strategic human resource management. *Human Resource Management Review*, *21*(3), 243–255. doi:10.1016/j.hrmr.2010.07.001

Luxury Institute. (2019). *'State of The Luxury Industry' survey shows wealthy shoppers around the world crave emotional and human connections with luxury brands*. Retrieved from https://www.globenewswire.com/news-release/2019/01/22/1703335/0/en/Luxury-Institute-s-State-Of-The-Luxury-Industry-Survey-Shows-Wealthy-Shoppers-Around-The-World-Crave-Emotional-and-Human-Connections-With-Luxury-Brands.html

Mallak, L. (1998). Putting organizational resilience to work. *Industrial Management (Des Plaines)*, *40*(6), 8–13.

Miller, D. (1992). Environmental fit versus internal fit. *Organization Science*, *3*(2), 159–178. doi:10.1287/orsc.3.2.159

Nia, A., & Zaichhkowsky, J. L. (2000). Do counterfeits devalue the ownership of luxury brands? *Journal of Product and Brand Management*, *9*(7), 485–497. doi:10.1108/10610420010351402

Prayag, G., Spector, S., Orchiston, C., & Chowdhury, M. (2019). Psychological resilience, organizational resilience and life satisfaction in tourism firms: Insights from the Canterbury earthquakes. *Current Issues in Tourism*, *1*(18), 1–18.

Scott, R. (2003). *Organizations: Rational, Natural and Open Systems* (5th ed.). Prentice Hall.

Sicard, M.-C. (2003). *Luxe, mensonges & marketing - Mais que font les marques de luxe?* (3rd ed.). Pearson Education.

Silverstein, M. J., & Fiske, N. (2003). Luxury for the masses. *Harvard Business Review*, *81*(4), 48–57. PMID:12687919

Smith, W. K., Binns, A., & Tushman, M. L. (2010). Complex business models: Managing strategic paradoxes simultaneously. *Long Range Planning*, *43*(2-3), 448–461. doi:10.1016/j.lrp.2009.12.003

Stoltz, P. G. (2004). Building resilience for uncertain times. *Leader to Leader*, *2004*(31), 16–20. doi:10.1002/ltl.58

Sutcliffe, K. M., & Vogus, T. J. (2003). Organizing for resilience. In K. S. Cameron, J. E. Dutton, & R. E. Quinn (Eds.), *Positive organizational scholarship: Foundations of a new discipline* (pp. 94–110). Berrett-Koehler.

Teece, D. J. (2012). Dynamic capabilities: Routines versus entrepreneurial action. *Journal of Management Studies*, *49*(8), 1395–1401. doi:10.1111/j.1467-6486.2012.01080.x

Teece, D. J., Pisano, G., & Shuen, A. (1997). Dynamic capabilities and strategic management. *Strategic Management Journal*, *18*(7), 509–533. doi:10.1002/(SICI)1097-0266(199708)18:7<509::AID-SMJ882>3.0.CO;2-Z

Truong, Y., McColl, R., & Kitchen, P. J. (2008). New luxury brand positioning and the emergence of masstige brands. *Journal of Brand Management*, *16*(5/6), 375–382.

Tully, S., & Caplin, J. (2008). Look who pays for the bailout. Meet the Henrys (high earners, not rich yet). *Fortune International*, *158*(8), 50.

Weick, K. E. (1993). The collapse of sensemaking in organizations. *Administrative Science Quarterly*, *38*(4), 628–652. doi:10.2307/2393339

Weick, K. E., & Sutcliffe, K. M. (2001). *Managing the unexpected: Assuring high performance in an age of complexity*. Jossey-Bass.

Xu, D., & Meyer, K. E. (2013). Linking theory and context: 'Strategy research in emerging economies' after Wright et al. (2005). *Journal of Management Studies, 50*(7), 1322-1346.

Zott, C., & Amit, R. (2010). Business model design: An activity system perspective. *Long Range Planning, 43*(2-3), 216–226. doi:10.1016/j.lrp.2009.07.004

ADDITIONAL READING

Deevy, E. (1995). *Creating the resilient organization: A rapid response management program*. Prentice Hall.

Duchek, S., Raetze, S., & Scheuch, I. (2019). The role of diversity in organizational resilience: A theoretical framework. *Business Research*. Retrieved from https://link.springer.com/article/10.1007/s40685-019-0084-8

Eppler, M. J., Hoffmann, F., & Bresciani, S. (2011). New business models through collaborative idea generation. *International Journal of Innovation Management, 15*(6), 1323–1341. doi:10.1142/S1363919611003751

Johnson, M. W., Christensen, C. M., & Kagermann, H. (2008). Reinventing your business model. *Harvard Business Review, 86*(12), 57–68.

Lattuch, F., & Young, S. (2011). Young professionals' perceptions toward organizational change. *Leadership and Organization Development Journal, 32*(6), 605–627. doi:10.1108/01437731111161085

Loughlin, C., & Barling, J. (2001). Young workers' work values, attitudes, and behaviours. *Journal of Occupational and Organizational Psychology, 74*(4), 543–558. doi:10.1348/096317901167514

McCann, J. (2004). Organizational effectiveness: Changing concepts for changing environments. *Human Resource Planning, 27*(1), 42–50.

Poole, M. S., & Van de Ven, A. H. (Eds.). (2004). *Handbook of organizational change and innovation*. Oxford University Press.

Priporas, C. V., Stylos, N., & Fotiadis, A. K. (2017). Generation Z consumers' expectations of interactions in smart retailing: A future agenda. *Computers in Human Behavior, 77*, 374–381. doi:10.1016/j.chb.2017.01.058

KEY TERMS AND DEFINITIONS

Business Model: Specify the revenue generation mechanism(s) for the firm. Given the value proposition and the position of the firm within the value network, formulate the competitive strategy by which the innovating firm will gain and hold advantage over rivals in a market segment.

Change Management: Process of continually renewing the direction, structure and capabilities of an organization to meet the ever-changing needs of external and internal customers.

Dynamic Environments: Rapidly changing conditions that affect organizations, such as consumer tastes, technology, or laws and regulations. Managers must react quickly, and organizations must be flexible to respond. Strategic initiatives emerge in response to these changing factors

Generation Z: Those individuals who were born in the decade following the widespread emergence of the World Wide Web, from the mid 1990s to the early 2000s.

HENRYs: High-earners-not–rich-yet.

Organizational Resilience: Ability to survive a crisis, and thrive in a world of uncertainty. A resilient organization has the capacity to adapt potential disturbances emerging, and the ability to turn crises into a source of strategic opportunity.

Chapter 2
Exploring the Organizational and Technological Implications on Strategic Business Model Change:
A Case Study of One Electronic Marketplace

João Roque
Polytechnic Institute of Gaya, Portugal

José Duarte Santos
https://orcid.org/0000-0001-5815-4983
Polytechnic Institute of Gaya, Portugal

Jorge Simões
https://orcid.org/0000-0002-7822-0068
Polytechnic Institute of Gaya, Portugal

Fernando Almeida
https://orcid.org/0000-0002-6758-4843
Polytechnic Institute of Gaya, Portugal

DOI: 10.4018/978-1-7998-4552-2.ch002

ABSTRACT

The purpose of this chapter is to identify and analyze the main organizational and technological factors that play a relevant role in a transformational strategic change inherent in changing the business model supported on the internet. An analysis was made of the different business models, as well as their connection to strategic management and how this is accomplished in the organizational and technological plan. This empirical study, based on the qualitative methodology, focuses on a single case study on a Portuguese company that recently changed its business model. The findings allowed the authors to assess the advantages and challenges posed by the transformation of an initial business based on a website that performs a comparison of prices for an integrated model based on a marketplace, in which customers can make their purchases and access all products, from different stores, in one place.

INTRODUCTION

The global economic environment has changed over the years as a result of globalization. One of the factors that promote increasing competitiveness is technology, namely new information and communication technologies (Radman & Belin, 2017; Zoroja & Bach, 2016). There is an increasing number of organizations that base their business on a service offering, which is a factor that promotes internationalization and also promotes a greater focus on people and the enhancement of their skills. These economic changes have favored the emergence of new approaches in organizations in several areas. Yasav (2015) states that the supply of information technology products/services has made it possible to support several of the changes that have been occurring, also affecting the demand side of the relationship with customers, since they also have at their disposal new capabilities that change the way they interact with the market.

The strategic development presents several forms like continuous, incremental, flow or transformational (Pearce & Robinson, 2014). Despite the less frequency of the latter form, the drastic changes that this form of strategic development places to companies tends to be more demanding and challenging. The Internet can be the lever for this option, giving rise to the appearance of new business models, providing opportunities, but also creating challenges for companies. Therefore, there is interest from the business world to study these movements about the companies, so that they can be more proactive in the idealization of the business model.

Initially, this study synthesizes and compares different concepts and definitions of business models, their link to strategic management and how they are explored in the organizational and technological plan. Continuously, it identifies and characterizes several business models and evidences specific models supported on the Internet. With the analysis of the models is expected to get to detect common elements that can constitute as factors key for when the company changes of business model. Also, the transformation of the derived company of a strategy that implicates to a digital component will be addressed by this study.

This study also carries out an empirical study supported by the qualitative methodology, with a single case study that focused on a Portuguese company that recently changed its business model. For this purpose, the authors used a semi-structured interview, documentation provided by the company and public documents about it. This study, of exploratory nature, intends to have as main contribution the identification of organizational and technological factors that are present in the transformation of a model of specific business and that can be incorporated in future quantitative studies, to be possible to perform an eventual validation and generalization. The adopted methodology allowed exploring the real context of an organization, using for that purpose qualitative and quantitative sources. According to Yin (2009), the case study is a research strategy that comprises a method that covers everything in specific approaches of data collection and analysis. It was important to use this methodology to understand the reasons that led the company analyzed to make strategic and organizational changes in its business model.

Finally, the findings are discussed according to the established dimensions of the semi-structured interview. After that, the conclusions are presented and some relevant indications for future research directions are given.

BACKGROUND

Business Model Concept

The concept of business model has gained importance mainly due to the growth of the knowledge economy, the growth of the Internet, e-commerce, the offshoring of many commercial activities and the restructuring of the industry (Teece, 2010).

The process of building a business model is based on key elements like strategic positioning and value chain (Porter, 1996). Throughout this process, entrepreneurs are encouraged to build a business based on strategic decisions and explore the relationship between the various elements through diverse combinations. The model is a relatively simple way that the organization has to set the limits of the main decisions that need to be taken, as well as what should not be done (Morris, Schindehutte & Allen, 2005).

For Timmers (1998), the business model is a description of the various actors, potential benefits for them and sources of revenue. Rappa (2004) states that a business model is a method of doing business and it describes how a company creates value, relates to its partners and generates revenue. In turn, Afuah and Tucci (2002) define a business model as being important to explain the competitive advantage and performance of the company. Consequently, this is the process by which companies can generate revenue to their customers from the efficient use of their resources.

A business model presents a company's value proposition (Osterwalder & Pigneur. 2002; Rappa, 2004) to a target audience (Osterwalder & Pigneur. 2002) and what is its marketing action plan to raise revenue (Osterwalder & Pigneur. 2002; Rappa, 2004). Osterwalder (2004) defines a business model as a method and a tool formed by a set of interrelated components that describe the logic by which the company earns money. In turn, Johnson, Christensen and Kagermann (2008) consider the existence of four interconnection elements: value proposition, revenue, key resources and key processes that together create and deliver value.

Laudon and Traver (2018) argue that a business model is supported by a set of planned activities, sometimes referred to as business processes, designed in such a way that the organization obtains profit. Technological evolution and the redefinition of information and communication technologies in companies in business processes have led companies to rethink their business models. Osterwalder (2004) suggests that the business model is at the center of the triangle formed by strategy, organization, and information and communication technology.

Al-Debei, El-Haddadeh and Avison (2008) analyzed seventeen definitions of business model and presented a definition that seeks to be generic and simultaneously incorporates the flexibility of the business model representation and it identifies the location of the business model within the digital business organization: "the business model is an abstract representation of an organization, be it conceptual, textual, and/or graphical, of all core interrelated architectural, co-operational, and financial arrangements designed and developed by an organization presently and in the future, as well as all core products and/or services the organization offers, or will offer, based on these arrangements needed to achieve its strategic goals and objectives" (pp. 8-9).

In fact, all companies have a business model, whether articulated or not, which means that they all need to define a consistent business model, subject to change through the evolution of the market and technology (Chesbrough, 2007). The concept of business model, although not fully implemented in some companies, is implicitly or explicitly present in all of them (Teece, 2010).

Table 1. Business models components

Model	Features	Authors
Activities	It involves knowing what activities to perform and when they should be performed.	Afuah & Tucci (2002); Shafer, Smith & Linder (2005)
Capabilities	Competencies of the company concerning its ability to convert its resources into value for the customer, revenue for the company, and generate competitive advantage.	Afuah & Tucci (2002)
Communication	It corresponds to the method that the company uses to communicate and influence its customers.	Osterwalder & Pigneur (2010); Petrovic, Kittl & Tekstenc (2001)
Cost structure	Indicates the relationship between the income that the company obtains and the costs that involve that income.	Afuah & Tucci (2002); Eyring, Johnson & Nair (2010); Osterwalder & Pigneur (2010); Petrovic et al. (2001); Shafer et al. (2005)
Distribution	It involves delivery, channels and promotion.	Osterwalder & Pigneur (2010); Petrovic et al. (2001)
Implementation	Consists of the process of actually executing the decision made previously regarding the value to the customer, scope, price, sources of income, and activities.	Afuah & Tucci (2002)
Legal Issues	They have to be considered in all dimensions of the business model since they can influence the overall view of the business model.	Alt & Zimmerman (2001)
Logistics	Answers all questions related to business value chain design.	Mahadevan (2000)
Market	Selection of the most appropriate market to operate the business.	Petrovic et al. (2001)
Mission	It includes the overview, strategic objectives and value proposal (product characteristics or service).	Alt & Zimmerman (2001)
Partners	Identification of suppliers, partners and position in the value chain.	Osterwalder and Pigneur (2010)
Price	Pricing strategy that enables profit from the value provided to customers.	Afuah & Tucci (2002)
Product or service	It is what satisfies the value proposition and generates the benefit proposed to the customer.	Petrovic et al. (2001); Stähler (2002)
Processes	Implies a greater detail regarding the mission and structure of a business model.	Alt & Zimmerman (2001); Eyring et al. (2010); Johnson et al. (2008); Shafer et al. (2005)
Production	Identifies how the elements are combined in the transformation process.	Petrovic et al. (2001)
Relationship with the consumer	Identification of the type of relationships that the company establishes with a specific customer segment.	Osterwalder & Pigneur (2010); Petrovic et al. (2001)
Revenues	Plan to ensure that the business will have an income. Analysis of the organization's sources of income.	Afuah & Tucci (2002); Alt & Zimmerman (2001); Eyring et al. (2010); Johnson et al. (2008); Mahadevan (2000); Osterwalder & Pigneur (2010); Petrovic et al. (2001); Stähler (2002)
Resources	Describes the elements needed for the transformation process and how to identify and purchase the required quantities.	Afuah & Tucci (2002); Eyring et al. (2010); Johnson et al. (2008); Osterwalder & Pigneur (2010); Petrovic et al. (2001); Shafer et al. (2005)
Strategic choices	It encompasses customers, value proposition, competitors, strategy, differentiation and mission.	Shafer et al. (2005)
Structure	Determines the roles and agents that are part of a business community, as well as the focus on industry, customers and products.	Alt & Zimmerman (2001)
Sustainability	Strategy adopted by the company to maintain its competitive advantage.	Afuah &Tucci (2002)
Target	Identification of target customer segments and their needs.	Osterwalder &Pigneur (2010)
Technology	It is necessary to take into account the technological advances and the impact this has on the design of business models.	Alt & Zimmerman (2001)
Value creation architecture	It consists of creating the promised benefit to the consumer in an efficient manner. It consists of market design, internal and external architecture.	Stähler (2002)
Value proposition	Identifies the value proposition for customers, vendors and business partners.	Afuah & Tucci (2002); Eyring et al. (2010); Johnson et al. (2008); Mahadevan (2000); Osterwalder & Pigneur (2010); Petrovic et al. (2001); Shafer et al. (2005); Stähler (2002)

Business Models Components

In the application of a business model, several components need to be thought and defined. It is not surprising that two businesses based on the same model have different results through the way they have internalized those components. However, it is also not consensual which components should be considered in the business model. Consequently, Table 1 presents the components considered as important by the established authors.

The analysis of the studied authors allows us verifying the existence of 25 components to be taken into consideration in the definition of the structure of a business. However, it can be seen that some components are more consensual among the authors. Therefore, it is highlighted: the analysis of the cost structure, the format of revenues, the necessary resources and the value proposition. A reduction of the components of the business model only to these four components can be considered too simplistic. However, this representation incorporates the basis of a business.

Business Models Classification

Timmers (1998) focused his studies on Internet supported business models and classified them based on two criteria: (i) functional integration (single function or multiple functions/integrated) and (ii) degree of innovation (lower or higher). In total, Timmers (1998) identified 10 generic types of business models. In turn, Afuah and Tucci (2002) classify the business models into seven types, using the company's revenue model as variables. Rappa (2004) proposes nine categories to classify the business models of Internet-based companies. Deitel and Deitel (2004) identify seven business models for the web and Turban et al. (2018) classify the models according to the type of revenue and how e-commerce is carried out.

Supported on the various models submitted by the above-mentioned authors, it is pertinent to classify the models based on the type of revenue and form of marketing. Therefore, Table 2 classifies the models based on the type of revenue. It should be noted that some models represent the same typologies, although their authors have different nomenclatures.

Table 2. Classification of business models based on the type of revenue

Model	Features	Authors
Advertising fees.	Companies charge others for allowing them to place a banner on their sites	Turban et al. (2018)
Commission (Afuah & Tucci, 2002) Transaction fees (Turban et al., 2018)	This model is based on the charging of a fee by a third party, usually referred to as an intermediary. Such intermediary may act as a Marketplace. Normally commissions are based on the volume of transactions.	Afuah & Tucci (2002); Turban et al. (2018)
Fee-for-Service (Afuah & Tucci, 2002) Utility (Rapa, 2004)	It is based on a time-based approach to payment depending on the time of use or payment depending on the content viewed.	Afuah & Tucci (2002); Rapa (2004)
License fees	Licensing fees may be applied annually or for every use.	Turban et al. (2018)
Referral (Afuah &Tucci, 2002) Affiliate (Rapa, 2004) Affiliate fees (Turban et al., 2018)	An entity offers financial incentives, usually a percentage of the profits to other entities to place a banner or something similar on its website that enables customers to be redirected to the associated entity's website. The company generates revenue by sending customers to another site, which is typically based as a percentage of sales or a flat rate.	Afuah & Tucci (2002); Rapa (2004); Turban et al. (2018)
Sales	The revenue comes from the products or services offered by the company through the Internet.	Turban et al. (2018)
Subscription fee	Users of the service pay a periodic fee (monthly or yearly) to subscribe to the service. The service provider can offer a free version and charge for a premium version.	Afuah & Tucci (2002); Rapa (2004); Turban et al. (2018)

Table 3 shows a classification of business models based on the form of marketing, the model being designated preferably based on Internet presence, when coexisting in the brick and mortar version.

Table 3. Classification of Internet presence business models based on the form of marketing

Model	Features	Authors
3rd party marketplace	Provides user interface and product catalog. It can also provide additional features such as payment, ordering, and logistics.	Timmers (1998); Turban et al. (2018)
Advertising	A site that provides content and services mixed with advertising messages in the form of banners.	Afuah & Tucci (2002); Voorveld et al. (2018)
Bartering	Websites that make it possible to offer one item in exchange for another.	Rapa (2004); Turban et al. (2018)
Brokerage	Category of models in which there is an entity that brings customers and sellers together and facilitates transactions. Usually, a commission is charged for each transaction made.	Rapa (2004); Turban et al. (2018)
Collaboration platforms	They provide a set of tools and information for collaboration between organizations.	Fernandes & Remelhe (2016); Timmers (1998)
Community	Based on the creation of a community of users who support the site through voluntary donations. Profit can also come from the purchase of ancillary products, voluntary contributions or even advertising and subscriptions.	Storvang et al. (2019); Weill & Vitale (2001)
Deep discounting	The organization offers discounts on the price of the products or services it trades, to appeal to those consumers who value the price highly in their purchase decisions.	Turban et al. (2018)
e-auction	Electronic implementation of the traditional auction mechanism. It may include contract, payment and delivery.	Timmers (1998); Ow et al. (2018); Turban et al. (2018);
e-mall	Includes a set of several online stores.	Timmers (1998)
e-shop (Timmers, 1998) Merchant (Rapa, 2004) Storefront (Deitel and Deitel, 2004)	It includes the promotion of the organization and its goods/services and the possibility to order and pay. Can include auctions. Rapa (2004) refers to a manufacturer who sells directly to consumers without intermediaries and Weill and Vitale (2001) refer to Direct to Customers.	Deitel & Deitel (2004); Rapa (2014); Timmers (1998); Turban et al. (2018)
e-procurement	Includes electronic search services for goods and services.	Piera et al. (2014); Timmers (1998)
Full-service provider	Providing a complete service in a given area (such as finance, health, etc.), directly and through partners, in an attempt to have the primary relationship with the consumer.	Weill & Vitale (2001)
Group purchasing	It is based on the concept of quantity discounts. The Internet model allows individuals to get together so they can gain a large-quantity advantage.	Turban et al. (2018)
Information brokers (Timmers, 1998) Value net integrator (Weill & Vitale, 2001) Infomediary (Rapa, 2004)	Services that provide information and advice. These entities may collect information about consumers and their consumer habits and sell that information.	Rapa (2004); Timmers (1998); Turban et al. (2018); Weill & Vitale (2001)
Markup	It is based on value addition in sales. Sales are made through price lists or auctions.	Afuah & Tucci (2002)
Membership	Business in which only members have access to the services provided, including access to certain information, entering into transactions, etc.	Turban et al. (2018)
Name-your-own-price	The customer indicates how much he is willing to pay and an intermediary looks for a supplier who meets the requirements.	Deitel & Deitel (2004); Turban et al. (2018)
Portal	These are websites that provide consumers with a wide range of options, from news, sports, weather information, and also a search tool that allows them to conduct searches on the web.	Deitel & Deitel (2004)
Price comparison	A business that enables consumers to compare prices charged by various suppliers for similar items. The profit comes from partnership with suppliers.	Deitel & Deitel (2004); Turban et al. (2018)
Product customization	Customers configure their products or services. The sales employee then assigns a price to the item and sells it.	Park & Yoo (2018); Turban et al. (2018)
Production	It is based on profits from production. The company transforms raw material into a higher-value product.	Afuah & Tucci (2002)
Referral (Afuah & Tucci, 2002) Affiliate (Rapa, 2004; Turban et al., 2018)	An entity offers financial incentives, usually a percentage of the profits to other entities to place a banner or something similar on its website that enables customers to be redirected to the associated entity's website. The company generates revenue by sending customers to another site. Revenue is generated through a percentage of sales or a flat rate. It provides buying opportunities for those who browse the Internet through click-through, linking the site directly to the merchant's site. The merchant only pays if he/she sells.	Afuah & Tucci (2002); Rapa (2004); Turban et al. (2018)
Shared Infrastructure	Brings together various competitors for them to cooperate, through the sharing of technology infrastructure.	Weill & Vitale (2001)
Shopping-cart technology	Technology that allows consumers to accumulate items they want to buy as they browse an electronic site.	Deitel & Deitel (2004)
Supply-chain improvers	Restructuring of the supply chain by organizations to increase collaboration, reduce delays, etc.	Turban et al. (2018)
Value chain integrator	It aims to integrate multiple steps in the value chain to explore the flow of information between these steps and thus add value.	Timmers (1998); Turban et al. (2018)
Value chain service provider	Services that specialize in a specific function of the value chain, such as logistics and electronic payments.	Timmers (1998); Turban et al. (2018)
Viral marketing	Recipients send product/service information to friends. It explores the connections between people to spread and become viral.	Turban et al. (2018)
Virtual communities	Services that require the registration of users. They focus on the additional value arising from communication between members. Profit can come from membership fees or advertising.	Granata & Scozzese (2017); Timmers (1998)

MAIN FOCUS OF THE CHAPTER

Organization Background

The "KuantoKusta" company[1] is located in the industrial center of Lionesa in the town of Leça do Balio, belonging to the district of Porto, Portugal. It is a technology company committed to the online shopping process. It was founded in May 2005 by the Pimenta brothers, who were emigrants in France and wanted to open a computer store in Portugal. While conducting a market survey to analyze the prices practiced in the country, they encountered the inexistence of a website that added prices and allowed them to be compared, creating an innovative business for the time. A price comparison site was then set up where the pay was made per click, and several well-known brand partners were raised for this purpose in which the remuneration of the business was made per click.

Over the course of 14 years, KuantoKusta has established itself as the national leader in price comparison and has always been the link between the user and the shops. Only those who managed to gain the trust of users and partner stores would be able to become one of the most influential channels of e-commerce in Portugal and take such important steps towards innovation, such as its transformation into a Marketplace. The adhesion to a new business model was driven by the growing advancement of the digital market of the country. Aware of what the user is demanding, the transformation arises, just thinking not only for the consumer but with the consumer (i.e., to ensure the best experience), so that from the purchase to the delivery of the product, satisfaction is full.

The new business model allowed the company to generate 515 million Euros in sales to approximately 115 partner stores and double the number of employees in 2018. The company grew by approximately 20% from 2017 to 2018 (JN, 2019). Among the articles sold on the platform, the strongest category is that of technology, although products in the health, beauty, clothing or fashion segments are also on sale (JN, 2019). The company counts in 2019 with approximately 40 employees, having as CEO Paulo Pimenta, and 4 team leaders.

Materials and Methods

Qualitative research is particularly important for the study of social relations, given the plurality of life universes. This plurality requires a new sensitivity to the empirical study of issues. The accelerated social change and the consequent diversity of the universes of life increasingly confront researchers with new social contexts and new perspectives. In fact, the traditional process of traditional deductive methodologies fails in the differentiation of issues. In this sense, research is increasingly forced to resort to inductive strategies: instead of starting from theories to empirical testing, what is required is 'sensitizing concepts' to address the social contexts to be studied. On the contrary, however, of a general misunderstanding, these sensitizing concepts are influenced by the existing theoretical knowledge. But, in this case, the theories result from empirical studies. According to Mills (2014), knowledge and practice are studied in the quality of local knowledge and practice.

Qualitative research methodologies are inspired, among others, by the assumptions of the constructivist paradigm. These methodologies consider that knowledge is constructed inter-subjectively through a close interaction between the knowledgeable subject and the object. At the methodological level, the interpretation of reality involves considering and capturing the meanings attributed by social actors to the different aspects of their interaction (Mills, 2014). The striking feature of these methodologies lies in the fact that the questions to be investigated are not defined on the basis of the operationalization of previously formulated variables or hypotheses but according to objectives of exploration, description, and understanding of phenomena in all their complexity, privileging a close and prolonged contact with the subjects in their natural environment. Consequently, the objective of the qualitative methodology is to describe and understand human behavior in its complexity, explaining the process by which social actors construct the meanings assigned to the social and, from there, elaborate heuristic concepts that reflect this reality. They seek to generate an interpretative understanding of reality to reveal a multiple and dynamic reality (Luttrell, 2009; Queirós, Faria & Almeida, 2017).

The authors conducted a semi-structured interview with the Chief Marketing Officer (CMO) of KuantoKusta. The use of a semi-structured interview allowed us to have a sufficiently adaptable script that does not follow a rigid model contrary to the process of conducting a structured interview. According to Merriam (2015), this approach allows us to deepen some more relevant questions and its flexibility offers an adaptation to the interviewee, his reactions or the context, which will allow a broader data collection. This approach enables us to explore in-depth the organizational and technological challenges of the changing business model undergone by KuantoKusta. Furthermore, the adoption of this methodology allows us to analyze the company's positioning and the challenges posed by the implementation of an electronic marketplace.

A semi-structured interview script was defined as suggested by Merriam (2015) (see Table 4). A total of 16 questions were considered and they are divided into four dimensions: (i) contextual; (ii) diagnosis; (iii) evaluative; and (iv) strategic. In the "contextual" dimension, the aim is to contextualize the organization, its target market, and strategy; in the "diagnosis" dimension, the aim is to focus on the initial phase of the company's development; in the "evaluative" dimension, the focus becomes the current business model and a comparative analysis is performed against the model previously adopted by the company; and in the "strategic" dimension, the business and technological challenges that the company will face in developing its business activity are explored.

Table 4. Interview questions

Dimension	Questions
Contextual	Can you please tell us a little about the history of the company, namely how the idea of launching this business in the market came about?
	What is the size of the company and its organizational structure?
	What were the key moments that marked the company's history?
	How is the business advertised?
Diagnosis	What was the business model initially developed by "KuantoKusta"?
	What were the biggest obstacles felt in the development of the business in the initial paradigm?
Evaluative	What is the new business model adopted? How is this business model implemented?
	What were the reasons for changing the business model of "KuantoKusta"?
	What are the objectives you expect to achieve with the new business model that you consider could not be achieved in the previous model?
	What are the organizational and technological elements that had to be changed to implement this new business model? Has a transition plan been made?
Strategic	How is "KuantoKusta" positioned in the market?
	What are the main competitors? What are the main differentiation factors?
	What is the growth forecast with the adoption of this new model?
	Will there be a need to hire more human resources and invest in more technological resources?
	What are the main challenges that the company will face in the coming years in the development of its activity?

SOLUTIONS AND RECOMMENDATIONS

Contextual

KuantoKusta launched in May 2005 the first price comparison website in Portugal. This was an innovative business for the time, which made millions of Portuguese make more economical purchases and effectively meet their needs. Currently, the company has approximately 40 employees distributed as follows: one CEO; four teams' leaders (marketing, sales, service and resources, content and technical department) and respective teams.

Throughout these 14 years, KuantoKusta has consolidated as the national leader in price comparison and has become a link between the user and the shops. Critical success factors in the company's activity were, firstly, the emergence of the idea, secondly, the partnerships made with major brands and, finally, the opening of the MarketPlace. Some key moments that mark the history of the company are highlighted, namely:

- 1st app launched in 2012. For KuantoKusta, it is essential to have a global digitization strategy and to build a presence in these media. Apps are increasingly part of our way of living and working and, consequently, access via an app is fundamental to the company's growth (Girish, 2018);
- Responsive website developed in 2014. With the growth of the variety of devices where websites are accessed (e.g., laptops, smartphones, tablets) it becomes unsustainable to have multiple versions of the same site that fit the size and resolutions of screens available on the market. In this sense, responsive web design is one of the technical solutions that allow an automatic adaptation to the screen width of the device where the content is being viewed. According to Almeida and Monteiro (2017), it is currently essential to have responsive websites to offer acceptable levels of User Experience (UX) and also to be suitable for search engines and increase its relevance;
- PriceBench launched in 2016. PriceBench is a specialized tool for collecting, processing and analyzing product data that turns the price management process more intelligent;
- Marketplace launched in 2018. On this platform, different stores can advertise their products, giving the customer a diverse range of options. For users, the marketplace allows a single site to offer goods from multiple sellers and to compare and choose the best price easily. Besides, through the use of the marketplace, the user can buy in several different stores and make only a single payment.

KuantoKusta makes little investment in marketing. The promotion of the business is done mainly through word-of-mouth. KuantoKusta considers that the traditional means of diffusion and communication of content fall short of the needs of the company. As a result, the Internet has become more relevant as a tool of research and information sharing and also influences the opinion of consumers especially through social networks. By investing in digital communication from its website and social networks, KuantoKusta is able to take advantage of word-of-mouth communication. This vision is shared by Maisam and Mahsa (2016) and Trusov, Bucklin and Pauwels (2009) that highlight the role of the word-of-mouth in the evaluation of products and services by consumers, in contrast to the information obtained through advertising media. Additionally, the findings obtained by Naz (2014) indicate that the impact of the word-of-mouth results from the involvement and interaction inherent in this type of communication to the extent that it results in greater consumer concentration.

Diagnosis

Initially, the company's activity consisted of an online price comparison site. The business model was based on the number of clicks performed by the user. The remuneration of the business was based on three indicators: cost per click (CPC), cost per mile (CPM), and cost per acquisition (CPA). The CPC is calculated according to the number of clicks on ads, the CPM by impressions, and the CPA is calculated based on the number of conversions. In most business agreements established by the company, remuneration is based on the CPC model. In this model, the advertiser pays for the number of visitors going from the site where the ad was made to his site. According to Islam (2019), this is the most widespread model in digital ads. As the budget is spent based on the number of clicks that an ad receives, this model is more indicated and easier to control (Tiwary, 2016).

The change in the business model implied both organizational and technological changes. The biggest obstacle felt by the company in the initial development of the business was to attract partners and obtain a return on the initial investment. The initial investment made by the company's founders was around 30 thousand Euros. According to public data provided by the company, turnover reached one million and 700 thousand Euros in 2017, and almost 30 million visits (Castro, 2018). On another perspective, the transactions generated for the partner stores reached 296 million Euros, 8.78% more than in 2016 (Castro, 2018). Curiously, the crisis felt in Portugal during the 2010-2014 period was a driver for business growth, because people started to worry more about comparing prices to increase their saves.

Evaluative

The new business model adopted by KuantoKusta is the marketplace. Through it, customers can make their purchases and access all products, from different stores, in one place. With this transformation, KuantoKusta becomes a platform that brings together stores and users in one place. Therefore, a customer who used to come to KuantoKusta just to compare prices can now buy all kinds of products, from different stores, without leaving the KuantoKusta website or without going to a physical store. With this new business model, the company seeks to reach a target of 1000 daily purchases. This change in the business model also implied significant changes in other components of a business model, such as the activities developed, communication process, cost structure, or value proposal. This has involved training employees for this new challenge and informing customers of this new paradigm. This was a challenge since the company's image was merely associated with a price comparison website.

It is also relevant to explore the motivations that drove this change. The company realized through formal and informal contacts with its customers and partners that a user, before deciding on an online purchase, needs information that goes far beyond the price of the product (e.g., store reliability, shipping conditions, delivery times, etc.). By aggregating this information in a marketplace, the purchase conditions become uniform, more transparent and secure. Therefore, the offer of an aggregator service that enables both a price comparator and an electronic marketplace was a catalyst for this change. Moreover, Bandara, Fernando and Akter (2017) and Hill (2018) advocate those complex aspects of security, privacy, authentication, and anonymity are particularly important for e-commerce. Additionally, the confidentiality, reliability, and protection of information against security threats are a critical prerequisite for the functionalities offered by an e-marketplace (Sfenrianto, Wijaya &Wang, 2018).

KuantoKusta realized that despite this strategic change, the essence of the company will continue to focus on price comparison. This has been a key element of notoriety and credibility in the market and has become a reference in e-commerce in Portugal. However, it is also recognized that this strategic change implied the alteration of organizational and technological elements. To this end, a check out model had to be created on the site, partnerships with online payment companies had to be developed, and the customer support process had to be improved. Additionally, more internal human resources were also required, particularly in terms of programming and systems administration.

Strategic

Innovation is an essential key concept for business development at KuantoKusta. At the moment the company is positioned as the most differentiating marketplace in Portugal, also standing out for being the most "friendly" for the end-user. According to Kim (2013), the "friendly" concept should incorporate multiple dimensions, such as usability, design, security, and robustness. In this sense, KuantoKusta designed an e-marketplace thinking about the interaction that the user will have through a smartphone. Several factors were considered in the implementation of the marketplace, namely: (i) readability, so that the user does not need to enlarge the screen to read what is written; (ii) perfect fit, by avoiding the use of a horizontal scroll bar for the complete visualization of the page; (iii) accessibility, avoiding the need for applications or software to navigate the marketplace; and (iv) light and intuitive layout, through the design of buttons and easy to click links.

Currently, the company considers that its main competitors are Dott,[2] Worten[3] and Fnac.[4] However, the main differentiation of KuantoKusta is the simultaneous provision of a price comparator and marketplace. Neither of its competitors offers both services at the same time. KuantoKusta is taking its first steps with its marketplace service, estimating business growth at around 30% by the end of 2019. This growth will necessarily be accompanied by greater investment in human and technological resources. At a technological level, the company intends to invest in servers and hardware. In terms of human resources, the company intends to have a more autonomous marketing department and to hire more human resources (e.g., commercial and technical) to serve the final customer.

KuantoKusta's biggest challenge is to be continuously innovating. This is a highly challenging and ever-changing business area. New players in this market often arise. Although the findings identified by Karakaya and Stahl (2009) indicate the knowledge in e-commerce and the existence of sufficient resources to become competitive in this market, in practice the resources have to be analyzed from a perspective of sustainability and comparative with other competitors. In the case of an e-marketplace, in particular, the entry barriers for the emergence of new competitors will be higher, since a key factor of competitive advantage is the establishment of partners. In this sense, it is essential for KuantoKusta to be in constant evolution and follows market trends, always looking for new partnerships alongside major brands.

FUTURE RESEARCH DIRECTIONS

Marketplaces are attractive to many entrepreneurs who seek in this business model a profitable and scalable solution to undertake on the Internet. However, this path needs to overcome some challenges to be successful. One of these challenges is the segmentation of the business, which is why more and more segmented e-marketplaces are emerging in specific sectors of activity. With this, these companies seek to be more specialized and present competitive advantages based on knowledge and proximity to the customer. Another challenge is the sustainability of the business in the medium and long term. It is, therefore, necessary that the existing partnerships can contribute to the sustainability of the business from a financial and organizational perspective.

Marketplaces offer companies the possibility of selling their products in a highly visible location without having to open their own store. For consumers, the convenience of finding everything in one place, with many more options and price offers, is a great attraction. However, for the customer to find what they want, it is important to filter the offers. Until the consumer makes his decision, there are several stores, products, brands, models and functions to search, compare and choose. In the middle of this process, the consumer may feel lost in front of so many options, feel unable to choose and give up the purchase. The solution is to organize the marketplace offers in a relevant way to the consumer. Through the use of Big Data and Artificial Intelligence techniques, e-marketplaces can identify consumer interests, behaviors, navigation and purchase history. Based on this learning, the customer receives personalized suggestions. This way, the experience becomes much more positive in the marketplace. In fact, artificial intelligence is today one of the most promising technologies in the ability to work and optimize all this dispersed information (Bughin et al., 2017). Despite its undeniable impact, some challenges must be overcome. One of them is the implication of artificial intelligence algorithms for regulation and their compliance with the rules established by the GDPR (Gal & Elkin-Koren, 2017; Tikkinen-Piri, Rohunen & Markkula, 2018).

CONCLUSION

The globalization and the advancement of information and communication technologies in recent decades have enabled the emergence of new businesses and new behavioral and market trends. Organizations need to follow this line of evolution, adding to their business advantages related to convenience, communication, and technology that will enable them to offer greater added value to the client. There are now more business models that lead organizations to have components of e-Business. It was seen the importance of the strategy to guide the organization towards common objectives, as well as the need for business modeling so that all stakeholders understand how the business works. Proper functioning at these levels will ensure that the operation of the organization at the process level is also aligned with the organization's strategy. The existence of feedback between the various levels of business logic is of great importance. There are several factors that lead to a company changing or transforming its initial business model, and in the case of the company under study ("KuantoKusta"), the main factors that led to the change in the initial business model were the need to follow the evolution of the market, closely following the evolution of its competitors, offer a service differentiator, being the only company that aggregates in the same site the comparison of prices, as well as the online purchase of the products intended.

The realization of this case study allowed us to know and explore the business model of the company KuantoKusta, thus being able to understand the reasons that led to the change of the initial business model. The approach used has allowed us to explore this phenomenon from multiple perspectives such as the contextual, diagnosis, evaluative, and strategic dimensions. In conclusion, we can say that the company is attentive to market trends, as well as to the needs of the end customer, offering them more and more easily more convenient and secure solutions to make their transactions and price comparisons. At the moment, with the adoption of the "Marketplace" business model, the end customer can get the best prices by comparing various brands and then purchase the desired product comfortably and safely.

The changes made by KuantoKusta in its business model implied organizational and technological changes. This study also underscores the current market competitiveness and accelerated business process in the electronic medium, which implies that organizations constantly reorganize their goals and establish ever-smaller life cycles for their products and services. Finally, organizations need to be aware of the change and enjoy the sustainable, fast, and cost-effective resources that e-business provides.

This study offers mainly practical contributions. It may be relevant for company managers who have in mind strategic changes in their business models, thus perceiving the greater implications, benefits, and risks inherent in these changes, as well as realizing that they can aggregate new business models to existing ones by increasing in this way value the company. However, there are also limitations mainly because the study addresses a single case study with its own specificities. In this sense, the challenges encountered are relevant and should be framed in the context of KuantoKusta and their applicability to other business areas or geographical contexts should be duly assessed considering the contextual conditions.

ACKNOWLEDGMENT

The authors would like to thank KuantoKusta's management team for their cooperation in making this study possible.

REFERENCES

Afuah, A., & Tucci, C. L. (2002). Internet business models and strategies: Text and cases. New York: McGraw-Hill.

Al-Debei, M., El-Haddadeh, R., & Avison, D. (2008). Defining the business model in the new world of digital business. In *Proceedings of the Fourteenth Americas Conference on Information Systems* (pp.1-11). Toronto, Canada: Association for Information Systems.

Almeida, F., & Monteiro, J. (2017). Approaches and Principles for UX Web Experiences. *Journal of Information Technology and Web Engineering, 12*(2), 49–65. doi:10.4018/IJITWE.2017040103

Alt, R., & Zimmermann, H.-D. (2001). Introduction to special section: Business models. *Electronic Markets, 1*(11), 3–9.

Bandara, R., Fernando, M., & Akter, S. (2017). The privacy paradox in the data-driven marketplace: The role of knowledge deficiency and psychological distance. *Procedia Computer Science, 121*, 562–567. doi:10.1016/j.procs.2017.11.074

Bughin, J., Hazan, E., Ramaswamy, S., Chui, M., Allas, T., Dahlstrom, P., Henke, N., & Trench, M. (2017). *Artificial intelligence the next digital frontier*. McKinsey Global Institute, Discussion Paper. Retrieved from https://www.mckinsey.com/~/media/McKinsey/Industries/Advanced%20Electronics/Our%20Insights/How%20artificial%20intelligence%20can%20deliver%20real%20value%20to%20companies/MGI-Artificial-Intelligence-Discussion-paper.ashx

Castro, C. (2018). *Crise ajudou negócio do KuantoKusta*. Retrieved from https://www.dinheirovivo.pt/empresas/mub-cargo-uber-das-mercadorias-chega-a-espanha-este-ano/

Chesbrough, H. (2007). Business model innovation: It's not just about technology anymore. *Strategy and Leadership, 35*(6), 12–17. doi:10.1108/10878570710833714

Deitel, H., & Deitel, P. (2004). The complete e-business and e-commerce programming training course. New Jersey: Prentice Hall.

Eyring, M. J., Johnson, M. W., & Nair, H. (2010). New business models in emerging markets. *Harvard Business Review, 89*(1-2), 88–95.

Fernandes, T., & Remelhe, P. (2016). How to engage customers in co-creation: Customers' motivations for collaborative innovation. *Journal of Strategic Marketing, 24*(3-4), 311–326. doi:10.1080/0965254X.2015.1095220

Gal, M. S., & Elkin-Koren, N. (2017). Algorithmic consumers. *Harvard Journal of Law & Technology*, *30*, 1–45.

Girish, R. (2018). *Why are businesses shifting to mobile apps in 2018.* Retrieved from https://www.fingent.com/blog/businesses-shifting-mobile-apps-2018

Granata, G., & Scozzese, G. (2017). The Influence of Virtual Communities in Marketing Decision. *International Business Research*, *10*(12), 191–196. doi:10.5539/ibr.v10n12p191

Hill, R. (2018). Theory of marketplace morality and impoverished consumers. *Marketing Theory*, *18*(3), 411–420. doi:10.1177/1470593117753983

Islam, T. (2019). *Cost per click: the most used model of online advertising*. Retrieved from https://charpotra.blogspot.com/2019/04/cost-per-click-most-used-model-of.html

JN. (2019). *KuantoKusta investe três milhões de euros para alargar plataforma de venda "online"*. Retrieved from https://www.jn.pt/inovacao/interior/kuantokusta-investe-tres-milhoes-de-euros-para-alargar-plataforma-de-venda-online-10615695.html

Johnson, M. W., Christensen, C. M., & Kagermann, H. (2008). Reinventing your business model. *Harvard Business Review*, *86*(12), 57–68.

Karakaya, F., & Stahl, M. (2009). After market entry barriers in e-commerce markets. *Journal of Electronic Commerce Research*, *10*(3), 130–143.

Kim, B. (2013). Responsive web design, discoverability, and mobile challenge. *Library Technology Reports*, *49*(6), 29–39.

Laudon, K., & Traver, C. (2018). *E-Commerce* (14th ed.). London: Pearson.

Luttrell, W. (2009). Qualitative educational research. Abingdon-on-Thames: Routledge.

Mahadevan, B. (2000). Business models for internet based e-commerce: An anatomy. *California Management Review*, *42*(4), 55–69. doi:10.2307/41166053

Maisam, S., & Mahsa, R. D. (2016). Positive word of mouth marketing: Explaining the roles of value congruity and brand love. *Journal of Competitiveness*, *8*(1), 19–37. doi:10.7441/joc.2016.01.02

Merriam, S. (2015). Qualitative research: A guide to design and implementation. New Jersey: John Wiley & Sons.

Mills, J. (2014). Qualitative methodology. Thousand Oaks, CA: Sage Publications.

Morris, M., Schindehutte, M., & Allen, J. (2005). The entrepreneur's business model: Toward a unified perspective. *Journal of Business Research*, *58*(6), 726–735. doi:10.1016/j.jbusres.2003.11.001

Naz, F. (2014). Word of mouth and its impact on marketing. *International Journal of Scientific and Research Publications*, *4*(1), 1–4.

Osterwalder, A. (2004). *The business model ontology a proposition in a design science approach* (Unpublished doctoral dissertation). Faculté des Hautes Études Commerciales, Université de Lausanne, Lausanne, Switzerland.

Osterwalder, A., & Pigneur, Y. (2002). An e-business model ontology for modeling e-business [paper presentation]. *15th Bled Electronic Commerce Conference*. Retrieved from: http://citeseerx.ist.psu.edu/viewdoc/download?doi=10.1.1.16.633&rep=rep1&type=pdf

Osterwalder, A., & Pigneur, Y. (2010). Business model generation. New Jersey: John Wiley & Sons.

Ow, T., Spaid, B., Wood, C., & Ba, S. (2018). Trust and experience in online auctions. *Journal of Organizational Computing and Electronic Commerce*, *28*(4), 294–314. doi:10.1080/10919392.2018.1517478

Park, M., & Yoo, J. (2018). Benefits of mass customized products: Moderating role of product involvement and fashion innovativeness. *Heliyon*, *4*(2), e00537. doi:10.1016/j.heliyon.2018.e00537 PMID:29560452

Pearce, J., & Robinson, R. (2014). Strategic management. New York: McGraw-Hill Education.

Petrovic, O., Kittl, C., & Tekstenc, R. D. (2001). Developing business models for e-business. *Proceedings of the International Conference on Electronic Commerce*.

Piera, C., Roberto, C., Giuseppe, C., & Teresa, M. (2014). E-procurement and e-supply chain: Features and development of e-collaboration. *IERI Procedia*, *6*, 8–14. doi:10.1016/j.ieri.2014.03.003

Porter, M. E. (1996). What is strategy? *Harvard Business Review*, *74*(6), 61–78. PMID:10158475

Queirós, A., Faria, D., & Almeida, F. (2017). Strengths and limitations of qualitative and quantitative research methods. *European Journal of Education Studies*, *3*(9), 369–387.

Radman, G., & Belin, A. (2017). Competitiveness in technology and innovation: How to keep on? *International Journal of Digital Technology & Economy*, *2*(1), 45–56.

Rappa, M. (2004). The utility business model and the future of computing services. *IBM Systems Journal*, *43*(1), 32–42. doi:10.1147j.431.0032

Sfenrianto, S., Wijaya, T., & Wang, G. (2018). Assessing the buyer trust and satisfaction factors in the e-marketplace. *Journal of Theoretical and Applied Electronic Commerce Research*, *13*(2), 43–57. doi:10.4067/S0718-18762018000200105

Shafer, S. M., Smith, H. J., & Linder, J. C. (2005). The power of business models. *Business Horizons*, *48*(3), 199–207. doi:10.1016/j.bushor.2004.10.014

Stähler, P. (2002). Business models as a unit of analysis for strategizing. In *Proceedings of the International Workshop on Business Models* (vol. 45, no. 7, pp. 2990-2995). University of Lausanne.

Storvang, P., Haug, A., & Nguyen, B. (2019). Stimulating consumer community creation through a co-design approach. *International Journal of Market Research*.

Teece, D. (2010). Business models, business strategy and innovation. *Long Range Planning*, *43*(2-3), 172–194. doi:10.1016/j.lrp.2009.07.003

Tikkinen-Piri, C., Rohunen, A., & Markkula, J. (2018). EU general data protection regulation: Changes and implications for personal data collecting companies. *Computer Law & Security Review*, *34*(1), 134–153. doi:10.1016/j.clsr.2017.05.015

Timmers, P. (1998). Business models for electronic markets. *Electronic Markets*, *8*(2), 3–8. doi:10.1080/10196789800000016

Tiwary, A. (2016). Know online advertising: All information about online advertising at one place. Bloomington: Partridge India.

Trusov, M., Bucklin, R., & Pauwels, K. (2009). Effects of word-of-mouth versus traditional marketing: Findings from an internet social networking site. *Journal of Marketing*, *73*(5), 90–102. doi:10.1509/jmkg.73.5.90

Turban, E., Outland, J., King, D., Lee, J. K., Liang, T.-P., & Turban, D. C. (2018). Electronic commerce 2018: A managerial and social networks perspective (9th ed.). New York: Springer. doi:10.1007/978-3-319-58715-8

Voorveld, H., van Noort, G., Muntinga, D., & Bronner, F. (2018). Engagement with social media and social media advertising: The differentiating role of platform type. *Journal of Advertising*, *47*(1), 38–54. doi:10.1080/00913367.2017.1405754

Weill, P., & Vitale, M. R. (2001). *Place to space: migrating to e-business models*. Boston: Harvard Business Press.

Yasav, S. (2015). The impact of digital technology on consumer purchase behavior. *Journal of Financial Perspectives*, *3*(3), 1–13.

Yin, R. K. (2009). Case study research: Design and methods (4th ed.). Thousand Oaks, CA: Sage Publications.

Zoroja, J., & Bach, M. (2016). Editorial: Impact of information and communication technology to the competitiveness of European countries - Cluster Analysis Approach. *Journal of Theoretical and Applied Electronic Commerce Research*, *11*(1), 1–10. doi:10.4067/S0718-18762016000100001

ADDITIONAL READING

Almeida, F., & Monteiro, J. (2017). The role of responsive design in web development. *Webology*, *14*(2), 48–65.

Beshore, B. (2018). *The messy marketplace: Selling your business in a world of imperfect buyers*. Boring Books.

Cang, H., & Wong, K. (2010). Adoption of e-procurement and participation of e-marketplace on firm performance: Trust as a moderator. *Information & Management*, *47*(5-6), 255–324.

Dakduk, S., Ter Horst, E., Santalla, Z., Molina, G., & Malave, J. (2017). Customer behavior in electronic commerce: A Bayesian approach. *Journal of Theoretical and Applied Electronic Commerce Research*, *12*(2), 1–20. doi:10.4067/S0718-18762017000200002

Dharmesti, M., & Nugroho, S. (2013). The antecedents of online customer satisfaction and customer loyalty. *Journal of Business and Retail Management Research*, *7*(2), 1–12.

Jolivet, J., Jullien, B., & Vinay, F. (2016). Reputation and prices on the e-market: Evidence from a major french platform. *International Journal of Industrial Organization*, *31*(45), 59–75. doi:10.1016/j.ijindorg.2016.01.003

Li, H., Fang, Y., Lim, K., Kai, H., & Wang, Y. (2018). Platform-based function repertoire, reputation, and sales performance of e-marketplace sellers. *Management Information Systems Quarterly*, *43*(1), 207–236. doi:10.25300/MISQ/2019/14201

Makkonen, J., Gracia, C., Koivistoinen, J., Saarinen, V., & Handgraaf, S. (2018). *The lean marketplace: A practical guide to building a successful online marketplace business*. Sharetribe.

Shiau, W., & Luo, M. (2012). Factors affecting online group buying intention and satisfaction: A social exchange theory perspective. *Computers in Human Behavior*, *28*(6), 2431–2444. doi:10.1016/j.chb.2012.07.030

Wei, K., Li, Y., Zha, Y., & Ma, J. (2019). Trust, risk and transaction intention in consumer-to-consumer e-marketplaces: An empirical comparison between buyers' and sellers' perspectives. *Industrial Management & Data Systems*, *119*(2), 331–350. doi:10.1108/IMDS-10-2017-0489

KEY TERMS AND DEFINITIONS

Customer Relationship Management: A set of practices, business strategies and customer-focused technologies that, from small companies and start-ups to medium and large organizations, can be used to manage and analyze interactions with their customers, anticipate their needs and desires, optimize profitability and increase the sales and assertiveness of their campaigns to attract new customers.

Decision Support System: A particular type of information system specially developed to support the need for information to support decision making in complex management and decision problems, including semi-structured or unstructured decision situations.

E-Marketplace: Proper place for buying and selling products. Currently, the term marketplace is used as a reference to a proper place of the Internet, a site, where different sellers virtually sell their products.

Enterprise Resource Planning: Integrated business management system that aims to plan company resources. The ERP functions as an enterprise database, which brings together in a single platform all operations in an integrated manner, such as manufacturing, logistics, finance, human resources, etc.

Supply Chain Management: Application that controls the flow of information and materials to maximize the company's results. In short, it is the management of the manufacturer's relationships with those who provide services to it, and ensures the quality and/or reduction of costs without any link in the chain breaking and damaging the final product.

Word-of-Mouth: Way to share information through oral communication between people. In marketing, it can be used as a powerful advertising strategy that enhances viral marketing when associated with social networks.

ENDNOTES

1. https://www.kuantokusta.pt
2. https://dott.pt
3. https://www.worten.pt
4. https://www.fnac.pt

Chapter 3
Digital Business Transformation in the Banking Sector

José Campino
ISCTE – Instituto Universitário de Lisboa, Portugal

Ana Brochado
ISCTE – Instituto Universitário de Lisboa, Portugal

Álvaro Rosa
ISCTE – Instituto Universitário de Lisboa, Portugal

ABSTRACT

Financial technology companies (fintechs) have gained tremendous importance in the last decade and particularly in the last four years. They have contributed with disruptive technological solutions and provided not only complementary but also substitute products to the traditional banking sector. New incumbents have been challenging banks already established and forced them to innovate in order to remain competitive. Indeed, banks have a heavy burden of slow processes, costly business models, and few innovative solutions. The authors collected 100 articles from Scopus related with the fintech and bank topics. This study adopted a hybrid design comprising a systematic qualitative review methods and narrative, supplemented by semantic network analysis. Based on the results of the systematic literature review, the authors explored the impacts that fintechs have had on traditional banking sector.

DOI: 10.4018/978-1-7998-4552-2.ch003

INTRODUCTION

New concepts of fintechs have appeared and became interesting due to the reputational challenge posed to traditional banking caused by the subprime crisis. Consumers have questioned the strategy of financial industry and the impacts it has had on the world economy (Dell'Atti, Trotta, Iannuzzi, & Demaria, 2017). Fintech companies have real impacts because their technological solutions are being broadly adopted in banking or retail being blockchain a case study even for cyber security (Kshetri, 2017). Fintechs impact the traditional banking system because they challenge the existent business model and provide much more technological solutions characterized by lower prices and higher accessibility. Fintech is a fast-growing sector with high potential and may be considered a disruption on the current state of technology. Consumers are adopting these services due to their advantages which constitute solutions for the future of banking and several other industries. Nonetheless, the risks associated with this new industry should also be considered. The current risks that fintech companies pose may affect consumers, companies and the entire financial stability (KPMG, 2019) because currently fintech offer a diverse range of services which can be a plain current account but also virtual investments in fiat or digital currencies (Brochado, 2018a). The examples are the Initial Coin Offerings (ICOs) which are an alternative investment form offering the possibility of direct financing from investors worldwide (Brochado, 2018b) and contributing to the democratization of entrepreneurship and access to capital markets (Chen, 2018).

The aim of this chapter is to study fintech developments and in particular the impacts they have had in shaping traditional banking business models recently challenged (Roland Berger, 2018). This paper aims at answering the following research question: What insights does current literature offer regarding the impact of fintechs in the banking sector?

The structure of this chapter is as follows: (i) next section offers a descriptive analysis of the impact of fintechs and digital solutions in banking; (ii) the methodology describes the approach used to collect the papers under analysis and the content analysis approach; (iii) the results section includes a descriptive, narrative and semantic analysis (iv) the chapter ends with conclusions and the avenues for future research.

THEORETICAL FRAMEWORK

The Fintech and the Traditional Banking

The concept of fintech is not consensual. Following the study of Schueffel (2016) fintechs are defined as "new financial industry that applies technology to improve financial activities" (p. 15). These new solutions gained hype after the European banks suffered several shocks which challenged their business model and have been affecting their profitability until today (Cheng & Mevis, 2018). This is confirmed by the historical prices of the Euro Stoxx for banks which still did not recover from values before the crisis. After the subprime crisis the strategies of central banks were to ease monetary policy reducing the interest rates and increasing the monetary base. This policy had not only consequences on credit expansion in order to create economic stimulus (Spyromitrosa & Tsintzos, 2019) but also on less opportunities for regular and even sophisticated investors because the interest rates on investments are much lower than before (e.g. regular savings, the LIBOR and EURIBOR are much lower which also impacts the availability of money and investments) (Kreidych, Roshchyna, & Kazak, 2018).

Traditional banking is characterized by a costly model of branches (Gomber, Kauffman, Parker, & Weber, 2018, p. 230), traditional lending, relationship deposits and traditional sources of revenue (e.g. interest rate charged and banking fees) (Chiorazzo, D'Apice, DeYoung, & Morelli, 2018). However, there are also drivers which support the appearance of fintech companies in an era of digital expansion with easy access to the internet. As per Gomber, Kauffman, Parker, & Weber (2018) and KPMG (2019), the main drivers of this technological revolution are: *(i) Technology innovation*: the pace of technological transformation is increasing very fast and technologies often interconnect with each other creating technological breakthroughs. As fintechs are based on IT structures, this technological improvement supports these companies; (ii) *Process Disruption*: the appearance of virtual currencies based in a blockchain process created a process disruption, making it the new model that should be adopted. Gomber, Kauffman, Parker, & Weber (2018) argued that "the entire financial services industry has been disrupted in fundamental ways" (p. 225); (iii) *Services Transformation*: a transformation in the service provided by financial companies has been noticed due to consumers' pressure and technological developments. The fintechs' service has been putting pressure on traditional service transformation; (iv) *Economies of scale in IT applications*: according to Lacity & Willcocks (2001) an example of economies of scale in IT is the outsourcing of IT systems to service providers. A higher investment in IT systems also improves the productivity of a company (Woudstra, Berghout, Tan, Eekeren, & Dedene, 2017).

Fintechs pose a direct challenge to the traditional banks which need to adapt to new consumers' trends from which fintech companies took advantage. Heavy traditional banking industry's legacy might be a burden posing a threat to a fast and successful adaptation to the new reality (Gomber, Kauffman, Parker, & Weber, 2018; Chiorazzo, D'Apice, DeYoung, & Morelli, 2018). According to Roland Berger (2018) there are also social factors such as: (i) unwillingness to change from both employees and management; (ii) risk of unacceptance from shareholders; and business factors such as: (i) lack of cooperation between business functions and IT. However, the pressure on banks to change their business model is increasing not only on a business perspective (threat from new digital incumbents) but also from a social perspective because clients are demanding bigger Corporate Social Responsibility (CSR) from banks. As an attempt to answer consumers' demands, banks are creating sustainable CSR policies (Costa-Climent & Martínez-Climent, 2018). Fintech companies were born in a context where CSR is demanded and they took advantage of this fact because a wide range of investments, such as ICOs, are on sustainable solutions and several fintech platforms allow investment in a broad range of "green" solutions. Complementary is the capacity of fintechs to finance Non-governmental Organizations (NGOs) and social causes worldwide due to their technology which captures the interest and investment of both companies searching for investing in social causes but also captures the interest of consumers (Freivogel, 2016). According to Roland Berger (2018) fintechs appear as the third driver of innovation in terms of relevance only after the "customer behavior" and "tech giants". Traditional banks are trying to adapt to this new reality by transforming their processes and making them more digital while cooperating with fintechs or acquiring them in order to integrate their innovations. According to the same report the fintechs are considered: (i) industry innovators, (ii) platform drivers and (iii) solution providers but currently not a direct substitute of the traditional banks as long as they can keep up the innovation pace.

The Interest on Fintechs

The banking sector is still recovering from the last financial crisis but has today achieved a steady position due to a feeling of safety caused by the central banks' measures. Although with several challenges such as poor growth, banks have achieved solid accomplishments revealed in market capitalization, tier 1 capital ratios or stable returns (McKinsey&Company, 2018). There are forces which drive innovation (e.g. technology expansion and permissive regulation) and promote the appearance of new market incumbents as the fintech companies that may affect banks profitability (Desai, V, V, & Jayakumar, 2019). Therefore, banks have been adapting and the ones digitalizing faster are the ones that are more prone to obtain bigger efficiency gains and thus stay competitive in the market (McKinsey&Company, 2018).

Figure 1. Worldwide interest in the topic "Fintech"

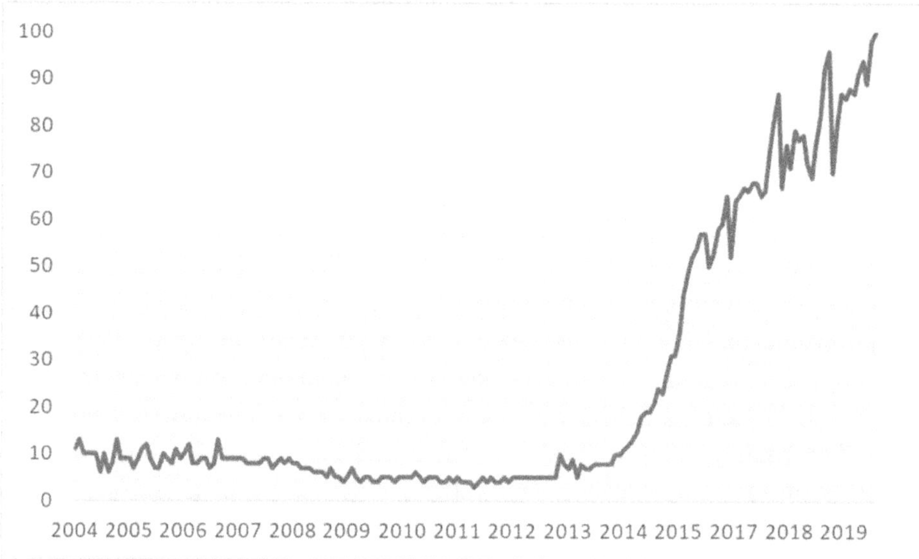

Source: Google Trends (https://www.google.com/trends). The numbers represent the popularity of the term selected in Google searches. The values range from 100 (most interesting) to 0 (no interest).

The interest in the new concept of fintech has been increasing and has had a rapid growth in popularity since 2013 as confirmed by Google Trends' data. On October 2019 the interest in the word "fintech" has 100 points which means maximum interest while the word "bank" has about 85 points. The word "bank" has stable levels of interest along the time period between the years of 2004 and 2011 ranging from 65 to 85 points. The word was mostly searched between the years of 2008 and 2010 during the financial crisis and had an interest peak close to 100 points on 2009.

Risks Posed by Fintechs to Traditional Banking

Currently the new incumbents are a real threat to the well-established banking system due to the substitute products and services offered (Vives, 2017). PWC (2016) estimated that 28% of the banking and payment businesses as well as 22% of the insurance, asset management and wealth management systems are at risk by 2020 due to the new competition. The reason is fintechs are operating concurrently with traditional banking particularly in the payments area, financial intermediation and cryptocurrencies. Fintechs focus on customer centricity due to the services provided. As a result, the importance of this concept increases as well as the adoption of fintechs' strategies by traditional industries with 48% of financial companies adopting fintechs' strategies into their business model (PWC, 2019). The most likely technologies which drive change in traditional business model of financial services organizations are artificial intelligence, big data, cloud and blockchain, all of them at the core of fintechs' business model (PWC, 2019). The pillars for a strong fintech ecosystem are a sustained demand for their services from consumers, companies and financial institutions, the access to talent which currently is more global, an enabling environment based on strong collaboration among incumbents, access to local and international markets and forces to a sustainable development as well as a favorable regulation (EY, 2018). The majority of these conditions are met today which urges the adaptation of traditional banking (Deloitte, 2017).

Figure 2. Worldwide interest in the topic "Bank"

Source: Google Trends (https://www.google.com/trends). The numbers represent the popularity of the term selected in Google searches. The values range from 100 (most interesting) to 0 (no interest).

Traditional Banking Adaptation to Fintech

Financial institutions must adapt and incorporate the fintechs' technological solutions into their business model particularly investing in IT and upgrading their core platforms (Andrade, 2019). Fintech companies put pressure on established financial companies on margins charged, loss of market share, information security and customer churn (PWC, 2016). Thus, more than half of banks and capital markets institutions have incorporated emerging technologies into commercial banking and personal loans, and an additional 20% plan to do so in the next two years (PWC, 2019). Some of these institutions use the Mergers and Acquisitions (M&A) scheme in order to absorb fintechs into their business model and consequently the M&A activity is growing since 2017 with the Q1+Q2 of 2019 amounting to USD 23.9 billion and about 160 deals completed worldwide (KPMG, 2019a). Currently financial institutions as well as technological, media and telecommunications comapanies are cooperating in order to create synergies and easily incorporate innovative solutions into their business model. Telecommunications companies have advantage offering customer centric products which have great success, but financial institutions are well-established in the market and have acquired licensing to operate in financial solutions. However, both sectors have a clear focus on customer retention which is the key to succeed, they have different visions on the main aspects of emerging technology to focus in order to do so. Whilst financial institutions prioritize the ease of use and the faster service and processes, telecommunications companies prioritize personal digital contact and personalized service but both sectors are focusing on trust (PWC, 2019). This highlights the main weaknesses of both sectors because telecommunications companies lack the close contact to the customer and financial institutions have much heavier processes and less user-friendly platforms than their counterparties. Despite the last financial crisis impact on financial institution's reputation (Vives, 2017), they still have great trust from consumers (EY, 2014) mainly due to the security measures taken and surely they have a great advantage in the activities which involve closer contact with the customer and require a great deal of trust and safety. Therefore, they are seen as having a great advantage of continuing to be privileged financial intermediaries (McKinsey&Company, 2018). It is consensual that financial institutions should focus on several areas in order to survive and be adaptable within the new technology world, namely: (i) becoming digital (Bughin, Deakin, & O'Beirne, 2019); (ii) optimize their business model (e.g. adopting robot advice, digital platforms, partnering with telecommunications companies); (iii) become more cost efficient; (iv) retain customers; (v) be able to attract talent; (vi) focus on specific business segments with tailor made solutions; (vii) being able to keep the pace with regulatory developments (PWC, 2016; Khanna & Martins, 2018; McKinsey&Company, 2018; PWC, 2019).

Fintechs' Deals, Investment and Market Volume by Geography

Geographically, the areas with higher investments in fintech (i.e. investment of Venture Capital, Private Equity and M&A) are the Americas (the United States of America account for 87% of the investment) and Europe followed by Asia Pacific (KPMG, 2019a). However, there are important developments, deals and interest in regions such as China, which is by far the most important country in terms of market volume (Ziegler, et al., 2019), and Russia due to a less developed capital market, less access to loans and capital controls. Concerning fintech hubs the United States of America (USA) and China lead the way by far being London the only European city represented in the top 10 (position 4) of fintech hubs (University of Cambridge, 2018). Globally, in the first half of 2019 fintechs represented an investment of USD 37.9 billion with 962 deals which represents a decrease from 2018 (USD 120 billion and 2590 deals) mainly due to a preference of investors for smaller deals, a decrease in investment in Asia, a more matured market in blockchain, an increase in banks' competitiveness in terms of digitalization and also investment in financial services from big technological companies (KPMG, 2019a). Nevertheless, there is an impressive growth in investment in alternative finance such as ICOs (Brochado, 2018b) and also in cryptocurrencies' market capitalization during the last 3 years (Brochado, 2018a) with an impressive valorization during 2017 and subsequent fall in 2018 followed by a slower valorization in 2019 which although smaller than the one occurred in 2017 is still much above the values previous to the first valorization as per the figure 3.

Figure 3. Market capitalization of bitcoin and altcoins

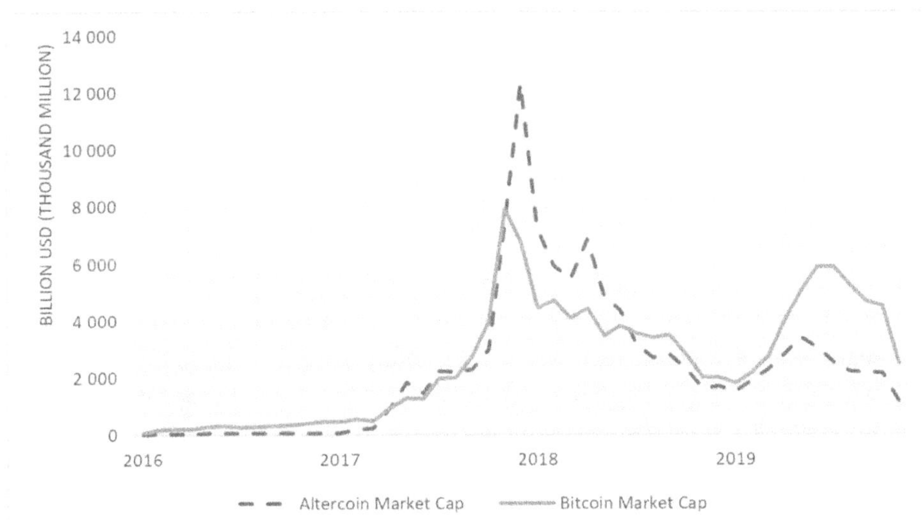

Source: https://coin.dance/

The year of 2018 registered the highest investment in blockchain and cryptocurrency with USD 5 billion of capital investment and 586 deals whereas the first half of 2019 has registered USD 1 billion and 171 deals (KPMG, 2019a). On 2017, a growth of 184% was registered compared to the previous year on staff active in blockchain industry, tendency maintained in 2018 with a growth of 165% (Q1+Q2) (Rauchs, Blandin, Bear, & McKeon, 2019). Fintech must be prepared for regulatory impacts (EY, 2017) creating ground to the appearance of RegTech, meaning, "any use of technology to match data to information taxonomies that are meaningful to both regulators and the companies they regulate, in order to automate compliance and oversight processes" (Schizas, et al., 2019). Most companies are present in the United Kingdom (UK) and the USA being the continental European representatives, Switzerland and Ireland (Schizas, et al., 2019). Investment in these companies fluctuates but 2018 represented USD 3.9 billion of investment and 123 deals whilst the first half of 2019 represented USD 1.5 billion of investment and 53 deals (KPMG, 2019a).

The USA is the largest market for fintech in the Americas and had a market growth of 88.5% each year between 2013 and 2017 representing a market volume of USD 42.81 billion of the global Americas market volume of USD 44.3 billion in 2017. Canada is the second most important market (2% of market volume) in Americas. Latin American countries represent 1% of the total market value (University of Cambridge, 2018a). Concerning investment in the activity, the American market represented USD 55.3 billion in 2018 and the 10 biggest fintech deals in the first half of 2019 also took place in the USA (Dun & Bradstreet, USD 6.9 billion; Investment Technology Group, USD 1 billion). The only two deals outside the USA happened in Canada (Shareworks by Morgan Stanley, USD 843.8 million; Wave Financial, USD 405 million), and Argentina (Prisma Medios de Pago, USD 725 million) (KPMG, 2019a).

In the European continent the UK is by far the largest contributor to the fintech's market volume with EUR 7.07 billion of a total of EUR 10.44 billion in 2017 which represents 68%. The percentage was higher before with 81% in 2015 and 73% in 2016 which means the distance between the UK and the rest of Europe is decreasing (Ziegler, et al., 2019). The market volume of fintech has been constantly increasing in Europe although it is still much smaller than in the USA and Asia (including China). Concerning investment in fintech companies, the European market accounts for USD 13.2 billion and 307 deals which represents a growth tendency, although the values for the first two quarters of 2019 were smaller when compared to the same period of 2018. Most representative deals happening in first half of 2019 happened in Germany (Concardis, USD 6 billion) and France (eFront, 1.3 billion), followed by several UK deals and one single deal in Norway (KPMG, 2019a). In terms of number of platforms operating in Europe the UK leads with 77 platforms, followed by Germany with 46 platforms, France with 46 platforms, Italy with 45 platforms, Spain with 39 platforms and the Netherlands with 32 platforms (Ziegler, et al., 2019).

China is the country with the highest market volume in the world but lacks in terms of investment. China represents a total of USD 358.3 billion with a global value for the entire Asian market of USD 361.9 billion in 2017. China's market volume growth trend is very clear and has been present since 2013 with a growth from USD 6 billion in this year to USD 358 billion in 2017 (University of Cambridge, 2018). After China, the most significant market volumes in Asia are represented by the counties of Australia (USD 1.5 billion), South Korea (USD 1.13 billion), Japan (USD 348.7 million) and India (USD 268.6 million) (University of Cambridge, 2018). Concerning the investments in fintech the Asian region accounted USD 3.6 billion and 102 deals which represents a growth tendency although with lower values in the first two quarters of 2019. Most relevant deals in the first half of 2019 happened in China (NCF Wealth Holdings, USD 2 billion; Shanghai Dianrong Financial Information Services, USD 100 million), South Korea (Blockchain Exchange Alliance, USD 200 million), Australia (Airwallex, USD 100 million), Indonesia (Akulaku, USD 100 million) and Vietnam (Momo, USD 100 million) (KPMG, 2019a).

Figure 4. Market volume by region in 2017

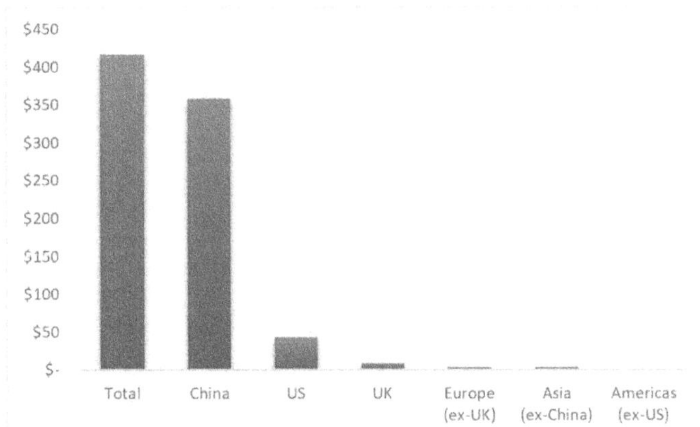

	Total	China	US	UK	Europe (ex-UK)	Asia (ex-China)	Americas (ex-US)
Market Volume (2017)	$416.42	$358.00	$42.81	$7.87	$3.75	$3.64	$1.53

The values are in billion (thousand million) USD. The exchange rate 1.11 EUR/USD was applied to the European values. Source: (University of Cambridge, 2018a), (Ziegler, et al., 2019), (University of Cambridge, 2018).

Business Models of Alternative Finance Companies

There are several business models for alternative finance companies which adoption varies depending on the region where platforms are incorporated. As per table 1, lending services dominate in terms of market volume across all regions being the only exception the "invoice trading" in Europe.

Table 1. Business models of Fintech per region with definitions

Americas	
Balance Sheet Consumer Lending	$ 15.3 billion
P2P Consumer Lending	$ 14.9 billion
Balance Sheet Business Lending	$ 7.3 billion

Europe	
P2P Consumer Lending	$ 1.56 billion
Invoice Trading	$ 597 million
P2P Business Lending	$ 520 million

Asia	
P2P Consumer Lending	$ 225 billion
P2P Business Lending	$ 98 billion
P2P Property Lending	$ 6.6 billion

Source: (University of Cambridge, 2018a), (Ziegler, et al., 2019), (University of Cambridge, 2018).

Balance Sheet Consumer Lending	The platform entity provides a loan directly to a consumer borrower.
P2P Consumer Lending	Individuals or institutional funders provide a loan to a consumer borrower.
Balance Sheet Business Lending	The platform entity provides a loan directly to a business borrower.
Invoice Trading	Individuals or institutional funders purchase invoices or receivable notes from a business at a discount.
P2P Business Lending	Individuals or institutional funders provide a loan to a business borrower.
P2P Property Lending	Individuals or institutional funders provide a loan secured against a property to a consumer or business borrower.

METHODOLOGY

This research aims to perform a systematic literature of current fintech research and to answer the question: What insights does current literature offer regarding the impact of fintech developments in the business model of the banking sector? A research on "banking" and "fintech" as search terms in the abstract, title or keywords in the database SCOPUS allowed the record of 100 relevant studies published in English. The search code used was (TITLE-ABS-KEY (bank AND fintech) OR TITLE-ABS-KEY (bank AND "Initial Coin Offerings") OR TITLE-ABS-KEY (bank AND crowdfunding) OR TITLE-ABS-KEY (bank AND digitalization) OR TITLE-ABS-KEY (bank AND "robot advice") OR TITLE-ABS-KEY (bank AND blockchain) OR TITLE-ABS-KEY (bank AND "artificial intelligence") OR TITLE-ABS-KEY (bank AND "big data") OR TITLE-ABS-KEY (bank AND "smart contract") OR TITLE-

ABS-KEY (bank AND "digital platform") OR TITLE-ABS-KEY (bank AND "digital transformation") OR TITLE-ABS-KEY (bank AND "virtual currency") OR TITLE-ABS-KEY (bank AND cryptocurrency)) AND (LIMIT-TO (SUBJAREA, "BUSI")) AND (LIMIT-TO (LANGUAGE, "English")) AND (LIMIT-TO (DOCTYPE, "ar") OR LIMIT-TO (DOCTYPE, "re")). The search was not restricted to chronological limits and was able to collect 102 papers but 2 of them focused on a different field of research, namely, medicine, and thus considered not relevant. Therefore, the 100 relevant papers have a date range from 2011 to 2019 excluding the year of 2013 where no paper was found. The papers from older years (i.e. 2011-2014) focus particularly on topics such as digital transformation, big data, crowdfunding or predictive models, respectively. Only in 2015 the fintech topic explicitly appears and in 2016 the research continues and expands also to blockchain related topics. The great majority of the papers are very recent and 85% were published between the years of 2017-2019. The information for each paper was recoded into an Excel spreadsheet, comprising the following columns: title of the paper, year, abstract, keywords, authors, authors' affiliations, and journal. The data was treated in Excel and complemented with further information when needed in order to have a more rigorous analysis. The authors also used the Scimago Journal and Country Rank in order to obtain quartiles and countries of several Journals analyzed.

This study adopted a hybrid design comprising the systematic qualitative review methods and narrative, supplemented by semantic network analysis. Using a systematic method, the authors document the geographical spread of the papers by author, year, research methods, and primary topical areas, thus providing a reproducible and reliable assessment of current progress in the research field. The narrative discussion indicates the research production within each of the topical areas, explores emerging themes and methods, and identifies knowledge gaps for future research directions. A semantic network analysis further explores connections among key topical areas. The authors also content-analyzed the papers' abstracts through Leximancer, a software program that automatically extracts semantic networks from qualitative data. Leximancer identified the connections among topics, having been successfully employed for literature review (Crofts & Bisman, 2010). This software generates conceptual maps based on co-occurrences of words in keyword lists. The analysis' reliability is secured by its stability (i.e., intercoder reliability) and reproducibility (i.e., high consistency in the way data are coded).

In order to make the research process clearer the authors developed a summary table with the procedures and steps taken in order to obtain the final results. Table 2 summarizes the steps but also the actions taken in each step and the outputs obtained.

Table 2. Summary of the procedures and steps taken along the research process

Procedure	Actions taken	Results
1. Perform a search on SCOPUS		
1.1. Select the search criteria (e.g. key-words, language, research field)	Work with SCOPUS in order to obtain the final code line	Code line providing the final results
1.2. Select the data to export (e.g. abstract, authors, journal's name)	Work with SCOPUS and select the relevant information	Final data selected
1.3. Export the results to a CSV file	Export the results to a CSV file and treat it in Excel	CSV file to be treated in Excel
2. Analyze the data collected		
2.1. Analyze the data exported and select relevant papers	Transform the CSV file into a workable Excel file and check data consistency. For example, be sure that all the papers collected are relevant	Workable Excel file
2.2. Complete the data if some consistency is necessary (e.g. DOI missing, authors missing)	Complement the data obtained due to possible missing information	Final Excel file
2.3. Complete the data with the information on journals' ranking from Scimago	Cross-check information with Scimago in order to complement the data obtained	Further information on the Excel file
3. Descriptive analysis		
3.1. Preform simple statistics on the data collected (e.g. number of articles per journal, leading institutions or countries)	Select the data necessary and perform simple statistics	Summary statistics tables
4. Analysis of key-words		
4.1. Perform statistics on the most frequent key-words used by the authors	Select the necessary data and perform simple statistics	Summary statistics tables
4.2. Build a word-cloud with the most frequent key-words	Select a software and build a word-cloud having into consideration the most relevant key-words	Word-cloud
5. Leximancer analysis		
5.1 Run Leximancer software based on the abstracts collected	Input the data collected from SCOPUS and program Leximancer	Outputs from Leximancer (i.e. conceptual map)
5.2 Analyze Leximancer's results including the final conceptual map	Download all the software's results and analyze them	Conceptual map analysis complemented by the remaining
5.3. Connect Leximancer's results with the literature	Deeply analyze the papers collected by its themes and connect them with the conceptual map	Final analysis connecting the papers collected with the Leximancer's results

RESULTS AND DISCUSSION

Number of Articles by Journal

Table 3 depicts the top 17 institutions publishing papers on this topic. The authors have selected a top 17 given the relevance of global results obtained because below the 17th institution analyzed the publications decreased to 1 and therefore became less relevant for the analysis. Besides, the top selected represents 47 of the 100 papers studied.

The institutions publishing more research about the banking and fintech topic are the journals Financial Innovation, European Research Studies Journal and the Journal of Payments Strategy and Systems. These institutions together published a total of 32% of the papers. There is an increasing interest on the topic and from 2018 onwards the papers published doubled when compared to the period between 2011 and 2017. Furthermore, there are more institutions publishing papers on this topic during most recent years which is confirmed by the fact that most of them have not published any paper between the years of 2011 and 2017 on the same topic. Further to this analysis, the authors used Scimago in order to find the journals' country of origin and also the quartile to which they belong according to Scimago Journal and Country Rank.

Table 3. Number of articles by Journal

	2011-2017	2018-oct, 2019	Total
FI	6	0	6
ERSJ	2	3	5
JPSS	0	4	4
JEB	0	3	3
BH	2	1	3
FRBSLR	0	3	3
SC	2	1	3
IJeBE	0	2	2
IJFR	0	2	2
BBS	0	2	2
CE	1	1	2
QAS	1	1	2
EM	0	2	2
IEEEP	2	0	2
JFE	0	2	2
IJRTE	0	2	2
EBOLR	0	2	2
Total	16	31	47

Note: FM = Financial Inovation; ERSJ = European Research Studies Journal; JPSS = Journal of Payments Strategy and Systems; JEB = Journal of Economics and Business; BH = Business Horizons; FRBSLR = Federal Reserve Bank of St. Louis Review; SC = Strategic Change; IJeBE = International Journal of e-Business Research; IJFR = International Journal of Financial Research; BBS = Banks and Bank Systems; CEQ = Contemporary Economics; QAS = Quality - Access to Success; EM= Electronic Markets; IEEEP = IEEE Potentials; JFE = Journal of Financial Economics; IJRTE = International Journal of Recent Technology and Engineering; EBOLR = European Business Organization Law Review

Table 4. Journals' Country and Rank by Scimago

	Quartile	Country
FI	Not available	China
ERSJ	Q2	Greece
JPSS	Not available	United Kingdom
JEB	Q2	Netherlands
BH	Q1	Netherlands
FRBSLR	Q2	United States of America
SC	Q2	United Kingdom
IJeBE	Q4	United States of America
IJFR	Not available	Canada
BBS	Q3	Ukraine
CE	Q3	Poland
QAS	Q3	Romania
EM	Q1	Germany
IEEEP	Q3	United States of America
JFE	Q1	Netherlands
IJRTE	Not available	India
EBOLR	Q2	Netherlands

Note: FM = Financial Inovation; ERSJ = European Research Studies Journal; JPSS = Journal of Payments Strategy and Systems; JEB = Journal of Economics and Business; BH = Business Horizons; FRBSLR = Federal Reserve Bank of St. Louis Review; SC = Strategic Change; IJeBE = International Journal of e-Business Research; IJFR = International Journal of Financial Research; BBS = Banks and Bank Systems; CEQ = Contemporary Economics; QAS = Quality - Access to Success; EM= Electronic Markets; IEEEP = IEEE Potentials; JFE = Journal of Financial Economics; IJRTE = International Journal of Recent Technology and Engineering; EBOLR = European Business Organization Law Review

Most journals belong to the quartiles (Q) 1 and 2. The Q1 represents 23% of top journals and Q2 29%. Q3+Q4 together represent 38% of top journals publishing about this topic with only one journal belonging to the Q4. Only 4 journals where not included in the Scimago ranking and thus cannot be considered in the current analysis. Concerning the journals' origin, most of them are from the Netherlands, the USA and the UK. The top 17 journals include 2 open source journals from China and India.

Leading Institutions with the Most Number of Authors

The authors have also collected information on institutions publishing articles on this topic dividing them into "Academic" and "Non-academic".

Table 5. Leading institutions with the greatest number of authors

	2011-2017	2018-oct, 2019	Total
University of Latvia	1	6	7
University of Jyväskylä	0	6	6
York University	0	6	6
White&Case	0	5	5
SRM Institute of Science and Technology	0	4	4
Rostov State University of Economics	0	4	4
Tarbiat Modares University	0	4	4
Karlsruhe Institute of Technology	0	4	4
Universitas Padjadajaran	0	4	4
Sun Yat-sen Business School	4	0	4
University of Zurich	4	0	4
University of Piraeus	4	0	4
Total	13	43	56

Table 6. Institutions' classification

	2011-2017	2018-oct, 2019	Total
Academic	68	149	217
Non-Academic	4	24	28
Total	72	173	245

There is a much higher number of authors and institutions publishing papers in more recent years than on the previous period between the years of 2011 and 2017 according to table 5. The top three institutions publishing research on the topic are the University of Latvia (Latvia), University of Jyväskylä (Finland) and the York University (Canada). Together they have published a total of 19 articles since 2011 and therefore represent 34% of the papers published by the top institutions. There is a clear tendency for the dominance of the academia concerning the publication of research. From all the 245 institutions studied 217 are academic. Nevertheless, there is also an increasing interest of non-academic institutions as only 4 institutions have published research between the period of 2011-2017 and since 2018 the number increased to 24. Among the non-academic institutions, mostly are consulting companies, central banks, national public agencies, technology companies and a law company. Most of the interest comes from central banks and national public institutions. Besides, consulting companies seem to be cultivating the interest on these topics as they are trendy and most likely profitable. A law company from New York, namely White&Case, is among the leader institutions in terms of authors.

Leading Countries for Papers and Authors

A relationship between countries-papers published and counties-authors was also established. Tables 7 and 8 depict these relationships and confirm the pattern between them. In both cases the top 3 countries in terms of authors and papers published belong to the USA, UK and Germany. These countries represent a total of 56% of the papers published and 52% of the authors. China is in the top of countries with the most authors, but India and Russia are in both rankings (authors and papers published). Lastly, Russia is present in both rankings and Switzerland in the countries for papers published ranking. Concerning Switzerland, it is interesting to notice that it represents a prosperous country for fintechs in Europe. This fact might be due to its strict laws which may work as safeguard for future expansion and also due to the fact that Switzerland is friendly to new technology innovation and a country historically known by its well-established banking sector.

Word Cloud with Most Frequent Keywords

The top three words of papers published are interconnected and constitute the real challenge for the banks' business model. Considering the word cloud in figure 5, it is visible that the most used keywords are banking, fintech and digital followed by the words finance, technology, lending and financial services, respectively. Therefore, the authors conclude that the most prominent topic in today's literature is the relation between the banks and fintechs.

Table 7. Leading countries for papers published

	2011-2017	2018-oct, 2019	Total
United States of America	5	12	17
United Kingdom	4	8	12
Germany	3	8	11
India	2	4	6
France	2	3	5
Spain	0	5	5
Russia	2	2	4
Canada	2	2	4
Switzerland	3	1	4
Italy	0	4	4
Total	23	49	72

Table 8. Leading countries for authors

	2011-2017	2018-oct, 2019	Total
United States of America	6	27	33
Germany	4	20	24
United Kingdom	4	13	17
India	5	9	14
France	4	7	11
Romania	3	7	10
Spain	0	9	9
Russia	3	6	9
Italy	0	8	8
China	8	0	8
Total	37	106	143

Table 9. Table with Most Frequent Keywords

	Frequency	Percentage
Banking	51	11%
Fintech	37	8%
Digital	36	8%
Finance	29	7%
Technology	29	7%
Lending	28	6%
Financial service	27	6%
Big data	21	5%
Innovation	17	4%
Regulation	17	4%
Blockchain	15	3%
Crowdfunding	15	3%
Payments	15	3%
Economics	13	3%
Markets	13	3%
Investment	12	3%
Strategy	11	2%
Digital transformation	9	2%
Information	9	2%
Artificial intelligence	7	2%
Bitcoin	7	2%
Machine learning	7	2%
Cryptocurrency	5	1%
Peer-to-peer lending	5	1%
Platform	5	1%
Secutiry	5	1%
Total	445	100%

Figure 5. Word cloud with the most frequent keywords

These topics are closely related with technology, finance and financial services because fintech companies are exactly characterized by these solutions. Moreover, the word big data is also very much cited because it is the base for the operations in new digital companies. There is also an interest in lending activities because it is banking activity's core and it is slowly being challenged by the new incumbents. Fintech companies are providing credit solutions based on big data, a new way of risk assessment and peer-to-peer lending with a much faster and cheaper model benefiting the consumer. With frequency table 9 as reference the authors conclude that most important topics discussed today fall within three categories: technology, services and regulation. Most of the words are related with technology such as digital, big data, innovation, blockchain, digital transformation, artificial intelligence and machine learning. These words suggest that fintech transformation is based on digital solutions which are supported by big data, artificial intelligence and machine learning and the core process of blockchain. The second most significant group of words is related with services such as financial services, lending, crowdfunding and payments. In sum, the literature is focusing on the analysis of traditional banking services already provided by fintech companies, such as lending and payments, and also on new services such as crowdfunding. Finally, the authors have found that regulation is also important for the studies on this topic as well as security which is related with cyber security and consumer protection.

Word Cloud with the Most Frequent Words in the Abstracts

The authors have used the software Leximancer in order to perform the papers abstracts' analysis. The main objective was to find the most frequent words and the probability of two words appearing together. The final result was the concept map in figure 6.

Figure 6. Conceptual map of research topics

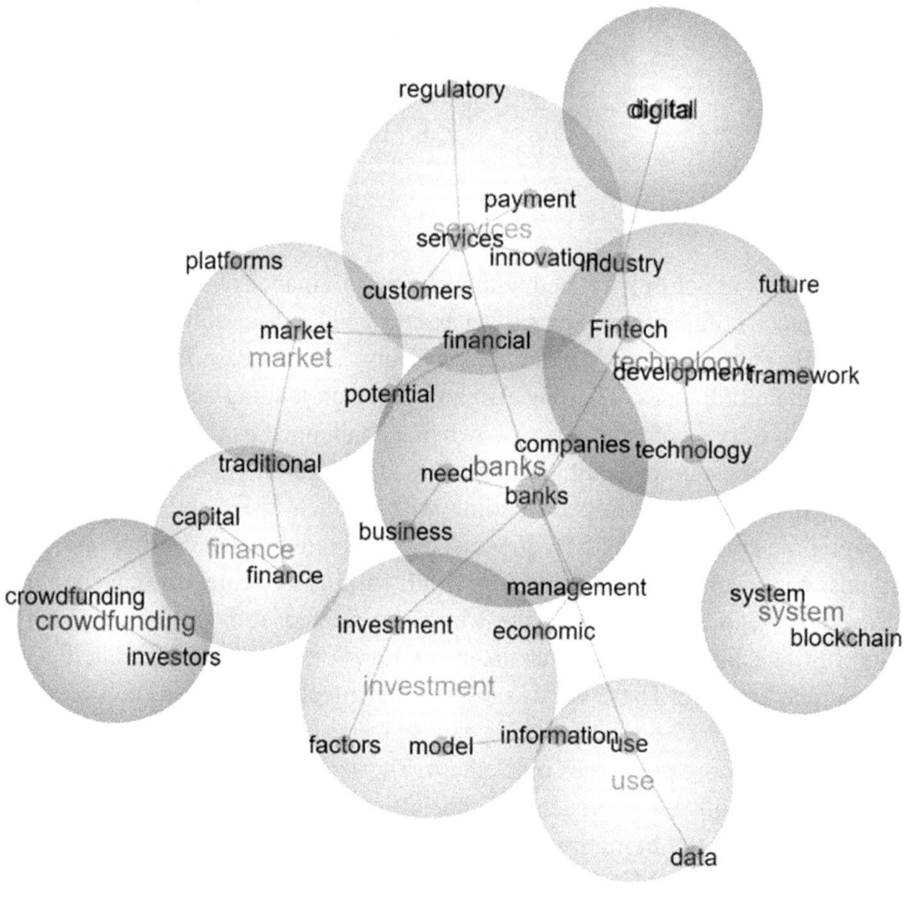

The size of the circles, its color and centeredness represent concepts' importance in the dataset. Therefore, most central, seemingly red-colored and bigger circles are the most important in the dataset at the same time that the lines connect the related concepts. A total of 10 key themes are represented in the map with their respective concepts' groups of related topics. In line with what was previously found, the authors conclude that most central concepts are the "banks" (count: 201; relevance: 100%), "technology" (count: 83; relevance: 41%) and "services" (count: 65; relevance: 32%). The concept of "banks" is related with several other relevant concepts such as "need", "business" and "financial". The same logic applies to the concept of "technology" which is related with other concepts such as "fintech", "future", "framework" and "development". The concept of "services" is related with the concepts: "customers", "financial", "innovation", "payment" and "regulatory". The remaining themes which are not as central as the previous ones are "digital" (count: 45; relevance: 22%) and "system" (count: 35; relevance: 17%) which is related with the concept of "blockchain". The theme "crowdfunding" (count: 19; relevance: 19%) is related with the concept of "investors" and also with "finance" (count: 29; relevance: 14%) through the topic "capital". The theme "market" (count: 55; relevance: 27%) is related with the concept of "platforms" and also shares the topic of "traditional" with the theme "finance". The theme "investment" (count: 33; relevance: 16%) is related with the concepts of "factors" and "model". "Information" and "data" topics are related with the theme "use" (count: 70; relevance: 35%). Table 10 systematizes the themes identified by Leximancer and the papers associated to them and used in authors' further analysis. The table also provides a brief summary of the main literature findings.

A further analysis revealed that the theme "banks" is related with the need to adapt to new circumstances because they are clearly being challenged by new incumbents (Jakšič & Marinč, 2019). Fintech companies offer substitute products to the traditional banking and with their new solutions can even reach populations to whom banks' service is expensive and hard to access (Kim & Hann, 2019; Nigam, Mbarek, & Benetti, 2019) being fintechs very important in less developed markets (Coetzee, 2018). Banks are adapting to digital solutions, having most of them a robust reediness for their adoption, (Auvinen, et al., 2019). Banks are competing but mainly partnering (Bömer & Maxin, 2018; Drasch, Schweizer, & Urbach, 2018) with fintechs which were already born digital (Iman, 2019). The adoption to new technologies such as blockchain (Min, 2019), big data and robot-advisors (Belanche, Casaló, & Flavián, 2019) will have impacts in the traditional banking structures (Semenyuta, Andreeva, Sichev, & Filippov, 2019), for instance, the need for very specialized work and less need for resources allocated to operational teams (Lavrinenko & Shmatko, 2019). Nevertheless, the implementation of these solutions will have also a strong positive impact replacing complex and costly banking

Table 10. Systematization of themes, papers and main findings

Theme	Leximancer's Relevance	Papers	Main findings
Banks	100%	Anagnostopoulos, 2018; Auvinen, et al., 2019; Belanche, Casaló, & Flavián, 2019; Bömer & Maxin, 2018; Coetzee, 2018; Drasch, Schweizer, & Urbach, 2018; Frias & Freire, 2019; Gohary, 2019; Gonzalez, 2019; Harvey & Branco-Illodo, 2019; Iman, 2019; Kim & Hann, 2019; Kovanen, 2019; Lavrinenko & Shmatko, 2019; Mehar, et al., 2019; Micheler & Whaley, 2019; Min, 2019; Nigam, Mbarek, & Benetti, 2019; Semenyuta, Andreeva, Sichev, & Filippov, 2019; Wolf & Redford, 2019; Jakšić & Marinč, 2019	(i) Banks are being challenged by new incumbents. (ii) Fintechs are expanding and offering substitute products reaching populations to whom the traditional services are expensive or hard to access. (iii) Banks are trying to adapt to this new competition and mainly partnering with fintechs. (iv) The existence and adoption of new technologies will impact traditional banking's structures such as less allocation of operational resources, a need for specialized work and leaner processes. (v) Cryptocurrencies are also impacting banks and central banks. Their proliferations urges for regulation.
Technology, use and system	41%, 35%, 17%	Addo, Guegan, & Hassani, 2018; Anagnostopoulos, 2018; Gohary, 2019; Gonzalez, 2019; Hassani, Huang, & Silva, 2018; Kovanen, 2019; Micheler & Whaley, 2019; Procházka, 2018; Stewart & Jürjens, 2018; Yoon & Jun, 2019; Ashta & Biot-Paquerot, 2018; Belanche, Casaló, & Flavián, 2019	(i) The theme use is closely related with the use of technology and is not relevant on its own. (ii) The use of technology is related with the use of blockchain systems. That is the reason to the association of the theme system. (iii) Technology is associated to fintechs and the products they offer. (iv) Literature states that blockchain is the main technology breakthrough behind the fintechs' success. (v) Traditional banks need to adapt to this technological developments.
Services	32%	Anagnostopoulos, 2018; Anagnostopoulos, 2018; Döderlein, 2018; Drasch, Schweizer, & Urbach, 2018; Larios-Hernández, 2017; Passi, 2018; Romanova, Grima, Spiter, & Kudinska, 2018; Stewart & Jürjens, 2018; Yoon & Jun, 2019; Zalan & Toufaily, 2017	(i) Refers to traditional financial services offered by banks and currently fintechs. (ii) Banks are under pressure from the market and fintech companies to offer innovative digital services. (iii) Although the regulation might be a burden it has been eased in order to facilitate banks to adopt innovative measures. (iv) The fintechs are used mostly by young and educated people being very fruitful in developing markets in which they allow the access to financial services.
Market, crowdfunding and finance	27%, 19%, 14%	Brown, Boon, & Pitt, 2017; Cumming, Meoli, & Vismara, 2019; Hoegen, Steininger, & Veit, 2018; Kim & Hann, 2019; Nigam, Mbarek, & Benetti, 2019; Prakash, Reddy, & Vasaswi, 2019; Zilber, Silveira, Carvalho, & Imbrizi, 2016	(i) The themes finance (financial services and financing), market (financial markets) and crowdfunding are interconnected with predominance for crowdfunding. (ii) Crowdfunding is also considered an alternative financing source which had an important increase because it overcomes the usual difficulties in the traditional financing forms.
Digital	22%	Bantouna, Poulios, Tsagkaris, & Demestichas, 2014; Japparova & Rupeika-Apoga, 2017; Larios-Hernández, 2017; Liu, Chen, & Chou, 2011; Meena, Sriram, & Sundaram, 2017; Zalan & Toufaily, 2017	(i) Connected with the themes technology and service once digital is related with the appearance of disruptive digital services. (ii) Traditional banks need to become digitalized in order to remain competitive. (iii) The digitalization of the economy is possible due to large amounts of data available. (iv) There are concerns about the digital inclusion but clearly digital services promote entrepreneurship and the financial inclusion of populations in less developed markets.
Investment	16%	Bodislav, Bran, & Popescu, 2018; Hoegen, Steininger, & Veit, 2018; Jung, Dorner, Weinhardt, & Pusmaz, 2018; Sigo, et al., 2018; Brown, Boon, & Pitt, 2017	(i) Refers to the alternative ways of investment which differ from the traditional ones. (ii) Literature refers to automated investment counseling and the use of big data in the investment process.

processes (Gonzalez, 2019) and facilitating several banking services such as payments (Gohary, 2019). The literature also highlights the need to foster entrepreneurship within banks' subsidiaries in order to nurture innovation and also to empower them to reinvent themselves (Wolf & Redford, 2019). Impacting banks and central banks are also the cryptocurrencies which have proliferated during the last years (Kovanen, 2019; Mehar, et al., 2019) and which advocate for more privacy (Harvey & Branco-Illodo, 2019) and independence from the central banks (Frias & Freire, 2019). These facts also urged for more regulation in fintech and cryptocurrencies' markets (Anagnostopoulos, 2018; Micheler & Whaley, 2019).

The theme "services" is mainly referred in the literature to identify financial services offered traditionally by banks and currently also by fintechs (Zalan & Toufaily, 2017; Anagnostopoulos, 2018). Literature confirms banks are under pressure to offer innovative and digital services which go in line with consumers' demands (Drasch, Schweizer, & Urbach, 2018; Yoon & Jun, 2019). The authors also confirmed that this innovation is considered to have positive effects on consumers and regulators (Anagnostopoulos, 2018). This pressure does not only come from fintech companies but also from the market which has been more flexible and prone to creating innovative services (Romanova, Grima, Spiter, & Kudinska, 2018). Although the regulation may still be seen as a burden to innovation (Döderlein, 2018), the new European Payment Services Directive (PSD2) regulation is an example of a regulatory measure which intends to increase the consumer protection at the same time that tries to homogenize and make the payment market more efficient (Passi, 2018). Literature also reveals that the fintech services, although clear substitutes to traditional banking, are still mostly used by younger and higher educated people (Stewart & Jürjens, 2018) being very fruitful in developing markets where the access to traditional financial services is very limited (Larios-Hernández, 2017).

Literature associates the theme "technology" with the fintech companies (Belanche, Casaló, & Flavián, 2019) and innovative services provided by them (Yoon & Jun, 2019) mostly related with payments (Kovanen, 2019). Insights are also provided on the impacts fintech technology has on traditional services (Anagnostopoulos, 2018; Gohary, 2019). The theme technology is frequently interconnected with the topic blockchain through the theme system. Therefore, the literature assumes blockchain systems have been the main technological breakthrough behind the recent fintech innovation (Gonzalez, 2019) and relates it with the expansion of technology and with a real disruption in the monetary system (Ashta & Biot-Paquerot, 2018). The banking system is already adopting technological solutions, such as blockchain (Hassani, Huang, & Silva, 2018), in order to keep up the pace with their competitors (Addo, Guegan, & Hassani, 2018; Stewart & Jürjens, 2018). Nonetheless, new technological solutions, pose a challenge to regulation which has been increasing in this area (Procházka, 2018) with the example of the Bank of England adopting itself digital solutions for regulatory purposes (Micheler & Whaley, 2019). The theme "digital" also appears in line with both previous themes as it is related with the appearance of new disruptive digital services (Zalan & Toufaily, 2017) and the need to adopt digital solutions (Liu, Chen, & Chou, 2011). The literature focuses on banks and states that digitalization processes are crucial for banks to guarantee their own development (Japparova & Rupeika-Apoga, 2017). The economy's digitalization is possible due to large amounts of data available and the capacity to process it (Bantouna, Poulios, Tsagkaris, & Demestichas, 2014). Nevertheless, digitalization raises also some concerns regarding exclusion because there is a clear positive correlation between age and income and the utilization of digital solutions (Meena, Sriram, & Sundaram, 2017). However, the new digital financial services are able to promote entrepreneurship and also financial inclusion (Larios-Hernández, 2017). The usage of the new technological financial services, the use of data and digital solutions are clearly increasing being the main reason for the existence of the theme use.

The themes "market", "finance" and "crowdfunding" appear interconnected in the literature. The theme "market" refers mainly to financial markets and the theme "finance" mainly refers to the financial services and to the financing of companies and investments. Crowdfunding is also associated with a type of market and an alternative way of financing projects (Zilber, Silveira, Carvalho, & Imbrizi, 2016; Kim & Hann, 2019). Crowdfunding is defined as a way used by "organizations and individuals to obtain investments they otherwise might not receive from more traditional sources such as banks, angel investors, and stock markets" (Brown, Boon, & Pitt, 2017, p. 1). There is an increase in the financing by crowdfunding (Prakash, Reddy, & Vasaswi, 2019) because it is a way of overcoming financing difficulties in projects which are unable to obtain financing via traditional forms (Cumming, Meoli, & Vismara, 2019; Nigam, Mbarek, & Benetti, 2019). The volume of crowdfunding increased 1000% in a small number of years and it is nearly outpacing the worldwide venture capital spending (Hoegen, Steininger, & Veit, 2018).

Finally, the literature refers the theme "investment" and associates it with alternative ways of investment (Brown, Boon, & Pitt, 2017). These alternative forms have different decision-making processes compared to the traditional ones (Hoegen, Steininger, & Veit, 2018). Furthermore, the literature refers new ways of automated investment counseling such as robot-advisor systems (Jung, Dorner, Weinhardt, & Pusmaz, 2018) and the use of big data in investment processes as a way of making better decisions (Bodislav, Bran, & Popescu, 2018; Sigo, et al., 2018).

The entire map proves the idea that the central topic is still banks and the services they offer which are being challenged by substitute products offered by new incumbents. Fintechs are prone at providing a consumer-focused service and therefore, there is a strong interest in topics such as technology which is identified as a future's trend and with new frameworks' development within fintech companies. These new revolutionary services are mostly digital and based on blockchain system which has captured banks' attention which have adopted some of fintech's processes mainly through cooperation. Although the traditional financial institutions are struggling to keep pace with innovation, they are putting the best effort on this in order to guarantee their survival.

Table with the Methodologies Used

The current section is dedicated to the analysis of the methodologies used in the papers considered for this research. The authors have divided the methodologies into: literature review; quantitative; qualitative; mixed; conceptual (e.g. new model); experimental. Furthermore, the type of data is analyzed and divided into: primary; secondary; both types of data. A summary of the analysis can be found in table 11.

The authors have concluded that the majority of the papers fit into the methodology of the literature review representing a total of 42 papers. The second type of research representing 29 papers of the sample is the quantitative research followed by the qualitative research methodology used in 23 of the sample papers. The remaining approaches still have low significance but there are mixed methods approaches, conceptual frameworks and experimental researches on this topic. The mostly used type of data is secondary data mainly due to the literature review papers but also due to the quantitative research which uses mainly this type of data. In sum, the secondary data is used in 77 of the papers analyzed while the primary data is used in 20 of the papers analyzed with a reduced number of papers using both types of data which accounts to 3 of the papers analyzed.

Table 11. Summary of the methodologies used

Methods	Papers	Secondary data	Primary data	Both data
Literature Review	42	42	0	0
Quantitative	29	23	4	2
Qualitative	23	9	14	0
Mixed	3	1	1	1
Conceptual	2	2	0	0
Experimental	1	0	1	0
Total	100	77	20	3

CONCLUSIONS AND FURTHER RESEARCH

Main Conclusions

The aim of this paper was to answer the following research question: what insights does current literature offer regarding the impact of fintech in the banking sector? Accordingly, the authors developed a systematic literature review. Fintech are gaining relevance in the last years as concluded by the analysis of Google Trends' data and also by the literature analysis. Internet interest on this topic has increased as well as the number of articles published and the number of authors, journals, private institutions and universities interested in the topic.

The literature proves that the USA, the UK and Germany are the most relevant countries in terms of research on current topic. These are the most important markets for the fintech (after China) and also the ones with the most developed educational system. Despite having several active authors interested on fintech and the Journal which publishes the most, China is still behind several countries in terms of authors and publications, namely, the emerging markets for fintech such as Germany, Italy, Spain, Eastern Europe and India. The most cited words in papers' keywords are consistent with current state of the fintech/banking market. The most prominent topics focus on banks, fintechs and finance. The interest is clear on services provided by fintech which are mostly similar to traditional banking's ones. Hence, there is strong interest in payments, financial services, lending and currency. Together with these concepts are technological ones such as big data, blockchain, artificial intelligence, data transformation and machine learning. The analysis also highlights the focus on regulation. Leximancer's concept map and literature associated with it proves the conclusions already found through the snapshot done previously.

Previous studies revealed that fintechs are indeed direct competitors of traditional financial institutions since they offer substitute products (PWC, 2016; Vives, 2017), while technological companies have the strong advantage of being completely digitalized, offering services and products in a much faster and cheap manner than financial institutions (PWC, 2019). Traditional financial institutions, particularly the banks, have a heavy burden of old processes and costly business models based on fees (Chiorazzo, D'Apice, DeYoung, & Morelli, 2018; Gomber, Kauffman, Parker, & Weber, 2018). After the last financial crisis (2007-2008) banks jeopardized their reputation and fintechs expanded based on the idea that there is no need for third party intermediation with blockchain based systems which can ultimately substitute central banks' role as currency issuers. Previous studies also stated that although fintechs have expanded and currently pose a direct threat to traditional banking they are not considered clear substitutes though (Roland Berger, 2018). Nonetheless, they are considered disruptive innovators and are forcing banks to rapidly adapt (Deloitte, 2017; PWC, 2019). Hence, banks are adapting in order to change their processes and focus on consumers' needs taking advantage of the trust on traditional and regulated institutions (EY, 2014). Banks are dealing with fintechs through acquisition or collaboration (KPMG, 2019a; PWC, 2019). Banks recognize the importance of concepts such as data, digital and technology and the necessity of integrating them onto their business model (Addo, Guegan, & Hassani, 2018; Hassani, Huang, & Silva, 2018; PWC, 2019). Simultaneously, fintech market is expanding and its three most relevant regions are China, the USA and the UK. Although the European market is expanding (e.g. in Germany, France, Italy, Spain or Netherlands) the UK is clearly the center for the European innovation in fintechs. The USA are an important market for fintechs but China is today the most prominent one globally.

Avenues for Future Research

Future studies on banks' digital transformation should focus on technologies and systems used in fintech industry currently being adopted by banks (e.g. blockchain, robot-advising, big data). Banks are thriving to adopt new technologies and solutions in order to improve old processes and remain competitive which is key to their survival and maintenance as key players in the financial industry. Therefore, technologies adopted and their purposes are of high importance. For instance, which is the use of blockchain in traditional banking and what risks and advantages does it pose? Have the banks adopting these technologies become more competitive and have they attracted more consumers? Besides pure fintech technologies, future studies should also focus on banks' adoption of digital solutions (e.g. home banking applications, digital customer support). Are banks offering more digital solutions to their clients? What is the percentage of traditional banks' clients actively using digital solutions and in what depth do they use them?

Financial institutions have several ways of dealing with fintechs but a model of cooperation has been preferred because it seems to allow traditional companies to easily adopt fintechs' technological solutions (Roland Berger, 2018; PWC, 2019). A future study on the models used by traditional financial institutions to deal with fintechs would be of interest. Which models have been adopted in the relation between traditional institutions and new incumbents? Do models of cooperation produce better results? Who has benefited the most with the cooperation?

The authors have found that new financial services still benefit from more permissive regulation than traditional banks (EY, 2018; Desai, V, V, & Jayakumar, 2019). Traditional institutions can benefit from regulation because it increases trust on them, but it may also jeopardize much of the innovation. There are also signs of openness in regulators in order to allow the traditional banks to adopt innovative solutions. Studies on regulation and the way it affects the new incumbents are interesting. Is regulation (or the lack of it) favoring fintech? How can fintechs protect and adapt themselves to possible future regulatory measures? Are banks taking advantage of regulatory openness?

There is clear evidence that investments are taking different forms and are also becoming digital due to the existence of new solutions and new markets which are replacing the traditional ones (Brochado, 2018b; Hoegen, Steininger, & Veit, 2018; Cumming, Meoli, & Vismara, 2019; Nigam, Mbarek, & Benetti, 2019; Prakash, Reddy, & Vasaswi, 2019). Examples of these new investments are crowdfunding and more recently the Initial Coin Offerings (ICOs) which use virtual currencies and tokens to attract investment. Therefore, further studies should also focus on studying the success factors of new fintech companies and in particular the success factors of these new investment vehicles. Which are the success factors of a completely digital company offering financial services? Which are the success factors of campaigns such as the ICOs which are completely digital, using virtual currencies and with a global reach?

MAIN RESEARCH LIMITATIONS

The database collected from SCOPUS is limited to 100 relevant papers and the great majority of them were published in the last 3 years. The conclusions would be stronger if a larger database was available and also if an older track record existed. In other words, this would result in more bibliography as well as an established group of researchers and consequently more consistency of the results. The current research is limited to a search on SCOPUS database. Consequently, it could be enlarged if other indexes are cross-checked among them and the number of articles included is increased. The SCOPUS search was limited to papers written in English for the sake of comparison among them and an easy and unbiased analysis. Although the largest majority is written in English several papers were lost in the analysis and consequently important information might also be lost. The search on SCOPUS is performed selecting several combinations of words which result in a final list of papers. Although the authors think that the sample is relevant, they might have not included important words to the search on the platform and thus some papers might not have been included in the analysis. The novelty of the topic is also cause of constant changes in concepts and market data. Therefore, the data presented in the theoretical framework might be outdated soon and requires constant updates to be relevant. This limitation increases due to the volatility of fintech business and constant valorization and depreciation of cryptocurrencies.

In sum, fintechs are clearly reshaping the traditional market of financial services by offering digital solutions and customer centric products. Traditional institutions are adapting to this new reality and are adopting technological solutions in order to remain competitive. Future studies on these topics will be important to understand how the market is moving and what the impacts of innovation are.

REFERENCES

Addo, P., Guegan, D., & Hassani, B. (2018). *Credit risk analysis using machine and deep learning models*. Risks. doi:10.3390/risks6020038

Anagnostopoulos, I. (2018). Fintech and regtech: Impact on regulators and banks. *Journal of Economics and Business*, *100*, 7–25. doi:10.1016/j.jeconbus.2018.07.003

Andrade, P. (2019). *Can Innovation be a sustainable competitive advantage for a bank?* ISCTE-IUL.

Ashta, A., & Biot-Paquerot, G. (2018). FinTech evolution: Strategic value management issues in a fast changing industry. *Strategic Change*, *27*(4), 301–311. doi:10.1002/jsc.2203

Auvinen, T., Sajasalo, P., Sintonen, T., Pekkala, K., Takala, T., & Luoma-aho, V. (2019). Evolution of strategy narration and leadership work in the digital era. *Leadership*, *15*(2), 205–225. doi:10.1177/1742715019826426

Bantouna, A., Poulios, G., Tsagkaris, K., & Demestichas, P. (2014). Network load predictions based on big data and the utilization of self-organizing maps. *Journal of Network and Systems Management*, *22*(2), 150–173. doi:10.100710922-013-9285-1

Belanche, D., Casaló, L., & Flavián, C. (2019). Artificial Intelligence in FinTech: Understanding robo-advisors adoption among customers. *Industrial Management & Data Systems*, *119*(7), 1411–1430. Advance online publication. doi:10.1108/IMDS-08-2018-0368

Bodislav, D., Bran, F., & Popescu, L. (2018). The business-automated data economy model, 2018 early update. *Quality - Access to Success*, 80-84.

Bömer, M., & Maxin, H. (2018). Why fintechs cooperate with banks—evidence from germany. *Zeitschrift fur die gesamte Versicherungswissenschaft*, 359-386. doi:10.100712297-018-0421-6

Brochado, A. (2018a). Snapshot da Indústria das Criptomoedas. Caderno do Mercado de Valores Mobiliários, 83-108.

Brochado, A. (2018b). Snapshot das Initial Coin Offerings (ICOs). Cadernos do Mercado de Valores Mobiliários, 53-76.

Brown, T., Boon, E., & Pitt, L. (2017). Seeking funding in order to sell: Crowdfunding as a marketing tool. *Business Horizons*, *60*(2), 189–195. doi:10.1016/j.bushor.2016.11.004

Bughin, J., Deakin, J., & O'Beirne, B. (2019). Digital transformation: Improving the odds. *The McKinsey Quarterly*.

Chen, Y. (2018). Blockchain tokens and the potential democratization of entrepreneurship and innovation. *Business Horizons*, *61*(4), 567–575. doi:10.1016/j.bushor.2018.03.006

Cheng, G., & Mevis, D. (2018). What happened to profitability? Shocks, challenges and perspectives for euro area banks. *European Journal of Finance*, 1–25. doi:10.1080/1351847X.2018.1470994

Chiorazzo, V., D'Apice, V., DeYoung, R., & Morelli, P. (2018). Is the traditional banking model a survivor? *Journal of Banking & Finance*, *97*, 238–256. doi:10.1016/j.jbankfin.2018.10.008

Coetzee, J. (2018). *Strategic implications of fintech on South African retail banks.* South African Journal of Economic and Management Sciences., doi:10.4102ajems.v21i1.2455

Coin Dance. (2019, October 25). *Coin Dance.* Retrieved from https://coin.dance/

Costa-Climent, R., & Martínez-Climent, C. (2018). Sustainable profitability of ethical and conventional banking. *Contemporary Economics*, 519-530. doi:10.5709/ce.1897-9254.294

Crofts, K., & Bisman, J. (2010). Interrogating accountability: An illustration of the use of Leximancer software for qualitative data analysis. *Qualitative Research in Accounting & Management*, *7*(2), 180–207. doi:10.1108/11766091011050859

Cumming, D., Meoli, M., & Vismara, S. (2019). Does equity crowdfunding democratize entrepreneurial finance? *Small Business Economics.* Advance online publication. doi:10.100711187-019-00188-z

Dell'Atti, S., Trotta, A., Iannuzzi, A. P., & Demaria, F. (2017). *Corporate Social Responsibility Engagement as a Determinant of Bank Reputation: An Empirical Analysis.* doi:10.1002/csr.1430

Deloitte. (2017). Beyond fintech: Eight forces that are shifting the competitive landscape. *Beyond fintech: Eight forces that are shifting the competitive landscape.*

Desai, K. R., V, M., V, V., & Jayakumar, K. (2019). Fintech Innovations and Its Impact on the Profitability of Selected Banks. *International Journal of Business and Management Invention*, 41-45.

Döderlein, D. (2018). What is the optimal mix between banks and fintechs in the payments architecture? *Journal of Payments Strategy and Systems*, 122-129.

Drasch, B., Schweizer, A., & Urbach, N. (2018). Integrating the 'Troublemakers': A taxonomy for cooperation between banks and fintechs. *Journal of Economics and Business*, *100*, 26–42. doi:10.1016/j.jeconbus.2018.04.002

EY. (2014). *Winning through customer experience*. EY Global Consumer Banking Survey.

EY. (2017). *Unleashing the potential of FinTech in banking*. Author.

EY. (2018). *FinTech ecosystem playbook*. Author.

Freivogel, C. (2016, June 29). *The social side of Fintech*. Retrieved September 2019, 22, from SwissBanking: https://www.swissbanking.org/en/services/insight/2.16/the-social-side-of-fintech

Frias, A., & Freire, E. (2019). Financial shielding that Bitcoin grants to capitals in the world. *Investment Management and Financial Innovations*, 49-61. doi:10.21511/imfi.16(3).2019.06

Gohary, E. E. (2019). The impact of financial technology on facilitating e-government services in Egypt. *Journal of Distribution Science*, 51-59. doi:10.15722/JDS.17.5.201905.51

Gomber, P., Kauffman, R. J., Parker, C., & Weber, B. W. (2018). On the Fintech Revolution: Interpreting the Forces of Innovation, Disruption, and Transformation in Financial Services. *Journal of Management Information Systems*, *35*(1), 220–265. doi:10.1080/07421222.2018.1440766

Gonzalcz, L. (2019). Blockchain, herding and trust in peer-to-peer lending. *Managerial Finance*, MF-09-2018-0423. Advance online publication. doi:10.1108/MF-09-2018-0423

Google. (2019, October 25). *Google Trends*. Retrieved from https://trends.google.com/

Harvey, J., & Branco-Illodo, I. (2019). Why Cryptocurrencies Want Privacy: A Review of Political Motivations and Branding Expressed in "Privacy Coin" Whitepapers. *Journal of Political Marketing*, 1–30. Advance online publication. doi:10.1080/15377857.2019.1652223

Hassani, H., Huang, X., & Silva, E. (2018). Banking with blockchain-ed big data. *Journal of Management Analytics*, 256-275. doi:10.1080/23270012.2018.1528900

Hoegen, A., Steininger, D., & Veit, D. (2018). How do investors decide? An interdisciplinary review of decision-making in crowdfunding. *Electronic Markets, 28*(3), 339–365. doi:10.100712525-017-0269-y

Iman, N. (2019). Traditional banks against fintech startups: A field investigation of a regional bank in Indonesia. *Banks and Bank Systems*, 20-33. doi:10.21511/bbs.14(3).2019.03

Jakšič, M., & Marinč, M. (2019). Relationship banking and information technology: The role of artificial intelligence and FinTech. *Risk Management*. Advance online publication. doi:10.105741283-018-0039-y

Japparova, I., & Rupeika-Apoga, R. (2017). Banking business models of the digital future: The case of Latvia. *European Research Studies Journal*, 864-878.

Jung, D., Dorner, V., Weinhardt, C., & Pusmaz, H. (2018). Designing a robo-advisor for risk-averse, low-budget consumers. *Electronic Markets, 28*(3), 367–380. doi:10.100712525-017-0279-9

Khanna, S., & Martins, H. (2018). *Six digital growth strategies for banks*. McKinsey Insights.

Kim, K., & Hann, I. (2019). Crowdfunding and the democratization of access to capital-an illusion? Evidence from housing prices. *Information Systems Research, 30*(1), 276–290. doi:10.1287/isre.2018.0802

Kovanen, A. (2019). Competing with bitcoin - some policy considerations for issuing digitalized legal tenders. *International Journal of Financial Research*, 1-16. doi:10.5430/ijfr.v10n4p1

KPMG. (2019). *Regulation and supervision of fintech: Ever-expanding expectations*. KPMG.

KPMG. (2019a). *The Pulse of Fintech. Biannual global analysis of investment in fintech*. KPMG.

Kreidych, I., Roshchyna, N., & Kazak, O. (2018). The application of monetary incentive policy in current economic conditions. *Baltic Journal of Economic Studies*, 129-139. doi:10.30525/2256-0742/2018-4-5-129-139

Kshetri, N. (2017). Blockchain's roles in strengthening cybersecurity and. *Telecommunications Policy*, 1–12. doi:10.1016/j.telpol.2017.09.003

Lacity, M. C., & Willcocks, L. P. (2001). *Global information technology outsourcing*. Wiley. doi:10.1108/17538290810857457

Larios-Hernández, G. (2017). Blockchain entrepreneurship opportunity in the practices of the unbanked. *Business Horizons*, *60*(6), 865–874. doi:10.1016/j.bushor.2017.07.012

Lavrinenko, A., & Shmatko, N. (2019). Twenty-first century skills in finance: prospects for a profound job transformation. *Foresight and STI Governance*, 42-51. doi:10.17323/2500-2597.2019.2.42.51

Liu, D., Chen, S., & Chou, T. (2011). Resource fit in digital transformation: Lessons learned from the CBC Bank global e-banking project. *Management Decision*, *49*(10), 1728–1742. doi:10.1108/00251741111183852

McKinsey&Company. (2018). *New rules for an old game: Banks in the changing world of financial intermediation*. McKinsey Global Banking Annual Review.

Meena, S. D., Sriram, M., & Sundaram, N. (2017). Digital financial inclusion is a need of the hour: An investigation amongst bank account holders in Vellore district of Tamil Nadu, India. *International Journal of Applied Business and Economic Research*, 1-6.

Mehar, M., Shier, C., Giambattista, A., Gong, E., Fletcher, G., Sanayhie, R., Kim, H. M., & Laskowski, M. (2019). Understanding a revolutionary and flawed grand experiment in blockchain: The DAO attack. *Journal of Cases on Information Technology*, *21*(1), 19–32. doi:10.4018/JCIT.2019010102

Micheler, E., & Whaley, A. (2019). Regulatory Technology: Replacing Law with Computer Code. *European Business Organization Law Review*. Advance online publication. doi:10.100740804-019-00151-1

Min, H. (2019). Blockchain technology for enhancing supply chain resilience. *Business Horizons*, *62*(1), 35–45. doi:10.1016/j.bushor.2018.08.012

Nigam, N., Mbarek, S., & Benetti, C. (2019). Can crowdfunding promote innovation in the wine industry? *International Journal of Entrepreneurship and Small Business*, *36*(3), 335–354. doi:10.1504/IJESB.2019.097741

Passi, L. (2018). An open banking ecosystem to survive the revised payment services directive: Connecting international banks and fintechs with the CBI globe platform. *Journal of Payments Strategy and Systems,* 335-345.

Prakash, K., Reddy, P., & Vasaswi, K. (2019). Equity crowdfunding in Europe - A new financial phenomenon for Gen-Z entrepreneurs. *International Journal of Recent Technology and Engineering*, 1944-1948.

Procházka, D. (2018). Accounting for bitcoin and other cryptocurrencies under IFRS: A comparison and assessment of competing models. *International Journal of Digital Accounting Research*, 161-188. doi:10.4192/1577-8517-v18_7

PWC. (2016). *Blurred lines: How FinTech is shaping Financial Services*. Global FinTech Report.

PWC. (2019). *Crossing the lines: How fintech is propelling FS and TMT companies out of their lanes*. Global Fintech Report.

Rauchs, M., Blandin, A., Bear, K., & McKeon, S. (2019). *2nd Global Enterprise Blockchain Benchmarking Study*. Cambridge Centre for Alternative Finance. doi:10.2139srn.3461765

Roland Berger. (2018, August). The digitalization race: Can financial service providers hack the pace? Third European Retail Banking Survey - Findings and recommendations. *Focus*. Retrieved September 21, 2019, from https://www.rolandberger.com/publications/publication_pdf/roland_berger_retail_banking_survey_en.pdf

Romanova, I., Grima, S., Spiter, J., & Kudinska, M. (2018). The payment services Directive II and competitiveness: The perspective of European fintech companies. *European Research Studies Journal*, 3-22.

Schizas, E., McKain, G., Zhang, B., Ganbold, A., Kumar, P., Hussain, H., & Yerolemou, N. (2019). *The Global RegTech Industry Benchmark Report*. Cambridge Center for Alternative Finance. doi:10.2139srn.3560811

Schueffel, P. (2016). *Taming the Beast: A Scientific Definition of Fintech*. SSRN., doi:10.2139srn.3097312

Semenyuta, O., Andreeva, A., Sichev, R., & Filippov, Y. (2019). Digital technologies in lending small and medium-size enterprises in Russia. International Journal of Economics and Business Administration, 40-52.

Sigo, M., Selvam, M., Balasundram, M., Kannaiah, D., Kathiravan, C., & Vadivel, T. (2018). Big data analytics-application of artificial neural network in forecasting stock price trends in India. Academy of Accounting and Financial Studies Journal, 1-13.

Spyromitrosa, E., & Tsintzos, P. (2019). Credit expansion in a monetary policy game: Implications of the valuation haircut framework. Finance Research Letters, 125-129. doi:10.1016/j.frl.2018.04.012

Stewart, H., & Jürjens, J. (2018). Data security and consumer trust in FinTech innovation in Germany. *Information and Computer Security*, 109-128. doi:10.1108/ICS-06-2017-0039

University of Cambridge. (2018). *The 3rd Asia Pacific Region Alternative Finance Industry Report*. Cambridge Centre for Alternative Finance.

University of Cambridge. (2018). *The Future of Finance is Emerging: New Hubs, New Landscapes*. Global Fintech Hub Report.

University of Cambridge. (2018a). *Reaching New Heights*. The 3rd Americas Alternative Finance Industry Report.

Vives, X. (2017). *The Impact of Fintech on Banking*. European Economy.

Wolf, C., & Redford, D. (2019). *Fostering entrepreneurship for innovation in African Banks' subsidiaries*. Africa Journal of Management. doi:10.1080/23322373.2019.1649558

Woudstra, U., Berghout, E., Tan, C.-W., Eekeren, P. v., & Dedene, G. (2017). *Resource Complementarity and IT Economies of Scale: Mechanisms and Empirical Evidence*. doi:10.1080/10580530.2017.1288527

Yoon, K., & Jun, J. (2019). Liability And Antifraud Investment In Fintech Retail Payment Services. *Contemporary Economic Policy, 191-194*. Advance online publication. doi:10.1111/coep.12281

Zalan, T., & Toufaily, E. (2017). The promise of fintech in emerging markets: Not as disruptive. *Contemporary Economics*, 415-430. doi:10.5709/ce.1897-9254.253

Ziegler, T., Shneor, R., Wenzlaff, K., Odorović, A., Johanson, D., Hao, R., & Ryll, L. (2019). Shifting Paradigms. The 4th European Alternative Finance Benchmarking Report.

Zilber, S., Silveira, F., Carvalho, L., & Imbrizi, A. (2016). Crowd funding as an alternative for new ventures funding in emerging countries. *International Business Management*, 575-584. doi:10.3923/ibm.2016.575.584

KEY TERMS AND DEFINITIONS

Altcoins: These refer to alternative coins to bitcoin. They surged after the bitcoin and are based on the same technology.

Cryptocurrency: Virtual currency not controlled by a central authority and which constitutes a digital asset. These currencies work usually through a blockchain technology.

Financial Institution: Every company which engages in businesses which deal with financial or monetary transactions. Banks are included into this category as well as financial intermediaries or wealth managers.

Fintech: Technological company providing financial services which are complementary and most times substitutes to the ones offered by traditional banking sector. These companies are characterized by its high investment in new digitalized business models.

Investment: In this chapter, investment means the amount invested in Fintech companies via several strategies, namely, venture capital or mergers and acquisitions (M&A).

Market Volume: Market volume refers to the total amount of transactions concluded in a determined period, for instance, the transactions amount which Fintech concluded in a specified market for a determined period.

P2P: Peer to peer activities are used to avoid intermediaries in the process because lender and borrower match without the need of an intermediary bank.

RegTech: Technological company specialized in the offer of new technological solutions in order to meet regulatory requirements.

Chapter 4
Competitive Cycles in a Hyper-Connected World:
Everything Flows

Alessandro Arbore
https://orcid.org/0000-0002-6505-2800
Bocconi University, Italy

ABSTRACT

This chapter presents a competitive framework suggesting a circular perspective in analyzing and managing competitive wars in a hyper-competitive and hyper-connected world. The author uses the expression "competitive cycles" to represent a typical journey of a competitive arena. The journey starts with the status quo, characterized by a direct confrontation on specific success factors (War of Position); eventually, this scenario is disrupted by the game-changing strategy of an insurgent (War of Movement). This leads to the next stage of the journey, the War of Imitation, ending up when the new game finally becomes the new status quo, that is, back to the War of Position. Then everything flows, until a new cycle, with its new rules, will start again. The digital tsunami is adding momentum and clock-speed to competitive cycles. In every moment of a firm's life, then, it is vitally important to be fully aware of its different wars. In fact, behind each of them lies distinctive rationales and dynamics, which call for specific strategic approaches.

DOI: 10.4018/978-1-7998-4552-2.ch004

INTRODUCTION: HISTORY REPEATS ITSELF

More than twenty years ago, D'Aveni introduced the expression hyper-competition to describe the vibrant and turbulent scenarios emerging during the 90s (D'Aveni, 1994). Then the digital revolution arrived, and –year after year- it dramatically amplified all those trends. We are now in the 20s and that hyper-competitive world has become a hyper-connected world.

Many things have changed, like never before, although the core principles of competition still apply (Porter & Heppelmann, 2014). Turbulence and uncertainty have become even bigger: the digital paradigm is adding momentum and clock-speed to "competitive cycles" (Valdani & Arbore, 2013).

What is exactly a "Competitive Cycle"? In 1725, the Italian scientist Giambattista Vico theorized that "the progress of things is made of historical courses and recurrences" (p. xxii): more simply, he was suggesting that history repeats itself. The idea of *circularity* in our destiny is actually a theme taken up by many throughout the ages, in many different disciplines. Consider the eternal return of Zarathustra in Nietzsche's thought, for instance. When referring to a competitive arena, we use the expression "competitive cycle", as explained below.

A competitive cycle starts from the status quo of an industry, characterized by a direct confrontation on specific success factors, sometimes referred to as critical or key success factors (KSF): within an industry, these are the winning weapons at a given time. Any direct confrontation leveraging on those weapons can be named a "War of Position". Soon or later, however, the status quo will be disrupted by a game-changing strategy of an insurgent company, which could be either an existing player or a complete outsider. Such an indirect, innovative attack will be named a "War of Movement": completely new weapons are introduced, and a new game starts. Afterwards, if the War of Movement is a successful one, then the industry will move to the third stage of a competitive cycle, that is, the "War of Imitation". Eventually, our circular journey will be completed when the new, disruptive game will become the new status quo: everything flows, as in Heraclitus' words, until a new cycle, with its new rules, will start again.

Proactive change, then, becomes the long-term orientation of successful companies. Still, it is important to remember that every revolution brings with it new opportunities as well as new risks: a manager must know when the time is right to start a revolution, or to join someone else's, or to keep the peace. To clarify these dynamics, also in the age of hyper-connection and digital competition, is the overarching goal of this chapter.

COMPETITIVE CYCLES IN ACTION: AN EVERGREEN PERSPECTIVE

From a theoretical perspective, the background of our framework emerges from three different streams of literature:

- The proactive firm, an idea that is conceptually rooted in the chaos and complexity theory (Kauffman, 1995; Kotter, 1996; Brown & Eisenhardt, 1998; Sanders, 1999). Proactive systems adapt to change overcoming environmental turbulence and entropy.
- The Resource Based View, holding that the value generated by a firm is contingent on its endowment of resources and capabilities (Penrose, 1959; Barney, 1991; Grant 1991; Prahalad & Hamel, 1994). The uniqueness of this endowment is at the core of the competitive advantage, whose sustainability is higher, the higher are the barriers raised to imitability. A strong link between the proactive firm and the resource based view lies in the concept of Dynamic Capabilities, which refers to the firm's 'ability to integrate, build, and reconfigure internal and external competencies to address rapidly-changing environments' (Teece, Pisano & Shuen, 1997).
- The innovation literature, in its broadest meaning: from the creative destruction of Schumpeter (1942) to the disruptive innovation of Christensen (1997). Many authors have highlighted how successful companies evolve by alternating phases of continuous improvement interrupted by phases of revolutionary innovation (Dosi, 1982; Foster, 1986; Tushman & O'Reilly, 1997; Iansiti, 1998; Christensen 1997, 2006). Here, the concept of ambidexterity is especially consistent with the proactive firm and the resource based view: ambidextrous organizations are not simply concerned with the exploitation of their resources and capabilities, but have a continuous commitment to regenerate them for exploring new, innovative strategies (O'Reilly & Tushman 2004).

Given these general backgrounds, the framework of the Competitive Cycles is discussed below. Both cutting edge and classic examples could help us to provide empirical cases to illustrate the idea. This section will start with a classic one: competitive cycles within the gaming console industry. Starting from that, the chapter will move to digital scenarios, because "managers and entrepreneurs must understand the finer points of digital competition, innovation, and power. But they must also master the fundamental principles of business and good governance that apply in any company and in any era" (Cusumano, Gawer & Yoffie, 2019, p. 12).

On December 3, 1994, in a sector that for years had been experiencing a dramatic decline, Sony launched its first PlayStation gaming console (PS), a breakthrough revolution in terms of technology, graphic performance, gaming experience, and positioning. Actually, with the advent of the personal computer, many analysts had pronounced the sector of video game consoles dead, especially those who clearly recalled the concept and the graph of the "industry life cycle" that was drilled into their heads in business school. Against all odds, Sony took a gamble that paid off by shattering every record: 100 million PlayStations sold by the end of 2005 (Edwards, 2007).

Of course, a triumph of this magnitude quickly attracted the attention of aggressive new enterprises. Above all, by Christmas 2001, Sony found itself facing a direct challenge from Microsoft's Xbox. This marked the beginning of what we call the War of Imitation, which led to a competitive escalation reminding the pages of the novel Fight Club. The reaction of Sony was the launch of the PlayStation 2, with more power and graphic performance. Then Microsoft reacted with its Xbox360, with more power and graphic performance. And Sony reacted with its PS3, with more power and graphic performance… At that time, its price was almost $600. On 9 July 2007, Sony Corporation issued a press release announcing that it was slashing the PlayStation3's price tag by $100, which was 17% less than the introductory price set in November 2006. At the same time, the company publicized the launch of a model with more memory at the previous price. The same day at a press conference in Tokyo, a Microsoft executive hastened to state that the company would not lower Xbox 360 prices. Nonetheless, on 7 August 2007 the Redmond firm announced a $50 price cut on the US market, to be followed two weeks later by a €50 reduction in Europe (approximately 13%). Similar moves by both companies would replay in October, November, and December (Waters, 2007). And again in 2008, 2009, and 2010 (Goldhill, 2013).

The strategic evolution in this arena suggests that Sony and Microsoft, at that time, were fighting what we called a War of Position. For PlayStation, the success of the initial version, which upended all the rules of play, were a distant memory. As later generations of consoles came on the scene, Sony reacted to competitor imitation by following the more typical and dangerous rationale of a War of Position. The company embarked on a path of continuous enhancements of the original success factors (power and graphic performance in their case) and lower prices to secure market share. Likewise, greater power and lower prices also marked Microsoft's strategy. As a result, the two players became trapped in the fight club with shrinking or even negative margins.

A reverse strategy was implemented by Nintendo. Unlike its rivals, this company started developing its consoles by following a different rationale. Using the terminology of this Chapter, Nintendo began playing a War of Movement. As a matter of fact, the Nintendo Wii system, launched in late 2006, rapidly took the leadership position in the sector (Statista Research Department, 2011).

Rather than adhering to sector orthodoxies and fighting with the typical weapons of the status quo, Nintendo started thinking "outside the box" in terms of the market and market demands. For example, unlike PS3 and Xbox360, the Wii did not have HD resolution. Following a new approach, the Wii no longer targeted young, expert users with dexterity in their digits to rival a virtuoso organist. Instead, the social and active side of electronic entertainment became the key concept for developing the product and related applications. The games got simpler in some respects, in order to lock in a wider audience (counter-segmentation), but they also made people actually get up and move rather than simply stay in their seats. Nothing could be farther from the "bits per second" mindset. Finally, by putting the predominance of power and performance into proper perspective, Nintendo realized a cost advantage over its competitors. The Wii's introductory price in 2006 was $250, compared to $599 for the PS3. That quickly translated into market leadership worth 30 billion dollars (Statista Research Department, 2011).

This classic case just gave us the practical background to highlight the three main seasons of a competitive cycle: a) the war of Movement, b) the war of Imitation, and c) the war of Position. A fundamental difference with respect to climactic seasons, however, is our control on the timing. In fact, every firm to some extent can play the role of either follower or driver of each season, depending on its proactive attitude and capabilities (Valdani & Arbore, 2013). At the end, if today's leaders want to be tomorrow's leaders, they have to make everything change. Similarly, if today's followers want to become tomorrow's leaders, they have to make everything change too.

How long a competitive cycle takes depends on the magnitude of the innovation in question. On one side, for example, there are marginal or incremental innovations, which activate what we can call low-impact Wars of Movement; on the other end, there are more disruptive or radical innovations, which create a true quantum leap, triggering high-impact Wars of Movement (Figure 1). LG ArtCool, for instance, was the first air conditioner introducing design as a new competitive weapon. Since the very first year, this was a successful intuition, totally unseen by the previous rules of competition and by the traditional orthodoxies within that industry. A sort of institutional blindness sometimes traps biases us toward maintaining the status quo, so that even the most obvious moves become invisible to our eyes. Nonetheless, the initiative of LG –which entailed a low risk– was also relatively easy to imitate: after the first, profitable year, other market leaders followed suit to explore the new value dimension for the unseen market segment. In the end, then, this is what defines a low-impact War of Movement: a marginal value innovation, with marginal risk and profits, and a relatively quick journey before moving back to the War of Position.

Conversely, the way Apple entered into the cellphone business can be seen as a high impact War of Movement: a radically new business model and value proposition that revolutionized the industry and generated long-term yields.

Figure 1. Competitive cycles and the magnitude of a War of Movement: a continuum
Source: Author, SDA Bocconi, 2020

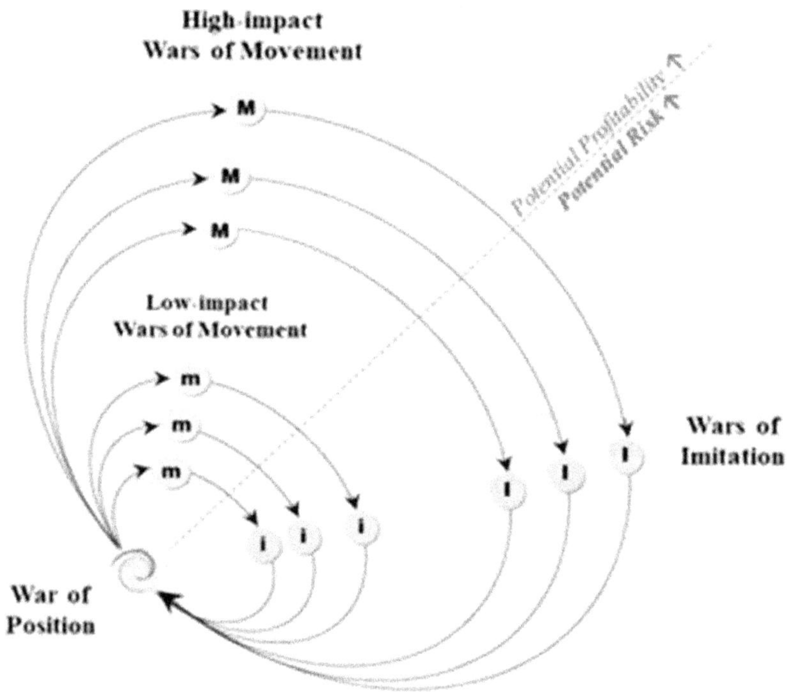

THE WAR OF MOVEMENT IN THE AGE OF HYPER-CONNECTION

As opposed to the War of Position, which is a zero-sum market-sharing scenario, the War of Movement is about market creation or market regeneration, so it can be a win-win scenario. Starting a War of Movement is about challenging some industry common wisdom and finding *new ways* to create value. Using Sun Tzu words, the ancient philosophers and theorists of the "art of war" (1963), it is about *winning without fighting*. Both Sun Tzu and Napoleon, in fact, suggested that when one's army is inferior in numbers or skill, it is critical to avoid a direct conflict and better to elude the enemy. The war of movement, indeed, is an indirect attack, using lateral, unorthodox logics to win an existing market or to invent a new one. Within an existing market, competitors are slow to react to less orthodox or indirect maneuvers for two reasons. The first involves the comfort of strategic routines. We are referring to a firm's behavior when it feels threatened, yet hesitates to take action for fear of having to deviate from its well-trodden path and reassuring way of doing things. The second reason is evident when firms that defend their own strategies refuse to admit that an attacker's less orthodox maneuver has any chance of success. These organizations will focus on finding objective evidence that supports their convictions --which are psychologically more reassuring and less stressful-- instead of activating resources and capabilities to enact an effective response.

How can we start a War of Movement then? "Give me a place to stand on, and I will move the Earth," said Archimedes. Indeed, to initiate a War of Movement, the "places to stand on" are as many as the management can imagine and –above all– they are not necessarily related to technology or R&D. The limit is vision and creativity, more than other resources. This section will try to provide a list of them, without the ambition of being exhaustive.

- **Rethinking the entire business model.** The most disruptive dimension for a War of Movement is probably the one reconsidering the entire business model within an industry. A business model is commonly defined as the way a firm creates, delivers, and captures value from a market. Before discussing new business models in the digital era, evergreen examples include low cost companies in the airline industry, Zara and the instant fashion model in the clothing industry, or the mass customization model of Dell in the IBM era of personal computers. In all these cases, the players starting a war of movement were able to challenge some industry common wisdom (e.g., service is a critical success factor to win the airline competition) and completely redefined the way to create and capture value from the market: winning without fighting.

With the arrival of the digital tsunami, there has been many wars of movement disrupting traditional business models. A possible classification is introduced below. It is worth to underline that these typologies are not necessarily mutually exclusive:

- **New, data driven business models**. A quite effective example of this kind is provided by The Weather Company (Gupta 2018). Its traditional business model was based on the revenues from the advertising broadcasted on their famous TV channel. But everything flows and the digital tsunami suddenly reduced the TV audience and made that model unprofitable. Then they launched a weather app for smartphones. Many users downloaded it, but they were not ready to pay for it: the Weather Company was still creating and delivering value to customers, but it was not able anymore to capture that value and generate revenues: the model was not profitable anymore. The turn-around arrived when they realized that bigger opportunities, in the current world, may arise when exploring and exploiting the value of data. Specifically, they started to generate and capture value when using the data from the app to help retailers and advertisers predict how the weather will affect consumer purchasing behavior. For this step, of course, they had to complement their original know-how with new competences on predictive analytics and artificial intelligence. Accordingly, they started a partnership with IBM, which eventually acquired them.

Further examples may come from many industries, including the insurance sector. Trov, for instance, was one of the first on-demand insurance companies that reinvented the way people protect their valuable objects: Trov's application enables customers to insure single items, for just the period of time they need, entirely from their mobile device. From the company point of view, the profitability of such a disruptive model is related to the access to large data sets which can be eventually leveraged for commercial benefits. Still, to remind that a war of movement also entails higher risks and a lot of experimentation, similar cases in the United Kingdom are not jet profitable to date.

For this War of Movement, then, the first goal becomes to collect big data. The second, and more critical one, is to transform data into valuable information. Information must then become a source of revenue flows and finally profits, with a lot of recursive learning and optimization happening along the way. While this logical funnel might sound obvious, more often the model looks like: "first I collect data and then I pray for profits to rain down from the sky". Sometimes Silicon Valley and Las Vegas look too close.

- **New, multi-source and multi-layer revenue models**. The best example here is probably Amazon. By leveraging on their customer base, brand trust, and infrastructure, they multiplied their business opportunities year after year. They started in 1995 with a wholesale model selling books online. Then, in 2000, they added the agency model, by transforming Amazon into a marketplace opened to third-party sellers. In 2005 they added the subscription model of Amazon Prime. In 2006 and 2007 they also added a pay-per-play model for movies and music. In 2007 they introduced a blade-and-razor model for electronic publishing: the Kindle was the razor and e-books were the blades for higher margins. Such a move was also very important because it represented their first attempt to explore a strategic extension to the hardware layer. A strategic advantage of Apple, for example, is to control both the hardware and the software layer of its value propositions (e.g., both the iPhone and its operating system, that is, a unique value ecosystem to create and capture value). Similarly, a strategic disadvantage of Samsung is the lack of control on the software layer, at least for the smartphone market, where Google controls the operating system and a relevant part of the ecosystem. Following this perspective, Amazon is trying to extend its control to the hardware layer too: the Kindle, then the Fire Phone, Fire Tablet, Fire Stick, and finally, since 2014, all the Echo devices (almost 20 devices by the end of 2019), with Alexa as the software layer, supporting also the advertising model introduced in 2011. Today Amazon has an incredibly reach multi-source and multi-layer revenue model. In the meanwhile, traditional competitors like Barnes & Nobles are still focused on their wholesale model only (just multichannel).

Finally, talking about new revenue models, a pretty common and successful one in the digital era is the freemium model, like in the case of Dropbox or LinkedIn. The offer is designed with two strategic layers: the free layer (like Dropbox gigabytes of cloud storage for free), having the goal of triggering interest and customer attraction, fostering brand awareness, positive world-of-mouth, and a rapid growth of the customer base; plus a premium layer (like extra services or extra gigabytes), with the goal to generate revenues, subsidizing the free layer and sustaining the entire profit model. Essentially, then, the cost of the free layer is a marketing cost to accelerate brand awareness, trial rates, and the diffusion of the new service. In this perspective, free users are «marketing agents», that can be activated with specific referral programs, like "member-get-member" campaigns, then reducing customer acquisition costs. In addition, in the presence of network externality, like for LinkedIn, free users increase the value of the overall offer, by definition. Finally, they are also a precious source for learning, testing, and improving the service (data, data, data). With a similar architecture, of course, the conversion rate between free and paid customers becomes the critical variable to evaluate the profitability of a freemium model.

- **New, outcome-based business models ("servitization" and pay-per-use models)**. An interesting game changer in the radiology business has been Medneo, a German company founded in 2011 (Kupe & Lange, 2013). Until 2010 the founders used to work for a large healthcare company selling premium magnetic resonance imaging machines to hospitals. With the severe economic downturn, however, many customers were delaying new orders. This prompted the idea of a change in the business model: instead of selling such expensive machines, they could offer physicians a way to obtain and pay just for the outcome, that is, the clinical images. In other words, they shifted to a pay-per-use model, or outcome-based models, moving from selling a product to selling a service. This shift is also known as "servitization" and has been recently explored also by companies like Philips, with a pay-per-lux model at the Amsterdam Schiphol Airport, and Michelin, with a "pay by the mile" model, a customized tire lease programs for trucks.

With outcome-based models, the seller is motivated to be more efficient and reliable in providing the outcome, which will buy with more confidence (Gupta, 2018). In addition, the innovative efforts of the company will be focused on the outcome, becoming more customer-focused than product oriented. Finally, and probably more disruptive, this model allows to expend the customer base, because it maximizes the affordability by eliminating any upfront fixed cost. On the other hand, the financial and organizational implications for a company are huge, which must entirely redesign its internal processes, roles, KPIs, and even the profit formula.

A further expression to describe this trend is "access over ownership": customers may receive access to the benefits of a product without owning it. When this concept meets the revenue model introduced next, that is platforms, then we find all the wars of movement leveraging the so-called "sharing economy" (see below).

- **New, platform-based revenue models**, including those sharing a specific asset. There is not a converging definition of business platform. In its broadest meaning, a platform is a system of connected and complementary products and services offered by a company to its customer base, generally involving also third parties (sometimes this is also referred to as an ecosystem). In this perspective, the Apple iPhone is a platform complementing the hardware with an ecosystem of services available through its operating system. A famous B2B example is shared by Porter and Happelmann (2014). In 2012, the farm equipment manufacturer John Deere launched the platform MyJohnDeer to interconnect their machines (equipped with sensors and gps localization) with owners, local agronomists, dealers, as well as with any other third party that could be useful to develop a unique value ecosystem. By crossing and analyzing all the data (see also "data driven business models"), the company was able to support farmers manage their fleet, reduce downtime inefficiencies, and save on fuel costs. Such a valuable system clearly increases switching costs (e.g. if moving to a competitor, all the historical data would be lost), then increasing loyalty and willingness to pay. This also reminds that our list of new business models is not mutually exclusive: the war of movement by John Deere is based on both data and a platform.

Strictly speaking, according to Cusumano et. al. (2019), a business platform connects two or more market actors or "sides". A classic example are the Yellow Pages, connecting retailers with buyers, but the digital revolution made building and scaling up platforms vastly simpler: eBay, Uber, or Airbnb are well known business models of this kind.

Specifically, a typical transaction platform creates value by reducing information asymmetries and transaction costs between supply and demand, while capturing value through agency fees, commissions, or subscription fees. By nature, then, platforms experience so-called indirect network effects: more buyers on a platform attract more sellers, and more sellers in turn draw in more buyers. For this reason, the player with the largest base might enjoy a tremendous competitive advantage, unless multi-homing is possible. Multi-homing refers to the possibility for the customer to join more than one platform at the same time. A person, for example, could sign in for more car-sharing services or home-delivery services, like Uber Eat and Deliveroo. In these cases, then, the first mover advantage becomes less relevant (but still relevant if the availability of historic data is crucial to create value). Overall, however, the platform assets that are hard to copy and imitate are the community and the resources its members own and contribute, be they rooms or cars or ideas and information (Van Alstyne et at., 2016).

It is now important to mention two critical aspects of platform-based business models. First, they grant the company less control on the quality of the customer experience, that is, in turn, on its final satisfaction and loyalty. Think at Groupon: the final satisfaction of its customer, for example, will depend on his experience at that restaurant, which cannot be fully controlled by Groupon. Rating systems may help, but they are not the final solution. The problem of control is even bigger if the architecture of the platform is open, like in the case of Facebook.

The second critical challenge of platform-based business models is reaching a critical mass of users able to activate network effects and positive feedbacks for takeoff. This is the so called chicken-or-egg dilemma: no Uber drivers ® no users; no users ® no Uber drivers. While specific literature might provide more detailed suggestions (Van Alstyne et at., 2016; Gupta 2018; Cusumano et. al. 2019), it is essential to underscore that the launch phase shall benefit from strategic actions that solely aim at getting started –even if they are not financially sustainable or practically scalable. This might include offering a compelling value proposition, even at a loss, simply to attract customers until critical mass is reached –e.g. having one's fleet of Uber cars and drivers, even at loss. Similarly, a platform company could subsidize one side of the platform –e.g. giving the Yellow Pages for free to families– in order to stimulate demand and to make money on the other side –e.g., local businesses for advertising. Freemium models, introduced above, can be an additional strategy to reach critical mass.

All in all, platform-based business models require a cultural and strategic shift, new integration capabilities, as well as competences for data analysis and data-driven relationship management. The goal is not anymore to sell products, but to create value ecosystems able to attract and retain a large base of loyal customers, so to multiply business opportunities with them. Given this goal, trust is a key ingredient. In addition, it is generally worthy to open the platform to third parties able to offer an increasing number of complementary services: this would further increase the value of the ecosystem, fostering network effects and customers' switching costs.

By attracting more and more loyal customers, the value for the company is captured by transforming such a large customer base into a large source of data (and trust) which, in turn, can be transformed into further business opportunities through multi-revenue models, like direct sales, subscriptions, commissions, data monetization, and so on.

- **Rethinking the channel and the value delivery strategy**. Without redefining the entire business model, a new channel strategy can serve as a "place to stand on" for breaking with the status quo. Franchising, introduced by Singer more than a hundred years ago, Luxottica, owning retailers for controlling the market for glasses, the first vending machines, Amazon's website, the postal system delivering Netflix DVDs before the streaming era: these are just a few of the most prominent cases of Wars of movement activated by reinventing the conventions about "value delivery". Today these possibilities are amplified by digital, mobile, ubiquitous, interconnected, and geo-localized technologies. Shell TapUp, for example, is a web-based application that allows to schedule orders for mobile fueling: it will be a Shell vehicle coming to you and not vice-versa. This experimentation, started in Rotterdam, already activated the preventive imitation of Exxon, which is now testing a similar service in some U.S. areas.
- **Rethinking the pricing strategy**. Here again we find Netflix, which challenged the previous status quo leaded by Blockbuster by debuting unlimited movie rentals at a flat rate. In some country, the mobile telephone market was revolutionized in the past with the introduction of pre-paid cards. Derivatives, such as futures and swaps, revolutionized the pricing of financial instruments and other goods. Today, blending this path with the digital opportunities, Starbucks is offering its successful "order and pay ahead" service, using its app and mobile payment system to drastically improve customer experience and increase price acceptability. British drug company Janssen-Cilag, a subsidiary of Johnson & Johnson, has led the way toward payment by results for medical treatment. The company offers to cover the cost of an expensive cancer drug if the patient fails to show adequate progress: the hospital would

pay for the drug only if the patient responds well. Sharing the risk increases price affordability for the hospital and this contributed to the success of this product.

Finally, one of the most extreme redesign of the pricing strategy refers to a case already mentioned: servitization (e.g. moving either to subscription-based models or pay-per-use models). This approach requires a complete redefinition of the business model, moving from selling products to selling "outcomes", as explained above.

- **Rethinking the organization model**. A new organizational format or reengineered processes are other aspects which can give rise to ample opportunities in the War of Movement. From Henry Ford's assembly lines to the Japanese industry's just-in-time, via customer-centered reengineering, these strategies have significantly impacted the trajectories of several sectors. Today is the era of agile and customer-centered organizations, like in the example of Vodafone, which is currently redefining its internal roles and processes in a more flexible way around customer needs, value, and innovation.
- **Rethinking customer needs, segmentation and positioning**. Creative segmentation, beyond the traditional criteria of a given industry, in a further land of opportunities for a war of movement. A classic example is the one of Swatch. In the past, there were two strategic groups in the watch industry: the one of functional, affordable models, with competitors like Casio, Texas Instruments and Sharp, and the strategic group of fashionable, luxury watches, with competitors like Rolex and Cartier. The positioning of Swatch was simply an untapped one: fashionable, but affordable. Winning without fighting, by crossing the borders of the previous conventional thinking. Today, in the digital era, Blue Apron was able to rethink customer needs in the cooking industry by creating a new market which is in-between gourmet restaurants and home cooking: "meal kit" delivery is a successful value proposition which is already facing the season of the war of imitation. Many players are growing in this new market, reminding us that the war of movement is generally a non-zero sum game: while the war of position is a win-lose game (or even lose-lose), a war of movement can be a win-win game.

According to Kotler and Trias de Bes (2003), an effective way to "dislocate" a market (dislocation is the process of generating a creative stimulus by provoking a discontinuity in conventional thought) is to focus one's creativity toward new untapped targets, new untapped needs, or new occasions. As for new occasions, for example, the authors include the possibility to think out of the box in terms of the time (e.g. Executive MBA at evening or during the weekend) as well as in terms of the place (e.g. music players for the swimming pool).

- **Rethinking the entire value proposition**. By looking at the previous dimension from the side of the product, instead of the market, a war of movement can start by entirely redesigning one's value proposition, as in the famous Blue Ocean approach (Kim & Mauborgne, 2005; 2017): what value drivers can we eliminate, introduce, reduce, or increase to move away from the industry standards? An example that the authors describe is the well know case of the Cirque du Soleil, providing a sophisticated and acrobatic ballet experience in the context of a circus setting, with dramatic story lines and eliminating the cost of the animals: that makes it a unique and profitable value proposition in a market that was shrinking. A War of Position, referring to this framework, is what the authors call the Red Ocean. A similar approach is the one suggested by Kotler and Trias de Bes (2003) to "dislocate" a product. According to the authors, six different areas of investigation are useful to suspend logical thought on a product and to inspire creative ideas: (a) replacement, (b) inversion, (c) combination, (d) exaggeration, (e) elimination, and (f) reordering. a) Replacement consists in eliminating or modifying one or more parts of the product by introducing components that are present in other non-related products. Examples are the replacement of watch hands and charging mechanisms with quartz technology. b) Inversion is the complex process of subverting the consumption or purchase of a product or service by affirming the opposite. By inverting the fast fashion value proposition, for example, some companies are promoting slow fashion, emphasizing quality, ethics, and sustainability. c) Combination instead means evaluating the possibility of adding one or more elements to the product or service to increase its potential to meet new needs and provide new solutions. Somehow, this is the land of hybrid innovation, combining –for instance– an air conditioner with a framework to display pictures, or it could be a piece of furniture that integrates a TV set, and so on. d) Exaggeration involves magnifying one or more elements of the product. Starting from the success of the Simpson's, for example, the TV sitcom South Park magnified the ingredient of being provocative. e) Elimination is removing one or more elements of the product or service. The iPhone, for instance, has been the first device eliminating the keyboard from mobile phones. f) Reordering, finally, is the dislocation of products with the aim of changing the order of one or more elements characterizing the traditional value proposition. For example, the traditional sequence when buying an airline ticket is the following: the company set the price, the customer decides whether to buy. By reordering this sequence, Priceline.com (known today as Booking.com) launched its first successful value proposition: the customer named their limit price, then the airline company decided whether to accept or not.

- A specific case of a war of movement redesigning the value proposition is a maneuver that introduces a completely **new, enhancing service and customer experience**. Still, it is worthy to remember that a successful war of movement shall translate into value for the company, not just for the customer. To put it differently, if the new enhancing service is too easy to imitate, for example, we would simply trigger a war of position, adding more and more features, increasing our costs, without moving away from competitors. We would create value for the customer without being able to capture part of that value. A positive example could be the one of Hointer stores: using an app, the customers can select the dresses they want to try; an automated system, then, will dispatch the items of the selected color and size directly to the dressing rooms. "Hointer found its shoppers, on average, try on twelve items instead of the usual three to five, which has in turn increased sales by 30 to 50%" (Gupta, 2018, p. 127). Introducing a new, enhancing service, then, the company was able to create value for the customer (enjoying a smother shopping experience), while capturing value as well, both increasing sales as well as exploiting a more efficient use of the space with half of the staff.

In keeping with the principles of the War of Movement, then, a firm's success depends primarily on how accurately it anticipates market changes and how quickly it responds to customer needs. It is not enough for a firm to simply win over market share from its competitors. The War of Movement, by its very nature, calls for a particular strategic predisposition for market creation and regeneration: generating value by creatively identifying new opportunities, new ideas, and new endeavors. As the circular nature of history confirms, innovation is the only way to avoid the financial stress of the War of Position, or worse still, the destabilizing effect of a competitor's War of Movement.

THE WAR OF IMITATION

Soon or later, an innovative firm starting a War of Movement stimulates other organizations to follow suit in a competitive War of Imitation. A new comer, for example, may recognize new opportunities for diversification, while retailers can see opportunities for downstream integration. The motivations and strategies, however, can be quite different when talking about a war of imitation played by other incumbent companies. The following cases can be observed:

1. Strategic reaction to the element of surprise, when success is suddenly clear. Many incumbents are taken by surprise when an outsider player starts some innovative War of Movement. This is what happened to Blockbuster, among the others. In these cases, the reaction of the traditional players is put off until sales and demand clearly skyrocket. Even in these cases the enterprise does not always react and chalks up the new model's success to a passing fad or is afraid of jeopardizing or cannibalizing sales of their current products. In these cases, the imitator only reacts when the changes in the market show a clear risk of suffering a loss in market share or losing dominance. At this time, however, it is often too late.
2. Strategic choice to wait until success is clear ("Wait and See Strategy"). In this case, the company makes a conscious choice to wait patiently for the innovation's market development. This is sometimes the case of companies owning a significant stock of resources and capabilities: they might prefer to leave the cost of market development to the innovating player. For instance, this was the strategy adopted by some European incumbents for high-speed mobile communication networks: they left to the followers the commercial burden to open the new market, while already owning the infrastructure. Economies of speed, of course, becomes critical here: it is about shifting from a first mover advantage to a fast mover advantage (a.k.a. fast follower strategy).

These companies, even if avoiding the typical risks of the first mover, are still open to a different risk, that is, waiting too long: indeed, their imitation may arrive too late, when margins, economies of experience, brand image or the number of early imitators have already seized most of the opportunities opened up by the first mover. A classic example could be the energy drink market, a typical market creation War of Movement: an exceptionally strong imitator like Coca-cola was unable to win against the first mover, Red Bull, especially effective in creating imitation barriers with branding.

3. Strategic choice for imitation even when success is not yet certain. In this interesting case, there may be several reasons behind such a choice (Lieberman & Asaba, 2006):
    a. Imitation based on "implicit information". In the presence of high uncertainty, some companies may observe the actions of the first movers and, especially if the latter are well-known players, they may decide to imitate, regardless of the information in their possession. Clearly, the assumption of the imitators is that the first movers have better information, but this is not necessarily the case. Once a critical mass of imitating companies is reached, there may be what some economists refer to as

information cascades, leading to "bandwagon pressures", as observed in the late 90s: so many companies decided to join the e-business bet, just because others were doing it, until the bubble burst at the beginning of 2000s.

b. Imitation for legitimacy or status. Some players follow the behavior of leading companies primarily to seek legitimacy from institutions and from their public, that is, to anchor their status to the one of other well-established companies. In this perspective, the imitation becomes a signal for the public and institutions in order to avoid a negative reputation or image on the market. Imitating green policies or corporate social responsibility initiatives can be a case in point.

c. Imitation as a preemptive defense of the status quo and to reduce rivalry levels. Another reason for an incumbent to follow a first mover, even before knowing the outcome of its War of Movement, is to defend its competitive position in front of uncertainty. For instance, if an innovator decides to explore a new market or a new technology, the imitator may decide to do the same immediately so, regardless of the action's success, their relative positions would remain the same.

Often, the aim of this strategy is to reduce the risk of uncertain scenarios which could be disruptive and not easy to imitate in a short period of time. If electric cars will become successful, for example, it would be too risky to join this game only at that time.

In some other cases, especially in concentrated markets, mutual imitation may become a form of tacit tolerance. Certain enterprises would imitate mutual presence in different markets or segments, for example, to have more points of contact, which would facilitate collusion since that would increase the possibility for retaliation.

A key point in the War of Imitation is understanding what could be the first and the second mover advantages as well as disadvantages, to better frame when and how the imitator can increase its chances to win its battle. First of all, the pioneer must sustain the high risks and uncertainties for opening unknown territories, which can be hostile lands. The benefits of this research, however, can be reaped by a second mover able to take advantage of its discoveries.

In fact, the imitator may:

- learn from the mistakes of the innovator and not spend their resources on developing products without market potential and instead draw on the experience of others, i.e. their products and services which better meet the needs and benefits expressed by customers;

- avoid or reduce financial efforts which are instead sustained by the first mover during the initial phases of their research and development and in systems engineering;
- focus attention and resources on the development of the technological process instead of focusing on the technology of the product or service, and in doing so improve both quality and production efficiency;
- avoid the trap of inertia innovators may fall into where they are less inclined to make improvements and incremental moves to the innovation;
- avoid costs for customer education and awareness of new products, which are instead sustained by the innovator;
- take advantage of the experience gained in other markets and leveraging on strategic synergies with its existing businesses. When Amazon entered the online advertising business in 2011, for example, they leveraged on their great availability of data and distinctive abilities to predict customers' purchasing behaviors and interests. They also leveraged on a competitive asymmetry with the leader Google, that is logistics: in 2019 they started to test "free samples delivery" as a new form of advertising.

On the other sides, the main disadvantages of the imitator could be: lower economies of scale and experience, especially if there are significant fixed costs and the volumes of the first mover are already high. Possible barriers to access the market, if the first mover was able to block distribution channels (downstream closure) or the access to strategic providers (upstream closure). Possible barriers related to the brand reputation of the first mover, as described in the case of Red Bull. Possible barriers related to technological or cultural standards, if the first mover was already able to become "the way" customers expect and the second mover cannot match it, as in the case of a proprietary platform. This is also related to a final point, that is, the existence of switching costs, locking-in the customers to the first mover, either for legal, technical, or psychological costs if changing their provider.

Accordingly, enabling factors for the War of Imitation are:

- lack of strong legal or technological mechanisms to protect secrets or patents of a War of Movement;
- easy access to customers in terms of value delivery and distribution channels;
- presence of multiple suppliers that may provide key raw materials or critical technologies to imitate the first mover;
- easiness to understand and to replicate the key value creation processes and procedures behind the success of a War of Movement (it has been hard, for example, to replicate the success of Zara for many followers in a War of Imitation);

- inability of the first mover –for its lack of capabilities or resources-- to build strong entry barriers against potential rivals, be any of the barriers mentioned above, from technical to reputational ones.

MARKET STRATEGIES AND DYNAMICS IN A WAR OF IMITATION

A War of Imitation can be played by pursuing different market strategies, depending on the relative position compared to the innovator. Successful options are:

1. Exercising market power, that is, a frontal attack to the first mover. This is an option when the imitator has a substantial advantage in terms of available resources and market position, as it was the case of Microsoft playing its War of Imitation against Netscape Navigator, the first leader for Internet browsers. Microsoft simply leveraged on its financial resources and market power from the operating system market to push the diffusion of its browser Explorer.
2. Market repositioning strategies, which can be implemented in one of the following forms, depending on both an external and internal analysis:
    a. Similar quality, lower price. Two conditions are required here: as for the internal analysis, the company shall have some clear cost advantage; otherwise, this move would only trigger a competitive escalation and the competitive dynamics already classified as lose-lose scenarios. The first reaction of Samsung to the iPhone, for example, was trying to offer something as close as possible to the innovator, but with a lower price, due to the large-scale cost advantage of the Korean company. Nonetheless, they understated the second condition, that is, the external analysis of customers' value chain: for the successful War of Movement started by Apple, its high symbolic price was part of the winning formula. Reducing this ingredient was not a winning strategy.
    b. Downgrading and impoverishment strategies. If the imitator recognizes the existence of a lower, still profitable segment, which might prioritize affordability over performance, then the imitator could downgrade some product features to offer a more accessible version of the value proposition, stimulating market growth and entrenching itself in the low end of the market. This is especially suitable when the first mover is strong on the value and performance dimensions, which could be an over-performance for part of the market. For example, in an article titled "How Wish grew to over $1 billion in revenue by inverting Amazon's strategy", the author explains: "Most of their products are unbranded, sold by various small

businesses directly to consumers, with no warranty or support from Wish. The shipping time can range from 4 to 12 weeks. The user experience (on web or mobile) is rather pedestrian. The prices, however, are rock-bottom." (Hollis, 2018).

c. Leapfrogging strategies: second, but better. The imitator can elicit customers interest by making incremental improvements to the pioneer's offering. Having more information about customer needs and preferences, or having an improved technology due to the time of entry, the imitator could enjoy a second mover advantage: it would be an incremental, innovative imitation. According to the New Your Times, for instance, the upcoming electric vehicles from Porsche will be capable of 800-volt charging that will offer 248 miles in 15 minutes, a step above (i.e., leapfrogging) the 480-volt Tesla systems, which supply up to 150 miles of travel in a half-hour (Voelk, 2018).

Leapfrogging strategies can be focused on specific value dimensions for specific segments. Blue Apron, for instance, started a market creation War of Movement with their "meal kit" concept, a value proposition across the borders of restaurants and home cooking (Tybout & Calkins, 2019). Many second movers, however, were quickly able to gain a distinctive positioning ("second but better") applying the idea of benefit segmentation. Among the others, HelloFresh emphasized a greater ease of preparation; Plated emphasized superior quality and taste; Purple Carrot claimed to be healthier and more environmentally friendly. All these moves, at the end, could leave the first mover in a tight spot.

With a similar marketing perspective, leapfrogging can also be applied to specific "category of users" or for specific "usage occasions". Intuitive Da Vinci, for example, was the first and successful robotic surgery system. At the end of 2018, after many years, Medtronic played their second mover strategy with the acquisition of Mazor Robotics, a system which is highly specialized on robotic spine and brain surgery: second but better for a specific "category of users" (neurosurgeons). Similarly, some players imitated the iPod value proposition by launching waterproof MP3-players, designed for "usage occasions" like swimming pools.

In all of these cases, it is important to verify if there are attributes that customers expect "the same way" as in the first-mover offer: if so, these will be must-have attributes and the imitator should first match the "standard" set by the first mover, like a dominant design. Only after matching these points-of-parity, then, they could try to win by leveraging on the specific points-of-difference described so far.

d. Enlarging the market by targeting and converting non-users. This repositioning strategy shall try to understand whether there are potential customers that the incumbent is not serving yet. Is so, why? Can we target them profitably? The success will depend on our ability to provide an answer and reduce the existing barriers to adopt. To that purpose, some innovative effort is generally required also in this case, that is, an innovative imitation is needed, in-between a war of movement and a war of imitation. Dell, for instance, is a well-known case of an insurgent company which reinvented the way former incumbents were selling notebooks, attracting a remarkable segment of non-users, that is, customers that could not afford these products before. So, at that time, having an unknown brand was not a problem for Dell to attract them.

e. Reconceptualization, for serving different needs (different and not better, as it was in the case of leapfrogging). Also this strategy is an innovative imitation and, specifically, a creative imitation that will move later on the need served. The product is reconceptualised by changing its intended use or application then. The Segway value proposition, for instance, has been imitated and reconceptualized to become Genny 2.0, a wheelchair to improve mobility of impaired persons. In the pharmaceutical industry, sometimes companies can change the dose of the molecule of an existing brand to serve different needs with a different brand.

In terms of competitive dynamics, the general risk with any repositioning strategy is the possibility that, if your market move is a successful one, then in turn, the first mover could imitate you as well. It is important to go back to the basics and asking: will I be able to defend my second mover strategy? Or will the leader easily imitate me, maybe leveraging on more resources, deeper know-how, or stronger marketing and sales? Few times, from this point of view, the first mover could actually pay a disadvantage for the strong brand associations related to its first, original positioning (Tybout & Calkins, 2019).

3. Lateral imitation strategy. This is the strategy pursued by a company either imitating a War of Movement in a different, untapped market; or innovating its business by copying ideas from other industries. The latter, then, is a further form of creative imitation.

Starting with the first case, Facile.it was the first online comparator in Italy. Still they were fast followers, since they were quickly imitating the innovators in the United Kingdom. After realizing the potential of these platforms as an effective market creation War of Movement, they adapted the same idea to the untapped Italian market. Here they are still among the market leaders. For this case, of coursc, the same considerations about competitive dynamics shared for repositioning strategies apply (e.g. Will the first movers in the U.K. follow me and hit me in Italy?).

Moving to the lateral imitation of "ideas" from different industries, this is a quite interesting case which can refer to many strategic dimensions. For example, it can be the imitation of a marketing strategy, as in the case of the Intel Inside campaign, successfully inspired to the DuPont ingredient marketing strategy introduced with Teflon. It can be the imitation of a business model, like in the case of the African start-up Hello Tractor, dubbed the "Uber for tractors". They successfully share tractors in Africa with the same model of Uber and now they are scaling-up in India, Pakistan and Bangladesh. Or it can be the imitation of anything else: Booking, for example, keeps improving customer experience with its app by importing ideas from the apps of players in any possible industry, from Tinder to Amazon.

Lateral imitation is especially important in our hyper-connected world, since consumers today tend to use benchmarks from a wide variety of players across industries to judge the quality of our value propositions. The expression "liquid (or fluid) expectations" can be used to describe this idea: "Whether you are a bank, a retailer, or a brand, consumers expect your web page to load as quickly as Google's, your delivery to be as fast as Amazon's, your products to be as flawless as Apple's, and your service to be as smooth as Uber's." (Gupta, 2018, p. 197).

CONCLUSION

We are leaving in extraordinary dynamic, hyper-connected, and turbulent ages. In similar scenarios, even if game-changing Wars of Movement are associated to the highest business opportunities, they are also related to the highest risks. Following a financial perspective, a company shall manage this trade-off by balancing its strategic wars and decisions: with a portfolio perspective, a hyper-connected company shall play more and different Wars at the same time. It is not Innovation Versus Imitation, for instance. It is both. In a given moment, there will be competitive fronts to be reinvented and to be created, with both low and high impact Wars of Movement, as reviewed in the specific section of this chapter. At the same time, there will be competitive fronts to join, with the most appropriate Wars of Imitation, as reviewed in the previous section. And there will be well-established fronts and revenue flows to defend, focusing of efficiency and perfect execution, which are the critical weapons in a War of Position.

The structural uncertainty of a hyper-connected and hyper-competitive world, in other words, requires guarding many fronts of our green betting table. All the chips on a War of Movement would expose the company to an excessive risk in the short term, while all the chips on a War of Position would expose the company to the greatest risk in the long term. Again, it is about balancing, exploring, learning, and being great at playing the three Wars at the same time.

Amazon can be seen as a company of this kind, continuously leveraging on distinctive assets, while learning and developing new capabilities. They started with a *War of Movement* reinventing the way to sell books. Then, in Sun Tzu's words, "opportunities multiply as they are seized". Soon they opened their platform to other vendors, exploring new business and revenue models. Today they are able to defend their e-commerce front from any direct attack in a *War of Position* thanks to huge economies of scale and scope, as well as tremendous efficiency in operations, logistics, and data management. At the same time, they are also great to play the *War of Imitation*, in many different ways. They quickly imitate vendors on their marketplace as soon as the data suggest selling a product directly, that is, balancing the agency and the wholesale model. Similarly, by looking at the data, they quickly imitate specific manufacturers by selling successful products with the AmazonBasic private label. They also played incremental imitation with Amazon Music, for instance, or following Google in the advertising business. At the same time, in a highly volatile and turbulent context, they keep experimenting and exploring new frontiers and new *Wars of Movement* every single day, with a "liquid" and inductive approach, in a restless effort to lead and drive their competitive cycles.

REFERENCES

Barney, J. (1991). Firm Resources and Sustained Competitive Advantage. *Journal of Management, 17*(1), 99–120. doi:10.1177/014920639101700108

Brown, S. L., & Eisenhardt, K. M. (1998). *Competing on the Edge.* Harvard Business School Press.

Christensen, C. M. (1997). *The Innovation's Dilemma.* Harvard Business School Press.

Christensen, C. M. (2006). The ongoing process of building a theory of disruption. *Journal of Product Innovation Management, 23*(1), 39–55. doi:10.1111/j.1540-5885.2005.00180.x

Cusumano, M. A., Gawer, A. A., & Yoffie, D.B. (2019). The Business of Platforms: Strategy in the Age of Digital Competition, Innovation, and Power. HarperCollins.

D'Aveni, R. (1994). *Hypercompetition.* Free Press.

Dosi, G. (1982). Technological paradigms and technological trajectories. A suggested interpretation of the determinants and directions of technical change. *Research Policy, 11*(3), 147–162. doi:10.1016/0048-7333(82)90016-6

Edwards, C. (2007). Sony's Surprising PS3 Price Cut. *Bloomberg*. Retrieved from: https://www.bloomberg.com/news/articles/2007-07-09/sonys-surprising-ps3-price-cutbusinessweek-business-news-stock-market-and-financial-advice

Foster, R. (1986). *Innovation: The Attacker's Advantage*. Summit Books. doi:10.1007/978-3-322-83742-4

Goldhill, O. (2013). Sony reignites console price war with Microsoft. *The Telegraph*. Retrieved from: https://www.telegraph.co.uk/technology/video-games/10112334/E3-2013-Sony-reignites-console-price-war-with-Microsoft.html

Grant, R. M. (1991). The resource based theory of competitive advantage: Implications for strategy formulation. *California Management Review*, *33*(3), 114–135. doi:10.2307/41166664

Gupta, N. (2018). *Driving Digital Strategy: a Guide to Reimagining your Business*. Harvard Business Review Press.

Hollis, S. (2018). *How Wish grew to over $1 billion in revenue by inverting Amazon's strategy*. Retrieved from https://jilt.com/blog/wish-growth/

Iansiti, M. (1998). *Technology Integration*. Harvard Business School Press.

Kauffman, S. (1995). *At Home in the Universe*. Oxford University Press.

Kim, W. C., & Mauborgne, R. (2005). *Blue Ocean Strategy: How to Create Uncontested Market Space and Make Competition Irrelevant*. Harvard Business School Publishing.

Kim, W. C., & Mauborgne, R. (2017). *Blue ocean shift: Beyond competing - proven steps to inspire confidence and seize new growth*. Macmillan.

Kotler, P., & Triasde Bes, F. (2003). *Lateral Marketing: New Techniques for Finding Breakthrough Ideas*. John Wiley & Sons.

Kotter, J. P. (1996). *Leading Change*. Harvard Business School Press.

Kupp, M., & Lange, K. (2012, May 20). Dearth of orders gave birth to Medneo. *Financial Times*.

Lieberman, M. B., & Asaba, S. (2006). Why Do Firms Imitate Each Other. *Academy of Management Review*, *31*(2), 366–385. doi:10.5465/amr.2006.20208686

O'Reilly, C., & Tushman, M. (2004). The Ambidextrous Organization. *Harvard Business Review*, *82*(4), 74–81. PMID:15077368

Penrose, E. (1959). The Theory of the Growth of the Firm. Oxford University Press.

Porter, M. E., & Heppelmann, J. E. (2014). How Smart, Connected Products Are Transforming Competition. *Harvard Business Review*, *92*, 64–88.

Prahalad, C. K., & Hamel, G. (1994). *Competing for the Future*. Harvard Business School Press.

Rivkin, J. W. (2000). Imitation of Complex Strategies. *Management Science*, *46*(6), 824–844. doi:10.1287/mnsc.46.6.824.11940

Sanders, T. I. (1998). *Strategic thinking and the new science: planning in the midst of chaos, complexity, and change*. Free Press.

Schumpeter, J. A. (1942). *Capitalism, Socialism, and Democracy*. Harper.

Statista Research Department. (2011). *Video game consoles: global market share 2006-2010*. Retrieved from: https://www.statista.com/statistics/272048/global-market-shares-of-game-consoles/

Sun Tzu. (1963). The Art of War (S. B. Griffith, Trans.). Oxford University Press. (Original work: roughly 5th century BC)

Teece, D. J., Pisano, G., & Shuen, A. (1997). Dynamic capabilities and strategic management. *Strategic Management Journal*, *18*(7), 509–533. doi:10.1002/(SICI)1097-0266(199708)18:7<509::AID-SMJ882>3.0.CO;2-Z

Tushman, M., & O'Reilly, C. A. (1997). *Winning through innovation: A practical guide to leading organizational change and renewal*. Harvard Business School Press. doi:10.1108/eb054591

Tybout, A. M., & Calkins, T. (Eds.). (2019). *Kellogg on Branding in a Hyper-Connected World*. John Wiley & Sons.

Valdani, E., & Arbore, A. (2013). *Competitive Strategies: Managing the Present*. Imagining the Future. doi:10.1057/9780230354586

Van Alstyne, M. W., Parker, G. G., & Choudary, S. P. (2016). Pipelines, Platforms, and the New Rules of Strategy. *Harvard Business Review*, *94*(4), 54–62.

Vico, G. (1976). *La Scienza Nuova e altri scritti*. UTET. (Original work: 1725, 1730, 1744)

Voelk, T. (2018, Mar. 6). Porsche Positions Itself Against Tesla, on the Road and Beside It. *The New York Times*.

Waters, R. (2007). Microsoft raises ante in price wars. *Financial Times*. Retrieved from: https://amp.ft.com/content/caf2b046-450f-11dc-82f5-0000779fd2ac

Chapter 5
Creating Value From Garbage:
A Marketing and Circular Economy Strategy for Sustainability

Cristina Calvo-Porral
https://orcid.org/0000-0002-5470-0729
University of La Coruña, Spain

ABSTRACT

We live on a finite planet with scarce resources, which entails major challenges such as the depletion of natural resources, the ecological footprint, and climate change. However, in the continued growth of global economy, the majority of companies' strategies and business models move away from sustainability while facing a big paradox: on one side, companies focus on economic development encouraging consumption, but on the other side, companies could play a key role in environmental issues, enhancing more sustainable consumption patterns. In this context, some companies have adopted marketing strategies that focus on turning garbage into value, as a way to tackle one of the major environmental issues. In this chapter, some of these companies and their marketing strategies are examined through a multiple case analysis. The main purpose of this chapter is to show that some companies are addressing one major environmental issue by turning garbage into value.

DOI: 10.4018/978-1-7998-4552-2.ch005

INTRODUCTION

The Sustainable Marketing Orientation

The consumption of natural resources has been increasing much faster than population, with environmental consequences such as climate change or pollution. In this context, the World Commission on Environment and Development (1987) defines development as sustainable if it "meets the needs of the present without compromising the ability of future generations to meet their own needs". Similarly, the concept of *sustainable marketing orientation* recognizes that nowadays consumption patterns are unsustainable; thus, requiring changes in consumer behavior (United Nations Environment Programme et al. 2005). Therefore, the sustainable marketing orientation proposes the offering of products and services marketed in a responsible way that does not adversely impact upon environment sustainability. Interestingly, this marketing orientation differs from the traditional market orientation that called for maximizing company profits through efficient management of resources and competitive marketing responsive to customer needs (Mitchell et al., 2010).

Likewise, some authors in the marketing area also defined the sustainable marketing orientation. For example, Hart (1995) conceptualized the sustainable marketing orientation as characterized by long-term marketing strategies that aim to meet market expectations while being environmentally responsible of natural resources. Other authors, such as Kilbourne (1998) highlighted that the sustainable marketing orientation emerged as an alternative to earlier managerial strategies, in order to focus on ecological sustainability rather than on economic efficiency. Accordingly, the sustainable marketing orientation develops actions and strategies so that only products and services that are considered as "*needs*" are commercialized and marketed, whereas those items considered as "*wants*" are not (Schor, 1998), encouraging consumers to develop a more resource-efficient way of consumption (Connolly & Prothero, 2003).

Sustainability Marketing

A major cause of damage to the natural environment is the high level of consumption in developed countries, since developed societies have overused natural resources. This fact puts pressure on marketing managers to make products become more sustainable and to develop a sustainable marketing orientation.

The concept of sustainability marketing is a consequence of the evolution of the sustainability agenda in the marketing area over the last 30 years (Kemper & Ballantine, 2019). In this vein, one of the first definitions of sustainability marketing is the one provided by Brundtland (1987) who conceptualized sustainability marketing as "the development that meets the needs of the present without compromising the ability of future generations to meet their own needs". Later, authors like defined sustainable marketing as "the process of planning, implementing and controlling the development, pricing, promotion and distribution of products in a way that satisfies customer needs, organizational goals and the process is compatible with eco-systems". Other authors point out that the concept of sustainable marketing goes beyond a product or commercial orientation to a broad societal view in order to create long-term relationships (Gordon et al., 2011); and that sustainability marketing takes into consideration societal and environmental issues at the start of the marketing process, instead of considering them as externalities, focusing on the transformational potential of marketing to change consumption and production (Belz & Peattie, 2009).

Likewise, current attempts for conceptualizing sustainability marketing include three dimensions of sustainable development: economic, social and environmental (Mitchell et al., 2010; Sung & Lee, 2011; Kemper & Ballantine, 2019). More specifically Sung and Lee (2011) report that *marketing sustainability orientation* is based on three dimensions. First one is the social dimension, which is related to the company's impact on society and on the individuals' well-being. Second dimension is the environmental component which focuses on the company's activities relative to natural resources and the company contribution to environmental sustainability. Finally, the third dimension is economic and refers to the value generation and financial performance of companies.

However, nowadays a debate exists around the concept of sustainability, allowing numerous interpretations. In this context, authors like Kemper & Ballantine (2019) indicate that the very principle of sustainability is to avoid creating waste, and about creating value multiple times and for the same material. So that sustainability marketing seeks to reduce and eliminate waste during production and consumption, while taking into consideration the environmental and social cost of a product (Kemper & Ballantine, 2019). Further, these authors support three different conceptualizations of sustainability marketing. In the first place, the *auxiliary sustainability* marketing, that focusses on the production of sustainable products and services. Secondly, the *reformative sustainability* marketing, which extends the previous definition to the promotion of sustainable lifestyles and consumption patterns. Finally, the *transformative sustainable* marketing extends the previous approaches to focus on the transformation of organizations and norms.

The Contradictory Nature of Sustainability and Marketing

Current consumption levels are unsustainable, and at the same time marketing is acknowledged to promote consumption, standing out as the antithesis to sustainability

(Van Dam & Apeldoorn, 1996; Prothero et al., 2010). For this reason, marketing has been severely criticized for contributing to environmental problems by promoting a culture of consumption instead of promoting a simpler way of living (Kilbourne, 1998). Similarly, marketing has been held responsible for creating and facilitating excessive purchasing behavior and the promotion of a hedonic attitude towards consumption (Kilbourne & Carlson, 2008), since the idea of limiting consumption is contrary to the prevailing philosophy of marketing (Varey, 2011).

The discussion about the contradictory relationship between sustainability and marketing has been ongoing since the 60s, and today some prior research questions whether marketing can actually be sustainable when it is based on an unrealistic model of continuous consumption that is environmentally unsustainable (Jones et al., 2008; Peattie & Peattie, 2009; Lim, 2016).

Nowadays, there is a need for a change in the marketing paradigm, in order to question how marketing can be sustainable and what means to be sustainable. In this context, some authors highlight the great potential of marketing in order to influence sustainable lifestyles and to produce sustainable products (Peattie & Peattie, 2009), the potential to make individuals think about consuming less and consuming differently (Prothero et al., 2010), as well as a great responsibility in promoting sustainable lifestyles and in demarking undesirable products and services (Kotler, 2011).

For example, some authors in the marketing area have promoted the production and commercialization of the so-called "*green*" products. These products could be defined as products or services that either conserve resources or that reduce waste (US Department of Commerce, 2010). But some authors noted that promoting "*green*" products ignores the great issue of overconsumption and that replacing products with green alternatives does not address the global issue of limited resources (Varey, 2011). Other authors have reported that companies should aim to maximize the economic lifecycle of their products and materials and design and commercialize product that are resource-efficient (Slowak & Regenfelder, 2017). Finally, some other authors indicate that sustainable marketing should drive a move from individual ownership to product use, in order to satisfy consumer needs through sharing and collaborative consumption, leasing and renting (Peattie, 2001; Polonsky, 2011). This change in the consumption paradigm implicates that consumers no longer want to own products; and instead, they prefer to "*pay per use*" different products and services, or that they prefer to share the products they own with other consumers.

BACKGROUND

Circular Economy: A Sustainable Strategy and Paradigm

The Concept of Circular Economy

Considering that natural resources are limited in quantity, there is an urgent need of methods and strategies for harnessing and using resources. In fact, nowadays, the dominant economic model –the "*consume-use-dispose*" model- is being challenged, since more sustainable methods of consuming and managing natural resources are required (Ranta et al., 2018). In this context, the circular economy strategy aims to transform in depth the way individuals use resources, replacing the existing open production system with a closed production system.

The circular economy provides an alternative model of consumption, based on the creation of closed production systems where resources are reused and kept in a loop of production and usage, allowing the creation of more value and for a longer period of time (Urbinati et al., 2017). In other words, the existing economic open system is based on a *linear consumption model*, where raw materials and natural resources are extracted, processed into final goods and then become waste after they have been consumed. Further, products are thrown away when they are no longer working or when they no longer satisfy the consumers' needs (Su et al., 2013).

However, in the *closed production model* resources are reused and kept in a loop of production and usage, allowing the generation of more value (Su et al., 2013; Urbinati et al., 2017). So, in a circular economy, products and materials continuously circulate in so-called loops as long as they can provide value (Ranta et al., 2018). Thus, the traditional linear flow of resources-products-waste could be replaced by a circular economy by a new pattern of resources-products-waste-renewable resources. Similarly, the circular economy strategy is closely related with the product life extension, product redistribution and reuse, as well as with remanufacturing and recycling (Urbinati et al., 2017).

So it can be stated that the circular economy strategy or paradigm has a critical role in conceiving garbage and waste as something to be metabolized in the same economy in order to create value (Crainer, 2013). In addition, the circular economy proposes a new way for companies to create customer value through the simultaneous creation of environmental and economic benefits (MacArthur, 2013).

The Principles of Circular Economy

The circular economy has gained great attention as a pathway towards more sustainable economic development. In their seminal work, Ghisellini et al. (2016) identified the main actions leading to circular economy, that were named as the "3R" principles of the circular economy, namely reduce, reuse and recycle, which clearly focus on the circulation of materials in the system.

In the first place, the *reduce* principle supports the minimizing of the overall amount of materials, energy used and waste generated in the economic system through the increase of efficiency in both production and consumption. This improved efficiency could be achieved by the improvement of technologies, the simplification of packaging or the usage of more power-efficient appliances (Su et al., 2013). Likewise, this principle aims to eliminate the need to reuse or recycle materials, while minimizing waste and environmental impact (Figge et al., 2014).

In the second place, the *reuse* principle supports that products or components that are not wasted are used again for the same purpose for which they were conceived (The European Parliament and the Council of European Union, 2008). In fact, reusing components and products requires fewer resources and less energy and labor than producing new ones (Castellani et al., 2015); and for this reason, reuse has the potential to increase overall resource efficiency.

Finally, the *recycle* principle is referred to any recovery operation by which waste materials are reprocessed into products, materials or substances whether for the original or for other purposes (The European Parliament and the Council of European Union, 2008). Therefore, recycling is a process through which used materials are treated so as to make them suitable for reuse, so that components and products are always transformed back into materials. However, when considering resource efficiency, recycling might be the least sustainable solution of the "3R" principles, given that is limited by the complexity of materials. Thus, these three principles underlie the efficient use of products and resources with the goal of maintaining them into the economy as long as possible, offering high value-added products and minimizing the production of waste (Urbinati et al., 2017).

In addition, other authors have pointed out a fourth principle of circular economy which is the *product-life extension*, meaning that companies should design and manufacture durable products that have a long lifetime, in order to reduce consumption. The similarities of the sustainability marketing and circular economy proposals are shown in Table 1.

Table 1. Foundations and proposals of sustainability marketing and circular economy

MARKETING ORIENTATIONS	FOUNDATIONS AND PROPOSALS
SUSTAINABLE MARKETING	Integration of environmental, social and economic concerns and practices into marketing activities. Proposes sustainable production and consumption, the reduction of consumption and wastage, and the development of sustainable ways of consumption.
CIRCULAR ECONOMY	Proposes an alternative model of consumption, based on the creation of closed production systems. Natural resources should be reused and kept in a loop of production and usage, allowing the creation of more value. Conceives garbage and waste as something to be metabolized in the economy in order to create value.

Finally, one interesting question is how consumers respond to such green economy products. Prior research on consumers' responses to circular products, such as recycled or remanufactured products have produced different results depending on the type of products examined (Anstine, 2000; Michaud & Llerena, 2011). In general terms, consumers' attitudes towards circular products are generally positive, but some studies have reported that consumers may respond negatively to these products (Anstine, 2000).

Examining the Concept and Value of Garbage

The Concept of Garbage

There is not a consensus on what constitutes garbage. Waste at the most fundamental level is simply what is discarded or unwanted. Some authors, such as Drackner (2005) report that waste or garbage could be considered as something that is discarded by individuals, implicating uselessness. In addition, garbage could be considered as a risk, since it involves the notion of garbage as a constant risk factor and a threat to humans and environment; and as a factor of negative aesthetics (Drackner, 2005).

Similarly, garbage has often been described as residue from production or consumption processes or the waste and discarded items of society (Brown, 2015). In this context, disposable goods could be defined as those products intended to be use once and discarded, such as for example disposable mops, diapers, disposable cups and so on (Brown, 2015). And much of these disposable goods that are filling landfills or are directly related to another environmental issue which is plastic, since a great amount of disposable goods and packaging are made of plastic (Brown, 2015).

On the other hand, what constitutes waste and garbage in a given society is highly variable and constitutes a quite subjective notion. In this vein, some authors such as Douglas (1996) highlight that the concept of garbage is culturally specific; and in turn, waste generation is not only a product of the society in which is generated, but is also deeply affected by the level of development and the rate of societal change (Brown, 2015). Similarly, waste is not considered the same across the world. This fact is due to different consumption patterns and cultural systems which substantially vary, influencing the production of waste in each society. Accordingly, the differences in what is considered as waste, how it is processed and how individuals react to garbage is influenced by several factors such as the rate of urbanization, patterns of consumption, lifestyle, revenue, the level of development and the size of population (OECD, 2013).

Finally, other authors report the existence of different types of waste, such as for example the electronic waste, which could be understood as those products that cease to have utility for the original customer for any reason, including technological obsolescence (Guide & Wassenhove, 2009). This electronic waste was mostly landfilled or incinerated, creating considerable damage to the environment.

The Value of Garbage

Discarded material and waste that was traditionally considered as garbage constitutes in fact potential value (Schindler & Demaria, 2019). Nowadays, and partially due to the circular economy paradigm waste and garbage are increasingly considered as a resource rather than an externality. In this context, authors such as Ackerman and Mirza (2001) highlight the beneficial aspects of waste, stating that the conception of garbage includes all the benefits which could be derived from people's garbage; and in turn, waste becomes an unused valuable resource, instead of a threat or risk factor.

However, prior research also indicates that a strategy for sustainability development must distinguish between wastes that are assets and wastes that are assaults (Ackerman & Mirza, 2001). That is, distinguishing between waste-based opportunities and waste-related dangers. The major difference between these two sides of waste is that products considered as waste vary immensely in toxicity: some wastage products are intensely hazardous and should only be handled with technical precautions and protections; while other wastage products can reasonably be seen as merely ugly resources which could be further exploited (Ackerman & Mirza, 2001).

METHODOLOGY

In the present chapter an explorative multiple case-study analysis is developed in order to examine different cases of creating value from garbage. Interestingly, the study of several cases could facilitate identifying and analyzing particular patterns and explain differences across cases by contrasting them to each other (Aaboen et al., 2012).

The multiple case-study method was chosen in order to examine the practices and strategies developed by companies in order to create value from garbage (Yin, 2009). Similarly, Schramm (1971) in his seminal work reported that the main purpose of the case studies is to illustrate a decision or a set of decisions, as well as why these decisions are taken, how they are implemented and with what result. Accordingly, in this chapter some decisions about addressing the waste global issue and how they are implemented are examined. Later, other authors indicated that the case study is a kind of empirical research that investigates a current phenomenon in depth (Yin, 2018); while the multiple-case study focuses on the same phenomena across cases (Aaboen et al., 2012). In this context, the present study focuses on a particular phenomenon that is the use of garbage as a valuable resource for manufacturing and producing new products.

Likewise, prior research reports that the multiple-case study method has much to contribute to the development and providing strong examples (Dubois & Araujo, 2007) and cases are chosen because of their relevance. Consequently, the multiple-case method developed here means a comparative analysis that deals with each case as an independent observation. More precisely, the cases for this study were selected on the basis of purposive sampling (Patton, 2002). According to Patton (2002) purposive sampling enables the selection of cases that are particularly informative in relation to the research. This resulted in a selection of four case companies from different countries that develop different initiatives to use garbage as the main resource. In addition, the four case companies that participated represent different product areas, production methods, sizes and locations; which will provide the study with insights from different categories of companies.

CASES OF VALUE CREATION FROM GARBAGE

Ecoalf: "Upcycling the Oceans"

Plastic pollution is the dominant type of debris throughout the marine environment, being the "plastic bottle" one of the most prominent disposable plastic items, which have become a symbol of waste produced. The reason is that a great majority of beverage containers –mostly water and soft drinks- are discarded immediately after use, and a great amount of these plastic containers become marine debris in their way to the ocean (Brown, 2015) with the consequence of at least eight million tons of plastic leak into the oceans every year (Magnier et al., 2019). But not only plastic bottles are causing this environmental damage, but also plastic bags that are used every year with a useful lifespan of less than 30 minutes, plastic fishing nets are left at the oceans or the electronic waste that is generated every year.

However, following the principles of circular economy, the plastic debris collected in the oceans could re-enter the production process (Magnier et al., 2019). In fact, the case of ocean plastic debris recycling highlights an environmental initiative that consists on trying to solve the damaging effects of the linear economy through the process of reclaiming, sorting and repurposing ocean detritus (Magnier et al., 2019).

In this context, some companies have started to use plastic debris from the oceans and recycle this plastic into new products, being one of these initiatives is the Spanish company Ecoalf. This company believes that waste has great value and demonstrates that it possible to transform garbage into fashion products and accessories. The founder, Javier Goyeneche, believed that the most sustainable strategy was to not use natural resources, so the company focused on recycling in order to create new recycled products, demonstrating that what some people call waste could be transformed into a collection of outerwear, swimwear, casual apparel, shoes and accessories.

The company vision and mission are to stop using natural resources and to think of waste and garbage as a valuable resource. Likewise, the company objective is to recover the residues that are destroying the Mediterranean and its habitat, and to transform them into quality threads to produce fabrics and clothing. And accordingly, the company strategy is named as "*trashion*", meaning that each recycled material could be processed and turned into a new product.

This goal was transformed into the company initiative "*upcycling the oceans*" which was put into practice on the east coast of Spain, in Alicante, Valencia and Castellon. This project aims to remove garbage and plastic debris from the oceans with the help of local fishermen in three differentiated stages. The first stage consists on seeking the collaboration of fishermen and training them, so that fishermen agree to place plastic containers in the ports where they could put all the waste caught in their nets. Currently each one of the 165 boats participating in the project is removing daily between four and six kilograms of waste from the seabed. In the second stage, the plastic residues are converted into flakes and pellets through the integration of sophisticated technological processes. And finally, in the third stage, the pellets are transformed into thread to manufacture the fabrics used by Ecoalf to make clothes and fashion accessories.

Therefore, through this project, Ecoalf collects the plastic and other wastage materials from the Mediterranean before it enters the oceans and is converted into micro-plastic, and then through a process of "*reverse logistics*" the company manufactures new products from recycled materials that include PET plastic bottles, fishing nets, used rubber tires, and other reused materials. So, this company creates new valuable products from plastic wastage.

Interestingly, Ecoalf needs 70 bottles to create 1 meter of fabric, and one of their jackets needs 80 bottles to be made. In order to make customers aware, all their clothing include the percentages of fabric used in the manufacturing process, also indicating the approximate number of bottles that have been recycled to produce the item.

TerraCycle: "Making Everything from Waste"

One of the major environmental issues today is that more than 80% of consumer goods end up in landfills due to two major reasons. On one hand, excessive garbage is generated and that perishable goods and their packaging have been designed for one-time use; and on the other hand, recycling today entails great difficulty since garbage is made up of very complex materials, with a lack of technology to give it a second life.

TerraCycle is a US company specialized in waste management that aims to tackle the garbage environmental issue. The founder of TerraCycle, Tom Szaky, came up with the idea of giving real economic value to garbage and trash by simply separating it, believing that "*the more garbage is separated, the more value is created*". Accordingly, the company mission is to treat garbage and waste "*one by one*", and then transform it into new raw materials in order to manufacture all kinds of products. The reason is that from a scientific viewpoint everything could be recycled, but the waste and garbage needs to be collected one by one, being this fact the major difficulty, since governments do not have the technology for this type of garbage collection. More precisely, TerraCycle is an example of creating value through recycling capability, considering waste and garbage as an established source of revenue, because recyclable materials are treated as valuable from the beginning. Further, the system developed by this company is based on collecting waste, separating recyclables from waste and processing the recyclables into new recycled materials.

The company was founded in 2001 as an organic fertilizer producer, using waste as the resource for production. More specifically, this company first began with a used soda bottles collection program for vermicompost. The program became a great success with 5,000 locations participating in the used bottles collection in only two years. Then, the company developed another collection program, with the following pattern: paying schools and not-for-profit organizations to collect waste considered non-recyclable sponsored by its producers, and upcycle the reclaimed products and packaging into new merchandise.

Throughout the years TerraCycle evolved into the world leader in the collection and recycling of waste streams and non-recyclable post-consumer waste that are traditionally considered not-recyclable (Urbinati et al., 2017), through the implementation of circularity and by employing innovative and creative technical processes to upcycle wastage materials. Interestingly, the reason why waste streams are not recycled and are instead sent to landfill or are incinerated is because the cost to collect and process them far outweighs the value generated from the recovered material.

This company operates in 24 countries through a nationally-operated voluntary collection programs, encouraging and explicitly stimulating consumers to adopt themselves a circular economy approach. So that it can be stated that TerraCycle is based on customers' environmental engagement. Then, TerraCycle recycles all these waste streams such as candy wrappers, pens, toothbrushes, cosmetic bottles and many others. And in the last stage, the company sells the recyclables to operators who can further process the recyclables into new materials. The company sell traditionally non-recyclable plastics to processors and end users, because these materials are not in high demand, it takes great effort to convince a company to use these materials in their supply chain.

Further, TerraCycle has created approximately 200 products from the materials recovered from those seemingly non-recyclable products and waste. In addition, TerraCycle products could be classified into two main groups. On one side, the "*upcycled products*" which are created from other waste items; and on the other side, "*recycled products and materials*" that is waste that is recycled into a raw material that can be used in products including playgrounds, plastic lumber, plastic pavers, bike racks, park benches and so on.

However, the company's mission is to "*eliminate the idea of waste*" in the context of a profitable business. In addition, the company is gradually altering the business model so that today the company tries not only to make everything recyclable but also to make everything from waste and garbage. In order to achieve this objective, TerraCycle operates in three different areas.

In the first place, the company focuses on "*making everything recyclable*"; and therefore, the major part of its business constitutes recycling the non-recyclable. The company claims that most packaging and products are considered non-recyclable because the costs of reclaiming material are higher than the value of the material; but TerraCycle manages to recycle those products and stimulate the process among consumers and companies, through the creation of national collection platforms for hard-to-recycle waste streams. These platforms are usually funded by companies, retailers, cities, distribution centers or even small businesses that are trying to improve their environmental performance. In addition, where possible, TerraCycle and their partners focus on how to integrate reclaimed materials into specific products.

The second area of activity of TerraCycle focuses on "*making everything from waste*". This is a natural consequence of the first operating area, because it means using the recycled wastage in the manufacturing of new products. The reclaimed material is used as a feedstock for other products, and in some cases it means running the whole supply chain. Finally, the third operating area of TerraCycle aims to "*eliminate the concept of waste*" by altering the current consumption patterns. The specific operations to this end are related with the process to implement durability into packaging of non-durable products. The first two actions are strongly interconnected, given that reusing, upcycling and in most of the cases recycling goods that are typically considered non-recyclable results with feedstock for other production being reclaimed from waste. Thus, the main value proposition of the company is the cooperation for collection and further usage of waste considered non-recyclable.

But, how does the company operate in order to collect waste and garbage?.

TerraCycle typically sets up national wastage collection platforms for hard-to-recycle waste streams. These platforms are usually funded by businesses and consumer product companies that are looking to enhance their environmental performance. More precisely, the company uses three different collection programs. In the first place, the company uses *collection programs* funded by brands, manufacturers, and retailers to collect and recycle waste considered non-recyclable. Secondly, the company develops municipal waste programs, providing "*zero waste*" solutions that range from city-wide to local programs to recycle non-recyclable products and packages. Finally, the company has set out a "*zero waste boxes*" program providing companies and consumers with a turnkey recycling solution in the form of a box for specific waste collection; so that the waste collected is then sent to TerraCycle.

There is a high level of circularity in TerraCycle business model, identified as resource recovery and circular sourcing. For example, BIC, the world leader in ballpoint pens production developed a partnership with TerraCycle to launch and develop a writing instruments recycling program. The main goal of this project was the organization of voluntary collection at schools, companies and universities for the writing instruments -regardless of whether they are BIC branded or not- in order to be recycled into new products. Currently this circularity program operates in seven European countries.

Consequently, the company was capable to make use of the rising environmental awareness of final consumers and the growing level of corporate social responsibility among popular brands. So, to date, over 80 million people in 21 countries have helped TerraCycle to divert approximately 5 billion pieces of waste from landfills and incineration. However, some critics indicate that this is not the solution to the problem of excessive waste generation, being a merely a cover-up for the company's customers unsustainable production patterns.

Rejuce: "Reducing Food Waste from Ugly Fruits"

More than one-third of the world's food produce goes to waste and never gets eaten every year, and the common practice of disposing food waste at landfills is not sustainable and results in depletion of limited landfill space, while generating greenhouse emissions. More specifically, more than a half of the food waste in manufacturing and farming could be classified as avoidable, accounting for £1.4 billion of losses in the UK. Further, a large portion of this waste is fruits and vegetables deemed unsuitable for consumers due to appearance and aesthetic standards. The reason is that in order to meet consumers' expectations, major food retailers often reject perfectly edible fruit and vegetables due to rigorous quality and aesthetic standards regarding the physical appearance and characteristics of fruits and vegetables, such as size, shape, color or weight (Stuart, 2009).

The issue of food waste has inspired a range of small businesses which use this waste, and specially these "wonky" fruits and vegetables to make new products, such as the case of Rejuce. This British company resulted from the identification that food waste could be used as material for new food products. More specifically the mission of the company Rejuce is to save perfectly edible fruit and vegetables from being thrown away, by turning them into cold fruit and vegetable pressed juice. So, this company reduces the amount of food waste by turning "wonky" edible food into a resource for a new food product, developing food waste separation, collection and food waste valorization, showing a great reuse capability.

Rejuce is a juicer company based in East London, founded in 2012 by chef Tom Fletcher, who discovered that each year over 400,000 tons of fresh fruit and vegetables were wasted by the food retail industry. One example of this food wastage is the New Spitalfields Market which alone produces between 15-30 tons of food waste every day. In this context, the company founder decided to use food surpluses from major distributors and wholesale markets "*not good enough to be sold, but too good to be thrown away*" to make healthy drinks; thus, producing and commercializing juices made from fresh fruit that would otherwise have been thrown away.

When the business started in 2012, the company was able to make an average of 400 liters of juice a day from ½ ton of food waste; and nowadays, the company is capable of processing 6 tons food waste a day and selling more than 100,000 bottles a year by saving edible food from going to waste. To date, the company has saved over 300 tons of discarded food products.

A network of suppliers provides the company with local and low cost ingredients, eliminating their own disposal costs in the process, being one of the major supplies the London based New Spitalfields Market, that produces tons of food waste every day. And regarding the company major customers, Rejuce supplies fruit and vegetable pressed juices mainly cafes, bars and venues predominantly in East London. In addition, the company sells its juices at summer festivals such as Greenman, Shambala, or End of the Road, among others, meaning a sales peak for a month or two for the company.

Rejuce is highly committed to sustainability throughout the business; and this commitment is often prioritized over commercial concerns. The primary goal of the company is to reduce food waste wherever possible; but in addition to the sustainable sourcing of fruits, Rejuce uses recycled PET bottles and eco-friendly labels, as well as sustainable transport.

Elvis and Kresse: "Manufacturing from Leftovers"

Other example of turning garbage into value is the British company Elvis & Kresse, since this company creates fashion accessories by re-engineering seemingly useless wastes. So, it uses waste as the primary source of production in order to design and manufacture bags, belts or wallets. In fact, the company's core mission is to reduce waste by reclaiming leftover or discarded materials and repurposing them into new fashionable products. The company founders Kresse Wesling and Elvis Henrit believe that each waste stream has the potential to live forever if it receives enough attention and innovation. Accordingly, the company design fashion accessories from waste always considering the best use of the material, and a market with an appropriate size to solve the specific waste problem.

More specifically, the principal raw material used by this company is genuine de-commissioned British fire brigade hoses that had become too damaged to get repaired and were otherwise destined for landfills in the United Kingdom. The reason is that fire hose is a complex material which cannot be shredded, melted, or recycled. Consequently, to date Elvis & Kresse has prevented fire hoses from ending up in landfills, with over 170 tons of material reclaimed, entirely eliminating fire hose waste in the UK. In addition, this company is strongly committed to repairing any of their products, further prolonging their life as much as possible.

However, when having solved this waste problem, the company then took on the larger problem of leather waste, since 800,000 tons of leather off-cuts that are generated by the global leather industry end up in landfill or incineration. In order solve this environmental issue, Elvis & Kresse partnered with the fashion company Burberry to rescue leather fragments to create a strong new material used for manufacturing fashion accessories. Further, over the last 13 years, Elvis & Kresse has grown to tackle more than 15 reclaimed materials, like upcycle fire hoses, leather waste, coffee sacs, parachute silk, auction banners, and printing blankets in order to manufacture their products; and more than 10 waste streams are used to create their products.

The innovativeness of Elvis & Kresse's business model lies in the fact that the company manufactures their products from waste streams that traditionally are not recyclable and constantly searches for new waste materials to reclaim.

RESULTS

In this section a comparison of the four cases under analysis is developed and summarized in Table 2. The overall performance of each case provides partial evidence that some companies with a sustainable marketing orientation consider garbage and waste as the main production resource.

More precisely, the companies under analysis have reacted to a market event -the garbage and waste global issue- treating it as a great opportunity instead of a threat, since these companies consider garbage as their main competitive factor. Further, the use of garbage as the main competitive advantage may be based on the following factors. In the first place, the easy access to an abundant and low valuable resource –such as plastic debris, food wastage or de-commissioned fire hoses- that nobody cares about. Secondly, the development or the access to a technology that allows the transformation of garbage into new products. Third, the founders' personal concerns and strong implication with the depletion of natural resources and environmental issues. Therefore, from the cases presented here it can be highlighted that these four companies' business models are based on solving different environmental issues through the enhancement of sustainable consumption patterns. Additionally, it can be stated that the conventional business model has been turned upside down, since an undesirable output for many companies such as garbage, is the main input for these four companies.

However, there are some interesting similarities and differences between the case companies under examination. One major similarity between these companies is that all of them follow a circular economy strategy, applying the principles of reduce, reuse and recycle. The second major similarity is that the companies under analysis carry out waste treatment, but using different technologies and procedures. Other interesting similarity is that their sustainability strategies and business models are based on their founder' personal interest on elimination the idea of waste. Conversely, regarding their differences, the cases under analysis differ regarding their product areas, industries and production methods; and in addition, these companies have different locations.

Table 2. Cases under research and their application of the principles of circular economy

CASE	Type of garbage/ Value created	Reduce	Reuse/ Recycle
ECOALF	-Plastic debris in the Mediterranean sea -Value: garments and accessories	-Capability to flexibly collect waste from oceans. -Diverts plastic bottles from improper disposal.	-Manufacturing capability for plastic and plastic debris and recycling materials derived from plastic
TERRACYCLE	-Any kind of garbage and waste which could be recycled	-Waste treatment that reduces waste incineration and landfilling. -Collection of waste and recyclables directly from households, reducing total solid waste which is directed to incineration. -Capability to flexibly collect recyclables from residents. -Recyclable materials have great value right from the beginning. -Increasing waste separation reduces waste management costs.	-Creates value through recycling. -Provides cheap recycled materials for manufacturing companies.
REJUCE	-Food wastage -Value: fruit and vegetable pressed juice	-Reduction of food waste -Reduction in overall wastefulness	-Turns major food waste into a new resource for new food products
ELVIS & KRESSE	-Unwanted and used fire-hoses -Value: Fashion garments and accessories	-Waste treatment that reduces waste incineration and landfilling. -Waste material has great economic value right from the beginning.	-Manufacturing capability for recycling fire-hoses and derived waste.

CONCLUSION

Through sustainable marketing companies introduce sustainability into the core marketing strategies and actions to ensure the reduction of consumption and waste; and to encourage consumers in developing a resource-efficient way of consumption, which includes the acceptance of consumption reduction.

Likewise, the circular economy strategy supports the transformation of the "*consume-use-disposal*" model, so that production and consumption waste is reused and incorporated into the economy to create more value; while encouraging the economic activities that reduce, reuse and recycle materials in production, distribution and consumption processes (Blomsma & Brennan, 2017). Consequently, companies should reuse product materials adopting a closed-loop system where resources are returned to the natural environment after use.

Considering these two complementary approaches, this chapter presents and analyzes four companies that are addressing some major environmental issues through turning garbage into value. Interestingly, these four companies – Ecoalf, TerraCycle, Rejuce, and Elvis & Kresse – not only reduce waste and help in tackling the wastage issue, but also are able to create valuable products from garbage; thus, going beyond the traditional production and consumption model.

FUTURE RESEARCH DIRECTIONS

The empirical evidence presented in this chapter is only explorative in nature; and in turn, further investigations are needed. In addition, the four companies analyzed in this chapter stem from secondary sources and are quite heterogeneous from each other, since they differ in the industry, dimension and country. Therefore, future research could focus on a more homogeneous sample of companies transforming garbage into value.

REFERENCES

Aaboen, L., Dubois, A., & Lind, F. (2012). Capturing processes in longitudinal multiple case studies. *Industrial Marketing Management*, *41*(2), 235–246. doi:10.1016/j.indmarman.2012.01.009

Ackerman, F., & Mirza, S. (2001). Waste in the inner city: Asset or assault? *Local Environment*, *6*(2), 113–120. doi:10.1080/13549830120052764

Anstine, J. (2000). Consumers' willingness to pay for recycled content in plastic kitchen garbage bags: A hedonic price approach. *Applied Economics Letters*, *7*(1), 35–39. doi:10.1080/135048500352068

Belz, F. M., & Peattie, K. (2009). Sustainability marketing: A global perspective. Academic Press.

Blomsma, F., & Brennan, G. (2017). The emergence of circular economy: A new framing around prolonging resource productivity. *Journal of Industrial Ecology*, *21*(3), 603–614. doi:10.1111/jiec.12603

Brown, D. P. (2015). Garbage: How population, landmass and development interact with culture in the production of waste. *Resources, Conservation and Recycling*, *98*, 41–54. doi:10.1016/j.resconrec.2015.02.012

Brundtland, G. H. (1987). *Our common future: The world commission on environment and development*. Oxford University Press.

Castellani, V., Sala, S., & Mirabella, N. (2015). Beyond the throwaway society: A life cycle-based assessment of the environmental benefit of reuse. *Integrated Environmental Assessment and Management*, *11*(3), 373–382. doi:10.1002/ieam.1614 PMID:25557152

Connolly, J., & Prothero, A. (2003). Sustainable consumption: Consumption, consumers and the commodity discourse. *Consumption Markets & Culture*, *6*(4), 275–291. doi:10.1080/1025386032000168311

Crainer, S. (2013). Squaring the circle. *Business Strategy Review*, *24*(4), 13–19. doi:10.1111/j.1467-8616.2013.00988.x

Douglas, M. (1966). *Purity and danger*. Routledge & Kegan.

Drackner, M. (2005). What is waste? To whom? An anthropological perspective on garbage. *Waste Management & Research*, *23*(3), 175–181. doi:10.1177/0734242X05054325 PMID:15988938

Dubois, A., & Araujo, L. (2007). Case research in purchasing and supply management: Opportunities and challenges. *Journal of Purchasing and Supply Management*, *13*(3), 170–181. doi:10.1016/j.pursup.2007.09.002

European Parliament and the Council of the European Union. (2008). Council directive 2008/98/EC on waste and repealing certain directives. *Official Journal* L312/3. Retrieved from https://eur-lex.europa.eu/legal-content/EN/TXT/?uri=celex%3A32008L0098

Figge, F., Young, W., & Barkemeyer, R. (2014). Sufficiency or efficiency to achieve lower resource consumption and emissions? The role of the rebound effect. *Journal of Cleaner Production*, *69*, 216–224. doi:10.1016/j.jclepro.2014.01.031

Fuller, D. A. (1999). *Sustainable marketing: Managerial-ecological issues*. Sage Publications.

Ghisellini, P., Cialani, C., & Ulgiati, S. (2016). A review on circular economy: The expected transition to a balanced interplay on environmental and economic systems. *Journal of Cleaner Production*, *114*, 11–32. doi:10.1016/j.jclepro.2015.09.007

Gordon, R., Carrigan, M., & Hastings, G. (2011). A framework for sustainable marketing. *Marketing Theory, 11*(2), 143–163. doi:10.1177/1470593111403218

Guide, V. D., & Wassenhove, L. N. (2009). The evolution of closed-loop supply chain research. *Operations Research, 57*(1), 10–18. doi:10.1287/opre.1080.0628

Hart, S. L. (1995). A natural resource-based view of the firm. *Academy of Management Review, 20*(4), 986–1014. doi:10.5465/amr.1995.9512280033

Jones, P., Clarke-Hill, C., Comfort, D., & Hillier, D. (2008). Marketing and sustainability. *Marketing Intelligence & Planning, 26*(2), 123–13. doi:10.1108/02634500810860584

Kemper, J. A., & Ballantine, P. W. (2019). What do we mean by sustainability marketing? *Journal of Marketing Management, 35*(3/4), 277–309. doi:10.1080/0267257X.2019.1573845

Kilbourne, W. E. (1998). Green marketing: A theoretical perspective. *Journal of Marketing Management, 14*(6), 641–655. doi:10.1362/026725798784867743

Kilbourne, W. E., & Carlson, L. (2008). The dominant social paradigm, consumption and environmental attitudes: Can macromarketing education help? *Journal of Macromarketing, 28*(2), 106–121. doi:10.1177/0276146708314586

Kotler, P. (2011). Reinventing marketing to manage the environmental imperative. *Journal of Marketing, 75*(4), 132–135. doi:10.1509/jmkg.75.4.132

Lim, W. M. (2016). A blueprint for sustainability marketing: Defining its conceptual boundaries for progress. *Marketing Theory, 16*(2), 232–249. doi:10.1177/1470593115609796

MacArthur, E. (2013). *Towards a circular economy. Economic and business rationale for an accelerated transition* (Vol. 1). Ellen McArthur Foundation. Retrieved from https://www.ellenmacarthurfoundation.org/assets/downloads/publications/Ellen-MacArthur-Foundation-Towards-the-Circular-Economy-vol.1.pdf

Magnier, L., Mugge, R., & Schoormans, J. (2019). Turning ocean garbage into products: Consumers' evaluations of products made of recycled ocean plastic. *Journal of Cleaner Production, 215*, 84–98. doi:10.1016/j.jclepro.2018.12.246

Michaud, C., & Llerena, D. (2011). Green consumer behaviour: An experimental analysis of willingness to pay for remanufactured products. *Business Strategy and the Environment, 20*(6), 408–420.

Mitchell, R. W., Wooliscroft, B., & Higham, J. (2010). Sustainable market orientations: A new approach to managing marketing strategy. *Journal of Macromarketing*, *30*(2), 160–170. doi:10.1177/0276146710361928

Organization for Economic Cooperation Development. (2013). *Municipal waste in OECD Factbook*. Paris: OECD Publishing. Retrieved from https://www.oecd-ilibrary.org/economics/oecd-factbook-2013/municipal-waste_factbook-2013-71-en

Patton, M. Q. (2002). *Qualitative research and evaluation methods* (3rd ed.). Sage Publishing.

Peattie, K. (2001). Towards sustainability: The third age of green marketing. *The Marketing Review*, *2*(2), 129–146. doi:10.1362/1469347012569869

Peattie, K., & Peattie, S. (2009). Social marketing: A pathway to consumption reduction? *Journal of Business Research*, *62*(2), 260–268. doi:10.1016/j.jbusres.2008.01.033

Polonsky, M. J. (2011). Transformative green marketing: Impediments and opportunities. *Journal of Business Research*, *64*(12), 1311–1319. doi:10.1016/j.jbusres.2011.01.016

Prothero, A., McDonagh, P., & Dobscha, S. (2010). Is green the new black? Reflections on a green commodity discourse. *Journal of Macromarketing*, *30*(2), 147–159. doi:10.1177/0276146710361922

Ranta, V., Aarikka-Stenroos, L., & Mäkinen, S. J. (2018). Creating value in the circular economy: A structured multiple-case analysis of business models. *Journal of Cleaner Production*, *201*, 988–1000. doi:10.1016/j.jclepro.2018.08.072

Schindler, S., & Demaria, F. (2019). Garbage is gold: Waste-based commodity frontiers, modes of valorization and ecological distribution conflicts. *Capitalism, Nature, Socialism*, 1–8. doi:10.1080/10455752.2019.1694553

Schor, J. B. (1998). *The overspent American: Why we want what we don't need*. Harper Perennial.

Schramm, W. (1971). *Notes on case studies of instructional media projects*. Institute for Communication Research. Retrieved from https://files.eric.ed.gov/fulltext/ED092145.pdf

Slowak, A. P., & Regenfelder, M. (2017). Creating value, not wasting resources: Sustainable innovation strategies. *Innovation (Abingdon)*, *30*(4), 455–475. doi:10.1080/13511610.2016.1192990

Stuart, T. (2009). *Waste: Uncovering the global food scandal*. Penguin Books.

Su, B., Heshmati, A., Geng, Y., & Yu, X. (2013). A review of the circular economy in China: Moving from rhetoric to implementation. *Journal of Cleaner Production*, *42*, 215–227. doi:10.1016/j.jclepro.2012.11.020

Sung, H., & Lee, J. (2011). Environmental management portfolio of Korean fashion brands. *Journal of Global Fashion Marketing*, *2*(1), 44–54. doi:10.1080/20932685.2011.10593082

United Nations Environment Programme (UNEP), Division of Technology, Industry and Economics, United Nations Global Compact (UNGC), & Utopies. (2005). *Talk the walk: Advancing sustainable lifestyles through marketing and communications*. Retrieved form http://wedocs.unep.org/handle/20.500.11822/8399

Urbinati, A., Chiaroni, D., & Chiesa, V. (2017). Towards a new taxonomy of circular economy business models. *Journal of Cleaner Production*, *168*, 487–498. doi:10.1016/j.jclepro.2017.09.047

U.S. Department of Commerce. (2010). *Measuring Green Economy Report*. Retrieved from https://www.commerce.gov/news/reports/2010/04/measuring-green-economy

Van Dam, Y. K., & Apeldoorn, P. A. (1996). Sustainable marketing. *Journal of Macromarketing*, *6*(2), 45–56. doi:10.1177/027614679601600204

Varey, R. J. (2011). A sustainable society logic for marketing. *Social Business*, *1*(1), 69–83. doi:10.1362/204440811X570563

World Commission on Environment and Development. (1987). *Our common future*. Oxford University Press.

Yin, R. K. (2009). *Case study research: Design and Methods* (4th ed.). Sage Publications.

Yin, R. K. (2018). *Case study research and applications: Design and methods* (6th ed.). Sage Publications.

KEY TERMS AND DEFINITIONS

Circular Economy: Provides an alternative model of consumption, based on the creation of closed production systems where resources are reused and kept in a "*loop of production*" and usage, allowing the creation of value for a longer period of time.

Garbage: What is discarded or unwanted by individuals, implicating uselessness.

Green Products: Products and services that either conserve resources or that reduce waste.

Recycle Principle: Refers to any recovery operation through which waste materials are reprocessed into products, materials or substances whether for the original or for other purposes.

Reduce Principle: Supports the minimization of the amount of materials, energy and waste generated in the economic system through the increase of efficiency in production and consumption.

Reuse Principle: Supports that products or components that are not wasted are used again for the same purpose for which they were conceived.

Sustainable Marketing: The marketing orientation that meets the needs of the present, without compromising the ability of future generations to meet their own needs.

Chapter 6
Key Strategic Drivers for Business Digital Transformation:
Systematic Literature Review

Ronnie Figueiredo
Universidade Europeia, Portugal & NECE, University of Beira Interior, Portugal

Raquel Soares
https://orcid.org/0000-0002-3483-3532
Business and Law Research Unit, Universidade Europeia, Portugal & UNIDCOM-IADE, Design and Communication Research Unit, Portugal & CiTUR, Portugal & University of Algarve, Portugal

João José de Matos Ferreira
https://orcid.org/0000-0002-5928-2474
NECE, Research Center in Business Sciences, University of Beira Interior, Portugal

ABSTRACT

The concept of digital transformation (DT) has reached a heightened demand level on the executives' agenda, especially when it is related to elements that influence the development and activities of contemporary firms being prevalent in discussions about industrial and social changes. This theme leads the authors to reflect on the key strategic drivers used by firms to carry out the qualitative process (prior experience)

DOI: 10.4018/978-1-7998-4552-2.ch006

of digital business transformation. It reinforces the purpose of understanding the key strategic drivers used by firms in recent years to guide the digital business transformation process. The systematic literature review was performed in the "WoS database," according to Boolean logic, aiming to capture the essential properties of the logical operators and sets of statements about the theme presented to compose the study. The results indicate a higher frequency for the big data and digitization drivers, followed by the innovation driver within the analyzed period.

INTRODUCTION

Recently, the concept of digital transformation (DT, hereafter) has reached a heightened demand level on the executives' agenda, especially when it is related to elements that influence the development and activities of contemporary firms, being prevalent in discussions about industrial and social changes.

Moreover, DT has affected entire sectors of the world economic system, such as the financial sector (regarded as one of the key drivers of the digital economy development) ranking second to telecommunications companies for investments in innovative information and communication technologies (Schepinin & Bataev, 2019).

The banking industry has been introducing technology into its strategy, seeking substantial gains from business digitalization, reducing operating costs, as well as risks and share of cash transactions, and increasing the value of electronic payments, besides the transformation of classic banking business models in Fintechs (Sloboda, Dunas, & Limański, 2018).

The "servitization" development is a driver of DT, especially in after sales service. For front-end processes, DT acts as a technology vehicle that renders it possible to meet the new requirements demanded by the customer. For back-end processes, DT is an opportunity to address internal efficiency and cost pressure resulting from "servitization" according to the requirements (Dombrowski & Fochler, 2018).

We are observing the development of new paradigms, not only for the interaction between consumer and business, but also for the interaction of different firms within the same business, where we attest the emergence of a new quality of institutional transformation characterized by the convergence of the digital and traditional economy (Kapustina, Pereverzeva, Stepanova, & Rusu, 2019).

The digitalization of the economy generates new business opportunities and the development of interstate investments cooperation, triggered by the strengthening of the globalization processes at all levels. Digital technologies have become the main "drivers" of financial market transformation, contributing to the development of information flows and the creation of new challenges in the future (Kozlova, Jacobsen, Golovkina, & Kupriyanova, 2019).

However, industrial DT does not progress at the same speed in all fields of application as numerous efforts to collect and exploit digital data were made long before the turn of the millennium (Gölzer & Fritzsche, 2017). Thus, the future impact of DT cannot be adequately predicted by simple quantitative extrapolations from previous experiences with the use of information technology. In this context, the study answers to the following research question:

RQ: What are the key strategic drivers used by firms to carry out the qualitative process (prior experience) of digital business transformation?

The study aims to investigate the key strategic drivers used by firms, recently, to guide the digital business transformation. It identifies and explores the main themes (business, DT and strategic drivers), contributing for the deepening of the literature through the identification of priority areas concerning the digital business transformation. The research was performed through a systematic literature review according to Lim, Davis, Tang, Shannon & Bonfield (2019); Palmatier, Houston & Hulland (2018) and Dolati Neghabadi, Evrard Samuel & Espinouse (2019) in the Web of Science database, applying the Boolean logic, in order to review and identify the main studies related to the proposed research problem and its future agenda.

The remaining of this chapter is organized as follows: section "background" presents the context of "digital transformation", section "research method" describes the methodology used, next section describes the results and discussions, and the "future research directions" are presented in the last section.

BACKGROUND

While digitization is a key factor of the fourth industrial revolution (Industry 4.0), organizations have different approaches to addressing this topic in order to gain a clearer picture of DT-related opportunities and challenges (Bienhaus & Haddud, 2018).

Our private and professional lives are fundamentally affected by digital technology (Mangematin, Sapsed, & Schüßler, 2014): the way we receive news, the choice and design of workplaces, how we connect with customers and product development stakeholders, how products are consumed, among others.

DT is a concept that changes the way firms work today. As a research field, it has introduced new approaches, structures, and case studies that should guide and help firms digitally transform their work and/or outcomes (Hrustek, Tomicic Furjan,

& Pihir, 2019). DTs are a cause of rapid and even disruptive change in most firms and future competitive environments, as they call for the emergence of new models, businesses, and fundamentally new markets.

Firms' transition from conventional to digital business models requires proper assessment of DT potential (Galimova, Gileva, Mukhanova, & Krasnuk, 2019). Thus, traditional firms must consider their structure and their roles in achieving new business goals (Kettunen & Laanti, 2017). In a broader sense, we it seeks to modify or adapt business models supported by technology and innovation that would trigger changes in external and internal environments (Kotarba, 2018) at both the professional and/or personal levels.

In the age of digitalization, the world's technological developments are growing at a steady pace, requiring firms to be agile in strategic decision-making to market changes as a guarantee of survival (Sahid, Maleh, & Belaissaoui, 2017).

This capability can be perceived by the expansion in the use of information and communication technologies (ICT, hereafter) over the past decade. Data that was previously unavailable for digital processing became obtainable, resulting in industry scanning with high granularity and low refresh rate (Gölzer & Fritzsche, 2017).

Information and communications technology (ICTs) are being used more than ever to evaluate firms within their market in order to overcome the competition and achieve competitive success (Shoniregun, 2004). So, having a solid strategy is vital to surviving in a competitive market, and many strategic approaches can help firms achieve the necessary competitive advantage. However, firms must consider the components that assist them in decision making and the necessary activities for firm management to maintain sustainability as markets and technologies change (Dabab & Weber, 2018).

Over the past few decades, the role of information technology (IT) has changed significantly from office and process automation to value adding and innovation through its use in business (Levstek, Hovelja, & Pucihar, 2018).

RESEARCH METHOD

The research was performed through a systematic literature review according to Lim, Davis, Tang, Shannon & Bonfield (2019); Palmatier, Houston & Hulland (2018) and Dolati Neghabadi, Evrard Samuel & Espinouse (2019) and in-depth content to review and to identify key studies related to the proposed research problem and their future agenda. The database used was the Web of Science, applying the proposed Boolean logic: (ABS (business AND transformation) AND TITLE-ABS-KEY (digital) AND TITLE-ABS-KEY (drivers)). 78 papers in the business and economics areas were identified by 2019. After the limitation on continuous publications, 47 papers were identified in the 2010 to 2019 range. The filters applied in the continuous limitation were English language and magazine papers. The years prior to 2009 did not present continuous publications, as the focus was on capturing the essential properties of logical operators and sets of statements about the theme presented to compose the initial proposal of the study, presented here.

RESULTS AND DISCUSSION

This section characterizes the articles resulting from the research, that is, the chronological evolution of the number of published papers, most cited papers, journals in which the papers are published, authors and their national geographic locations.

Papers, Sources, Authors and Countries

The publications' evolution can be observed in Figure 1. Since 2010, the publication on the theme has been ongoing, presenting an average of 2.25 articles per year in the range of 2010 and 2013. From 2014, the number of annual publications is higher than the average of the previous range, being 6.33 per year. In 2014, 2015, 2018 and 2019 (partial) the number of publications increases to an average of 7.25 per year. The year of 2018 presents the highest number of publications, 8.

Figure 1.

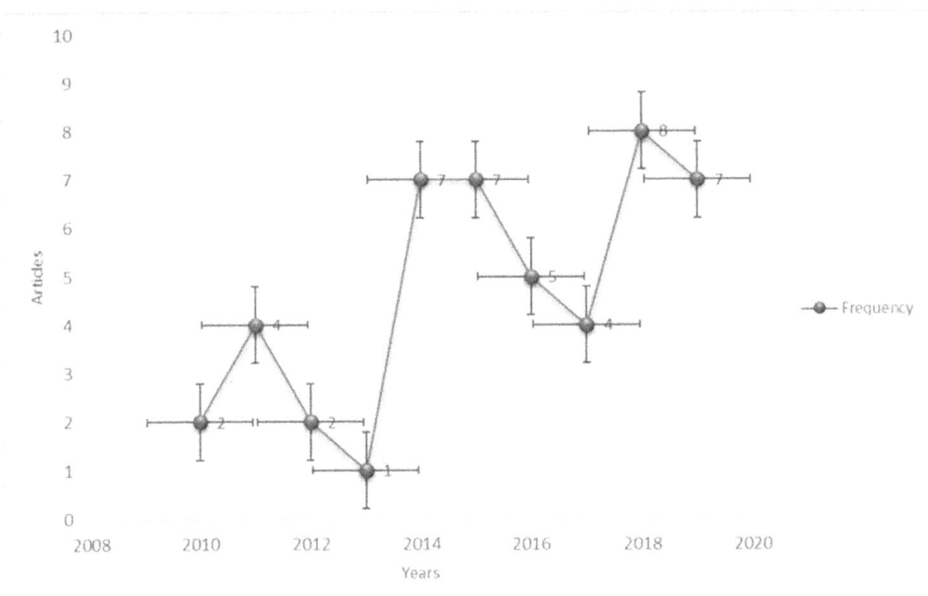

Table 1.

Journals	#Citations
Journal of Strategic Information Systems	*166*
Business Strategy and the Environment	*103*
Small Business Economics	*81*
Current Issues in Tourism	*52*
Tourism Geographies	*36*
Journal of Manufacturing Technology Management	*32*
Strategy and Leadership	*23*
Africa Journal of Management	*19*
Journal of Technology Transfer	*18*
Equality, Diversity and Inclusion	*14*

Regarding papers' citations, the most cited two papers in the study, 2014 and 2015, together, reached 269 citations. In 2014, is the year with the highest number of studies with citations, contributed 140 citations, followed by 2015 with 198 citations. Three studies developed in the areas of tourism, diversity and inclusion totaled 102 citations while the other 7 studies related to management, business and strategy totaled 442 citations, 77% of citations. Table 1 presents the 10 journals with the highest number of citations.

Concerning the authors, in this research the most cited study was Loebbecke & Picot (2015) and the least cited was Daya (2014). Figure 2 shows the authors' results and their evolutions over time.

Figure 2. Authors results and evolutions over time

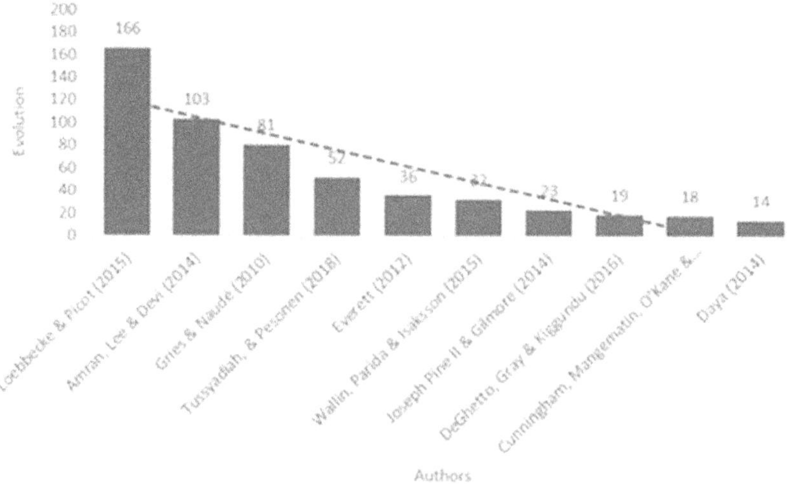

Table 2.

Country	#Papers
USA	13
United Kingdom	06
Germany	05
France	03
India	03
Ireland	03
Denmark	03
Finland	02
Italy	02
Malaysia	02

Figure 3. The top 10 countries with the highest number of papers

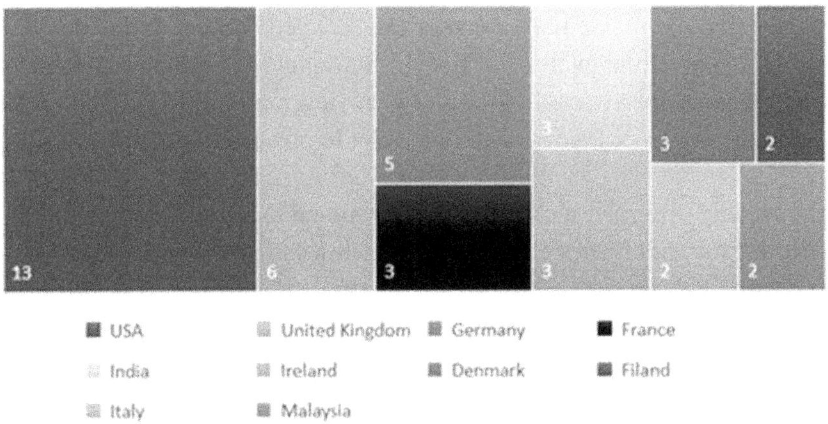

KEY STRATEGIC DRIVERS FOR DIGITAL BUSINESS TRANSFORMATION

The ongoing DT on industry has been studied primarily from the viewpoint of cyber-physical systems solutions as drivers of change. Accordingly, with the introduction of new digital technologies in industry, Gölzer & Fritzsche, (2017) argue that the focus is on understanding the changes in data management. Furthermore, they acknowledge that, so far, the existing business structures within and in-between firms drive in most cases the organization of data processing activities in operations management. Nevertheless, the opposite can take regarding the growing importance of Big Data in the DT context, i.e. business structures will evolve based on the potential to develop value streams offered through new data processing solutions. Moreover, Zimmermann, Schmidt, Sandkuhl, Wißotzki, Jugel, & Möhring (2015) point out that new business information systems integrate emerging Internet of Things (IoT) infrastructures and components. To leverage and extend previous Enterprise

Architecture efforts to enable business value, organizations need to integrate IoT architectures, due to the diversity of IoT technologies and products. Both architecture engineering and actual information systems and business models management are complex and presently integrating beside the IoT synergistic subjects, such as Enterprise Architecture in context with services and cloud computing, semantic-based decision support through ontologies and knowledge-based systems, big data management, as well as mobility and collaboration networks. Kotarba (2018) presents in his study a scope of changes in the morphology of business models in contemporary organizations that have occurred in the last decades, caused by the massive technological development, framed under the DT concept. Concerning the advent of digital technology, Mangematin, Sapsed, & Schüßler (2014) analyze the disassembly and reassembly dynamics in selected creative industries. So, the authors argue that a joint analysis of how institutional logics, business models and creative processes are affected by digital technology and how they interrelate in producing stability or change is central in order to provide a full understanding of:

(i) the broadly observed sectoral or organizational lock-in effects; and
(ii) the transformation and innovation possibilities.

Data visualization is an essential tool to drive end-user adoption and change management activities within data initiatives and particularly in digital environments. In this context, Magee (2016) develops a data-driven approach to the sales engagement cycle, which can essentially improve performance. It uses an analytical approach to determine customer needs and sales "signals" by adjusting sales engagement to market needs. It also develops a prototype in IBM Digital Sales Europe to test the effectiveness of a data-driven approach to territory management. Digitization and big data analytics redesign business models and affect employment among knowledge professionals - as it was done in automation for manufacturing workers. Loebbecke & Picot (2015) consider the mechanisms underlying the way digitization and big data analytics drive business and society transformation. They emphasize that digitization and big data analytics become ubiquitous, desirable and harmful as the consequences. With multiple mechanisms at stake, many current business models and jobs will be replaced - including the processes, skills and jobs that currently require higher education and skill levels. In digital endeavors, companies often experiment several business models before converging on to a specific and focused model they choose to follow. Gupta & Bose (2018) develop an integrative framework that identifies strategic learning and its impact on the digital model adopted by the firm as a key factor for business model transformation. Further, it is also noted that the interactions of strategic learning with the operating environment reciprocally impacts the operating environment for all firms in that particular product-market analyzed domain. Lammers, Tomidei, & Regattieri (2018) present through the results from a systematic literature review, a set of triggers for digital transformations across the key industries. Australia example is introduced as well as its five key service industries, namely mining, manufacturing, agriculture and construction. The results of this research indicate that triggers for DT vary expressively across different industries. Amran, Lee & Devi (2014) investigate the increasing of business complexity, associated with improved DT, leading firms to be involved and to contribute for the sustainability agenda. These authors conclude that the corporate social responsibility anchored in the vision and/or mission, as well as strategic alliances promoted with non-governmental organizations is positively associated to corporate social responsibility. Gries & Naudé (2010) provide an endogenous growth model to clarify the role of startups in digital economic transformation. The authors apply the Lewis' model distinction between a traditional and modern sector, supporting it through micro-foundations. The model shows how opportunity-driven entrepreneurship can drive DT in modern and traditional sectors through innovation. The explosive growth of peer-to-peer accommodation (P2P) is potentially transforming the digital and competitive landscape of the accommodation industry. Tussyadiah, & Pesonen (2018) explore market characteristics and factors that drive and hinder the use of P2P accommodation in collaborative consumption. Two relevant factors that drive P2P accommodation are identified: social appeal (desire for community and sustainability) and economic appeal (cost savings based on business digitization). Thus, barriers include issues of trust, efficacy and familiarity with the system and cost. Everett (2012) examines the transformation of food production sites into touristic experience spaces. It is also recognized how producers change the traditional production patterns to ease the growing demand of digital consumption. Wallin, Parida & Isaksson (2015) note that manufacturing firms are increasingly striving to combine products and services into integrated offerings. However, firms' success in this process of transformation is related to the presence of routines and structured processes, which authors conceptualize as Product-Service System (PSS) design. Joseph Pine II & Gilmore (2014) identify insights and consider them as key elements in the digitization business process and recognize that business executives should think differently about how they create economic value for their technology-using customers. DeGhetto, Gray, & Kiggundu (2016) state that as Africa emerges, grows and begins to create a more positive outlook on joint efforts to rethink the future. Accordingly, authors consider the participation of actors such as academics, executives, leaders, and policymakers to be imperative for the transformation in a sustainable way. Cunningham, Mangematin, O'Kane, & O'Reilly (2016) realize that attraction factors such as control, ambition, and personal motivation in career can influence the scientists becoming principal researchers in organizations. Daya (2014) proposes to create diverse and inclusion environments in organizations and identifies "senior leadership", "organizational climate", "organizational belonging", "communication", and "transparency" as core inclusion elements that need to be transformed at the organizational-level.

According to the systematic review, the Table 3 presents the most applied Key Strategic Drivers in the digital business transformation process.

Table 3.

Drivers	Definitions	Authors
Digitization and Big Data	Business structures will evolve based on the potential to develop value streams offered through new solutions of data processing.	Gölzer& Fritzsche (2017)
Internet of Things (IoT)	New business information systems integrate emerging IoT infrastructures and components.	Zimmermann et al.(2015)
Technological Models	A new scope of the changes in the business models' morphology caused by the massive technological development.	Kotarba (2018)
Data Visualization	Data visualization is an essential tool for driving end-user adoption and change management activities.	Mangematin et al. (2014)
Data Engagement and Orientation	A data-driven approach to the sales engagement cycle, whereas engagement can fundamentally improve performance.	Magee (2016)
Digitization and Big Data	Mechanisms underlying the way digitization and big data analytics drive the business and society transformation.	Loebbecke & Picot (2015)
Strategic Learning	Interactions of strategic learning with the operating environment reciprocally impacts the operating environment for all companies in that particular product-market domain.	Gupta & Bose (2018)
Sectorization	DT's drivers vary significantly across different sectors of the economy.	Lammers, Tomidei, & Regattieri (2018)
Social and Corporate Responsibility	The value of corporate social responsibility anchored in business strategy is positively associated with DT.	Amran, et all. (2014)
Innovation	Opportunity-driven entrepreneurship can drive DT in the modern and traditional sectors through innovation.	Gries & Naudé (2010)
Digitization and Big Data	Market characteristics and factors that drive and hinder the P2P accommodation based on economic appeal (cost savings based on business digitization).	Tussyadiah, & Pesonen (2018)
Digital Consumption	The increasing demands of digital consumption influence the change of traditional production, transforming production sites into spaces of experience.	Everett (2012)
Inovação	Business success in transformation is related to the presence of structured routines and processes, known as innovation capabilities of product service system (PSS).	Wallin, Parida & Isaksson (2015)
Insights	Identifying insights is considered a key element in the digitization business process.	Joseph Pine II & Gilmore (2014)
Actors' Integration	The integration of diverse actors, academics, executives, leaders and policy makers creates a new sustainable perspective.	DeGhetto, Gray, & Kiggundu (2016)
Scientific Research	Attracting factors such as career control, ambition and personal motivation can influence the training of researchers in organizations.	Cunningham, Mangematin, O'Kane, & O'Reilly (2016)
Diverse Environments	Creating diverse environments in organizations needs to be managed for DT along with organizational-level inclusion elements: "leadership", "climate", "organizational belonging", "communication" and "transparency".	Daya (2014)

Figure 4 presents the frequency of the Key Strategic Drivers in the digital business transformation process.

Figure 4.

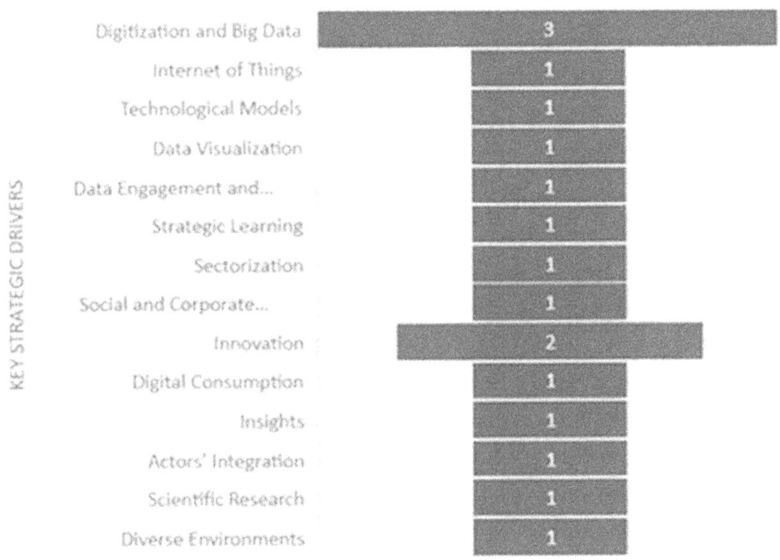

DISCUSSION AND CONCLUSION

Gölzer & Fritzsche (2017), in their study, present the issue of DT in businesses: "... the future impact of DT cannot be predicted adequately by simply quantitative extrapolations from previous experiences with the use of information technology." because, as the authors suggest, industry's DT does not progress with the same velocity in all fields of application, since countless efforts to collect and explore digital data were carried out long before the turn of the millennium.

Numerous studies have emerged since this challenge was launched. Although there is no consensus on the qualitative and quantitative DT approaches yet, we intend to systematize the existing literature in this field of study. Thus, we found fourteen approaches used in the "qualitative process" of DT: digitization and big data, IoT, technological models, data visualization, data engagement and orientation, strategic learning, sectorization, social and corporate responsibility, innovation, digital consumption, insights, actors' integration, scientific research and diverse environments.

We realize that digitization and big data drivers, as well as innovation, are the most frequently used in the DT process. This result is understood by the technical immediacy of the organizational change processes, the implementation cost and the exponential gain.

The qualitative process as well as previous experiences underlying the digital business transformation are the distinctive parts, being the first technologic approach, including processes and technologies for gathering data, information analysis and business decision making. The second part includes a behavioral approach based on organizational values and social and corporate responsibility. A set of technological and behavioral capabilities.

Evidence that DT theories can be used in digital business transformation processes is also found. It shows consensual relationships as well as in divergent ones, triggering reflections about the different business models and their impacts.

The research has direct implications for the industry literature, particularly for identifying the drivers used by firms to affect the DT process. Similarly, it also provides the opportunity for the scientific community to learn about the main subjects covered in the literature, discoveries, uncertainties and the future agenda.

The study has limitations, highlighting that only one database was used to collect papers that were in the basis of this research. Although WoS is presented as an international reference database, collecting papers from other databases and sources could provide further insights about key strategic drivers for DT phenomenon.

FUTURE RESEARCH DIRECTIONS

A new book chapter can be developed to identify the key strategic drivers for digital business transformation in Portugal, in a different sector. Another option is developed studies to create value streams in Digital Supply Chain. More one is investigating about framework to start a digital process in SMEs can be develop.

ACKNOWLEDGMENT

This research was supported by the NECE - Research Center in Business Science at UBI (University of Beira Interior) and CINTURS - Research Center for Tourism, Sustainability and Well-being at UAlg (University of Algarve) in partnership with Universidade Europeia (Business and Law Research Unit) Lisbon.

REFERENCES

Amran, A., Lee, S. P., & Devi, S. S. (2014). The influence of governance structure and strategic corporate social responsibility toward sustainability reporting quality. *Business Strategy and the Environment*, *23*(4), 217–235. doi:10.1002/bse.1767

Bienhaus, F., & Haddud, A. (2018). Procurement 4.0: Factors influencing the digitisation of procurement and supply chains. *Business Process Management Journal*, *24*(4), 965–984. doi:10.1108/BPMJ-06-2017-0139

Cunningham, J. A., Mangematin, V., O'Kane, C., & O'Reilly, P. (2016). At the frontiers of scientific advancement: The factors that influence scientists to become or choose to become publicly funded principal investigators. *The Journal of Technology Transfer*, *41*(4), 778–797. doi:10.100710961-015-9400-4

Dabab, M., & Weber, C. (2018). Business intelligence and data analytics as a driver of dynamic capability strategic approach. *PICMET 2018 - Portland International Conference on Management of Engineering and Technology: Managing Technological Entrepreneurship: The Engine for Economic Growth, Proceedings*, 1–9. 10.23919/PICMET.2018.8481750

Daya, P. (2014). Diversity and inclusion in an emerging market context. *Equality, Diversity and Inclusion*, *33*(3), 293–308. doi:10.1108/EDI-10-2012-0087

DeGhetto, K., Gray, J. R., & Kiggundu, M. N. (2016). The African Union's Agenda 2063: Aspirations, challenges, and opportunities for management research. *Africa Journal of Management*, *2*(1), 93–116. doi:10.1080/23322373.2015.1127090

Dolati Neghabadi, P., Evrard Samuel, K., & Espinouse, M. L. (2019). Systematic literature review on city logistics: Overview, classification and analysis. *International Journal of Production Research*, *57*(3), 865–887. doi:10.1080/00207543.2018.1489153

Dombrowski, U., & Fochler, S. (2018). Servitization as a key driver for Digital Transformation of manufacturing companies' Spare Parts Service. *Proceedings of the 2018 IEEE International Conference on Service Operations and Logistics, and Informatics*, 291–296. 10.1109/SOLI.2018.8476713

Everett, S. (2012). Production places or consumption spaces? The place-making agency of food tourism in Ireland and Scotland. *Tourism Geographies*, *14*(4), 535–554. doi:10.1080/14616688.2012.647321

Galimova, M., Gileva, T., Mukhanova, N., & Krasnuk, L. (2019). Selecting the path of the digital transformation of business-models for industrial enterprises. *IOP Conference Series. Materials Science and Engineering*, *497*(1), 012071. Advance online publication. doi:10.1088/1757-899X/497/1/012071

Gölzer, P., & Fritzsche, A. (2017). Data-driven operations management: Organisational implications of the digital transformation in industrial practice. *Production Planning and Control*, *28*(16), 1332–1343. doi:10.1080/09537287.2017.1375148

Gries, T., & Naudé, W. (2010). Entrepreneurship and structural economic transformation. *Small Business Economics*, *34*(1), 13–29. doi:10.100711187-009-9192-8

Gupta, G., & Bose, I. (2018, June). Strategic learning for digital market pioneering: Examining the transformation of Wishberry's crowdfunding model. *Technological Forecasting and Social Change*, *146*, 865–876. doi:10.1016/j.techfore.2018.06.020

Hrustek, L., Tomicic Furjan, M., & Pihir, I. (2019). Influence of Digital Transformation Drivers on Business Model creation. *2019 42nd International Convention on Information and Communication Technology, Electronics and Microelectronics*, 1304–1308. 10.23919/MIPRO.2019.8756666

Joseph Pine, B. II, & Gilmore, H., J. (. (2014). A leader's guide to innovation in the experience economy. *Strategy and Leadership*, *42*(1), 24–29. doi:10.1108/SL-09-2013-0073

Kapustina, I., Pereverzeva, T., Stepanova, T., & Rusu, I. (2019). Convergence of institutes of retail traditional and digital economy. *IOP Conference Series. Materials Science and Engineering*, *497*(1), 012120. Advance online publication. doi:10.1088/1757-899X/497/1/012120

Kettunen, P., & Laanti, M. (2017). Future software organizations – agile goals and roles. *European Journal of Futures Research*, *5*(1), 1–15. doi:10.100740309-017-0123-7

Kotarba, M. (2018). Digital transformation of business models. *Foundations of Management*, *10*(1), 123–142. doi:10.2478/fman-2018-0011

Kozlova, N., Jacobsen, B., Golovkina, S., & Kupriyanova, M. (2019). Russian-German investment relations in the context of digital transformation of the state and financial sector of the economy. *IOP Conference Series. Materials Science and Engineering*, *497*(1), 012122. Advance online publication. doi:10.1088/1757-899X/497/1/012122

Lammers, T., Tomidei, L., & Regattieri, A. (2018). What Causes Companies to Transform Digitally?*Portland International Conference on Management of Engineering and Technology*, 1–8.

Levstek, A., Hovelja, T., & Pucihar, A. (2018). IT Governance Mechanisms and Contingency Factors: Towards an Adaptive IT Governance Model. *Organizacija, 51*(4), 286–310. doi:10.2478/orga-2018-0024

Lim, J., Davis, A., Tang, A. R., Shannon, C. N., & Bonfield, C. M. (2019). Caregiver stress in children with craniosynostosis: A systematic literature review. *Child's Nervous System, 35*(2), 217–225. doi:10.100700381-018-3959-7 PMID:30155782

Loebbecke, C., & Picot, A. (2015). Reflections on societal and business model transformation arising from digitization and big data analytics: A research agenda. *The Journal of Strategic Information Systems, 24*(3), 149–157. doi:10.1016/j.jsis.2015.08.002

Magee, B. (2016). Evaluating data driven practices in sales environments: User engagement and sales results. *Journal of Decision Systems, 25*(sup1), 622–631. doi:10.1080/12460125.2016.1192084

Mangematin, V., Sapsed, J., & Schüßler, E. (2014). Disassembly and reassembly: An introduction to the Special Issue on digital technology and creative industries. *Technological Forecasting and Social Change, 83*(1), 1–9. doi:10.1016/j.techfore.2014.01.002

Palmatier, R. W., Houston, M. B., & Hulland, J. (2018). *Review articles: purpose, process, and structure.* Academic Press.

Sahid, A., Maleh, Y., & Belaissaoui, M. (2017). An agile framework for ITS management in organizations. A case study based on DevOps. *ACM International Conference Proceeding Series.* 10.1145/3167486.3167556

Schepinin, V., & Bataev, A. (2019). Digitalization of financial sphere: Challenger banks efficiency estimation. *IOP Conference Series. Materials Science and Engineering, 497*(1), 012051. Advance online publication. doi:10.1088/1757-899X/497/1/012051

Shoniregun, C. A. (2004). Classification and taxonomy of TEISMEs. *ACM International Conference Proceeding Series, 60*, 196–200. 10.1145/1052220.1052245

Sloboda, L., Dunas, N., & Limański, A. (2018). Contemporary challenges and risks of retail banking development in Ukraine. *Banks and Bank Systems, 13*(1), 88–97. doi:10.21511/bbs.13(1).2018.09

Tussyadiah, I. P., & Pesonen, J. (2018). Drivers and barriers of peer-to-peer accommodation stay–an exploratory study with American and Finnish travellers. *Current Issues in Tourism*, *21*(6), 703–720. doi:10.1080/13683500.2016.1141180

Wallin, J., Parida, V., & Isaksson, O. (2015). Understanding product-service system innovation capabilities development for manufacturing companies. *Journal of Manufacturing Technology Management*, *26*(5), 763–787. doi:10.1108/JMTM-05-2013-0055

Zimmermann, A., Schmidt, R., Sandkuhl, K., Wißotzki, M., Jugel, D., & Möhring, M. (2015). Digital enterprise architecture-transformation for the internet of things. *Proceedings of the 2015 IEEE 19th International Enterprise Distributed Object Computing Conference Workshops and Demonstrations*, 130–138. 10.1109/EDOCW.2015.16

ADDITIONAL READING

Amaral, I., Soares, R. R., & Proença, J. F. (2018). Business Model Innovation: Towards a conceptual framework. *Tourism & Management Studies*, *14*(1), 80–93. doi:10.18089/tms.2018.14107

Figueiredo, R., & Castro, M. S. (2020). How Can Marketing Intelligence Support Tourism Companies to Increase Their Competitiveness? In Multilevel Approach to Competitiveness in the Global Tourism Industry (pp. 278-289). IGI Global. doi:10.4018/978-1-7998-0365-2.ch016

Figueiredo, R., & de Matos Ferreira, J. J. (2019). Spinner Model: Prediction of Propensity to Innovate Based on Knowledge-Intensive Business Services. *Journal of the Knowledge Economy*. Advance online publication. doi:10.100713132-019-00607-2

Figueiredo, R., Neto, J. V., Ferreira, J. J., Quelhas, O. L. G., & Lima, G. B. A. (2019). Knowledge creation and knowledge transfer: An perspective under the kibs vision for evaluating the innovative capacity. *Informação & Informação*, *24*(1), 300–325. doi:10.5433/1981-8920.2019v24n1p300

Figueiredo, R., Neto, J. V., Quelhas, O. L. G., & de Matos Ferreira, J. J. (2017). Knowledge Intensive Business Services (KIBS): Bibliometric analysis and their different behaviors in the scientific literature. *RAI Revista de Administração e Inovação*, *14*(3), 216–225. doi:10.1016/j.rai.2017.05.004

Figueiredo, R., Quelhas, O., Vieira Neto, J., & Ferreira, J. J. (2019). The role of knowledge intensive business services in economic development: A bibliometric analysis from Bradford, Lotka and Zipf laws. *Gestão & Produção*, *26*(4), e4356. doi:10.1590/0104-530x4356-19

Soares, R. R., Zhang, C., Proença, J. F., & Kandampully, J. (2017). Why Are Generation Y Consumers the Most Likely to Complain and Repurchase? *Journal of Service Management*, *28*(3), 520–540. doi:10.1108/JOSM-08-2015-0256

KEY TERMS AND DEFINITIONS

Big Data: Big data is a combination of structured, semi structured and unstructured data collected by organizations that can be mined for information and used in machine learning projects, predictive modeling and other advanced analytics applications.

Data Visualization: Data visualization is the graphical representation of information and data.

Digital Transformation: Digital transformation is the integration of digital technology into all areas of a business, essentially changing how businesses operate and deliver value to customers.

Employee Engagement: Employee engagement is defined as the emotional investment employees make in their organizations.

Innovation: Innovation is the process of translating an idea or invention into a good or service that creates value or for which customers will pay.

Internet of Things (IoT): IoT is a physical object that connects to the Internet. It can be a fitness tracker, a thermostat, a lock or appliance – even a light bulb.

Strategic Drivers: Strategic drivers are forces that shape an organization's strategy.

Strategic Learning: Strategic learning can be seen as encompassing strategies for learning on the individual level, aiming at positively affecting the learner's autonomy.

Chapter 7
Does the Bargaining Power of Vertical Parties Improve or Worsen the Effect of Family Influence on Long-Term Performance?
A Socioemotional Wealth View

Rubén Martínez-Alonso
https://orcid.org/0000-0001-7389-762X
University of Almería, Spain

María J. Martínez-Romero
https://orcid.org/0000-0001-7891-1558
University of Almería, Spain

Julio Diéguez-Soto
https://orcid.org/0000-0001-5116-5604
University of Málaga, Spain

Alfonso A. Rojo-Ramírez
https://orcid.org/0000-0002-1295-7614
University of Almería, Spain

DOI: 10.4018/978-1-7998-4552-2.ch007

ABSTRACT

Grounding in the socioemotional wealth approach, this chapter explores the effect of family influence on long-term performance. Moreover, this study also examines the moderating role of the bargaining power of vertical parties, namely supplier (SBP) and customer (CBP) bargaining power, on the preceding relationship. By utilising a panel dataset of 3,118 observations of Spanish private manufacturing firms in the 2007–2016 period, the chapter finds that family influence negatively impacts long-term performance. The findings also reveal that CBP mitigates the negative effect of family influence on long-term performance. In this light, CBP is found to be a potential environmental factor that enables family influenced firms enhancing their long-term performance.

INTRODUCTION

In today's complex, rapidly changing and fiercely competitive environment, long-term performance has become a critical indicator of firm continuity and survival (Diéguez-Soto, Manzaneque, & Rojo-Ramírez, 2016b; Martínez-Alonso, Martínez-Romero, & Rojo-Ramírez, 2019). This is why, there is a vast previous literature focused on the influence of family influence on firm performance (Anderson & Reeb, 2003; O'Boyle, Pollack, & Rutherford, 2012; Villalonga & Amit, 2006, among others). However, the empirical findings obtained up to now regarding the interplay between family influence and firm performance have not been conclusive at all (e.g., Bertrand & Schoar, 2006; Gómez-Mejía, Cruz, Berrone, & De Castro, 2011), especially for private companies (Martínez-Romero, Martínez-Alonso, & Casado-Belmonte, 2020a; Sciascia & Mazzola, 2008). Consequently, the question of how and why family influence impacts on privately held firm performance is still largely unresolved and additional investigation is required (Sharma & Carney, 2012), providing a research avenue for contingent factors that might enlighten the former interplay (Chrisman, Chua, Pearson, & Barnett, 2012; Yeniaras, Sener, & Unver, 2017).

A possible contingent factor in the family influence-performance relationship might be the bargaining power of vertical parties (Porter, 1980). In this regard, bargaining power is usually defined as a function of the required costs to substitute a stakeholder (Porter, 1980). Thus, supplier (SBP) and customer (CBP) bargaining power may be relevant referent marks for family managers, as the particular aims and discretion of the latter might be significantly affected by the level of the former power (Kotlar, De Massis, Fang, & Frattini, 2014a; Urbinati, Franzo, De Massis, & Frattini, 2017). However, to the best of our knowledge, no studies have empirically examined the moderating role that SBP and CBP exert on the family influence–firm performance relationship.

Drawing on the socioemotional wealth (hereafter SEW) approach (Berrone, Cruz, & Gómez-Mejía, 2012; Gómez-Mejía, Haynes, Núñez-Nickel, Jacobson, & Moyano-Fuentes, 2007; Martínez-Romero & Rojo-Ramírez, 2016), we argue that, as family influenced firms pursue not only economic but also non-economic goals (Martin & Gómez-Mejía, 2016; Martínez-Alonso, Martínez-Romero, & Rojo-Ramírez, 2018), they will exert a negative effect on firm performance. That is, as family influenced firms tend to prioritize the fulfilment of affective needs over the achievement of purely financial goals (Martínez-Romero, 2018; Martínez-Romero & Rojo-Ramírez, 2017), they will detrimentally affect firm performance. Additionally, we argue that the bargaining power of vertical parties might be considered as a threat for the SEW endowment of family influenced firms, which may perceive that vertical parties might compromise their family wealth (De Massis, Kotlar, Mazzola, Minola, & Sciascia, 2018; Kotlar, Fang, De Massis, & Frattini, 2014b) and their survival in the long-term (Kotlar, De Massis, Frattini, & Kammerlander, 2020; Kotter, 1979), conditioning thus, their performance outcomes.

Therefore, and based on the aforementioned arguments, we intend to answer two questions in the present chapter. First, we revisit the question of how and why family influence impacts on firm performance in a context of private firms. Second, we examine when and to what extent SBP and CBP affect the decision-making processes in family influenced firms and drive changes in firm performance. To that end, we address the moderating influence of SBP and CBP in the family influence-firm performance relationship.

To test these hypotheses, we utilized a sample of 603 Spanish private manufacturing firms and used distinct econometric models, following a panel data structure from 2007 to 2016. Family influence is defined as a situation in which a family has a substantial ownership stake and managerial presence in the firm that enable the family to impact strategic actions (Chua, Chrisman, & Sharma, 1999). Long-term performance is measured by the mean of return on assets (ROA) (Rutherford, Kuratko, & Holt, 2008) in a 3-year period (t, t+1, and t+2) (Diéguez-Soto et al., 2016b).

This study makes at least three important contributions. First, we explore the interplay between family influence and long-term performance, providing a better understanding on this relationship, which has been scarcely analysed in prior literature. Second, we examine the moderating effect of SBP and CBP, which are both contingent variables that may enlighten the family influence-firm performance interplay. Third, this chapter analyses private firms, which are underrepresented in prior research despite being prevalent and playing a significant role in the economies worldwide.

This chapter presents the following structure: first, the theoretical background and hypotheses development are outlined; the research methods follow and thereafter results are displayed; finally, the chapter comes to an end with the discussion.

THEORETICAL BACKGROUND AND HYPOTHESES DEVELOPMENT

Family Influence and Long-Term Performance

Recent decades have witnessed a growing scholarly attention in analysing the performance of family influenced firms (Basco, 2013; Mazzi, 2011; Yeniaras et al., 2017) and whether the latter perform better than their non-family counterparts (Allouche, Amann, Jaussaud, & Kurashina, 2008; Carney, Van Essen, Gedajlovic, & Heugens, 2015; Kotey, 2005). This growing interest is not surprising, since family influenced firms constitute the backbone of most economies worldwide (La Porta, Lopez-De-Silanes, & Shleifer, 1999; Martínez-Alonso et al., 2019). However, despite numerous attempts by family firm researchers to examine how family characteristics affect firm performance (e.g., Kim & Gao, 2013; Zattoni, Gnan, & Huse, 2015), empirical evidence is still scarce regarding the impact of family influence on long-term performance.

Previous literature (e.g., Gómez-Mejía et al., 2007) argues that strategic decisions in family influenced firms are strongly conditioned upon family owners and managers' preferences and decisions, which are driven primarily by the desire of preserving the family's SEW (Chrisman & Patel, 2012; Gómez-Mejía, Makri, & Larraza-Kintana, 2010). SEW is defined as the set of non-financial aspects of the firm that meet the family's affective and social needs, including the ability to exercise family control and influence, fulfil desires of belonging, identity and intimacy, discharge familial obligations, preserve the family's social capital, sustain the emotional attachment of family members to the firm and renew family ties through dynastic succession (Berrone et al., 2012; Gómez-Mejía et al., 2007; Kotlar et al., 2014a). Up to now, SEW preservation has been widely recognized as the pivotal frame of reference for strategic decision-making in family influenced firms (Vandekerkhof, Steijvers, Hendriks, & Voordeckers, 2018; Zellweger, Nason, Nordqvist, & Brush, 2013). Because of this, family influenced firms tend to prioritize family goals over purely financial objectives (Chrisman & Patel, 2012; Gómez-Mejía et al., 2010), which may lead these firms toward the fulfilment of affective needs, rather than acting under effectiveness principles (Martínez-Romero, 2018; Martínez-Romero & Rojo-Ramírez, 2017). This particular behaviour is expected to affect family's strategic choices for achieving higher or lower levels of long-term performance (Sciascia,

Mazzola, & Kellermanns, 2014). In this regard, family influenced firms will adopt risky choices that preserve SEW even if they are supposed to reduce long-term performance, but they will also avoid risky decisions that may increase long-term performance to the detriment of SEW (Berrone, Cruz, Gómez-Mejía, & Larraza-Kintana, 2010; Chrisman & Patel, 2012).

For instance, family influenced firms are often reluctant to hire and delegate authority to external CEOs who may improve the innovative behaviour and professionalization of the firm (Cruz, Gómez-Mejía, & Becerra, 2010; Diéguez-Soto, Duréndez, García-Pérez-de-Lema, & Ruiz-Palomo, 2016a; Gómez-Mejía et al., 2014) in order to maintain family control. Furthermore, if nepotism is the accepted norm (Dyer, 2006), family members who may lack the talent, knowledge and skills to run a successful business may be placed in key management positions (Le Breton-Miller, Miller, & Lester, 2011; Miralles-Marcelo, Miralles-Quirós, & Lisboa, 2014), which may jeopardize long-term performance. Similarly, problems associated with self-control and altruism may adversely affect the quality of family managers and the recruitment of non-family managers (Gedajlovic, Lubatkin, & Schulze, 2004; Lubatkin, Schulze, Ling, & Dino, 2005), while increasing agency costs and the difficulty of monitoring long-term performance (Dyer, 2006; Schulze, Lubatkin, Dino, & Buchholtz, 2001). Family influenced firms may also avoid promising projects, risky investments in R&D, and potential collaborations with external stakeholders that can enhance long-term performance if they are perceived as a loss of control over the firm and a transfer of discretionary power over outsiders (Block, Miller, Jaskiewicz, & Spiegel, 2013; Diéguez-Soto, Manzaneque, González-García, & Galache-Laza, 2019; Pérez-González, 2006).

Moreover, SEW preservation may give rise to other negative aspects such as managerial entrenchment (Gómez-Mejía, Núñez-Nickel, & Gutierrez, 2001), dysfunctional relationships (Berrone et al., 2012), succession biases (Carney, 2005) and interpersonal conflicts (Sirmon, Arregle, Hitt, & Webb, 2008). Indeed, these aspects appear to be particularly acute in multigenerational family influenced firms, i.e., second generation and older firms (Sciascia et al., 2014). This is due to the lower quality of family relationships in later generations as a result of less intentional trust (Steier, 2001) and a wide diversity of goals, values, and commitments (Stockmans, Lybaert, & Voordeckers, 2010), which makes it challenging for a family to maintain a shared vision (Suess-Reyes, 2014), and thus may erode long-term performance.

Thereby, to preserve the family's SEW, family influenced firms might be willing to tolerate a higher risk of poor long-term performance (Berrone et al., 2010; Gómez-Mejía et al., 2007), since when SEW threatened, family's decisions might be driven on a non-economic rationality basis. This brings us to our first hypothesis:

H1: Family influence is negatively related to long-term performance.

The Moderating Role of the Bargaining Power of Vertical Parties

Although we hypothesized a negative impact of family influence on long-term performance, we argue that such impact might be weakened by the bargaining power of vertical parties.

The bargaining power of vertical parties is generally described as the ability to impose conditions on their transactions with other firms (Porter, 1980). These conditions can cover different aspects such as discounts, payment deferrals, quality requirements, delivery times, sales returns, complaints, etc. Specifically, this chapter focuses on analysing the bargaining power of two vertical parties commonly associated with firms, namely, SBP and CBP. While SBP refers to the cost of replacing a supplier, CBP relates to the cost of serving a customer (Porter, 1980). Prior research (e.g., Bruijl, 2018; Kotlar et al., 2014b; Porter, 1980) has indicated that the bargaining power of vertical parties is indirectly related to firm performance, since an increase in such power renders suppliers and customers to put pressure on prices or costs, leading to a decrease in the firms' ability to appropriate value and thus, may reduce the obtained outcomes. Accordingly, firms may see increased SBP and CBP as potential environmental threats that may negatively affect their long-term performance (Kotlar et al., 2014b; Porter, 1980).

In fact, these environmental threats seem to be even more pronounced in family influenced firms, which may perceive that their long-term financial welfare is compromised (De Massis et al., 2018; Kotlar et al., 2014b) and that their survival is at risk (Kotlar et al., 2020; Kotter, 1979). As previously mentioned, family influenced firms are guided not only by economic objectives, but also by family goals (Gómez-Mejía et al., 2007). The latter goals arise from the desire to meet the family's affective and social needs, that is, to preserve the SEW endowment of the family influenced firm. Although SEW preservation is usually the most important goal in family influenced firms (Gómez-Mejía et al., 2007; Gottardo & Moisello, 2015; Martin & Gómez-Mejía, 2016), economic objectives continue playing an important role in family decision-making, since economic success itself is a prerequisite for the accomplishment of family goals (Chrisman & Patel, 2012; Gottardo & Moisello, 2015; Martínez-Romero & Rojo-Ramírez, 2017). Hence, increased SBP and CBP may be perceived as more direct threats to family influenced firms compared to their non-family counterparts.

Managers of non-family influenced firms are assumed to perceive high SBP and CBP only as indirect antecedents of performance, since they tend to pursue purely financial goals and to be reluctant to address factors that are beyond their control (Pfeffer, 1972; Porter, 1980). On the contrary, family managers are likely to perceive such environmental concerns with greater intensity in their pursuit of control over decision-making (Kotlar et al., 2014b), which, as we have noted, is shaped by the interplay of economic and non-economic goals (Gómez-Mejía et al., 2007). In this respect, increased SBP and CBP may reduce family managers' freedom and authority to maintain control, exercise managerial discretion and make strategic decisions over time, since firms will have to satisfy higher demands from their vertical parties, will have reduced opportunities to negotiate volumes and prices, and will find it increasingly difficult to break the relationship (Kotter, 1979). As a result, resources that are critical to the firms' activities would be more difficult to acquire from alternative sources and the firm would have to respond to customer demands in a more careful way (Alves, Sousa, & Machado, 2020; Kotter, 1979; Pfeffer, 1972). Thus, these environmental threats may directly compromise the family's ability to exercise control over decision-making, which may also condition the achievement of superior long-term performance (Chrisman & Patel, 2012; Ferreira & Sousa, 2020; Martínez-Romero, Martínez-Alonso, Casado-Belmonte, & Diéguez-Soto, 2019). In this light, when dealing with high SBP and CBP, family influenced firms may be expected to take more risks in their strategic decision-making than their non-family counterparts, and therefore, respond more vigorously to these environmental threats. This is because family managers will feel the additional concern related to the fact that whether the firm fails, the SEW and the family itself will be severely damaged (Chrisman & Patel, 2012; Gómez-Mejía et al., 2010; Martínez-Alonso et al., 2018).

Nevertheless, prior literature (e.g., Staw, Sandelands, & Dutton, 1981) has pointed out that it is not easy for firms to respond effectively to environmental threats. In this vein, Sirmon et al. (2008) stated that family influenced firms, due to family influence in the firm, have some advantages over other businesses when it comes to responding to a threat. Sirmon and colleagues highlighted that family influenced firms are characterized by maintaining long-term strategies and goals as opposed to short-term inefficiencies, by having open communication channels and more organic structures that facilitate the implementation of firm strategies, as well as establishing extensive interactions among all its members (Chirico, Sirmon, Sciascia, & Mazzola, 2011; Patel & Fiet, 2011; Zellweger, Eddleston, & Kellermanns, 2010). These advantages associated to family influenced firms are particularly useful in reducing the rigidity linked to three general factors, i.e., information overload, centralized decision-making, and over-emphasis on efficiency, which inhibit effective responses to threats (Sirmon et al., 2008; Staw et al., 1981).

In view of the foregoing, we argue that high SBP and CBP may mitigate the negative effect of family influence on performance outcomes, inasmuch as it contributes to align economic and family goals (Gómez-Mejía, Patel, & Zellweger, 2018). Hence, we expect that family influenced firms dealing with increased SBP and CBP will have a less negative effect on long-term performance. Stated formally:

H2a: Greater SBP weakens the negative effect of family influence on long-term performance.
H2b: Greater CBP mitigates the negative effect of family influence on long-term performance.

Figure 1 summarizes the relationships investigated in this chapter.

Figure 1. Theoretical model
Source: Own elaboration

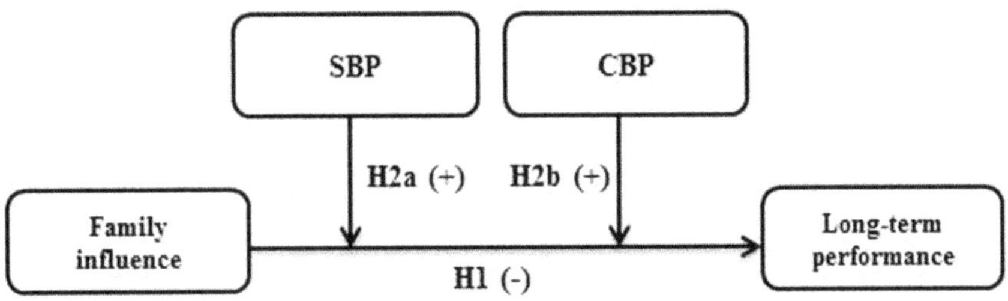

METHODOLOGY

Sample and Data

The data used to test our hypotheses are from the Spanish Business Strategies Survey (SBSS). This survey is conducted by the SEPI Foundation in cooperation with the Spanish Ministry of Industry. The SBSS has surveyed an average sample around 1,800-2,000 firms annually since 1990 by means of a questionnaire with 107 questions. The SBSS comprises a broad set of variables on Spanish firms operating in twenty manufacturing subindustries, covering significant information on firms' characteristics, activities, strategies, and stakeholders, among others. In particular, this dataset has been utilised by many scholars to explore management and performance issues in family influenced firms (e.g., Diéguez-Soto et al., 2016b; Kotlar et al., 2014a; Martínez-Alonso, Martínez-Romero, & Rojo-Ramírez, 2020).

The SBSS was developed with the aim of guaranteeing the representativeness of the Spanish manufacturing industry. The reference population of this survey is those firms with at least ten employees dedicated to one of the activities belonging to divisions 10 to 32 of the CNAE-2009, excluding division 19 (activities related to oil refinery and fuel processing). Firms within the SBSS are chosen through a combination of random sampling (firms from 10 to 200 employees) and census systems (firms of more than 200 employees). Since the sample is updated every year to incorporate nascent firms and to exclude those firms that disappear, the dataset is an unbalanced panel of firms. In total, the sample used in this chapter consists of a panel dataset of 3,118 firm-year observations corresponding to 603 Spanish private manufacturing firms for the period from 2007 to 2016.

An SBSS question allows identifying family influenced firms considering both family ownership and family management. Table 1 shows that 53.49% of the firms in the sample are family influenced firms, while the remaining 47.29% are non-family influenced firms. Table 1 also reports the distribution of firms by territorial subdivision and by industry. Summing up, slightly more than 50% of the sample firms are located in the east and the centre of Spain, and most of the firms in the sample operate in the metal products (13.14%) and foodstuffs and snuff (12.35%) subindustries.

Variables and Measures

Dependent Variable

In this chapter, firm performance is assessed by means of the ROA, defined as the earnings before interest and tax divided by total assets. ROA is a widely used measure of financial performance in family influenced firms, and is especially appropriate for manufacturing firms (Mazzi, 2011; Minichilli, Corbetta, & MacMillan, 2010; Schepers, Voordeckers, Steijvers, & Laveren, 2014). Therefore, based on the foregoing considerations, long-term performance is calculated as the average ROA over a three-year period (t, t+1, and t+2) (Diéguez-Soto et al., 2016b).

Independent Variable

As said, we consider that a family influences a firm when the family has both a substantial ownership stake and managerial presence in the firm in order to affect its strategic actions (Chua et al., 1999). Consequently, we use a binary measure of family influence that scores 1 whether there is a family with majority ownership in the firm and at least one member of that family actively participates in the top managerial team, and 0 otherwise (Kotlar et al., 2014b). Several studies (e.g., Cruz & Nordqvist, 2012; Diéguez-Soto, Garrido-Moreno, & Manzaneque, 2018; Sirmon et al., 2008) have adopted analogous measures of the influence of the family in the firm.

Table 1. Sample Description

Family vs. Non-Family Influenced Firms		
Family influenced firms	1,643	52.71%
Non-family influenced firms	1,475	47.29%
Total	3,118	100.00%
Territorial Subdivisions		
1. Northwest	381	12.22%
2. Northeastern	412	13.21%
3. Madrid	227	7.27%
4. Center	525	16.85%
5. East	1,097	35.19%
6. South	367	11.76%
7. Canarias	109	3.50%
Total	3,118	100.00%
Industry		
1. Meat industry	128	4.12%
2. Foodstuffs and snuff	385	12.35%
3. Drinks	95	3.03%
4. Textiles and clothing	174	5.57%
5. Leather and footwear	91	2.90%
6. Timber industry	93	2.99%
7. Paper Industry	129	4.14%
8. Graphics	126	4.03%
9. Chemical and pharmaceutical products	220	7.06%
10. Rubber and plastic	181	5.81%
11. Non-metallic mineral products	164	5.27%
12. Ferrous and non-ferrous metals	83	2.67%
13. Metal products	410	13.14%
14. Agricultural and industrial machinery	218	6.99%
15. Computer, electronic and optical products	52	1.66%
16. Electrical machinery and material	125	4.01%
17. Motor vehicles	172	5.53%
18. Other transport equipment	63	2.02%
19. Furniture industry	123	3.95%
20. Other manufacturing	86	2.77%
Total	3,118	100.00%

Source: Own elaboration

Moderating Variables

SBP and CBP are often conceptualised through two factors: the significance of the purchase/sale and the criticality of the products purchased/sold (Caniëls & Gelderman, 2007; Kotlar et al., 2014b; Porter, 1980). Nevertheless, this chapter only addresses the importance of the purchase/sale because the SBSS does not provide information on the criticality of those products, and thus, the two abovementioned factors cannot be used together to construct more precise measures of SBP and CBP. In this respect and following Nieto, Santamaria, and Fernandez (2015), SBP is calculated as the percentage of purchases that a firm make from its three major suppliers. In the same way, CBP is measured as the percentage of sales to the firm's three main customers. Concretely, scores near 100 denote that a firm has up to three suppliers/customers in total (high SBP and CBP), whereas scores near zero imply that a firm deals with a high number of suppliers/customers (low SBP and CBP) (Kotlar et al., 2014a).

Control Variables

Additionally, we include several one year lagged control variables to rule out alternative explanations. First, to control for organizational inertia (Kelly & Amburgey, 1991), we add *firm size* (i.e., total assets) and *firm age* (i.e., number of years since the firm's inception and the observation year). Moreover, because of the skewness of both firm size and age, a logarithmic transformation of these control variables is applied (Arzubiaga, Kotlar, De Massis, Maseda, & Iturralde, 2018). Second, we include *leverage*, calculated as the ratio of the firm's debt to total assets, with the aim of capturing the effect of financial resources on organizational outcomes (Diéguez-Soto et al., 2019), since firms with greater financial resources have more financial slack to achieve higher long-term performance. Third, as R&D is widely acknowledged to be a key determinant of long-term performance (Martínez-Alonso et al., 2019), we add *R&D intensity*, calculated as the ratio of the firm's R&D expenses over total sales. Following previous research (e.g., Artz, Norman, Hatfield, & Cardinal, 2010), we employ a two-year lagged expression of this variable. Fourth, to control for environmental factors, we include *competitor market power*, measured as the market share of the four main competitors in each of the firm's main market. Fifth, since disparities among subindustries may lead to different firm performance (Chang & Wang, 2007; Muñoz-Bullón & Sanchez-Bueno, 2011), we control for *industry effects*, by adding a group of twenty dummy variables representative of each subindustry (see Table 1 for a more detailed description). Finally, in order to control for *territorial specificities or context conditions* (Camagni & Capello, 2013), we include dummy variables depicting seven Spanish territorial subdivisions (Nomenclature des Unités Territoriales Statistiques, NUTS1) (see Table 1).

Analytical Method

The panel structure of the sample, i.e., repeated cross-sectional observations of firms over time, enables the utilisation of a panel data methodology. This estimation technique allows controlling for unobservable heterogeneity. Differences among firms may give rise to distinctive behaviours influencing strategic decision-making processes, which are not easily observable or measurable and thus, cannot be incorporated within a model. The employment of panel data makes it possible to control for this heterogeneity by capturing the first differences and therefore, eliminating the individual effect to avoid any bias in the results.

In particular, the models were estimated using random-effects GLS regression analysis. Although when using panel data designs, it is usual to discriminate between random- and fixed-effects models, applying, for instance, the Hausman test; the fact that some key control variables in our models, i.e., industry and territorial subdivisions dummies, do not change over time impede the choice of fixed-effects (Ashwin, Krishnan, & George, 2015; Diéguez-Soto & López-Delgado, 2019; González, Guzmán, Pombo, & Trujillo, 2013).

RESULTS

Table 2 reports the mean values, standard deviations, and correlations coefficients among the variables used in the models. Multicollinearity seems not to be a problem in our study. Every correlation coefficient is well below the 0.80 threshold above which multicollinearity hazards might arise (Gujarati & Porter, 2008). To further alleviate any remaining multicollinearity concerns, the moderating variables were centred around the mean before calculating the interaction terms (Aiken & West, 1991; Cohen, Cohen, West, & Aiken, 2003). We also found that individual values of the variance inflation factor and condition index did not exceed 1.16 and 1.56, respectively, remaining under the suggested thresholds (Hair, Black, Babin, & Anderson, 2010).

Table 3 presents the results of the random-effects GLS regression analysis. Model 1 includes the control variables. To test H1, the independent variable *family* influence is added in Model 2. The estimated coefficient representing the effect of *family influence* on *long-term performance* is negative and significant. Subsequently, to check the proposed moderating effects (H2a and H2b), we first introduced both moderators *SBP* and *CBP* in Model 3 and then, in sequential steps, the interaction effects *family influence x SBP* and *family influence x CBP* in Models 4 and 5, respectively. As can be seen in Model 3, the influence of both *SBP* and *CBP* on long-term performance was not statistically significant. Nevertheless, the direct effect of

Table 2. Descriptive and correlation matrix

Variable	Mean	SD	1	2	3	4	5	6	7	8	9
1. Long-term performance	.10	.12	1.00								
2. Firm size	16.08	2.11	-.03**	1.00							
3. Firm age	3.32	.60	-.03**	.13***	1.00						
4. Leverage	-.87	.64	.04***	.05***	-.12***	1.00					
5. R&D intensity	.01	.02	-.06***	.08***	.10***	.04***	1.00				
6. Competitor market power	20.71	28.84	.02	.04**	.06***	-.02	.06***	1.00			
7. Family influence	.53	.50	-.01	-.13***	-.10***	-.06***	-.10***	-.08***	1.00		
8. SBP	44.95	22.71	.01	-.06***	-.12***	-.04***	-.15***	-.06***	.05***	1.00	
9. CBP	44.21	27.83	.05***	-.01	-.09***	.01	-.02	-.07***	-.09***	.25***	1.00
Variance inflation factor				1.07	1.07	1.03	1.03	1.02	1.08	1.16	1.14
Condition index				1.10	1.17	1.24	1.27	1.31	1.40	1.41	1.55
Note. SD, standard deviation. * $p < 0.1$,** $p < 0.05$, *** $p < 0.01$.											

Source: Own elaboration

moderating variables is not relevant for testing moderation (Baron & Kenny, 1986); instead, when the moderator is not related to the dependent variable, it is easier to interpret the interaction term (Martínez-Alonso et al., 2020; Michiels, Voordeckers, Lybaert, & Steijvers, 2014). H2a and H2b postulate that *SBP* and *CBP* positively moderate the family influence-long-term performance relationship. On the one hand, H2a was not supported due to the interaction effect *family influence x SBP* was not statistically significant. On the other hand, H2b was supported because of CBP is found to mitigate the negative influence of *family influence* on *long-term performance*. Finally, a full model (Model 6) in which both interaction terms are introduced simultaneously, enables corroborating the obtained findings.

To provide a more nuanced picture of the moderating effect of CBP in the family influence-long-term performance relationship, the interaction effect is represented graphically in Figure 2. This figure shows that for high CBP values, firms with family influence perform better in the long-term than firms with no family influence; however, when the opposite effect occurs, i.e., low CBP values, firms with no family influence display greater long-term performance than firms with family influence.

Last, as an additional robustness test, we re-estimate Models 1-6 by utilising an alternative measurement of long-term performance, i.e., the mean ROA in a four-year period (t, t+1, t+2, and t+3) (Martínez-Alonso et al., 2019). The obtained results (Table 4) show that the direct impact of family influence on long-term performance (Model 8) and the interaction effect of family influence and CBP (Model 11) are less significant as compared to the main analysis (Table 3). Moreover, the interaction term of family influence and SBP remains non-significant (Model 10).

Table 3. Random-effects regressions results

	Model 1	**Model 2**	**Model 3**	**Model 4**	**Model 5**	**Model 6**
			Main effect			
Family influence (β_1)		-0.0100** (0.0058)	-0.0101** (0.0058)	-0.0098** (0.0058)	-0.0101** (0.0058)	-0.0102** (0.0058)
			Moderators			
SBP (β_2)			-0.0001 (0.0001)	-0.0001 (0.0002)	-0.0001 (0.0001)	-0.0001 (0.0002)
CBP (β_3)			0.0002 (0.0001)	0.0001 (0.0001)	-0.0002 (0.0001)	-0.0002 (0.0002)
			Moderating effects			
Family influence x SBP (β_{12})				0.0001 (0.0002)		-0.0001 (0.0002)
Family influence x CBP (β_{13})					0.0005*** (0.0002)	0.0005*** (0.0002)
			Controls			
Firm size	-0.0757 (0.0115)	-0.0966 (0.0115)	-0.1010 (0.0115)	-0.1020 (0.0116)	-0.0932 (0.0115)	-0.0914 (0.0115)
Firm age	-0.0227*** (0.0063)	-0.0232*** (0.0063)	-0.0234*** (0.0063)	-0.0234*** (0.0063)	-0.0242*** (0.0063)	-0.0242*** (0.0063)
Leverage	0.0053 (0.0041)	0.0050 (0.0041)	0.0051 (0.0041)	0.0051 (0.0041)	0.0054 (0.0041)	0.0054 (0.0041)
R&D intensity	-0.2563** (0.1104)	-0.2561** (0.1104)	-0.2590** (0.1106)	-0.2600** (0.1107)	-0.2574** (0.1104)	-0.2561** (0.1105)
Competitor market power	0.0001 (0.0001)	0.0001 (0.0001)	0.0001 (0.0001)	0.0001 (0.0001)	0.0001 (0.0001)	0.0001 (0.0001)
Territorial subdivisions	Included	Included	Included	Included	Included	Included
Industry dummies	Included	Included	Included	Included	Included	Included
Intercept	0.1785*** (0.0234)	0.1859*** (0.0238)	0.1892*** (0.0251)	0.1870*** (0.0239)	0.1907*** (0.0238)	0.1908*** (0.0238)
Number of observations	3,118	3,118	3,118	3,118	3,118	3,118
Number of firms	603	603	603	603	603	603
Wald chi^2	40.89***	43.80***	44.20***	44.30***	52.13***	52.30***
R^2: within	0.0155	0.0149	0.0145	0.0146	0.0152	0.0150
between	0.0201	0.0219	0.0235	0.0233	0.0303	0.0309
overall	0.0194	0.0227	0.0228	0.0227	0.0253	0.0256

Note. Dependent variable: long-term performance. Standard errors are indicated in parentheses. * $p < 0.1$, ** $p < 0.05$, *** $p < 0.01$.

Source: Own elaboration

Figure 2. Interaction: Family influence and CBP
Source: Own elaboration based on the two-way interactions' method of Dawson (2014)

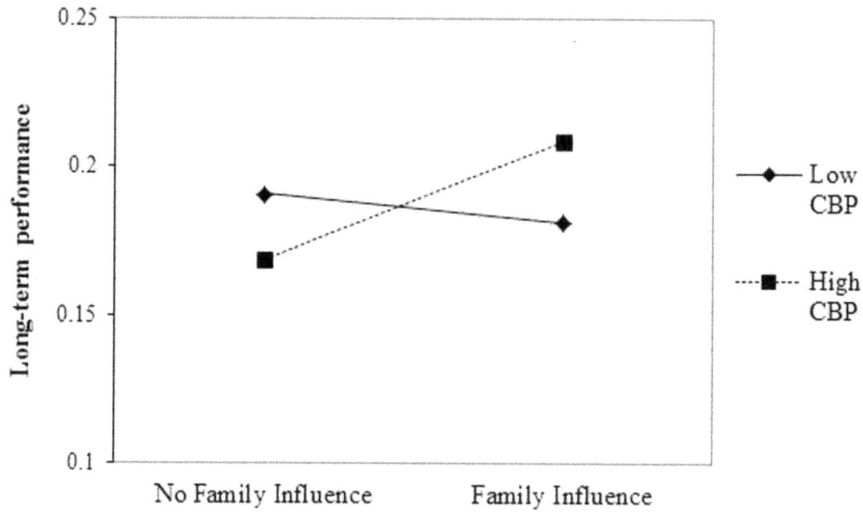

DISCUSSION

The present chapter analyses the relationship between family influence and firm performance, specifically long-term performance, in the context of private firms. Additionally, this study investigates two moderating factors, i.e., CBP and SBP, which might affect the abovementioned relationship. Based on the SEW approach (e.g., Gómez-Mejía et al., 2007), this chapter provides theoretical argumentation for the abovementioned relationships and subsequently, tests them empirically. The obtained results confirm what was previously hypothesized: family influenced firms exert a negative effect on long-term performance. Moreover, the findings reveal that the family influence-firm performance relationship is contingent upon the CBP. Finally, we were not able to find significant outcomes for the moderating effect of SBP in the interplay between family influence and firm performance.

Contributions

Our study makes several relevant contributions to literature. First, we offer a better comprehension of the direct effect of family influence on firm performance, which has shown controversial results in prior literature to date (Basco, 2013; O'Boyle et al., 2012; Yeniaras et al., 2017). In this regard, either positive (e.g., Allouche et al., 2008; Anderson & Reeb, 2003), negative (e.g., Bertrand & Schoar, 2006;

Table 4. Robustness test results

	Model 7	Model 8	Model 9	Model 10	Model 11	Model 12
Main effect						
Family influence (β_1)		-0.0093* (0.0055)	-0.0095* (0.0055)	-0.0094* (0.0055)	-0.0101** (0.0055)	-0.0102** (0.0056)
Moderators						
SBP (β_2)			0.0001 (0.0001)	0.0001 (0.0002)	-0.0001 (0.0001)	0.0001 (0.0002)
CBP (β_3)			0.0001 (0.0001)	0.0001 (0.0001)	-0.0002 (0.0001)	-0.0002 (0.0001)
Moderating effects						
Family influence x SBP (β_{12})				-0.0001 (0.0002)		-0.0002 (0.0002)
Family influence x CBP (β_{13})					0.0005*** (0.0002)	0.0005*** (0.0002)
Controls						
Firm size	-0.0372 (0.0111)	-0.0564 (0.0111)	-0.0571 (0.0112)	-0.0558 (0.0112)	-0.0514 (0.0112)	-0.0468 (0.0112)
Firm age	-0.0222*** (0.0064)	-0.0228*** (0.0064)	-0.0230*** (0.0064)	-0.0230*** (0.0064)	-0.0238*** (0.0064)	-0.0240*** (0.0064)
Leverage	0.0049 (0.0038)	0.0047 (0.0038)	0.0048 (0.0038)	0.0048 (0.0038)	0.0052 (0.0038)	0.0053 (0.0038)
R&D intensity	-0.1627* (0.1009)	-0.1605* (0.1009)	-0.1601* (0.1011)	-0.1593* (0.1012)	-0.1567* (0.1010)	-0.1539* (0.1010)
Competitor market power	0.0001 (0.0001)	0.0001 (0.0001)	0.0001 (0.0001)	0.0001 (0.0001)	0.0001 (0.0001)	0.0001 (0.0001)
Territorial subdivisions	Included	Included	Included	Included	Included	Included
Industry dummies	Included	Included	Included	Included	Included	Included
Intercept	0.1717*** (0.0236)	0.1792*** (0.0240)	0.1801*** (0.0241)	0.1806*** (0.0241)	0.1842*** (0.0241)	0.1849*** (0.0241)
Number of observations	2,771	2,771	2,771	2,771	2,771	2,771
Number of firms	603	603	603	603	603	603
Wald chi^2	42.17***	45.12***	45.28***	45.41***	53.29***	54.61***
R^2: within	0.0164	0.0152	0.0152	0.0151	0.0167	0.0167
between	0.0258	0.0292	0.0297	0.0299	0.0347	0.0359
overall	0.0240	0.0280	0.0280	0.0282	0.0316	0.0326

Note. Dependent variable: long-term performance. Standard errors are indicated in parentheses. * $p < 0.1$, ** $p < 0.05$, *** $p < 0.01$.

Source: Own elaboration

Gómez-Mejía et al., 2001) and even non-significant association (e.g., Sciascia & Mazzola, 2008), between family influence and firm performance has been found. The inconsistency in prior research has been attributed to different reasons, such as for example, the wide range of performance indicators (Anderson & Reeb, 2003; Dyer, 2006; Villalonga & Amit, 2006) and the obviated of the multifaceted nature of performance (Kim & Gao, 2013; Mazzi, 2011; Yeniaras et al., 2017). In an attempt to shed some light on the abovementioned mixing findings, we focus on a specific measure of performance, namely long-term performance, which has been theoretically analysed in different studies (e.g., Martínez-Alonso et al., 2018), but not empirically tested in many investigations (the studies of Diéguez-Soto et al. (2016b) and Martínez-Alonso et al. (2019) are notable exceptions). Thus, this article provides a better comprehension of whether family influence leads to generating better or worse long-term effects with regard to firm performance, emphasizing the long-term instead of the short-term perspective and findings.

Second, we go a step further in the family-performance relationship. That is, we go beyond the conceptual framework that examines the effect of family influence on long-term performance by introducing SBP and CBP as moderating variables in such relationship. In this vein, we answer the call of Chrisman et al. (2012), searching for moderating (and mediating) factors, which might help to unravel the intricate relationship between family influence and firm performance. Furthermore, we also answer the call of Zattoni et al. (2015) looking for studies that go beyond input-output models. Thereby, although prior research has analysed the direct effect of both SBP and CBP on firm performance, revealing a negative incidence of the bargaining power of vertical parties on firm economic and financial outcomes (e.g., Bruijl, 2018), the moderating effect of such bargaining power on the relationship between family influence and long-term peformance has not been previously explored. Thus, to the best of the authors' knowledge, this is the first study analysing the abovementioned relationships. In doing so, this chapter provides new insights to the current debate on performance dissimilarities between family influenced firms and their non-family counterparts. In this vein, the present chapter eases the understanding of why the findings concerning the impact of family influence on firm performance are conflicting yet (Stewart & Hitt, 2011). Likewise, by introducing the moderating effect of both CBP and SBP, this study addresses the question raised by Dyer (2006) regarding what type of family firm, in terms of its dependency to customers and/or suppliers, is able to generate greater firm performance.

Third, our chapter is focused on private firms, whose economic and financial data are normally difficult to gather, due to the inexistence of adequate databases (Sciascia et al., 2014). Because of the scarce longitudinal datasets for private firms, most prior research regarding the effect of family influence on firm performance has mainly focused on public firms, even though most firms worldwide are private firms (Basco, 2013; Mazzi, 2011; Sharma & Carney, 2012). Moreover, private and public firms may be based on distinct assumptions and governance mechanisms (Lubatkin et al., 2005). Although there exists some relevant research focused on the performance of private family and non-family firms (e.g., López-Delgado & Diéguez-Soto, 2015), there is still limited literature devoted to enlightening the performance issue on private firms (Sharma & Carney, 2012). Therefore, we also answer the call for further research on the continuous family firm performance debate (Martínez-Romero et al., 2020a).

Finally, but not less important, our study contributes to the literature on management by revealing that certain environmental factors, i.e., CBP, lead to differential results depending on the type of firm considered. In other words, the same stimuli is interpreted differently in family and non-family influenced firms, which contributes to our comprehension of the strategic behaviour of family influenced firms (Kotlar et al., 2014a). While for non-family influenced firms the reduction of customers' dependency has favourable effects on firm performance, for family-influenced firms happens just the opposite, the degree of concentration of the firm's major customers contributes to improve their firm performance. Thus, the family firms' networks with their customers are distinct in some way from those of non-family firms. Family firms usually have strong relationships with their customers and family firm' continuity priority makes more likely the establishment of long-term mutually beneficial stable relationships with customers than non-family influenced firm (Carney, 2005). However, stronger relationships with customers may result in a fragile situation for non-family firms if these partners own higher market power (Chrisman, Chua, & Kellermanns, 2009).

Implications for Practitioners

Our findings also have important implications for practitioners. First, to the extent the emotional endowment of family influenced firms has a detrimental effect on performance outcomes, firm advisors and consultants should notify family firm members about the negative consequences resulting from putting too much emphasis on non-economic goals to the detriment of economic objectives. Second, firm advisors and consultants should encourage family influenced firms to put emphasis on knowing their bargaining power with respect to that of vertical parties, particularly customers, inasmuch as family influenced firms could make the most of their bargaining power to achieve enhanced performance outcomes. In view of the results, family influenced firms should try to create trusting and long-standing relationships with their stakeholders (Berrone et al., 2012; Miller & Le-Breton-Miller, 2005).

Limitations and Future Research Avenues

Despite the relevance of the obtained findings, this chapter presents certain limitations that in turn, lead to novel avenues for future research. First, we have focused our analysis on the incidence of family influence on long-term performance, thus, making a distinction between family and non-family influenced firms (Carney et al., 2015; Kotey, 2005). However, current studies are highlighting the importance of distinguishing between different types of family influenced firms to deepen into family firm heterogeneity (Neubaum, Kammerlander, & Brigham, 2019; Rau, Sabine, Schneider-Siebke, & Gunther, 2019; Rojo-Ramírez & Martínez-Romero, 2018). Thus, future studies should analysed how different sources of family firm heterogeneity influence firm performance (Martínez-Romero, Martínez-Alonso, Rojo-Ramírez, & Diéguez-Soto, 2020b; Memili & Dibrell, 2019). Second, in line with prior research (e.g., Kotlar et al., 2014b), and due to the limitations of the ESEE database, our measures of SBP and CBP rely on only one dimension: the importance given to the three major suppliers/customers (Harrigan, 1983; Lustgarten, 1975). Yet, we were not able to evaluate the criticality of the goods purchased/sold (Porter, 1980). Consequently, a refinement of these measurements is likely to provide more robust and significant results. Third, we used a sample of Spanish private manufacturing firms to test our hypotheses, and thus, our findings could be affected by country-specific bias. Although it is true that globalization reduces differences across countries around the globe, future research may be developed to test whether our findings continue corroborating in other areas or not.

As concluding remarks, our findings reveal that family influence negatively impacts on long-term performance and that such relationship is weakened by CBP. These findings shed some light in the intricate family-performance relationship, by going beyond input-output models, through the inclusion of CBP as a contingent moderating factor.

REFERENCES

Aiken, L. S., & West, S. G. (1991). *Multiple regression: testing and interpreting interactions*. Sage Publications.

Allouche, J., Amann, B., Jaussaud, J., & Kurashina, T. (2008). The Impact of Family Control on the Performance and Financial Characteristics of Family Versus Nonfamily Businesses in Japan: A Matched-Pair Investigation. *Family Business Review*, *21*(4), 315–329. doi:10.1177/08944865080210040104

Alves, G. M., Sousa, B. M., & Machado, A. (2020). The Role of Digital Marketing and Online Relationship Quality in Social Tourism. In J. Santos & Ó. Silva (Eds.), *Digital Marketing Strategies for Tourism, Hospitality, and Airline Industries* (pp. 49–70). IGI Global. doi:10.4018/978-1-5225-9783-4.ch003

Anderson, R. C., & Reeb, D. M. (2003). Founding-family ownership and firm performance: Evidence from the S&P 500. *The Journal of Finance*, *58*(3), 1301–1329. doi:10.1111/1540-6261.00567

Artz, K. W., Norman, P. M., Hatfield, D. E., & Cardinal, L. B. (2010). A longitudinal study of the impact of R&D, patents, and product innovation on firm performance. *Journal of Product Innovation Management*, *27*(5), 725–740. doi:10.1111/j.1540-5885.2010.00747.x

Arzubiaga, U., Kotlar, J., De Massis, A., Maseda, A., & Iturralde, T. (2018). Entrepreneurial orientation and innovation in family SMEs: Unveiling the (actual) impact of the Board of Directors. *Journal of Business Venturing*, *33*(4), 455–469. doi:10.1016/j.jbusvent.2018.03.002

Ashwin, A. S., Krishnan, R. T., & George, R. (2015). Family firms in India: Family involvement, innovation and agency and stewardship behaviors. *Asia Pacific Journal of Management*, *32*(4), 869–900. doi:10.100710490-015-9440-1

Baron, R. M., & Kenny, D. A. (1986). The moderator–mediator variable distinction in social psychological research: Conceptual, strategic and statistical considerations. *Journal of Personality and Social Psychology*, *51*(6), 1173–1182. doi:10.1037/0022-3514.51.6.1173 PMID:3806354

Basco, R. (2013). The family's effect on family firm performance: A model testing the demographic and essence approaches. *Journal of Family Business Strategy*, *4*(1), 42–66. doi:10.1016/j.jfbs.2012.12.003

Berrone, P., Cruz, C., & Gómez-Mejía, L. R. (2012). Socioemotional Wealth in Family Firms: Theoretical Dimensions, Assessment Approaches, and Agenda for Future Research. *Family Business Review*, *25*(3), 258–279. doi:10.1177/0894486511435355

Berrone, P., Cruz, C., Gómez-Mejía, L. R., & Larraza-Kintana, M. (2010). Socioemotional Wealth and Corporate Responses to Institutional Pressures: Do Family-Controlled Firms Pollute Less? *Administrative Science Quarterly*, *55*(1), 82–113. doi:10.2189/asqu.2010.55.1.82

Bertrand, M., & Schoar, A. (2006). The role of family in family firms. *The Journal of Economic Perspectives*, *20*(2), 73–96. doi:10.1257/jep.20.2.73

Block, J. H., Miller, D., Jaskiewicz, P., & Spiegel, F. (2013). Economic and Technological Importance of Innovations in Large Family and Founder Firms: An Analysis of Patent Data. *Family Business Review, 26*(2), 180–199. doi:10.1177/0894486513477454

Bruijl, G. H. T. (2018). *The Relevance of Porter's Five Forces in Today's Innovative and Changing Business Environment.* Available online at SSRN: https://ssrn.com/abstract=3192207

Camagni, R., & Capello, R. (2013). Regional Innovation Patters and the EU Regional Policy Reform: Toward Smart Innovation Policies. *Growth and Change, 44*(2), 355–389. doi:10.1111/grow.12012

Caniëls, M. C. J., & Gelderman, C. J. (2007). Power and interdependence in buyer supplier relationships: A purchasing portfolio approach. *Industrial Marketing Management, 36*(2), 219–229. doi:10.1016/j.indmarman.2005.08.012

Carney, M. (2005). Corporate Governance and Competitive Advantage in Family-Controlled Firms. *Entrepreneurship Theory and Practice, 29*(3), 249–265. doi:10.1111/j.1540-6520.2005.00081.x

Carney, M., Van Essen, M., Gedajlovic, E. R., & Heugens, P. P. M. A. R. (2015). What do we know about private family firms? A meta-analytical review. *Entrepreneurship Theory and Practice, 39*(3), 513–544. doi:10.1111/etap.12054

Chang, S.-C., & Wang, C.-F. (2007). The effect of product diversification strategies on the relationship between international diversification and firm performance. *Journal of World Business, 42*(1), 61–79. doi:10.1016/j.jwb.2006.11.002

Chirico, F., Sirmon, D. G., Sciascia, S., & Mazzola, P. (2011). Resource orchestration in family firms: Investigating how entrepreneurial orientation, generational involvement, and participative strategy affect performance. *Strategic Entrepreneurship Journal, 5*(4), 307–326. doi:10.1002ej.121

Chrisman, J. J., Chua, J. H., & Kellermanns, F. (2009). Priorities, Resource Stocks, and Performance in Family and Nonfamily Firms. *Entrepreneurship Theory and Practice, 33*(3), 739–760. doi:10.1111/j.1540-6520.2009.00324.x

Chrisman, J. J., Chua, J. H., Pearson, A. W., & Barnett, T. (2012). Family Involvement, Family Influence, and Family-Centered Non-Economic Goals in Small Firms. *Entrepreneurship Theory and Practice, 36*(2), 267–293. doi:10.1111/j.1540-6520.2010.00407.x

Chrisman, J. J., & Patel, P. C. (2012). Variations in R&D investments of family and nonfamily firms: Behavioral agency and myopic loss aversion perspectives. *Academy of Management Journal*, *55*(4), 976–997. doi:10.5465/amj.2011.0211

Chua, J. H., Chrisman, J. J., & Sharma, P. (1999). Defining the family business by behavior. *Entrepreneurship Theory and Practice*, *23*(4), 19–39. doi:10.1177/104225879902300402

Cohen, J., Cohen, P., West, S. G., & Aiken, L. (2003). *Applied Multiple Regression / Correlation Analysis for the Behavioral Sciences* (3rd ed.). Lawrence Erlbaum Associates.

Cruz, C., & Nordqvist, M. (2012). Entrepreneurial orientation in family firms: A generational perspective. *Small Business Economics*, *38*(1), 33–49. doi:10.100711187-010-9265-8

Cruz, C. C., Gómez-Mejía, L. R., & Becerra, M. (2010). Perceptions of benevolence and the design of agency contracts: CEO-TMT relationships in family firms. *Academy of Management Journal*, *53*(1), 69–89. doi:10.5465/amj.2010.48036975

Dawson, J. F. (2014). Moderation in management research: What, why, when and how. *Journal of Business and Psychology*, *29*(1), 1–19. doi:10.100710869-013-9308-7

De Massis, A., Kotlar, J., Mazzola, P., Minola, T., & Sciascia, S. (2018). Conflicting Selves: Family Owners' Multiple Goals and Self-Control Agency Problems in Private Firms. *Entrepreneurship Theory and Practice*, *42*(3), 362–389. doi:10.1111/etap.12257

Diéguez-Soto, J., Duréndez, A., García-Pérez-de-Lema, D., & Ruiz-Palomo, D. (2016a). Technological, management, and persistent innovation in small and medium family firms: The influence of professionalism. *Canadian Journal of Administrative Sciences*, *33*(4), 332–346. doi:10.1002/cjas.1404

Diéguez-Soto, J., Garrido-Moreno, A., & Manzaneque, M. (2018). Unravelling the link between process innovation inputs and outputs: The moderating role of family management. *Journal of Family Business Strategy*, *9*(2), 114–127. doi:10.1016/j.jfbs.2017.11.007

Diéguez-Soto, J., & López-Delgado, P. (2019). Does Family and Lone Founder Involvement Lead to Similar Indebtedness? *Journal of Small Business Management*, *57*(4), 1531–1558. doi:10.1111/jsbm.12422

Diéguez-Soto, J., Manzaneque, M., González-García, V., & Galache-Laza, T. (2019). A study of the moderating influence of R&D intensity on the family management-firm performance relationship: Evidence from Spanish private manufacturing firms. *BRQ Business Research Quarterly*, *22*(2), 105–118. doi:10.1016/j.brq.2018.08.007

Diéguez-Soto, J., Manzaneque, M., & Rojo-Ramírez, A. A. (2016b). Technological Innovation Inputs, Outputs and Performance: The Moderating Role of Family Involvement in Management. *Family Business Review*, *29*(3), 327–346. doi:10.1177/0894486516646917

Dyer, W. G. (2006). Examining the "Family Effect" on Firm Performance. *Family Business Review*, *19*(4), 253–273. doi:10.1111/j.1741-6248.2006.00074.x

Ferreira, L., & Sousa, B. B. (2020). Understanding the Role of Social Networks in Consumer Behavior in Tourism. In C. Ramos, C. Almeida, & P. Fernandes (Eds.), *Handbook of Research on Social Media Applications for the Tourism and Hospitality Sector* (pp. 367–384). IGI Global. doi:10.4018/978-1-7998-1947-9.ch021

Gedajlovic, E., Lubatkin, M. H., & Schulze, W. S. (2004). Crossing the threshold from founder management to professional management: A governance perspective. *Journal of Management Studies*, *41*(5), 899–912. doi:10.1111/j.1467-6486.2004.00459.x

Gómez-Mejía, L. R., Campbell, J. T., Martin, G., Hoskisson, R. E., Makri, M., & Sirmon, D. G. (2014). Socioemotional Wealth as a Mixed Gamble: Revisiting Family Firm R&D Investments With the Behavioral Agency Model. *Entrepreneurship Theory and Practice*, *38*(6), 1351–1374.

Gómez-Mejía, L. R., Cruz, C., Berrone, P., & De Castro, J. (2011). The Bind that Ties: Socioemotional Wealth Preservation in Family Firms. *The Academy of Management Annals*, *5*(1), 653–707. doi:10.5465/19416520.2011.593320

Gómez-Mejía, L. R., Haynes, K. T., Núñez-Nickel, M., Jacobson, K. J. L., & Moyano-Fuentes, J. (2007). Socioemotional Wealth and Business Risks in Family-controlled Firms: Evidence from Spanish Olive Oil Mills. *Administrative Science Quarterly*, *52*(1), 106–137. doi:10.2189/asqu.52.1.106

Gómez-Mejía, L. R., Makri, M., & Larraza-Kintana, M. (2010). Diversification Decisions in Family-Controlled Firms. *Journal of Management Studies*, *47*(2), 223–252. doi:10.1111/j.1467-6486.2009.00889.x

Gómez-Mejía, L. R., Núñez-Nickel, M., & Gutierrez, I. (2001). The role of family ties in agency contracts. *Academy of Management Journal*, *44*(1), 81–95.

Gómez-Mejía, L. R., Patel, P. C., & Zellweger, T. M. (2018). In the Horns of the Dilemma: Socioemotional Wealth, Financial Wealth, and Acquisitions in Family Firms. *Journal of Management, 44*(4), 1369–1397. doi:10.1177/0149206315614375

González, M., Guzmán, A., Pombo, C., & Trujillo, M. A. (2013). Family firms and debt: Risk aversion versus risk of losing control. *Journal of Business Research, 66*(11), 2308–2320. doi:10.1016/j.jbusres.2012.03.014

Gottardo, P., & Moisello, A. M. (2015). The impact of socioemotional wealth on family firms' financial performance. *Problems and Perspectives in Management, 13*(1), 67–77.

Gujarati, D., & Porter, D. (2008). Basic econometrics (5th ed.). Boston: McGraw-Hill Education.

Hair, J. F., Black, B., Babin, B., & Anderson, R. E. (2010). *Multivariate data analysis* (6th ed.). Prentice Hall.

Harrigan, K. R. (1983). A Framework for Looking at Vertical Integration. *The Journal of Business Strategy, 3*(3), 30–37. doi:10.1108/eb038975

Kelly, D., & Amburgey, T. L. (1991). Organizational inertia and momentum: A dynamic model of strategic change. *Academy of Management Journal, 34*(3), 591–612.

Kim, Y., & Gao, F. Y. (2013). Does family involvement increase business performance? Family-longevity goals' moderating role in Chinese family firms. *Journal of Business Research, 66*(2), 265–274. doi:10.1016/j.jbusres.2012.08.018

Kotey, B. (2005). Are performance differences between family and non-family SMEs uniform across all firm sizes? *International Journal of Entrepreneurial Behaviour & Research, 11*(6), 394–421. doi:10.1108/13552550510625168

Kotlar, J., De Massis, A., Fang, H., & Frattini, F. (2014a). Strategic reference points in family firms. *Small Business Economics, 43*(3), 597–619. doi:10.100711187-014-9556-6

Kotlar, J., De Massis, A., Frattini, F., & Kammerlander, N. (2020). Motivation Gaps and Implementation Traps: The Paradoxical and Time-Varying Effects of Family Ownership on Firm Absorptive Capacity. *Journal of Product Innovation Management, 37*(1), 2–25. doi:10.1111/jpim.12503

Kotlar, J., Fang, H., De Massis, A., & Frattini, F. (2014b). Profitability Goals, Control Goals, and the R&D Investment Decisions of Family and Nonfamily Firms. *Journal of Product Innovation Management, 31*(6), 1128–1145. doi:10.1111/jpim.12165

Kotter, J. P. (1979). Managing External Dependence. *Academy of Management Review*, *4*(1), 87–92. doi:10.5465/amr.1979.4289188

La Porta, R., Lopez-De-Silanes, F., & Shleifer, A. (1999). Corporate Ownership Around the World. *The Journal of Finance*, *54*(2), 471–517. doi:10.1111/0022-1082.00115

Le Breton-Miller, I., Miller, D., & Lester, R. H. (2011). Stewardship or agency? A social embeddedness reconciliation of conduct and performance in public family businesses. *Organization Science*, *22*(3), 704–721. doi:10.1287/orsc.1100.0541

López-Delgado, P., & Diéguez-Soto, J. (2015). Lone founders, types of private family businesses and firm performance. *Journal of Family Business Strategy*, *6*(2), 73–85. doi:10.1016/j.jfbs.2014.11.001

Lubatkin, M. H., Schulze, W. S., Ling, Y., & Dino, R. N. (2005). The effects of parental altruism on the governance of family-managed firms. *Journal of Organizational Behavior*, *26*(3), 313–330. doi:10.1002/job.307

Lustgarten, S. H. (1975). The Impact of Buyer Concentration in Manufacturing Industries. *The Review of Economics and Statistics*, *57*(2), 125–132. doi:10.2307/1923993

Martin, G., & Gómez-Mejía, L. R. (2016). The relationship between socioemotional and financial wealth: Re-visiting family firm decision making. *Management Research: The Journal of the Iberoamerican Academy of Management*, *14*(3), 234–243. doi:10.1108/MRJIAM-02-2016-0638

Martínez-Alonso, R., Martínez-Romero, M. J., & Rojo-Ramírez, A. A. (2018). Technological innovation and Socioemotional wealth in family firm research: Literature review and proposal of a conceptual framework. *Management Research: The Journal of the Iberoamerican Academy of Management*, *16*(3), 270–301. doi:10.1108/MRJIAM-01-2018-0803

Martínez-Alonso, R., Martínez-Romero, M. J., & Rojo-Ramírez, A. A. (2019). Examining the Impact of Innovation Forms on Sustainable Economic Performance: The Influence of Family Management. *Sustainability*, *11*(21), 6132. doi:10.3390u11216132

Martínez-Alonso, R., Martínez-Romero, M. J., & Rojo-Ramírez, A. A. (2020). The impact of technological innovation efficiency on firm growth: The moderating role of family involvement in management. *European Journal of Innovation Management*, *23*(1), 134–155. doi:10.1108/EJIM-09-2018-0210

Martínez-Romero, M. J. (2018). *Financial performance and value creation in privately held family businesses: the influence of socioemotional wealth* (Doctoral thesis). Almería.

Martínez-Romero, M. J., Martínez-Alonso, R., & Casado-Belmonte, M. P. (2020a). The influence of socioemotional wealth on firm financial performance: Evidence from small and medium privately held family businesses. *International Journal of Entrepreneurship and Small Business, 40*(1), 7–31. doi:10.1504/IJESB.2020.106930

Martínez-Romero, M. J., Martínez-Alonso, R., Casado-Belmonte, M. P., & Diéguez-Soto, J. (2019) (Forthcoming). Family management and firm performance – The interaction effect of technological innovation efficiency. In *Intrapreneurship and Sustainable Human Capital: Digital Transformation through Dynamic Competences*. Springer.

Martínez-Romero, M. J., Martínez-Alonso, R., Rojo-Ramírez, A. A., & Diéguez-Soto, J. (2020b). Understanding Family Firm Profitability Heterogeneity. Differences Within Family Managed Firms and the Interaction Effect of Innovative Effort. In C. Camison & T. González-Cruz (Eds.), *Competitiveness, Organizational Management, and Governance in Family Firms* (pp. 305–329). IGI Global. doi:10.4018/978-1-7998-1655-3.ch013

Martínez-Romero, M. J., & Rojo-Ramírez, A. A. (2016). SEW: Looking for a definition and controversial issues. *European Journal of Family Business, 6*(1), 1–9. doi:10.1016/j.ejfb.2015.09.001

Martínez-Romero, M. J., & Rojo-Ramírez, A. A. (2017). Socioemotional wealth's implications in the calculus of the minimum rate of return required by family businesses' owners. *Review of Managerial Science, 11*(1), 95–118. doi:10.100711846-015-0181-9

Mazzi, C. (2011). Family business and financial performance: Current state of knowledge and future research challenges. *Journal of Family Business Strategy, 2*(3), 166–181. doi:10.1016/j.jfbs.2011.07.001

Memili, E., & Dibrell, C. (2019). *The Palgrave Handbook of Heterogeneity among Family Firms* (E. Memili & C. Dibrell, Eds.). doi:10.1007/978-3-319-77676-7

Michiels, A., Voordeckers, W., Lybaert, N., & Steijvers, T. (2014). Dividends and family governance practices in private family firms. *Small Business Economics, 44*(2), 299–314. doi:10.100711187-014-9594-0

Miller, D., & Le-Breton-Miller, I. (2005). *Managing for the Long Run: Lessons in Competitive Advantage from Great Family Businesses*. Harvard Business School Press.

Minichilli, A., Corbetta, G., & MacMillan, I. C. (2010). Top management teams in family-controlled companies: "Familiness", "faultlines", and their impact on financial performance. *Journal of Management Studies*, *47*(2), 205–222. doi:10.1111/j.1467-6486.2009.00888.x

Miralles-Marcelo, J. L., Miralles-Quirós, M. M., & Lisboa, I. (2014). The impact of family control on firm performance: Evidence from Portugal and Spain. *Journal of Family Business Strategy*, *5*(2), 156–168. doi:10.1016/j.jfbs.2014.03.002

Muñoz-Bullón, F., & Sanchez-Bueno, M. J. (2011). Is there new evidence to show that product and international diversification influence SMEs' performance? *EuroMed Journal of Business*, *6*(1), 63–76. doi:10.1108/14502191111130316

Neubaum, D. O., Kammerlander, N., & Brigham, K. H. (2019). Capturing Family Firm Heterogeneity: How Taxonomies and Typologies Can Help the Field Move Forward. *Family Business Review*, *32*(2), 106–130. doi:10.1177/0894486519848512

Nieto, M. J., Santamaria, L., & Fernandez, Z. (2015). Understanding the Innovation Behavior of Family Firms. *Journal of Small Business Management*, *53*(2), 382–399. doi:10.1111/jsbm.12075

O'Boyle, E. H., Pollack, J. M., & Rutherford, M. W. (2012). Exploring the relation between family involvement and firms' financial performance: A meta-analysis of main and moderator effects. *Journal of Business Venturing*, *27*(1), 1–18. doi:10.1016/j.jbusvent.2011.09.002

Patel, P. C., & Fiet, J. O. (2011). Knowledge combination and the potential advantages of family firms in searching for opportunities. *Entrepreneurship Theory and Practice*, *35*(6), 1179–1197. doi:10.1111/j.1540-6520.2011.00497.x

Pérez-González, F. (2006). Inherited control and firm performance. *The American Economic Review*, *96*(5), 1159–1588. doi:10.1257/aer.96.5.1559

Pfeffer, J. (1972). Interorganizational Influence and Managerial Attitudes. *Academy of Management Journal*, *15*(3), 317–330. doi: 10.2307/254856

Porter, M. E. (1980). *Competitive strategy*. Free Press.

Rau, S. B., Schneider-Siebke, V., & Gunther, C. (2019). Family Firm Values Explaining Family Firm Heterogeneity. *Family Business Review*, *32*(2), 195–215. doi:10.1177/0894486519846670

Rojo-Ramírez, A. A., & Martínez-Romero, M. J. (2018). Required and obtained equity returns in privately held businesses: The impact of family nature—evidence before and after the global economic crisis. *Review of Managerial Science*, *12*(3), 771–801. doi:10.100711846-017-0230-7

Rutherford, M. W., Kuratko, D. F., & Holt, D. T. (2008). Examining the Link and Performance: Can the F-PEC Untangle the Family Business Theory Jungle? *Entrepreneurial Theory and Practice*, *32*(6), 1089–1110. doi:10.1111/j.1540-6520.2008.00275.x

Schepers, J., Voordeckers, W., Steijvers, T., & Laveren, E. (2014). The entrepreneurial orientation–performance relationship in private family firms: The moderating role of socioemotional wealth. *Small Business Economics*, *43*(1), 39–55. doi:10.100711187-013-9533-5

Schulze, W. S., Lubatkin, M. H., Dino, R. N., & Buchholtz, A. K. (2001). Agency relationships in family firms: Theory and Evidence. *Organization Science*, *12*(2), 99–116. doi:10.1287/orsc.12.2.99.10114

Sciascia, S., & Mazzola, P. (2008). Family Involvement in Ownership and Management: Exploring Nonlinear Effects on Performance. *Family Business Review*, *21*(4), 331–345. doi:10.1177/08944865080210040105

Sciascia, S., Mazzola, P., & Kellermanns, F. W. (2014). Family management and profitability in private family-owned firms: Introducing generational stage and the socioemotional wealth perspective. *Journal of Family Business Strategy*, *5*(2), 131–137. doi:10.1016/j.jfbs.2014.03.001

Sharma, P., & Carney, M. (2012). Value Creation and Performance in Private Family Firms: Measurement and Methodological Issues. *Family Business Review*, *25*(3), 233–242. doi:10.1177/0894486512457295

Sirmon, D. G., Arregle, J.-L., Hitt, M., & Webb, J. W. (2008). The role of family influence in firms' strategic response to competitive threat of imitation. *Entrepreneurship Theory and Practice*, *32*(6), 979–998. doi:10.1111/j.1540-6520.2008.00267.x

Staw, B. M., Sandelands, L. E., & Dutton, J. E. (1981). Threat Rigidity Effects in Organizational Behavior: A Multilevel Analysis. *Administrative Science Quarterly*, *26*(4), 501–524. doi:10.2307/2392337

Steier, L. (2001). Family Firms, Plural Forms of Governance, and the Evolving Role of Trust. *Family Business Review*, *14*(4), 353–367. doi:10.1111/j.1741-6248.2001.00353.x

Stewart, A., & Hitt, M. A. (2012). Why Can't a Family Business Be More Like a Nonfamily Business?: Modes of Professionalization in Family Firms. *Family Business Review*, *25*(1), 58–86. doi:10.1177/0894486511421665

Stockmans, A., Lybaert, N., & Voordeckers, W. (2010). Socioemotional Wealth and Earnings Management in Private Family Firms. *Family Business Review*, *23*(3), 280–294. doi:10.1177/0894486510374457

Suess-Reyes, J. (2014). Family governance - Literature review and the development of a conceptual model. *Journal of Family Business Strategy*, *5*(2), 138–155. doi:10.1016/j.jfbs.2014.02.001

Urbinati, A., Franzo, S., De Massis, A., & Frattini. (2017). Innovation in Family Firms: A Review of Prior Studies and a Framework for Future Research. In A. Brem & E. Viardot (Eds.), *Revolution of Innovation Management* (pp. 213–246). London: Palgrave Macmillan. doi:10.1057/978-1-349-95123-9_8

Vandekerkhof, P., Steijvers, T., Hendriks, W., & Voordeckers, W. (2018). Socio-Emotional Wealth Separation and Decision-Making Quality in Family Firm TMTs: The Moderating Role of Psychological Safety. *Journal of Management Studies*, *55*(4), 648–676. doi:10.1111/joms.12277

Villalonga, B., & Amit, R. (2006). How do family ownership, control and management affect firm value? *Journal of Financial Economics*, *80*(2), 385–417. doi:10.1016/j.jfineco.2004.12.005

Yeniaras, V., Sener, P., & Unver, S. (2017). Is market learning the missing link between family involvement – firm performance relationship? A resource-based perspective. *The International Entrepreneurship and Management Journal*, *13*(2), 575–604. doi:10.100711365-016-0417-4

Zattoni, A., Gnan, L., & Huse, M. (2015). Does Family Involvement Influence Firm Performance? Exploring the Mediating Effects of Board Processes and Tasks. *Journal of Management*, *41*(4), 1214–1243. doi:10.1177/0149206312463936

Zellweger, T. M., Eddleston, K. A., & Kellermanns, F. W. (2010). Exploring the concept of familiness: Introducing family firm identity. *Journal of Family Business Strategy*, *1*(1), 54–63. doi:10.1016/j.jfbs.2009.12.003

Zellweger, T. M., Nason, R. S., Nordqvist, M., & Brush, C. G. (2013). Why do family firms strive for nonfinancial goals? An organizational identity perspective. *Entrepreneurship Theory and Practice*, *37*(2), 229–248. doi:10.1111/j.1540-6520.2011.00466.x

ADDITIONAL READING

IEF, & Red de Cátedras de Empresa Familiar. (2015). La Empresa Familiar en España (2015). Instituto de la Empresa Familiar. Barcelona, Spain.

IEF. (2018). *Red de Cátedras de Empresa Familiar*. Barcelona, Spain: Factores de Competitividad y Análisis Financiero en la Empresa Familiar. Instituto de la Empresa Familiar.

Iozzi, A., & Valletti, T. (2014). Vertical Bargaining and Countervailing Power. *American Economic Journal. Microeconomics*, *6*(3), 106–135. doi:10.1257/mic.6.3.106

Mazzola, P., Sciascia, S., & Kellermanns, F. W. (2013). Non-linear effects of family sources of power on performance. *Journal of Business Research*, *66*(4), 568–574. doi:10.1016/j.jbusres.2012.01.005

Mensching, H., Kraus, S., & Bouncken, R. B. (2014). Socioemotional wealth in family firm research - A literature review. *Journal of International Business and Economics*, *14*(4), 165–172. doi:10.18374/JIBE-14-4.11

Miller, D., Le Breton-Miller, I., Lester, R. H., & Cannella, A. Jr. (2007). Are family firms really superior performers? *Journal of Corporate Finance*, *13*(5), 829–858. doi:10.1016/j.jcorpfin.2007.03.004

Peneda de Oliveira, C., & Sousa, B. M. (2020). Green Consumer Behavior and Its Implications on Brand Marketing Strategy. In V. Naidoo & R. Verma (Eds.), *Green Marketing as a Positive Driver Toward Business Sustainability* (pp. 69–95). IGI Global. doi:10.4018/978-1-5225-9558-8.ch004

Sousa, B. B., & Magalhães, F. C. (2019). An Approach on Attachment in Public Marketing and Higher Education Management Contexts. In C. Machado & J. Davim (Eds.), *Higher Education and the Evolution of Management, Applied Sciences, and Engineering Curricula* (pp. 151–171). IGI Global. doi:10.4018/978-1-5225-7259-6.ch006

Zellweger, T. M. (2017). *Managing the Family Business. Theory and Practice.* Edward Elgar Publishing.

KEY TERMS AND DEFINITIONS

Customers: People or firms that buy goods or services from other firms.

Family Goals: Array of non-economic utilities that derive from the pursuit of family's SEW and that are likely to reflect the values, attitudes, and intentions of a business family in the firms' strategic decision-making.

Family Managers: Family members of a family influenced firm who hold managerial posts.

Family Owners: Family members of a family influenced firm who hold firm shares.

Long-Term Performance: Economic outcomes obtained in the long-term as a result of the interaction between firms' characteristics, actions and environment.

Strategic Decision-Making: The process of developing and implementing decisions that will influence the long-term welfare and survival of the firm.

Suppliers: Firms that provide goods and services that another person or organization needs.

Vertical Parties: Organisations that are in upstream or downstream positions in the supply chain relative to a firm.

Chapter 8
Business Performance Valuation and Value Creation

Maria Fernanda Matias
ESGHT, Universidade of Algarve, Portugal

Ana Isabel Martins
https://orcid.org/0000-0003-4768-3411
ESGHT, Universidade of Algarve, Portugal

Sandra Rebelo
ESGHT, Universidade of Algarve, Portugal

ABSTRACT

The globalization of the economy, the evolution of technology, and the increasing level of competition have imposed constant change to companies, namely on the continuous improvement of their functioning and organization, in the permanent updating of their products, and in the attitude towards the satisfaction of their customers. This pressure for change has led to the emergence of new approaches and management methods. One of these new approaches, called value management, is based on the concept of value, which translates a relationship between the satisfaction of a product or service and the resources necessary for its execution. This study presents the main tools for monitoring performance, highlighting the most expressive indicators of business performance. Before, however, brief reflection will be made on management oriented towards value creation.

DOI: 10.4018/978-1-7998-4552-2.ch008

INTRODUCTION

The globalization of the economy, the evolution of technology and the increasing level of competition have imposed constant changing to companies, namely on the continuous improvement of their functioning and organization, on the permanent updating of their products and on the attitude towards the satisfaction of their customers. This pressure for change has led to the emergence of new approaches and management methods. One of these new approaches, called Value Management, is based on the concept of value, which translates a relationship between the satisfaction of a product or service and the resources necessary for its execution.

The systems for evaluating and monitoring business performance are fundamental for the development of an efficient resource management that, in turn, will contribute to the pursuit of the company's strategic and operational objectives and to the creation of value. In recent decades, several systems with numerous specificities have emerged, with a more or less multidimensional character and, even, assuming the form of a performance index, particularly useful for comparing companies.

Despite the existing theoretical and empirical research on business performance, several authors (e.g. Choong, 2013; Lebas & Euske, 2011; Meyer, 2011; Neely, Gregory & Platts, 2005) advocate the need to study and rethink the meaning and way to measure performance. Neely *et al.* (2005) defined the performance valuation as the process of quantifying the efficiency and effectiveness of companies' actions, through metrics that capture the efficiency and/or effectiveness of those actions. Effectiveness refers to the level of success meeting customer needs, while efficiency corresponds to how company resources are used to meet customer needs. In this context, efficiency valuation approaches identify the misuse of resources in order to eliminate waste or optimize those resources for better results.

In this study, it is intended to present in a summary the main tools for monitoring and valuating performance, highlighting the most expressive indicators of business performance. Before, however, brief reflection will be made on management oriented towards value creation.

VALUE CREATION-ORIENTED MANAGEMENT

In the early eighties, few companies adopted the notion of shareholder value. The idea that the main responsibility of management is to add value gained great momentum and general acceptance only from 1986, when the book *Creating Shareholder Value* was published by Rappaport in the United States. Over the next ten years (nineties) market globalization, intensifying competition and the huge wave of privatizations promoted the notion of shareholder value as the main measure of performance around the world.

For long time, earnings were the main measure of performance of companies and managers. Indeed, even today, many of the evaluation models are based on earnings obtained and many of the evaluation parameters are defined based on net income, rate of income retention, dividend distribution rate, etc. Maximizing shareholder value is the politically correct attitude taken very often by managers. Shareholder value prevails in management reports, specialty magazines, and meetings of financial analysts, speeches and presentations.

With the development of value creation perspective, there was an increase in the use of cash flows in detriment of earnings. Rappaport (1998) identifies some of the most pressing gaps in earnings or incomes, since incomes are significantly dependent on accounting methods, do not reflect investment needs or the true value. The increase in net income does not necessarily imply an increase in economic value for shareholders. Shareholder value increases only when the rate of return on new investments is higher than the rate of return on alternative investments with similar risk. However, increases in income can be recorded even when investments provide lower return rates than the cost of capital, that is, when there is a loss of value.

It is therefore verified that traditional performance valuation measures based on accounting logic, such as the growth of earnings or sales, may not imply shareholder value creation. Given the existence of significant differences between cash flows and income, analysts assessed the need to reconcile analysis methodologies. In this context emerged the so-called new performance indicators such as Economic Value Added (EVA) or Market Value Added (MVA) (Young & O'Byrne, 2001).

EVA was created by financial advisor Stern Stewart & Co. in 1982, and is a measure for valuing the financial performance of a company that highlights the economic result created or added and which, in this way, is directly related to the value created for the shareholder. A company adds economic value when it can generate a higher income than the cost of its capital. EVA has been gaining increasing importance for companies as an indicator of performance and management valuation, as it highlights the capital invested and its costs and incomes obtained from its management.

The MVA was created by the Boston Consulting Group, and constitutes a cumulative measure of value, since it corresponds to the capitalized value (for the current moment) of EVA values.

From another perspective: MVA corresponds to the difference between invested capital (accounting value) and the market value of that investment.

According to Esperança and Matias (2005) in another perspective, the company can also create value by optimizing its capital structure, minimizing its cost of capital. Theoretical and empirical research on the capital structure, especially since the publication of Modigliani and Miller's work in 1958, have revealed that the issue relating to the existence of an optimal structure, and the factors that determine it, is not peaceful. The traditional approach to the capital structure advocates the existence of an optimal combination of equity and debt that minimizes the weighted average cost of capital (WACC) and therefore maximizes its market value.

According to a more financial approach (focused on net income), which assumes that (1) the costs of equity (k_e) and debt (k_d) are invariable with the level of indebtedness of the company, (2) $k_e > k_{d,}$ and (3) that the level of indebtedness is measured through the Debt/Equity ratio, the WACC decreases as the level of indebtedness increases, since the company finances itself with a higher proportion of capital with lower cost.

According to this approach, the company should maximize the level of indebtedness in order to bring the WACC closer to the cost of debt (k_d). Consequently, the company maximizes its market value when financing exclusively with debt.

Business reality reveals that this approach is unrealistic. First, because there are legal and functional reasons that promote the existence of equity in companies. Second, because it makes no sense to admit that the costs of equity and debt remain constant for any level of indebtedness. Higher levels of indebtedness are associated with higher levels of financial costs (even if k_d remains constant), which promotes increased financial risk and investors tend to reflect this increased risk in the required return.

According to a more economic approach (focused on operating income), which assumes that (1) the WACC and the cost of debt (k_d) are invariable with the level of indebtedness of the company, (2) $k_e > k_d$, and (3) that the cost of equity (k_e) grows linearly with indebtedness, the market value of the company is not affected by its capital structure because the increase in required return by shareholders is compensated by the use of a higher proportion of external capital (debt) with lower cost. In this way, it is not possible to determine an optimal capital structure.

The traditional perspective of the capital structure is then an intermediate position between the approaches of net income and operating income, arguing that the optimal capital structure of the company can be explained through the market reaction to his uses of external capital (Esperança & Matias, 2005).

Moreover, the concept of value is not consensual among the various stakeholders of the company. For example, for shareholders the value is associated to earnings, for customers to the level of satisfaction, for employees to motivation, well-being or participation in the company, for managers to efficiency, effectiveness or recognition, for the state to contributions in terms of employment and taxes and for creditors to the capacity to fulfill the commitments made.

However, there is some agreement on the fact that the value creation depends essentially on the ability of the company to present characteristics that differ itself from its competitors. A company must innovate and manage differences in terms of performance (on quality, costs, productivity, profits, etc.), adaptability (anticipating changes in its industry with the introduction of new technologies or production processes) and opportunity (by creating new businesses, new markets and/or new products).

There has been in recent years an evolution in the concept of value creation, which differs from that previously presented. In fact, this is an approach that records that the global capitalist system, we experience, is not meeting the needs of society, that social inequalities, at least in the most developed countries, have been accentuated, as well as environmental problems. People are aware that companies are managed according to maximizing the wealth of their owners and that they are not socially responsible.

This new view of management advocates a better adjustment between the objectives of companies and the interests of the various stakeholders, not restricted to shareholders. For example, according to Thomas (2005), the relevance that the West attributes to money and monetary values led to the creation of a production system that destroys nature and society. Porter and Kramer (2011) also reinforce the idea that citizens consider businesses to prosper based on the expense of the communities in which they are integrated.

The creation of shared value (CVC) conceives a new management model, according to which alignment and coherence between a new attitude of social environmental responsibility and the company's core business will contribute to increasing its results. Porter and Kramer (2011) do not advocate the existence of rivalry between businesses and citizens; on the contrary, companies are essential tools to meet the needs of the community. The concept of creating shared value, which is based on principles of competitiveness, provides for a new form of relationship between society and companies, that is, a capitalism of shared value, in which companies can create economic value, creating social value, leveraging their unique resources and competences. The authors define the concept of CVC as "*... policies and operating practices that enhance the competitiveness of a company while simultaneously advancing the economic and social conditions in the communities in which it operates*" (p.66).

CVC fills in the concepts developed by Michael Porter over time, namely the concept of value chain and clusters.

Michael Porter introduced, in the eighties of the 20th century, the value chain as an instrument for analyzing the fundamental skills to compete in the industry, from obtaining raw materials to the availability of the product to the consumer and to the after-sales relationship, in particular in the aspects where the company generates value (Porter, 1985). In other words, the company should know in depth the skills and resources available to it and which it should develop, i.e. the ones that are determinant to its performance. It argues that the company will gain competitiveness if its customers perceive the product, or service offered by the company, as having more value than the competition.

Conceived the value chain, Porter publishes in 1990 the book *The Competitive Advantage of Nations*, introducing the theory of clusters, whose theoretical bases date back to the 19th century, as a central element of industrial policy. The author presents the cluster as a new way of thinking about the economy, pointing out new attributions to companies, government entities and institutions, in order to improve competitiveness. The key elements of a cluster are companies producing goods or services, suppliers of specialized goods and services (components, machinery and technical support), financial support institutions and companies acting in related industries, and may include other organizations, including quality control agencies and universities. Porter argues that the competitiveness of a nation or region depends on the innovation capacity of industries. In turn, these will be productivity determinants of companies, suggesting that the competitive advantage is also obtained outside the company.

Porter and Kramer (2011) consider that companies have three ways to create shared value opportunities: redesign products and markets; redefining productivity in their value chain and activating the development of the local cluster and, claiming "*not all profit is equal. Profits involving a social purpose represent a higher form of capitalism, one that creates a positive cycle of company and community prosperity*" (p.75).

The CVC approach is more ambitious than that of stakeholders. The CVC argue that managers will be challenged to measure the company's performance by observing the value created from the perspective of stakeholders involved, not restricting themselves to purely economic performance measures, i.e., "*..., this perspective is about creating a higher level of well-being for the stakeholders involved in a system of value creation led by the firm*" (Harrison & Wicks, 2013, p. 98).

PERFORMANCE MONITORING INSTRUMENTS

Over times, several methods and/or tools [1] for evaluating the performance of companies have been developed. Ducq and Vallespir (2019a; 2019b) present the comparison over 60 models or approaches for measuring organizational performance systems and Tezza, Bornia and Vey (2010) compare 140 approaches. Resuming the most important, until the eighties performance was basically analyzed through economic and financial ratios or indicators such as profit, sales volume, sales profitability, per-employee sales, ROI (return on investment), ROA (return on assets) or ROE (return on equity), appreciated either in the simple way or through additive or multiplier models like Dupont or EVA (economic value added). For many authors these metrics were very limited, because they focused on the inner and past of companies, focusing essentially on organizations and processes (Tezza *et al.*, 2010; Chenhall & Langfield-Smith, 2007), not integrating or measuring all critical factors of corporate success.

Subsequently, the critics pointed out to financial metrics combined with changes in the business environment (Melnyk, Bititci, Platts, Tobias & Andersen, 2014), which led to the development of a more sophisticated set of tools, which combine financial and non-financial indicators. The following stand out: the Strategic Measurement and Reporting Technique (SMART Pyramid) from Cross and Lynch (1988); the Performance Measurement Matrix from Keegan, Eiler and Jones (1989); the Results-Determinants Framework from Fitzgerald, Johnston, Brignall, Silvestro and Voss (1991); the Balanced Scorecard (BSC) from Kaplan and Norton (1992); the Input-Process-Output-Outcome Framework from Brown (1996) and the Performance Prism (PP) from Neely and Adams (2001), for example.

These tools measure a company's performance multidimensionality, but do not offer a global performance index that allows to compare companies to each other. Multidimensionality is captured through multiple indicators, with the risk of dispersing the attention of managers and the loss of focus (Neves & Lourenço, 2009). Eventually, a summary measure of performance can be created, from a subjective weighted average of the evaluation of the various dimensions analyzed, as suggested by Kaplan and Norton (1992; 1996), within the scope of the BSC. This implies a priori attribution of subjective weights to the various variables analyzed in each of the performance evaluation methods, which has generated a lot of controversy and can skew comparisons between companies.

These limitations have motivated the use[2] of frontier methods that return a global performance index, the calculation of which requires the estimation of an efficiency frontier and the measurement of the deviation of each unit from it. Although in recent decades several performance evaluation methodologies have developed based on the concept of frontiers, Stochastic Frontier Analysis (SFA) and Data Envelopment Analysis (DEA) are the most used (Coelli, Rao, O'Donnell & Battese, 2005).

There are many models or approaches that allow the assessment of business performance. The main characteristics of the most popular management tools are presented briefly.

Economic and Financial Ratios or Indicators (Ratio Analysis)

The evaluation of business performance is based heavily on the definition of performance measures, on the vast majority consisting of ratios or indicators, and it is therefore considered relevant to reflect on some problematic issues associated with their use.

Indicators or ratios allow to assess various characterizing aspects of an enterprise at any given time and/or its evolution over several periods. They also allow the comparison of the values obtained for the company with those of other companies in the same industry and/or with the average values of the industry.

It is implicitly assumed, in this type of analysis, that the ratios used have the appropriate statistical properties, namely proportionality (the relationship between the numerator and the denominator is linear with constant equal to zero) and normality (the values under study have a normal distribution). However, a high number of studies reveal that non-proportionality and non-normality are the rule and not the exception, where the data constantly present high asymmetries and numerous extreme values, and the incorrect assumption of these properties promote serious implications for financial analysts and managers. For example, when there is no normality, both due to the existence of asymmetries or by the presence of extreme values, the average financial ratios of an industry should not be used as reference values for a company (Martins, 2001).

It is generally accepted that the ratios eliminate the influence of the dimension factor. However, there are many authors who dispute how often they are considered in financial analysis, without taking appropriate precautions regarding their limitations.

Authors such as Lev and Sunder (1979) and Whittington (1980) argue that the dimension factor is only circumvented in the presence of proportionality between components (numerator and denominator). In addition, while some authors, such as, Horrigan (1965) and Bird and McHugh (1977) argue that non-normality (i.e., the existence of asymmetries in the distributions of the ratios) is caused by non-proportionality, Trigueiros (1995; 1997) argues that the distributions of inverted symmetric ratios present marked asymmetries, so a direct relationship between non-proportionality and non-normality should not be established.

According to Lev and Sunder (1979), the main purpose of using ratios in financial information analysis is the control of the dimension factor. Considering y being the variable under study and x the variable that reflects the dimension factor (such as: assets, sales or number of employees, for example), the control of the dimension is only successful in the presence of perfect proportionality, that is, when:

$$y = \beta x$$

Lev and Sunder (1979:190)

With $x \neq 0$ and β constant. In this case, the analysis of the evolution of the ratio in time or the comparison between companies makes perfect sense, since the $y/x=\beta$ ratio simultaneously reflects the marginal effect and the average effect of x variations on the value of y.

By the way, according to McLeay (1986) the industry ratios can be presented according to two calculation methods:

1. Average value, where the ratio is calculated according to the simple arithmetic average of the ratios of each company, according to the expression:

$$\bar{r} = \frac{1}{n}\sum\left(y_i / x_i\right)$$

McLeay (1986:78)

2. Aggregate value, where the ratio is calculated with the aggregate numerator and denominator of the various companies under study, namely:

$$\bar{y} / \bar{x} = \sum y_i / \sum x_i = \frac{1}{n}\sum y_i / \frac{1}{n}\sum x_i$$

McLeay (1986:78)

Being that:

$$\bar{y} / \bar{x} = \bar{r} + \frac{\Sigma\left(y_i - \bar{r}x_i\right)}{\Sigma x_i}$$

McLeay (1986:79)

We can also verify that the differences between the values of $\bar{y} / \bar{x}$ and $\bar{r}$, depend on the covariance between the ratio and its denominator, since:

$$\frac{1}{n}\Sigma\left(r_i - \bar{r}\right)\left(x_i - \bar{x}\right) = \bar{y} - \bar{r}\,\bar{x}$$

McLeay (1986:90) and thus

$$\bar{y} / \bar{x} = \bar{r} + \frac{1}{\bar{x}}\operatorname{cov}(r, x)$$

McLeay (1986:90)

The values resulting from these two calculation methods will only be similar, subject to conditions of perfect proportionality between variables *y* and *x*.

As already mentioned above, the ratio analysis method promotes the need to compare the values of a company's ratios with certain reference ratios. Reference ratios are all values that serve as a comparison pattern in the analysis performed. The following three types are essentially identified: (1) from the company itself for previous periods for evolution analysis and/or predefined projections or objectives for performance analysis compared to the forecast; (2) of competing companies in order to identify the relative position of the company; (3) and the industry values in order to identify the relative position of the company.

Traditionally, the industry values are calculated based on the mean values of the industry, therefore, any extreme deviations in relation to these average values, can affect the future performance of companies, since, in these cases, decision-making elements warn of the need for convergence of their current ratios to the reference ratios. This type of convergence practice is often called "adjusting ratios".

The adjustment of ratios can be achieved by manipulating financial information, through accounting techniques and policies, such as the criterion of valuation of inventories, the depreciation and amortization method or by the valuation of fixed assets or through other management decisions in terms of investment, commercial, financing or distribution policies. It will be important to note that the divergences between the ratios or indicators of an enterprise and the benchmarks may not represent instability in relation to the average of its industry, but only reflect a strategic position of the company according to its objectives.

Indeed, the ratio analysis method has a significant set of limitations, which can be synthesized as follows:

- The lack of universal reference values causes a high subjectivity that affects the analysis.
- The ratios allow quantifying facts and detecting anomalies, but generally fail to explain satisfactorily the identified inaccuracies.
- The ratio analysis only makes sense when elaborated within the economic and social context in which the company belongs, making it very complex, or even impossible, to compare ratios between companies from different industries or countries.
- The information obtained through a ratio is minimal. The method assumes the study of the evolution of the same ratio in time and its interconnection with other ratios. For example, a high current ratio may represent a strong liquidity situation (good management) or an excess of cash funds, which do not generate income (poor management).

- Two identical values for the same ratio, obtained in different periods, or between different companies, may not reflect the same reality, as compensation may occur between their components.
- A ratio that presents a positive value (which may seem like a good situation) may conceal an unfavorable situation because it results from components with simultaneously negative signals, i.e. $-y/_{-x} \geq 0$;
- Ratios may be affected by one-off operations that coincide with exercise closures or seasonal variations.
- The definition of the average values of the industry, as a standard reference value for a company, will only be acceptable if the data complies with the statistical properties necessary, namely proportionality and normality.
- The possibility of calculating numerous ratios causes the need to select a more limited set of ratios that allows an analysis in which: a) the information lost by limiting the number of ratios used is minimized (for this, it is necessary that the final set of selected ratios maintain most of the variance observed in the original set of ratios considered); and b) the redundant information between the selected ratios is minimized (for this, it is necessary that the final set of selected ratios presents the lowest correlation between them and the absence of multicollinearity).

The evaluation of business performance is carried out through Key Performance Indicators (KPI). A KPI is a measurable value that demonstrates the degree of achievement of business objectives, that is, effectiveness. Companies define KPI in several areas to value their success in terms of overall performance or by departments such as sales, marketing, human resources, and technicians, among others. Although the vast majority of economic and financial KPI are ratios and indicators, KPI can be of financial or non-financial nature and can be expressed in terms of monetary units (€), relative (%), time units (years, months, days, hours), count (number) or indexes (levels of satisfaction, quality, productivity, occupation, etc.). Given the specificity of certain businesses, there are KPI traditionally associated with certain activities or industries in addition to those considered general and common to any business. Some examples are presented in Table 1.

Table 1. Examples of KPI

Economic and Financial	**Hospitality and Tourism**
Current ratio	Average occupancy rate
Equity ratio	Total available rooms
Inventory turnover	Average daily rate
Return on equity	Revenue per available room (RevPar)
Return on investment	Marketing cost per booking
Banking	Website conversion rate
Solvency	**Environment**
Financial margin	Water consumption
Business margin	Water recycling rate
Public Health	Energy consumption
Crude birth rate	Energy saving rate
Child mortality rate	Eco-efficiency of solid waste
Life expectancy	Hazardous waste rate
Regular smokers	**Construction**
Alcohol consumption	Changes to the project index
Communications	Concluded tasks
Telephone line penetration rate	Rework index
Internet traffic	Impact on the environment
High-speed internet coverage	Construction process wastes
Number of dial-up	Cost predictability

Source: the authors

SMART Pyramid

The Strategic Measurement Analysis and Report Technique (SMART) Pyramid, conceived in 1988 by Cross and Lynch, arises from the dissatisfaction of industrial managers towards traditional financial performance measures. According to Cross and Lynch (1988), industrial managers considered that they did not hold the information needed to make important business decisions. In this sense, the authors sought to create a system that would guide and define success through key indicators, linking the strategy to the operational centers.

The SMART Pyramid performance measurement system integrates strategic objectives and operational performance dimensions into a pyramid-shaped structure with four levels, according to Figure 1.

Figure 1. SMART Pyramid
Source: Cross & Lynch (1988) apud Neely et al. (2007, p.146)

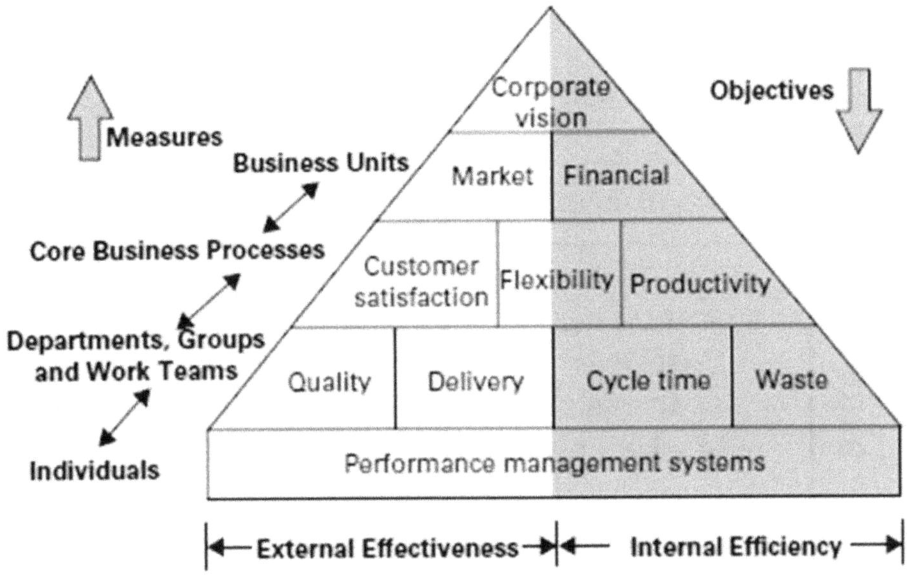

The top of the pyramid corresponds to the first level. In this is presented the strategic vision of the organization. In the second level, the objectives of each business unit are indicated in terms of market and financial results. In the third level, the operating systems of each business unit are defined and specified measures such as customer satisfaction, flexibility of operations and productivity of employees. Finally, at the base of the pyramid, the fourth level presents the evaluation indicators of operations centers regarding to quality, delivery of products to customers, time and cost of manufacture. The right side of the pyramid reflects internal efficiency measures, while the left side reflects external measures of effectiveness.

The authors expect that the pyramid form confers the notion of flowing measures where the measures related to operations centers reflect the corporate view, as well as the objectives of internal and external business units. This implies a communication of objectives in downward direction of the pyramid and the communication of performance indicators in ascending direction.

Performance Measure Matrix (PMM)

Believing that performance measures trigger management actions, Keegan *et al.* (1989) developed a performance measurement system with matrix shape called performance measure matrix (PMM). This presumes that performance measures derive from the strategy and from a multidimensional environment, vertically and horizontally integrated, in a complete understanding between relationships and spending behaviors, as Figure 2.

Figure 2. Performance Measure Matrix
Source: Keegan et al. (1989) apud Neely et al. (2007:145)

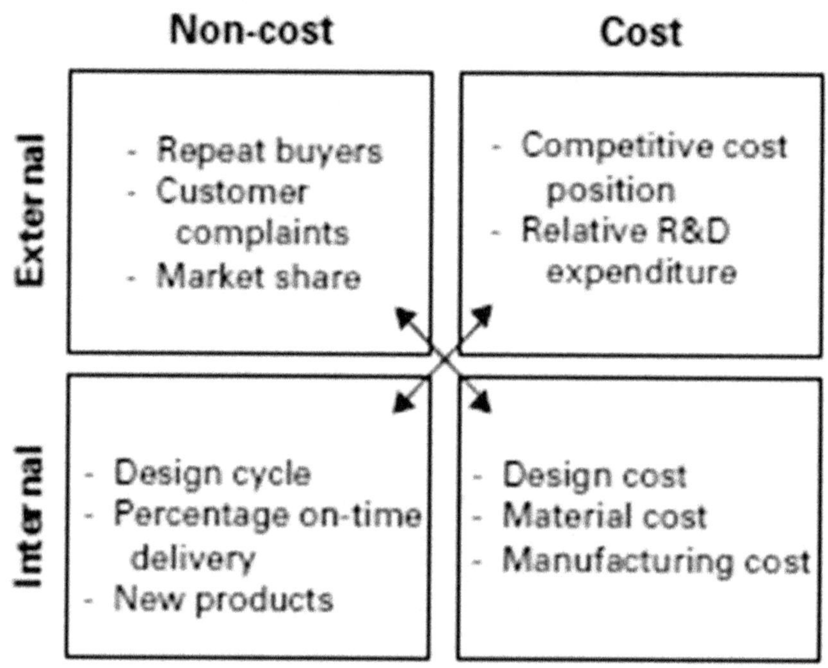

PMM is considered a simple system that focuses not only on results but also on its determinants. It analyzes, in an integrated way, four different categories of performance measures, combining financial and non-financial perspectives, with internal and external perspectives, thus showing a more balanced performance measurement system than the traditional ones.

Neely *et al.* (2007) consider this model more comprehensive and flexible, which allows accommodating all possible performance measures of an organization, as well as identifying omissions or aspects that need greater attention to increase the organization performance.

The Results-Determinants Framework (RTF)

After analyzing the performance of services industry, Fitzgerald *et al.* (1991) developed a performance measurement system based on results (competitiveness and financial performance) and its determinants (quality, flexibility, resources used and innovation), as shown in Table 2, called the Results-Determinants Framework (RTF).

This system explicitly exploits the relationship of casualty between results and their determinants. The results stem from past business performance from specific determinants, whose indicators will serve as a control and basis for identifying key performance factors to change and to improve future performance.

Table 2. Results-Determinants Framework

	Dimension of Performance	Type of Measure
RESULTS Lagging Indicators	**Competitiveness**	Relative market share and position
		Sales growth
		Measures of the customer base
	Financial performance	Profitability
		Liquidity
		Capital structure
		Market ratios
DETERMINANTS Leading Indicators	**Quality of service**	Reliability responsiveness
		Aesthetics/appearance
		Cleanliness/tidiness
		Comfort
		Friendliness
		Communication
		Courtesy
		Competence
		Access
		Availability
		Security
	Flexibility	Volume flexibility
		Delivery speed flexibility
		Specification flexibility
	Resource utilization	Productivity
		Efficiency
	Innovation	Performance of the innovation process
		Performance of the individual innovations

Source: Adapted from Fitzgerald et al. (1991, p.8)

However, RTF system does not include the performance dimensions for customers and human resources, so it does not allow a truly balanced view of performance.

Balanced Scorecard (BSC)

The Balanced Scorecard (BSC) integrates traditional business performance management and monitoring systems, functioning as an integrated management system, connecting the various areas and processes of the company.

Created in 1992 by Robert Kaplan and David Norton as a result of a study on organizational performance valuation systems, BSC was first presented in *The Balanced Scorecard – Measures that Drive Performance*, causing a strong impact on strategic management worldwide.

BSC can be understood as a tool or methodology that translates the mission and vision of companies into a comprehensive set of performance measures, which serves, at the same time, as the basis to a measurement and strategic management system. BSC enables managers to identify critical activities that allow creating value for all stakeholders of the company (Kaplan & Norton, 1996).

Its main objective is to provide, at all levels of management, a global and integrated view of organizational performance from four value perspectives, as shown in Figure 3.

Figure 3. Balanced Scorecard
Source: Kaplan & Norton (1996, p. 9)

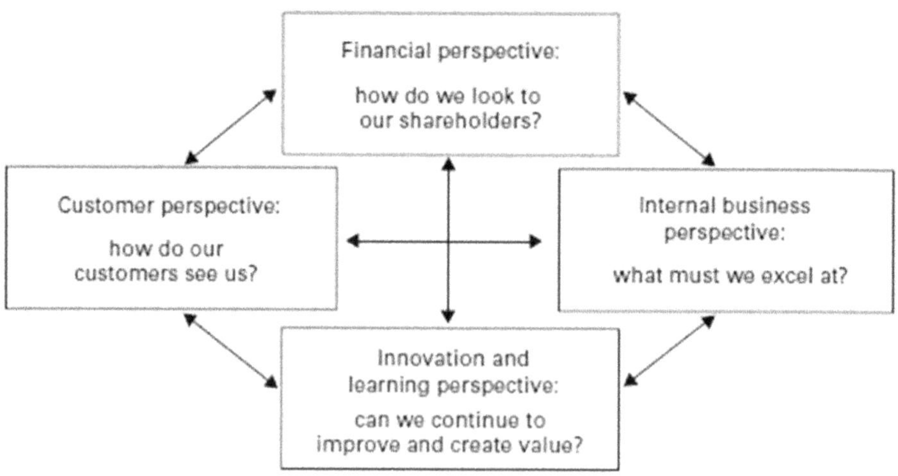

- **Financial:** evaluates the company's performance in terms of profitability and return on invested capital.
- **Customer:** evaluates the company's performance regarding the consolidation of its relationship with customers, in order to ensure the achievement of financial objectives in the long term, in a sustained form.
- **Internal Business:** evaluates the company's performance in terms of how it organizes its processes and executes its activities, ensuring the efficiency and effectiveness with which it meets the customers and financial objectives.
- **Innovation and Learning:** evaluates the company's performance in terms of its ability to create conditions for sustained long-term growth and to obtain necessary skills to achieve its strategic objectives.

The BSC explores the cause-effect relationship between these four perspectives and their objectives and allows to define, according to the company's strategy, objectives, critical factors, performance indicators and actions to be developed, for each of them.

The evaluation of business performance through BSC is carried out by KPI previously selected by the managers involved in the process. Given the existence of numerous ratios or indicators, it is necessary to pre-select KPI consistently with the strategy outlined and to allow an evaluation of the degree of achievement of the objectives defined by the company. Its authors advise the use of a maximum of 25 KPI, of financial and non-financial nature, otherwise the company cannot concentrate efforts on a too wide range of objectives.

The KPI in BSC context can be grouped according to critical factors within each of the four value perspectives. The most common critical factors are as follows:

- Profitability (which can group the following KPI: return on equity, return on sales, earnings per share, etc.).
- Growth (market share, sales growth rate, turnover, etc.).
- Value creation (EVA, MVA, etc.).
- Satisfaction (levels of customer or employee satisfaction, number of awards and incentives, meeting deadlines, etc.).
- Loyalty (number of repeat buyers, sales to regular customers, etc.).
- Efficiency (lead times, productivity, equipment usage levels, etc.).
- Quality (number of defective products, number of complaints, quality levels, etc.).
- Innovation (number of new ideas or new products, etc.).
- Technology (investment in new technologies, number of computerized jobs, etc.).

- Qualification (employee qualification levels, investment in training, number of training hours per employee, etc.).

The Input-Process-Output-Outcome Framework

The input-process-output-outcome framework, also called the Macro Process Model, was designed by Brown (1996) focusing on the company's main process and on the assumption that each stage of the business process is inducing the performance of the next stage.

According to Figure 4, Brown's model (1996) divides the operational process into five sequential stages: inputs, processing system, outputs, outcomes and goals and identifies measurement indicators for each stage.

The sequence of stages demonstrates how inputs affect the performance of processing systems, which in turn influence outputs, then results and, ultimately, defined objectives, assuming a linear relationship between each part.

Figure 4. Input-Process-Output-Outcome Framework
Source: Brown (1996) apud Neely et al. (2007, p. 147)

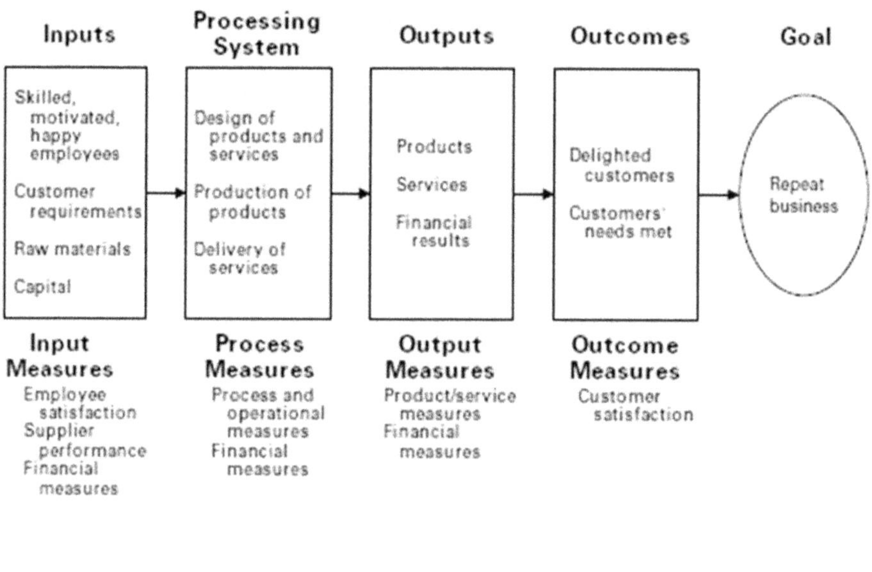

Neely *et al.* (2007) consider that one of the strengths of this model corresponds to the differentiation between output and outcome indicators, which has gathered great reception in the public sector.

Performance Prism (PP)

In response to performance analysis models based on one or two stakeholders (shareholders and customers), Neely and Adams (2001) present an integrated performance evaluation tool, focused on creating value for various stakeholders (investors, customers, workers, suppliers, regulatory entities and communities) and not focused on strategy, called Performance Prism (PP).

Neely and Adams (2001) consider that the strategy should derive from the analysis of stakeholders and that there is a reciprocal interest relationship between organizations and their stakeholders, as stated in Figure 5.

Figure 5. Performance Prism: relationship of interests
Source: Neely and Adams (2001, p. 13)

Stakeholder Satisfaction (Stakeholder wants & needs)		Stakeholders		Stakeholder Contribution (Organization wants & needs)
• Fast, Right, Cheap & Easy	←	• Custumers & Intermediaries	→	• Trust, Unity, Profit & Growth
• Purpose, Care, Skills & Pay	←	• Employees	→	• Hands, Hearts, Minds & Voices
• Trust, Unity, Profit & Growth	←	• Suppliers	→	• Fast, Right, Cheap & Easy
• Legal, Fair, Safe & True	←	• Regulators & Communities	→	• Rules, Reason, Clarity & Advice
• Return, Reward, Figures & Faith	←	• Investors	→	• Capital, Credit, Risk & Support

The PP considered by Neely, Adams and Crowe (2001) as second-generation performance tool, serves essentially to assist in the selection of performance measures and analyzes performance multidimensionality, from five perspectives, in which each of them corresponds to one of the faces of a prism, as shown in Figure 6.

Each face of the prism questions a fundamental aspect of the organization, which allows managers to analyze the challenges in managing organizational performance. The questions posed by the authors on each face of the prism are as follows:

- **Stakeholder satisfaction:** who are the key stakeholders and what do they want and need?

Figure 6. Performance Prism: 5 perspectives
Source: Neely, Kennerley & Adams (2007, p. 155)

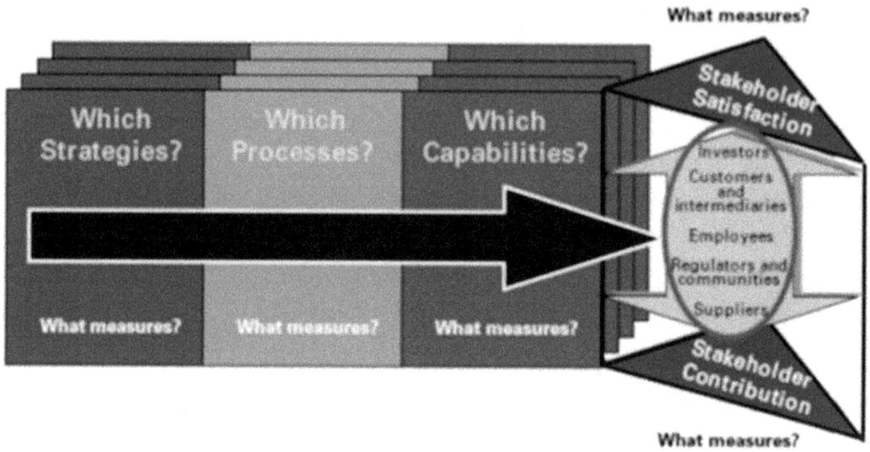

- **Strategies:** what strategies do we have to put in place to satisfy the wants and needs of these key stakeholders?
- **Processes:** what are the critical processes required to carry out these strategies?
- **Capabilities:** what capabilities do we need to operate and enhance these processes?
- **Stakeholder contribution:** what contributions do we require from our stakeholders if we are to maintain and develop these capabilities?

The answer to these questions allows us to understand the determinants of value creation for the organization, that is, the factors that create value for their stakeholders, and in turn, those that will guide organizational practices to undertake by managers. Thus, in the authors' opinion, it is a tool that allows to provide a balanced image of the business, which highlights external (stakeholders) and internal measures (strategy, process and capacity) and allows the use of financial and non-financial measures, as well as measures of efficiency or effectiveness of the organization.

Frontier Methods

Frontier methods are based on the concept of production frontier for calculating a relative efficiency index that allows comparison between various units (organizations). Based on the inputs and outputs of each unit, a production function is established, and an efficiency frontier is built, consisting of the units considered efficient. These serve as benchmarks to less efficient units. After plotting the efficient frontier, each unit's current performance is compared with its benchmarks, resulting in an efficiency index for each unit ranging from 0 to 1 (equivalent to 0 and 100%). The units considered efficient have an index of 1 while units considered non-efficient have a lower index.

Thus, frontier methods, in addition to evaluating the performance of each organization, are also a benchmarking technique, which allows the detection of management failures and support for improvement decisions.

In recent decades, multiple methodologies of estimation of frontier efficiency have been developed, and can be classified into two large groups: parametric and non-parametric: the parametric approach has as main characteristic the imposition of a functional form on technology to explain the levels of efficiency of companies; the non-parametric approach does not establish an initial production function. Through linear programming techniques, the non-parametric methodology determines a frontier of efficiency from the companies of best practice, and non-efficient companies are situated below the border. The non-parametric approach assumes that there are no random errors in the sample, attributing all residuals from the estimation process to inefficiency. These methods, inspired by Farrell's work (1957), analyze the relative efficiency of organizations with regard to the transformation of multiple inputs into outputs. Among the parametric methods, the most used is the Stochastic Frontier Analysis (SFA), while in non-parametric stands out the Data Envelopment Analysis (DEA) (Coelli *et al.*, 2005).

Stochastic Frontiers: Stochastic Frontier Analysis (SFA)

Introduced by Aigner, Lovell and Schmidt (1977) and Meeusen and van den Broeck (1977), in independent papers, SFA is a parametric method of efficiency analysis that requires the prior definition of the functional form of the production function, i.e. the specification and estimation of an equation representing the process of transformation of resources (inputs) into goods or services (outputs). Thus, the SFA allows the measurement of the error that may be due to both statistical noise factors, including uncertainty or unfavorable or favorable events, not controlled by the organization, as well as the inefficiencies of the organization, which result from factors controlled by managers. These components allow to control the presence of exogenous factors to the productive system.

The SFA is based on the micro-economic concept of the production function, which represents as much output as possible for a certain amount of inputs.

Coelli *et al.* (2005) points out as a disadvantage to this method the dependence on the definition of a production function and the fact that it requires the estimation of the statistical distribution of the error, which can strongly influence the results, besides implying complex calculations.

Data Envelopment Analysis (DEA)

Developed by Charnes, Cooper and Rhodes (1978), DEA is a multifactorial non-parametric linear programming methodology that analyzes, based on the observed performance, the relative efficiency of independent units (companies, agencies, departments, etc.) named Decision Making Units (DMU). Based on the inputs (resources) and outputs (results) of each unit, establishes an empirical production function and using linear programming builds an efficiency frontier, consisting of units considered efficient. The units considered efficient are the ones that present best practices, that is, those that present the best combination of inputs and outputs and serve as benchmarks to less efficient units.

Based on their benchmarks, units considered inefficient can reduce their level of inefficiency. In the input perspective, by verifying the level of resources that can be reduced by maintaining the level of results (input orientation), or in the perspective of outputs, valuating the level of results that can be increased maintaining the level of resources used (output orientation) (Coelli *et al.*, 2005).

DEA methodology essentially presents two standard approaches: (1) the CCR Model – created by Charnes, Cooper and Rhodes (1978), which allows an objective valuation of overall efficiency, identifying the sources and estimating amounts of identified inefficiencies, conceiving a global productivity measure, known as productive efficiency index. This model is based on constant returns to scale; (2) the BCC Model – developed by Banker, Charnes and Cooper (1984), which assumes that the units evaluated present variable returns to scale, distinguishes between technical and scale efficiency, estimates pure technical efficiency, for a given scale of operations, and identifies whether increasing, decreasing and constant returns to scale are present for future exploration. From this model results a measure of technical efficiency. For each of these approaches there are numerous variants, depending on the restrictions considered (Banker, Janakiraman & Natarajan, 2004a; Banker, Cooper, Seiford, Thrall & Zhu, 2004b).

In this context, the concept of global technical efficiency (GTE) can be decomposed into two components: pure technical efficiency (PTE) and scale efficiency (S), then:

$$GTE = PTE \times S$$

The pure technical efficiency index reflects the (under)utilization or waste of resources and the scale efficiency index reflects the possibility of the DMU has (or not) adopted the optimal production scale, i.e. the presence (or not) of constant returns to scale.

The efficiency index obtained by the CCR model (to which the condition of constant returns to scale is imposed) represents the overall technical efficiency, which measures the inefficiencies associated to the relationship between inputs and outputs, as well as the scale of operations. The efficiency index obtained by the BCC model represents only pure technical efficiency (Thanassoulis, 2003).

The scale efficiency index (S) is calculated based on the previous indexes, i.e. S=GTE/PTE. Regardless of the model used, it is known that GTE £ PTE. In order to analyze the type of return to scale of each DMU, the indexes GTE, PTE and S are calculated, and when:

GTE = 1: DMU is global and technically efficient. In this case PTE=S=1, which represents that the DMU used inputs in the appropriate proportions (PTE=1) and operated on an efficient production scale (S=1), that is, according to constant returns to scale.

GTE < 1: DMU is global and technically inefficient. Inefficiencies can derive from technical inefficiencies (PTE) or scale (S). It should be noted that when GTE=PTE ð S=1, the frontiers estimated by the two models match in the presence of constant returns to scale. When S < 1, the DMU is considered to be inefficient in terms of scale. In this case, in order to ascertain the type of scale (increasing or decreasing), DMU is evaluated relatively to a non-increasing return to scale frontier (more restrictive than that produced by the BCC model). Considering N the efficiency index for this frontier, when:

N = PTE: DMU operates on decreasing returns to scale. The frontiers produced by BCC models and non-increasing returns to scale match and correspond to the most restrictive frontier, i.e. the latter.

N ≠ PTE: DMU operates on increasing returns to scale. The frontiers produced by BCC models and non-increasing returns to scale do not match, a situation recorded with inefficient observations only when increasing returns to scale occur.

In short:

Constant returns to scale: GTE = PTE
Increasing returns to scale: GTE < PTE and N ≠ PTE
Decreasing returns to scale: GTE < PTE and N = PTE

Coelli *et al.* (2005) point out as the main advantage, the fact that DEA is a flexible, easy-to-use and computationally simple methodology given the possibility of: a) the use of multiple inputs and outputs, even if they have different units of measure; b) be implemented without knowing the algebraic form of the relationship between outputs and inputs, that is, it is possible to estimate a production frontier without knowing the nature of the outputs and inputs function; c) do not require the specification of weights for inputs and outputs a priori, since they are calculated in the model for each DMU, in order to maximize their efficiency index.

An efficiency index of 100% is expected to reflect a unit of good practices that serves as a reference and determines the objective values to the remaining DMU (considered inefficient). Thus, it is important to analyze the context in which such classification is obtained. To understand better the ranking results produced by the general models (CCR and BCC), it is possible to complement the analysis using several extensions of DEA models, such as super-efficiency models, inverted frontier or compound index, for example. Boussofiane, Dyson and Thanassoulis (1991), Adler, Friedman and Sinuany-Stern (2002), Meza and Lins (2002) and Leta, Mello, Gomes and Meza (2005) present, among others, these methods as a way of promoting discrimination in DEA models.

Tezza *et al.* (2010) present a comparison of numerous models or approaches about its scope, type, focus, level of measurement and degree of complexity. Table 3 presents a similar comparison of presented models included in this study.

Table 3. Comparison of presented models or approaches

Model or Approach	Classification Criteria				
	Scope	Type	Focus	Measure	Complexity
Ratio Analysis	CO	PR	FI, NF	ST, TA, OP	MD
SMART Pyramid	CO	PR	FI, NF	ST, TA, OP	MD
Performance Measure Matrix	CO	TE	FI, NF	ST	LW
The Results-Determinants Framework	SE	PR	FI, NF	ST, TA	MD
Balanced Scorecard	CO	TE	FI, NF	ST	HI
The Input-Process-Output-Outcome Framework	CO	TE	FI, NF	ST, TA	MD
Performance Prism (PP)	CO	TE	FI, NF	ST	HI
Frontier Methods	CO	PR	FI, NF	ST, TA, OP	HI

Source: Adapted from Tezza et al. (2010)

Considering:

Scope
CO: corporate approach which comprise general structure issues of the company (strategies, internal relationships with customers and suppliers, project organizations, information processing, etc.) and production and labor organization; SE: suitable to services industry.

Type
TE: purely theoretical studies, classified as theoretical-conceptual; PR: practical studies that validate some concepts and are classified as experimental, evaluation research (survey), case study or action research.

Focus
FI: financial; NF: non-financial (related to quality, innovation, response time, productivity and flexibility).

Level of Measurement
ST: strategic level focused on the future, which evaluate the strategies underlying the business and allied to the achievement of macro objectives in the long term; TA: tactical level focused on monitoring variations in operational performance, measuring groups of individuals or processes and related to administrative controls and decisions about control operations; OP: operational level focused on actions that result in an immediate response, feedback and routine measures.

Degree of Complexity
LW: low; MD: medium; HI: high.

CONCLUSION

Market globalization, which has promoted increased competition, growing sophistication in the offer of products and services and exponential technological development, has greatly contributed to the unquiet environment experienced in recent years in the business world. The global (economic and financial) crises experienced in recent years have forced companies to fight for survival, in a highly competitive environment, demanding from these differentiation policies on diversification, innovation and modernization of their distribution network, products, work processes, structures or organizational image. The liberalization of markets in several economies has broken down the most significant barrier to the entry of new competitors and internationalization, increasing the level of competition, increasing the competitive pressure for reducing margins and increasing efficiency and creating value, in order to maintain market shares. Value Management is currently an essential factor for the survival of companies, and its permanent performance monitoring and control is essential. More than ever.

The review presented shows that the context in which business performance measurement is developed is changing, as well as the approaches used for its evaluation, which try to overcome the limitations of the more traditional approaches, focused essentially on accounting indicators or financial results.

Several authors encourage the use of models of performance and efficiency evaluation based on multiple factors, given the complexity of the business reality. In recent years, is seen the evolution of the focus and scope of the models, which abandoned the traditional focus (accounting or financial) and incorporated approaches with a broader vision, focused on the individual, out of organizations and for their stakeholders. In fact, the degree of complexity of the models accompanied the increased complexity of organizations.

The performance of production units is often evaluated through indicators of productive efficiency. The general concept of efficiency is related to how resources are used in the production process. Technical efficiency is related to the evaluation of observed combinations of inputs and outputs, compared to the best possible technological alternatives. Technical efficiency essentially reflects the efficiency of the production process in converting resources into results. It is considered that a company has technical efficiency if, from a given set of resources and existing technology, it can produce as much as possible result (or if for a certain level of result and based on the available technology, it can produce it with as few resources as possible).

Frontier methodologies have been strongly used in recent years, as they allow the obtaining of a global efficiency index by estimating an efficiency frontier and calculating deviations from each company or unit in relation to this frontier. Operating on the frontier line means operating with the optimal combination of existing resources. The evaluation of the distance between the current position of each company in relation to the frontier represents its indicator of (in)efficiency.

Approaches such as the Balanced Scorecard and the Performance Pyramid are two excellent examples of performance measurement models focused on business strategy. These models combine the strategic planning process in performance evaluation, incorporating the definition of goals, performance objectives and identification of the most appropriate strategies.

The environment in which companies and other organizations develop is currently very dynamic and requires a permanent adjustment of business strategies. The permanent change in business strategies requires a permanent adaptation of performance measures. There is therefore a need for flexibility in performance measurement systems, resulting in the permanent adaptation of existing models or creativity for the creation of new models that fit the dynamics of the current market and the challenges facing businesses and other organizations.

REFERENCES

Adler, N., Friedman, L., & Sinuany-Stern, Z. (2002). Review of ranking methods in the Data Envelopment Analysis context. *European Journal of Operational Research, 140*(2), 249–265. doi:10.1016/S0377-2217(02)00068-1

Aigner, D., Lovell, C. A. K., & Schmidt, P. (1977). Formulation and estimation of stochastic frontier production function models. *Journal of Econometrics, 6*(1), 21–37. doi:10.1016/0304-4076(77)90052-5

Banker, R., Charnes, A., & Cooper, W. (1984). Some models for estimating technical and scale inefficiencies in data envelopment analysis. *Management Science, 30*(9), 1078–1098. doi:10.1287/mnsc.30.9.1078

Banker, R., Cooper, W., Seiford, L., Thrall, R., & Zhu, J. (2004b). Returns to scale in different DEA models. *European Journal of Operational Research, 154*(2), 345–362. doi:10.1016/S0377-2217(03)00174-7

Banker, R., Janakiraman, S., & Natarajan, R. (2004a). Analysis of trends in technical and allocative efficiency: An application to Texas public school districts. *European Journal of Operational Research, 154*(2), 477–491. doi:10.1016/S0377-2217(03)00183-8

Bird, R., & McHugh, A. (1977). Financial ratios – an empirical study. *Journal of Business Finance & Accounting, 4*(1), 29–45. doi:10.1111/j.1468-5957.1977.tb00159.x

Boussofiane, A., Dyson, R., & Thanassoulis, E. (1991). Applied Data Envelopment Analysis. *European Journal of Operational Research, 52*(1), 1–15. doi:10.1016/0377-2217(91)90331-O

Braz, R. G. F., Scavarda, L. F., & Martins, R. A. (2011). Reviewing and improving performance measurement systems: An action research. *International Journal of Production Economics, 133*(2), 751–760. doi:10.1016/j.ijpe.2011.06.003

Brown, M. G. (1996). *Keeping Score: Using the Right Metrics to Drive World-Class Performance*. Productivity Press Inc.

Charnes, A., Cooper, W. W., & Rhodes, E. (1978). Measuring the efficiency of decision-making units. *European Journal of Operational Research, 2*(6), 429–444. doi:10.1016/0377-2217(78)90138-8

Chenhall, R. H., & Langfield-Smith, K. (2007). Multiple perspectives of performance measures. *European Management Journal, 25*(4), 266–282. doi:10.1016/j.emj.2007.06.001

Choong, K. (2013). Has this large number of performance measurement publications contributed to its better understanding? A systematic review for research and applications. *International Journal of Production Research*, 1–24.

Coelli, T. J., Rao, D. S. P., O'Donnell, C. J., & Battese, G. E. (2005). *An Introduction to Efficiency and Productivity Analysis* (2nd ed.). Springer.

Cross, K. F., & Lynch, R. L. (1988). The SMART way to define and sustain success. *National Productivity Review, 9*(1), 23–33. doi:10.1002/npr.4040080105

Ducq, Y. M. S. R., & Vallespir, B. (2019a). A state of the art and comparison of approaches for performance measurement systems definition and design. *International Journal of Production Research, 57*(15-16), 5026–5046. doi:10.1080/00207543.2018.1506178

Ducq, Y. M. S. R., & Vallespir, B. (2019b). General enterprise performance measurement architecture. *International Journal of Production Research*. Advance online publication. doi:10.1080/00207543.2019.1692158

Esperança, P., & Matias, F. (2005). *Finanças Empresariais*. Publicações Dom Quixote.

Farrell, M. J. (1957). The measurement of productive efficiency. *Journal of the Royal Statistical Society. Series A (General), 120*(3), 253–290. doi:10.2307/2343100

Fitzgerald, L., Johnston, R., Brignall, S., Silvestro, R., & Voss, C. (1991). *Performance Measurement in Service Business*. CIMA.

Harrison, J. & Wicks, A. (2013). Stakeholder theory, value and firm performance. *Business Ethics Quarterly, 23*(1).

Horrigan, J. (1965). Some empirical bases of financial ratio analysis. *The Accounting Review*, 558–568.

Kaplan, R., & Norton, D. (1992). The balanced scorecard-measures that drive performance. *Harvard Business Review, 70*(1), 71–79. PMID:10119714

Kaplan, R., & Norton, D. (1996). *The balanced scorecard: Translating strategy into action*. Harvard Business Review Press.

Keegan, D. P., Eiler, R. G. & Jones, C. (1989, June). Are your performance measures obsolete? *Management Accounting*, 45-50.

Lebas, M., & Euske, K. (2011). A conceptual and operational delineation of performance. In A. Neely (Ed.), *Business performance measurement - Unifying theories and integrating practice* (2nd ed., pp. 125–139). Cambridge University Press.

Leta, F., Mello, J., Gomes, E., & Meza, L. (2005). Métodos de melhora de ordenação em DEA aplicados à avaliação estática de tornos mecânicos. *Investigação Operacional, 25*, 229–242.

Lev, B., & Sunder, S. (1979). Methodological issues in the use of financial ratios. *Journal of Accounting and Economics, 1*(3), 187–210. doi:10.1016/0165-4101(79)90007-7

Martins, A. (2001). *O Método dos Rácios no Sector Bancário em Portugal - Avaliação da normalidade e da proporcionalidade* (Unpublished master's thesis). Faculdade de Economia, Universidade do Algarve.

McLeay, S. (1986). The ratio of means, the means of ratios and other benchmarks: An examination of characteristic financial ratios in the French Corporate Sector. *Journal of the French Finance Association, 7*(1), 75–93.

Meeusen, W., & van den Broeck, J. (1977). Efficiency Estimation from Cobb-Douglas Production Functions with Composed Error. *International Economic Review, 18*(2), 435–444. doi:10.2307/2525757

Melnyk, S. A., Bititci, U., Platts, K., Tobias, J., & Andersen, B. (2014). Is performance measurement and management fit for the future? *Management Accounting Research, 25*(2), 173–186. doi:10.1016/j.mar.2013.07.007

Meyer, M. (2011). Finding performance: the new discipline in management. In A. Neely (Ed.), *Business performance measurement - unifying theories and integrating practice* (2nd ed., pp. 113–124). Cambridge University Press.

Meza, L., & Lins, M. (2002). Review of methods for increasing discrimination in Data Envelopment Analysis. *Annals of Operations Research, 116*(1/4), 225–242. doi:10.1023/A:1021340616758

Modigliani, F., & Miller, M. (1958). The cost of capital, corporation finance and the theory of investment. *The American Economic Review, 48*(3), 261–297.

Neely, A., Adams, C., & Crowe, P. (2001). The performance prism in practice. *Measuring Business Excellence, 5*(2), 6–13. doi:10.1108/13683040110385142

Neely, A., Gregory, M., & Platts, K. (2005). Performance measurement system design: A literature review and research agenda. *International Journal of Operations & Production Management, 25*(12), 1228–1263.

Neely, A., Kennerley, M., & Adams, C. (2007). Performance measurement frameworks: a review. In A. Neely (Ed.), *Business Performance Measurement – Unifying theories and integrating practice* (2nd ed., pp. 143–162). Cambridge University Press. doi:10.1017/CBO9780511488481.010

Neely, A. D., & Adams, C. (2001). Perspectives on performance: The performance prism. *Journal of Cost Management, 15*(1), 7–15.

Neves, J. C., & Lourenço, S. (2009). Using data envelopment analysis to select strategies that improve the performance of hotel companies. *International Journal of Contemporary Hospitality Management, 21*(6), 698–712. doi:10.1108/09596110910975963

Nudurupati, S. S., Bititci, U. S., Kumar, V., & Chan, F. T. S. (2011). State of the art literature review on performance measurement. *Computers & Industrial Engineering, 60*(2), 279–290. doi:10.1016/j.cie.2010.11.010

Porter, M. (1985). *Competitive Advantage: Creating and Sustaining Superior Performance*. Free Press.

Porter, M. (1990). *The Competitive Advantage of Nations*. Macmillan. doi:10.1007/978-1-349-11336-1

Porter, M., & Kramer, M. (2011). Creating Shared Value. *Harvard Business Review, 89*(1/2), 62–77.

Rappaport, A. (1998). *Creating Shareholder Value – a guide for managers and investors* (2nd ed.). Free Press.

Tezza, R., Bornia, A. C., & Vey, I. H. (2010). Sistemas de medição de desempenho: Uma revisão e classificação da literatura. *Gestão & Produção, 17*(1), 75–93. doi:10.1590/S0104-530X2010000100007

Thanassoulis, E. (2003). *Introduction to the Theory and Application of Data Envelopment Analysis: a foundation text with integrated software* (2nd ed.). Kluwer Academic Publishers.

Thomas, C. (2005). Poverty, development, and hunger. In J. Baylis, S. Smith, & P. Owens (Eds.), *The Globalization of World Politics: An Introduction to International Relations* (3rd ed., pp. 559–581). Oxford University Press.

Trigueiros, D. (1995). Accounting identities and the distribution of ratios. *The British Accounting Review*, *27*(2), 109–126. doi:10.1006/bare.1994.0006

Trigueiros, D. (1997). Non-proportionality in ratios: An alternative approach. *The British Accounting Review*, *29*(3), 213–230. doi:10.1006/bare.1996.0042

Whittington, G. (1980). Some basic properties of accounting ratios. *Journal of Business Finance & Accounting*, *7*(2), 219–232. doi:10.1111/j.1468-5957.1980.tb00738.x

Young, D., & O'Byrne, S. (2001). *EVA and Value-Based Management: a practical guide to implementation*. Mc-Graw Hill.

ENDNOTES

1. Several authors reviewed the enterprise performance measurement systems (e.g. Braz *et al.*, 2011; Nudurupati *et al.*, 2011; Tezza *et al.*, 2010).
2. For more details, see Coelli *et al.* (2005).

Chapter 9
Business Policy:
A Systems Approach to Corporate Governing

Pedro B. Água
https://orcid.org/0000-0003-1886-9938
CINAV, Portuguese Naval Academy, Portugal

Andre Vilares Morgado
https://orcid.org/0000-0001-7256-8509
AESE Business School, Portugal

ABSTRACT

The purpose of this chapter is to explore improvements in existing corporate governing practices that are currently being implemented through methods that lag behind most of the recent developments taking place in the field of computer science. The authors suggest taking on board systems modeling by adopting a computer-assisted policy design based on system dynamics simulators. Implementing a system thinking approach to business organizations allows the designing of virtuous strategies by simulating organizational behavior. In addition, this approach may also help to mitigate unintended consequences, like risks and outcomes which may surprise the firm, particularly from the board-level perspective. The originality of the present work arrives from merging several approaches that have been around for many years, however not combined in the context of the business policy conceptual framework. Therefore, it brings together recent developments in the fields of business policy, systems thinking, and computer-assisted policy design.

DOI: 10.4018/978-1-7998-4552-2.ch009

INTRODUCTION

The purpose of this conceptual chapter is to explore the improvement of existing corporate governing practices and policies. These practices and policies are critical for the competitiveness and sustainability of business organizations. However, the present design of such policies is done through methods that lag behind most of the recent developments taking place in the field of computer science. Data modeling and simulation have been developed to such an extent that leverages the sophistication and usefulness of management simulators. The authors of this chapter suggest taking on board such approaches to enhance the adoption of computer-assisted policy design based on system-dynamics simulators.

Organizations share the same nature of complex systems and, most often, top management is not able to find analytical mathematical solutions to solve governing problems. One of the possible ways to deal with these kinds of issues and themes is through the building of 'what if scenarios', that is to say, by testing what would happen to critical variables when changing system parameters. Such may be accomplished through a business simulation.

Implementing a system thinking approach (Checkland, 1981; Forrester, 1961) to business organizations allows the design of virtuous strategies by simulating the organizational behavior (Senge, 1990). Also, this approach may help to mitigate unintended consequences, like different sorts of risks and outcomes, which may surprise the organization from the board-level perspective.

The adopted theoretical framework departs from the business policy body of literature, a seminal approach to corporate strategy, before being replaced by other more practical, but perhaps less comprehensive and robust streams of thought (Warren, 2012). The field of business policy has early contributions from scholars belonging to Harvard Business School (Andrews, 1981; Andrews & David, 1971; Christensen, Andrews, Bower, Hamermesh & Porter, 1973). Later on, some European authors (Valero & Lucas, 1991; Valero & Figueroa, 2011) contributed to the development and evolution of such a conceptual model which conceives organizations as political entities, claiming that the adequate approach for governing organizations should include a comprehensive political approach. The authors argue that such dynamics can be modeled through complex systems simulation.

The focus of this chapter is governing, an action verb, as opposed to governance, a noun or substantive. The former is closer to the practitioner, the later to regulations and compliance. While compliance aspires to the minimum requirements, the practitioner must actively engage in the process of governing as a daily activity. Despite the offered contribution to increasing the competitiveness of the firm, the authors also intend to contribute to reducing the gap between practitioners and academics.

By departing from a well-established business policy conceptual model, the authors aim to explore policies and strategies ensuring more robustness into organizational strategic development. The managerial implications of this approach are many. Firstly, organizations are complex systems, and as such, a complex systems approach is potentially the most adequate method for modeling organizational behavior. Secondly, as the simulator is built based on a system dynamics approach, different scenarios can be tested, which resembles a safe lab. Finally, testing several scenarios allow selecting organizational policies based on a better-informed basis, where potential unintended consequences are identified, even before compromising large amounts of scarce resources.

The originality of the present work arrives from merging several approaches that have been around for many years, but have not yet been combined in the context of any corporate governing conceptual framework. It, therefore, brings together recent developments in the fields of business policy, systems thinking and computer-assisted policy design.

The authors believe that the offered view is of value for any business leaders facing decision-making responsibilities and organizational developers in charge of organizational policy design. In contrast, the approach here developed may be understood as being quite generic, due to not contemplating any sort of adaptation to a specific business sector or organization. Hence, some tailoring and contextual insights will be requested to capture what is unique to the organization under consideration.

THE BUSINESS POLICY MODEL

Senior managers aim to achieve the desired future situation for their organization, supposedly a better one than the current one in relative terms. This action demands to approach the organization from a holistic way, to ensure that unintended consequences are minimized. Among several possible approaches, Christensen et al. (1973) set up the seminal roots for a holistic organizational approach—the business policy approach (Gómez & Rocha, 2019)—consisting originally of three governance areas: (i) corporate strategy, (ii) executive structure, and (iii) incentive system. Later on, Valero and Lucas (1991) developed the Business Policy Model, a framework that builds on top of the work of Christensen et al. (1973), and conceives the work of the senior leader as embracing four main areas of governance, together with the development of specific procedures that provide detailed steps for the analysis, choice, and implementation of the organization's desired future. The four key governing areas are: (i) Business, (ii) Directing Structure, (iii) Incentive System, and (iv) Institutional Configuration. Distinguishing these four aspects is useful to preserve a holistic approach to the enterprise organization (Calleja & Melé, 2017).

Choosing the business means deciding to carry out the particular content of the activities or operations that, when related, allow the best possible evolution of an organization's results. Business is something very specific and may refer to performance results, others than sole profit. Bringing people together and putting them to work is one of the basic pillars of senior management's attention. Hence, creating a Directing Structure means entrusting individuals with particular parts of what needs to be done to effectively move the organization forward.

Professional commitment is attained by employing adequate Incentive Systems, which demands senior management to seek procedures that help people carry out their work, that is to say, to guarantee dedication and devotion across the entire organization. Getting people to work professionally, contributing with new ideas through creativity and knowledge is one of the expected goals. The challenge is to ensure that everyone contributes positively to an organization-wide performance.

The fourth key aspect is the Institutional Configuration, which is related to three key topics: (i) Initiative, (ii) Money, and (iii) Power. The Institutional Configuration refers to determinants of company viability on its whole. In this sense, Money dictates financing for new Initiatives. Power is an enabler, or sometimes a disabler, of Initiatives across the firm, as it may foster or restrain the level of organizational Initiatives. The Institutional Configuration is of utmost importance for organizational sustainability and where the critical dimensions of Initiative, Money, and Power are at play, sometimes facing complex dynamics (Valero & Figueroa, 2011). Such sustainability is even more critical whenever an organization engages in a 'change process', as could be the case of a managerial turnaround or an ambitious strategic move.

The Valero and Lucas (1991) Business Policy Model suggests that management may be more humanistic, and practical, being this a good alternative to the traditional schools of strategic management that promotes a narrow approach to general management, focusing almost exclusively on short term profit. The Business Policy Model has the virtue of connecting a humanist vision of business with the role of business in society.

The Language of Systems

Organization and government of social groups constitute the field of study addressed by Valero and Figueroa (2011, p. 25). Any social group is a system, more or less complex, with its structure that dictates how the system will react to a certain stimulus when posed in its environment. Causality arises from the systems underlying structure. Any two variables may exhibit a causal relationship when immersed in a system, which forces to consider causal models as belonging to the language of systems. It is also necessary to avoid confusing the cause with the effect, calling for a continuous verification of which operations fit together, which are defined as harmonic relationships, and which do not fit, which are defined as non-harmonic (Valero & Lucas, 1991, p. 97).

In the construction of complex system models, such as companies or other sorts of organizations, it is necessary to distinguish systemic thinking from event-oriented thinking. In event-oriented thinking, causal relationships are understood as linear chains of events. From this perspective, the causes are the facts that originate the effects.

Distinctly, in systemic thinking, the behavior of the system emerges from the structure of the system, that is, from the feedback links within it. Thus, the effects are not originated from the variables or nodes per se, but the emerging forces behind the recurrent effects of the feedback links. And in general, the effects are going to affect the variables that at a previous moment in time were their causes.

The difference between understanding the world as made by linear relationships of cause and effect or circular relationships of cause and effect is critical to understand where system dynamics arise from.

Even if this idea seems simplistic, it makes all the difference in the way one thinks about the world and organizations. These feedback loops are responsible for many surprising effects that no one has thought of and that can often cause organizations to collapse (however, sometimes also leads to good outcomes, even if no one has thought about them beforehand).

The Business Policy Model can be classified as a formal written and verbal model. In this chapter, the authors attempt to make the model more practical, transforming it into a causal model, which can be discussed from new perspectives and lead to better decisions and policy design.

Models are not validated in terms of truth, but they can be evaluated in terms of their usefulness in what regards supporting policy and decision-making (Sterman, 2000, p. 846). Taking the Latin word *simulare*, simulation means the imitation of a situation or process, generally to support better decisions (Roberts et al., 1983). Hence, a business policy simulator is a possible way to make the Business Policy Model more practical in its use. Simulators are used to develop professionals in other areas such as piloting aircraft. If an airplane pilot has thousands of hours before sitting down to guide a real plane, why does one entrust organizations to executives who do not have such sort of extensive training?

There have been different approaches to systems modeling in terms of language and grammar (Forrester, 1961; Checkland, 1981). Some use rich descriptive graphics, while others look for more objective and systematic representation, but without losing their meaning. The use of causal loop diagrams is such an example. In its most common form, a causal relationship is represented by an arrow with a '+' or '-' sign that connects two parameters. Appendix 1 provides an introduction to the language and grammar of causal diagrams and its formulation.

The Fundamental Equation of the Institutional Configuration

The firm is a joint action, constructive and progressive, pursues specific purposes in which profit is paramount (Valero & Figueroa, 2011, p. 9). As long as that is true, it may be a necessary but not a sufficient condition. This is reinforced by the words of Valero and Lucas (1991, p. 153) who argue that it is the lack of a good business that causes the company to fail because, sometimes, there is someone who kills it. This suggests that great care should be given to the Institutional Configuration area, in particular.

Taking the four main governing areas of the Business Policy Model, a simplified causal loop diagram can be built by addressing first the three nuclear concepts which constitute the Institutional Configuration.

To have Initiative is to have the desire to do something, to set it in motion and to ensure that the matter goes well and sustainable (Valero & Lucas, 1991, p. 164). The Initiative has the meaning of a proposition or idea that serves to initiate something, the ability to devise, invent or undertake something. In this sense, Initiative may be witnessed by the number of products, services or projects (external or internal) initiated. Although one can model 'Initiative' in general, for reasons of simplicity, it is considered in a strict sense, as the number of specific initiatives that can be started and developed over time. It is important to be aware that an evolution of the causal model can incorporate successive layers of detail to capture different aspects of the Initiative concept beyond the strict one used in this chapter, a fact noted by González-Toruño (2005).

To ensure consistency, system dynamic models should be grounded on reasonable assumptions (in a simulator these assumptions can be many). The first step is to search for relationships between the fundamental organizational variables within the area of Institutional Configuration, by answering the question: how are Initiative, Money and Power related? Although they may vary, such change implies a transformation in the complete Institutional Configuration. The sustainability of the company depends on it. They are independent variables, but due to being elastically related, a status quo regarding their harmony or balance is desired and allows good sustainable results. In this sense, the authors of this chapter considered the exploratory working hypothesis that follows as a reasonable working proposition:

$$\text{Initiative} = \text{Money} \times \text{Power}$$

or

$$I = M \times P$$

This expression considers that both Money and Power are means, not ends in themselves. These are necessary means or conditions, but not sufficient per se, to support the Initiative:

$$\text{Initiative} = f\,(\text{Money, Power})$$

The Initiative (which is affected and affects the Power and Money), is a fundamental component of the Institutional Configuration and has a crucial impact on the business sustainability. The conceptual application of the Business Policy Model begins with the business governing area, from which a business structure is designed and an adequate Incentive System is put in place to sustain a desirable level of professional commitment. The most decisive, conditioning, however, is the Initiative, and to get it through it needs adequate stability of Money (the stability of equity, ownership and financial commitments) and Power, but at the same time the Initiative will affect (positively or negatively) these same Power and Money. Having the business in a steady-state situation, gains will come from the proper use of Power by "the person at the top" who allows for improving the Initiative and the Money (Palacios, 2006).

On the contrary, making Money or Power ends in themselves would lead us to a debate in the field of moral philosophy which, despite its interest, is not the purpose of this chapter. In the end someone from the "top" will have to integrate and manage all these variables within a specific company whose social purposes include selling useful goods and services, creating and distributing wealth.

The above equation, and within the scope of this document, could potentially be referred to as the fundamental equation of the Institutional Configuration. The meaning that can be drawn from such equation is that, if the organization does not have enough Money, or enough Power, it is not possible to undertake enough organizational initiatives and consequently affect business performance. Another interpretation is that the more Money and Power within the organization, ceteris paribus, the more initiatives can be realized with the desirable consequences for the development of the business and its contribution for the performance of the organization implanted in its environment, which is in its market, economic and social contexts.

In reality, Initiative, Money and Power, are three elements featuring some degree of interdependence: the serious lack of one is not solved by the abundance of the other two. Neither Initiative, nor Money, nor Power can sustain the Business alone. The level of overlap is such that it could be said that, to carry out a specific Initiative, enough Power and Money is needed in addition to it.

Still, in complex systems, the effect can become the cause. Hence, the Initiative is going to affect Power and Money recursively, and in addition, perhaps instead of a single equation, a system of equations is needed for a more complete mathematical representation of the systemic performance of the three components of the Institutional Configuration governing area.

Systemic Thinking and the Business Policy Model

Valero and Figueroa (2011, p. 20) suggest that the work of the "person at the top" faces a lot of chance. These vertex people act on the causes that produce the organizational movement or advance toward what is intended to be achieved, that is the organizational mission and goals. Governing the destiny of the organization is therefore related to the configuration of action from its causes, and taking into account the four governing areas of the Business Policy Model.

The present chapter aims, not only to build a conceptual landmark but also to support corporate governing advancement more practically, delivering foreseeable benefits for the design of better governing policies. Hence, one can begin by elaborating a mathematical and causal theory leading to modeling from systemic thinking (Senge, 1991). Figure 1(a) means that the more Money the more initiatives are possible, but the more initiatives consume Money and less Money is left for other initiatives, thus closing a cycle of negative feedback that tends to balance.

Figure 1(b) presents such a negative feedback cycle which always seeks a position of equilibrium over time, that is, the search for some level of equilibrium [see Figure 1(c)]. It must be said that in this first systemic model the authors are not yet establishing the difference between different types of Money: endogenous Money and exogenous Money. For future developments of this model, it should be considered, since the most stabilizing institutional Money is the endogenous (capital and reserves), and an organization has to be careful not to be affected or compromised by the exogenous Money, that may end up affecting the company, an issue stressed by Valero & Figueroa, (2011, pp. 146-147).

The variable "Power" is now introduced. The more Money the more Power [see Figure 2(a)], and with more Power, conditions are created for more Initiatives to succeed [see Figure 2(b)]. It must be said that despite more Money available, such Money is not necessarily put to good use. One will have a Power derived from Money, but one will still need a Power capable of harmonizing the whole. If Power fails, both

Figure 1. Initiative and Money forms a negative link or a balanced "L", whose dynamics tend to seek a point of equilibrium

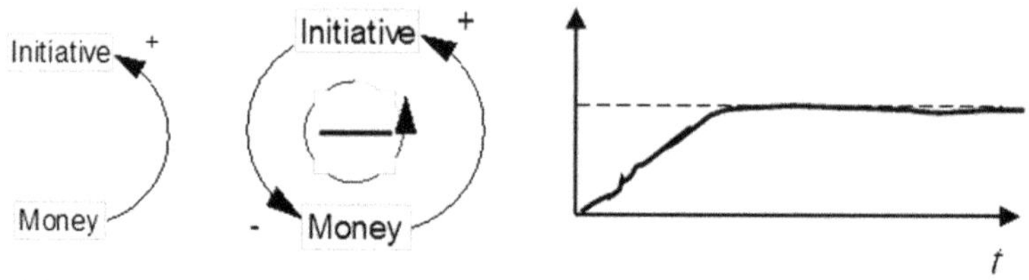

(a) (b) (c)

Money and the Initiative tend to flee. A single person in action who will concentrate the Initiative, the Money and the Power, can disarm the whole organization. This closes another negative causal loop, going through Power >> Initiative >> Money >> Power. Systems theory suggests that a system with many negative feedback loops ends in an over stabilized state, which explains, for example, why sometimes there is so much resistance to change in organizations. Conversely, if the system contains just one or a few negative links, the system may easily become an unstable system (this explains why small actions can sometimes destabilize a system or organization).

A negative feedback loop is defined by an odd number of negative influences, while a positive or reinforcing bond does not contain negative signal influences, or has an even bigger number of negative influences, as presented in Figure 2.

Figure 2. The addition of the Power affects the stability of the system

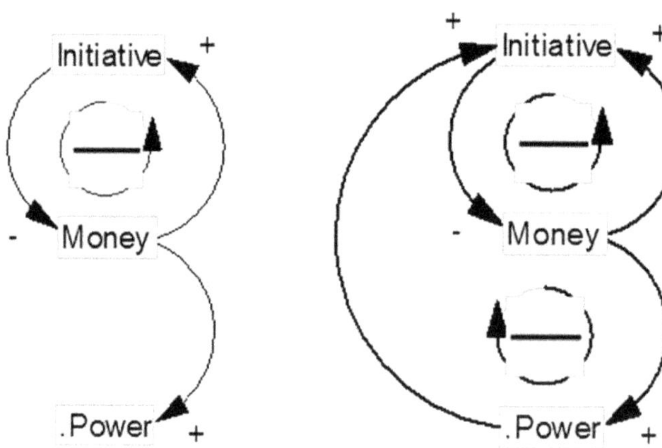

(a) (b)

Considering now the positive or reinforcing loops, generally these exhibit a growth behavior until some limit is imposed on the system and stops such growth. Alternatively, a positive link can also cause declining behavior, as exhibited in Figure 3.

Figure 3. The two basic behaviors of reinforcement or positive links

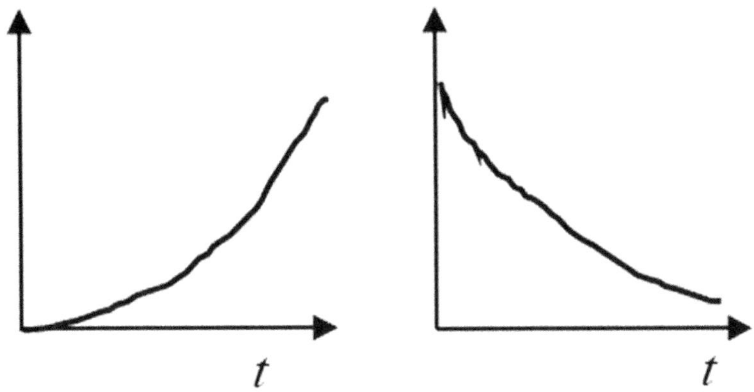

Following the same causal logic, the more the Initiative increases the more the Business potential gets increased. According to Valero and Figueroa (2011), the more Economic Added Value generated and accumulated by means of the Initiative, which energizes and orients it, the more new and better activities and the more value is created. Both factors (Initiative and Business) drive the development loop, while they are balanced by the Institutional Configuration, which structure, stabilize and facilitate the development of this dynamic.

With more Business, the more the Money level is reinforced (through sales of products, services or projects, with profit), improving the financial situation of the company (see Figure 4), which in turn will affect, in various ways, the balance of Power in the company compared to its external environment (e.g. vis-à-vis banks, shareholders and other stakeholders with potential influence on the company).

Valero and Lucas (1991, p. 160) suggested that *governing well demands knowledge on the relative weight of the various powers and to compensate them in such a way as to contribute to the stability of the same powers.*

By adding the effects of an appropriate Directing Structure, as well as an appropriate Incentive System, the model is further developed through the addition of more elements and their interrelationships (Forrester, 1961). Figure 5 shows the four governing areas of the Business Policy Model, in which the fundamental variables of the Institutional Configuration area are visible: Initiative, Money and Power.

Figure 4. The interrelationships between the three key components of the Institutional Configuration

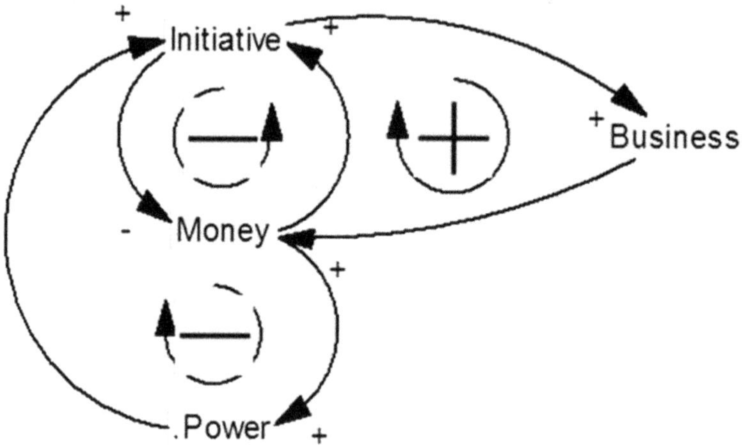

Figure 5. The simplified causal model of the Business Policy Model

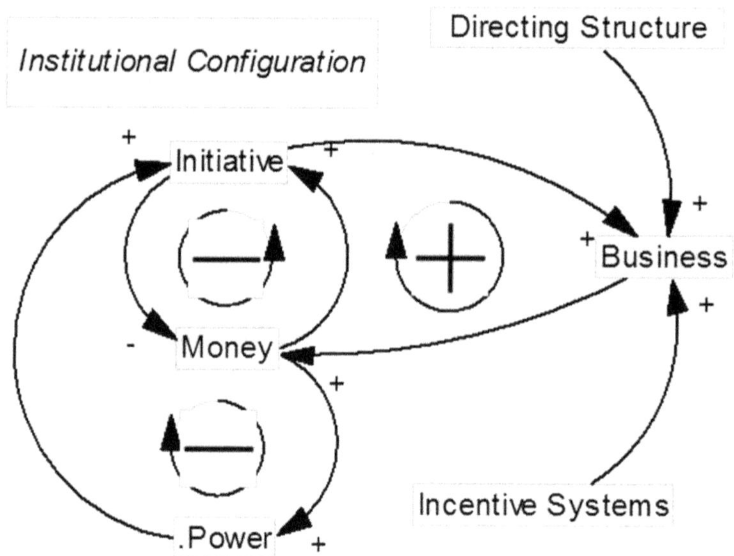

Building a System Dynamics Simulator

A simple model allows to considering relationships featuring known systemic effects, such as those resulting from systems archetypes (Senge, 1990), and infer possible side effects when adopting concrete solutions or policies for organizational problems. A more robust approach is the building of a business policy simulator, which allows testing solutions or scenarios, that is to say, concrete policies to be implemented by the organization. Among the several existing systems modeling languages, the system dynamics methodology is an adequate one and serves the purpose of this study.

Systems dynamics is a complex system modeling methodology, developed by Jay Forrester at the Massachusetts Institute of Technology, in the fifties of the twentieth century, and allows the language of causal diagrams to be translated into the level and flow diagrams (stocks and flows), also known as Forrester Diagrams. The 'grammar' is simple, comprising four basic elements: level, flow, valves and sources or drains. With these elements and establishing causal interconnections, diagrams that represent the structure of the system under study can be built. All systems that vary with time can be represented only by levels and flows. These two types of variables are necessary and sufficient to describe systems.

The simplified business policy block system presented in Figure 4 can be modeled as exhibited in Figure 6. The authors used a system dynamics modeling software for this purpose, the Vensim PLE (from Ventana Systems, Inc.). The mathematical equations used for structuring the dynamic model are presented in Annex B.

To improve the accuracy of a model one can include calibration parameters, such as Kp, which is present in Figure 6. In this model, Kp is a proportionality factor that seeks to translate the relationship between Money and Power, in the sense that, for a certain level of Money, Power evolves proportionately with Kp. Kp has a similar meaning to the K factor in the equation:

$$P.V = n.K.T$$

This equation relates pressure and volume of a gas, with temperature by Boltzmann constant K. Similarly, Kp needs to be estimated for the specific organization under modeling, alongside what is the appropriate range to provide an adequate proportionality.

Systems dynamics models can be complicated by the number of variables, their interconnections and mathematical modeling. Still, the software packages for system dynamics contain several tools that allow for the analysis of the model itself, from reality checks to plotting causal influence diagrams. These tools are of considerable help in the modeling process. Figure 7 shows which variables influence the Initiative.

Figure 6. The Forrester diagram applied to the context of the Institutional Configuration

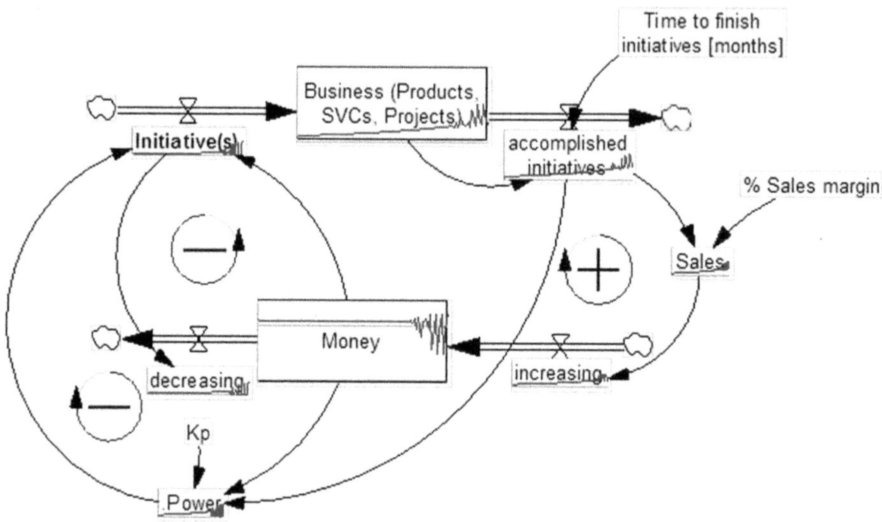

Figure 7. Chains of cause and effect

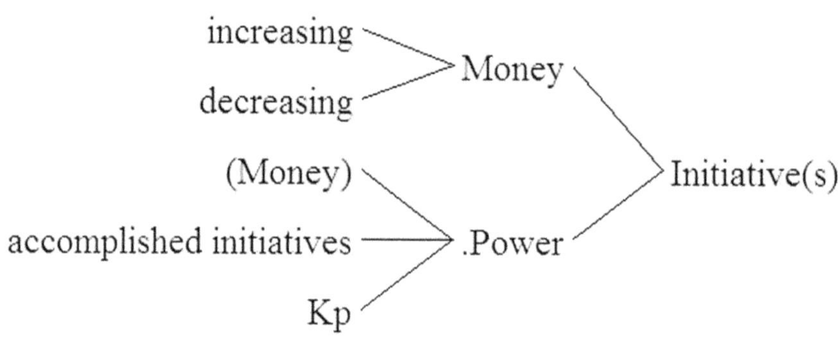

Questions such as "which variables are immediately affected by a specific model parameter?" can, therefore, be answered. Figure 8 shows the variable Money affecting the variables on its right-hand side. On a first level Power and Initiative take a stance, which by their turn will influence the variables Business and Initiative.

Figure 9 presents three graphs resulting from a first simulation using the described system dynamics model. This figure exhibits the behavior pattern over time of the three fundamental variables of the Institutional Configuration and shows the result of the interaction of certain levels of Initiative, Power and Money in the organization (i.e. the system), having oscillations or non-linear behaviors. This is useful for

Figure 8. The variable Money and its chain of different influences

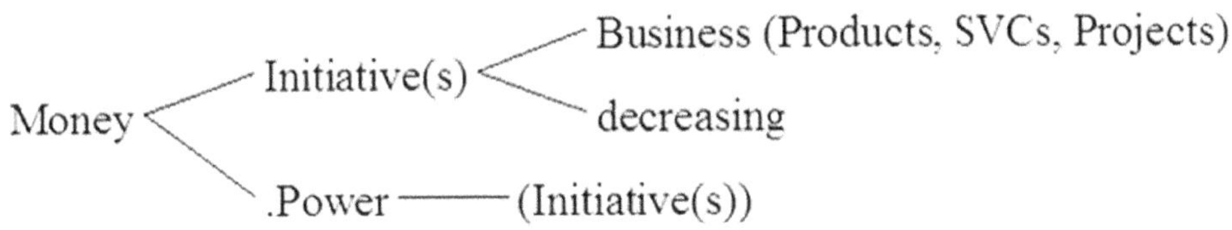

investigating scenarios and developing knowledge about specific policies under consideration. For example, Valero and Lucas (1991, p. 159) argue that the key to the company's self-continuation, from the point of view of Power, is to achieve its stability within the company and between the company and its external endeavor. But what will this stability do to the other components of the Institutional Configuration, or the other areas of the Business Policy Model? Answers to these questions may be obtained by analyzing the output of the business simulation.

By changing numerical values on input variables it is possible to observe the effects taking place on output variables over time. Simulations may have different time horizons, from the short term where the behavior for one or two years can be observed, to the long term involving larger periods.

Scenario Generation

An outcome of the decision-making process is strengthened if it is possible to obtain patterns of behavior over time that shows the achievement of chosen objectives; produce appropriate policies and plans to achieve such objectives and define the business in which the company wishes to be (Christensen et al., 1973, p. 125). Having a simulator that allows for experiments or scenarios to be tested can support different hypothetical organizational policies for different scenarios and look at how the variables of interest evolve with a view to achieving the chosen objectives: either in an organizational transformation, launching new products, internationalization decisions or other strategic changes the organization may consider. Such experiments and scenarios are tested by selecting variables to change (within reasonable ranges) and observing the results. This can be done by changing only one input variable at a time or several variables simultaneously to find optimal performance responses, thus enabling the design of optimal policies to be achieved. Systems theory suggests that the optimal performance of the system rarely corresponds to the maximum performance of a local optimal. In other words, maximizing the performance of one or all of the local variables does not guarantee the optimal performance of the system (organization) as a whole, which can be made visible through simulation.

Figure 9. Behavior over time of critical variables

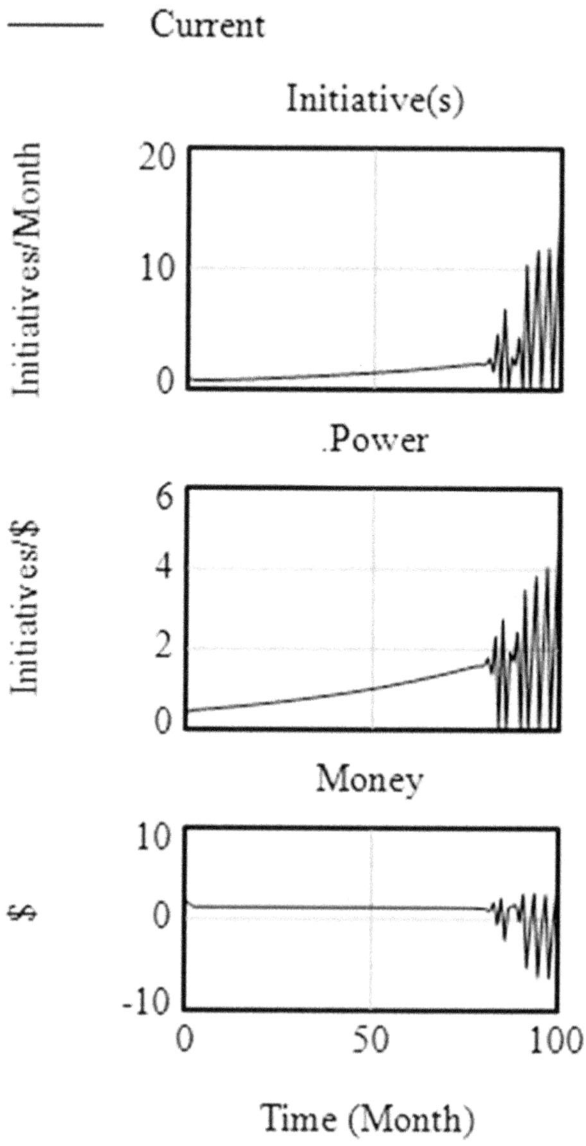

Regarding scenario generation may be useful to follow a process, like for instance the one proposed by Schwartz (1996), by adopting specific procedures for the generation of these scenarios. The same author suggests that to develop scenarios it is advisable to start from the inside out, and back from the outside in.

THE BUSINESS POLICY SYSTEMIC MODEL

An organization, mercantile or not, is an open system. This is, as opposed to a closed system, a system that exchanges resources (matter, energy or information) with its surrounding environment, as presented in Figure 10.

Figure 10. The company as an open system connected to its environment

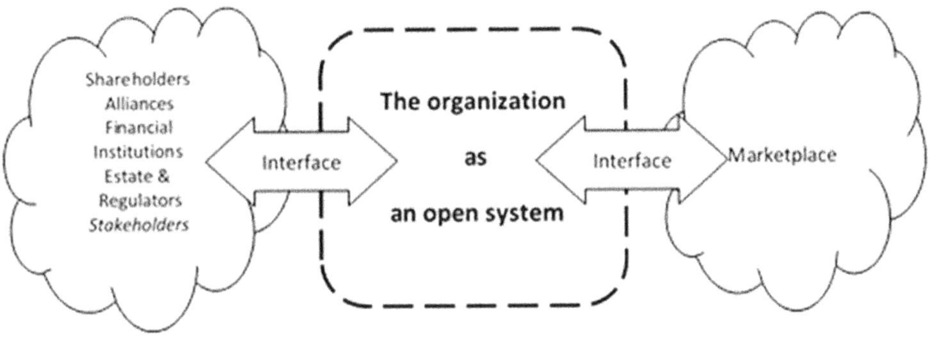

Thus, it may be useful to look at the graphic form of the Business Policy Model, as an open system in its environment and where the four areas of government become visible, as exhibited in Figure 11. It represents the interaction with the environment from the Institutional Configuration to the left, and the interaction with the market made through the Business, to the right. There are other points of interrelation of the organization with its environment but, as a first approach, this is a possible first architecture.

Figure 11. The Business Policy Model configured as an open system

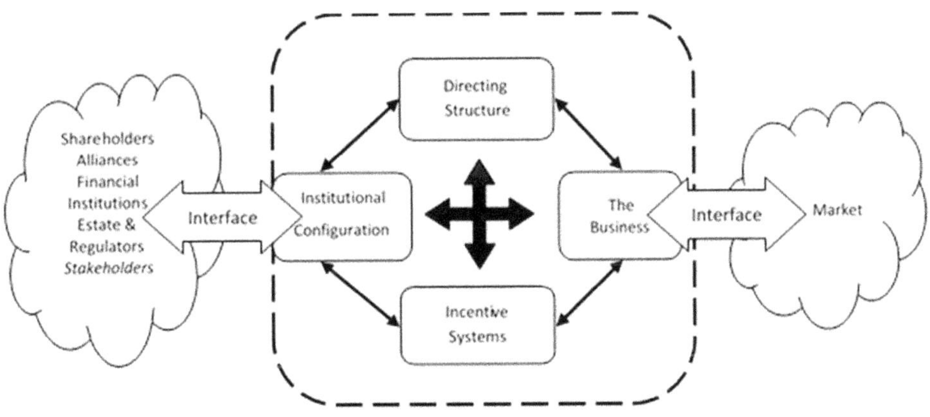

One possible way to look at the development of a systemic model is to conceive the first layer of causal relationships between a few relevant variables, as done, and then add more layers of detail, that is to say, adding more variables. The development of an enterprise policy simulator is a task that can take several years. Some suggestions or clues of possible ways to further develop the simulator after this first model are presented, pointing out possible evolutions for the model from its current point of development. Each governing area of the Business Policy Model will be considered separately.

Variables Influencing the Business

Figure 12 attempts to identify relevant variables that influence the Business area within the Business Policy Model. The influence of the following five areas of operations must be included in the development of the systemic model: design, production, commercial, finance and support (Valero & Lucas, 1991, p. 27).

At the same time, business growth will affect the other three areas of the Business Policy Model (Figure 13).

Figure 12. A representation of the relationships that affect the Business

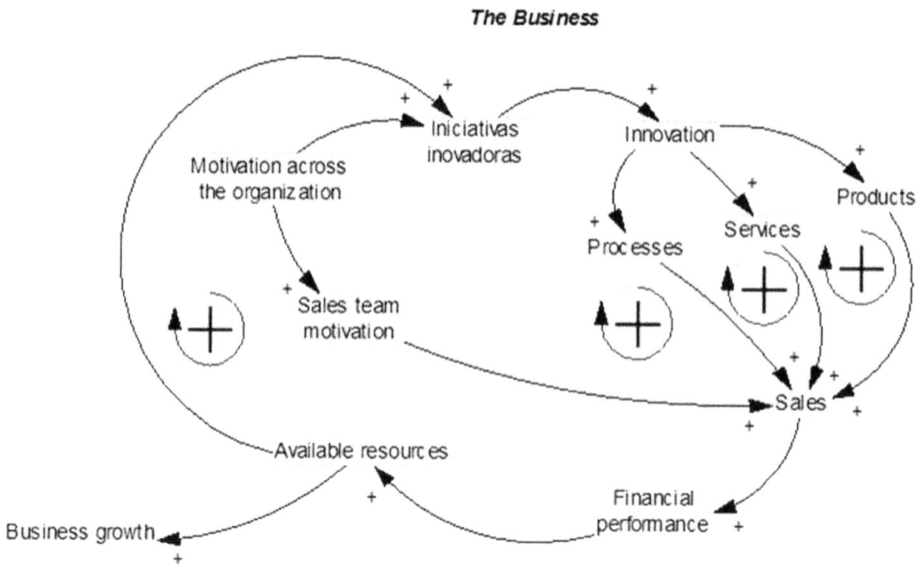

Figure 13. The complexity increases with the effects of business dynamics in the other three areas of the Business Policy Model

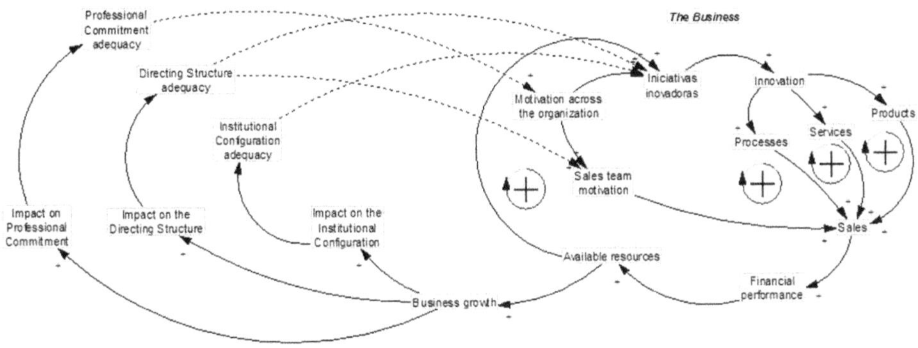

Variables Influencing the Directing Structure

A starting point is to look at the optimization of the Directing Structure. At the same time, the Directing Structure depends not only on the nature of the Business but, among other variables, on the geography where it operates and its specific communication cultures, information flows and promptness with which information is needed for good and timely decision-making and action. For example, it is relevant to think that instability in systems typically originates from temporary information delays when in the presence of feedback loops (Forrester, 1961). Relevant questions could be "what are the variables that influence the Directing Structure to optimize (perhaps maximizing) the Business?" Figure 14 suggests a structure.

Figure 14. Representation of the Directing Structure

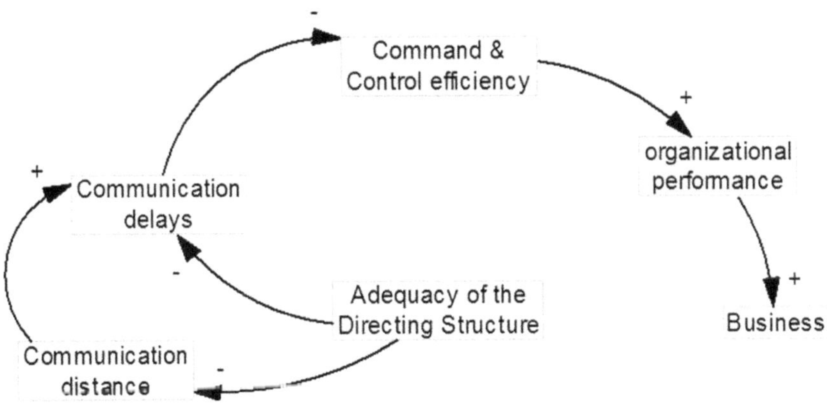

Variables Influencing the Incentive System

This is a topic where perhaps the difference between the approaches of the physical sciences and engineering and the approaches of the social sciences are greater, not least because ethics in the organizations come into play, which demands clear criteria regarding what can be done, what is to be done, and what must be done (Christensen et al., 1973, p. 524). Nevertheless, it is still possible to establish reasonable relationships using qualitative to quantitative conversions, within certain ranges. For instance, to use qualitative scales with descriptive levels to which numerical values can be assigned to make mathematical simulations possible.

According to Valero and Lucas (1991) governing—closely related to directing—consists of leading a company from a present situation to a better future situation, in relative terms. Therefore, good governance must set strategic objectives that are compared with the organization's current reality, generally evidencing gaps. The gap analysis is followed by decisions and, consequently, actions that will change the present reality of the company, in a link that closes on itself, bringing it closer to the strategic objectives or desirable future state through different possible paths, as presented in Figure 15.

Figure 15. The governing loop

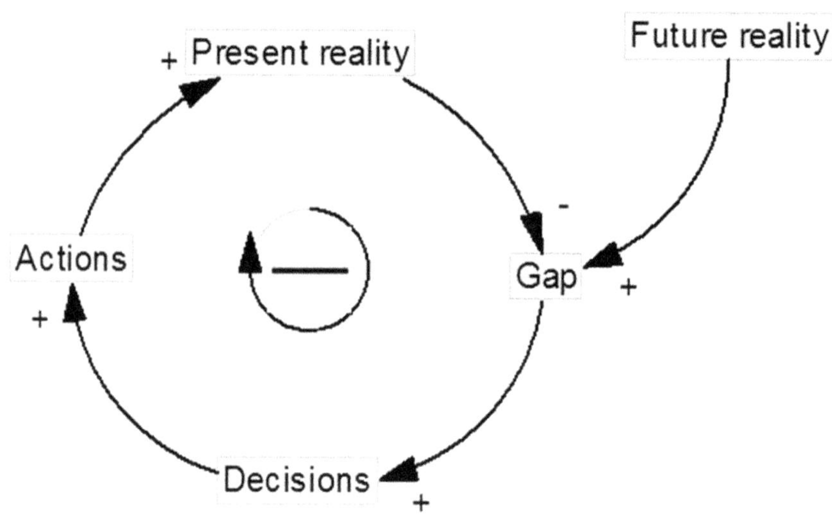

By taking measurements it is possible to compare the "where one would like the organization performance to be" with the "where the current organization is" in a variable by variable basis (or set of variables), which can be managed with a view to eliminating the undesirable difference. For example, Juan Palacios (2006) suggested that one could conceive a scale of Power in the organization, and suggested a way of doing it. This is the type of relationships that in a first approach can be useful towards a more complete model of a Business Policy Simulator.

Sterman (2000, p. 890) argues that all models (formal or only mental) are partial and incomplete representations of reality. Moreover, the dynamics of the model's variables will show nonlinearities, instabilities and collateral unintended effects, resulting from the political decision scenarios facing the company (Fisher, 2005). This is a point to be analyzed to identify additional relevant parameters to include in the simulator as soon as it is possible to look for its enhancement.

Outside Variables Influencing the Institutional Configuration

To build the simulator is necessary to take into account the issue of control, shareholders, regulatory bodies and to identify critical causal relationships that may impact the model. For example, if the concentration of Power within the organization is not high, what sort of relationship the general manager will establish with the shareholders and how it will be represented in the board of directors (whose power is dependent on multiple factors such as the greater or lesser concentration of capital)? Another set of questions that can be modeled is the following: "What are the behaviors of the variables that influence and maximize the stability of Power?"; "Is a situation of considerable Power differences better? Or is it preferable to have a situation where all the powers are balanced?" Figure 16 illustrates how these variables may impact the Institutional Configuration.

Other causal relationships of interest for the model may be legal and regulatory variables that may affect the organization via the Institutional Configuration. Experience may provide some policy orientation, but a model that can be simulated allows for clarification and elimination of doubts.

Naturally, this set of relationships can be added to the model, affecting the performance of the Institutional Configuration. In this scenario, it is verified that a new loop emerges, perhaps dangerous, because it is a loop of reinforcement that, for good or bad, will reinforce positive behaviors, but also negative ones. This is an output variable that will require sensitivity analysis to clarify how certain policies would be reinforced with this new loop. Figure 17 represents variables influencing Institutional Configuration.

Figure 16. Additional variables with impact on the Institutional Configuration

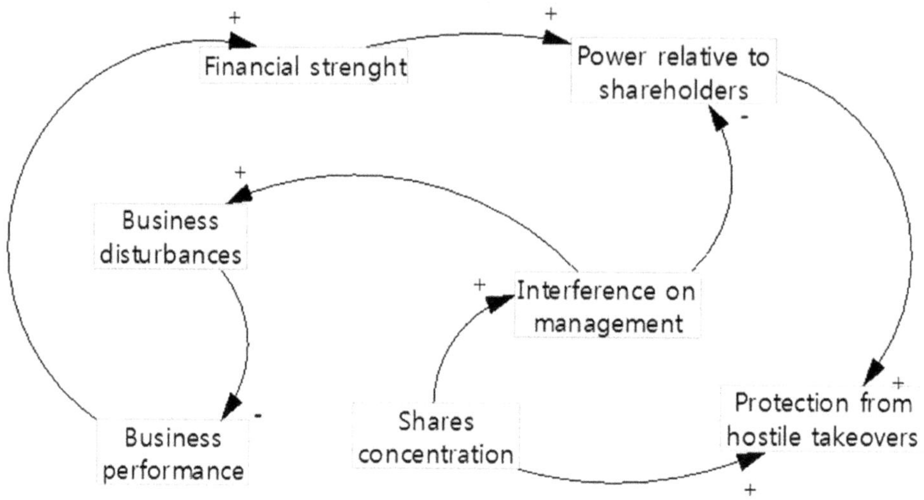

Figure 17. The systemic representation of the theme of Institutional Configuration can be developed with more variables and detail

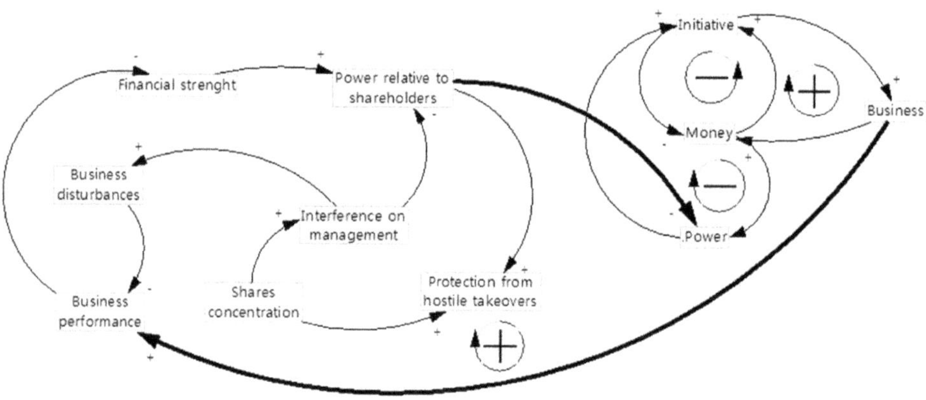

The purpose of the diagram presented in Figure 17 is not to present a complete model of the Institutional Configuration, but to help identify which additional variables should be added to the model.

The development of a model that is more detailed, and satisfying, may take years and will result from a team effort of people familiar with the Business Policy Model, to capture multiple perspectives and thus strengthen it. The diagram will become even more complex with the interconnection (integration) of the four areas of the Business Policy Model, but it must not be forgotten that this is the nature of the organizational systems, highly complex by definition. Also, the system dynamics model must be continuously validated by field practitioners, to capture the multiple perspectives and thus strengthen it. This effort should aim to reinforce the systemic character of the Business Policy Model (Valero & Figueroa, 2011, p. 11).

CONCLUSION

Decision and action are not exactly two stages of a great cycle, but the dimensions within which the leadership movement occurs, in which any future choice advances (Valero & Figueroa, 2011, p.29). Valero and Lucas (1991, p.25) argue that action is more important than the decision itself, even if it is necessary beforehand to decide. Decision and action have their origin and are recreated in the initiative or multiple initiatives across the organization.

To model an organization, taken as a system, demands formalization. Mental models are not fully shared with others. On the contrary, formal models, because they have graphic, mathematical or other representation can be shared, which facilitates the discussion more objectively as to their validity and application to possible approaches to problems and their solutions, making decisions more accurately. Besides, no model can predict the future. Some models are more useful than others in helping to address the developing future, in the sense that some models allow a greater understanding of how to govern and lead organizations into the future.

The Business Policy Model conceptually synthesizes the complex reality of the firm into four dimensions that allow for a vision that is both global and governable, from which the various management tools can be integrated. It highlights the political side of corporate governing and the work of senior management. Within the scope of complex systems, causal models that include system thinking and system dynamics allows to understand and model the complexity that takes place within business organizations. Therefore, such a modeling approach is suggested as a possible way to generate scenarios and support the design of computer-assisted policies, taking the Business Policy Model as a reference.

Top management and the board of directors govern because they lead the political, social, economic processes of the firm. At the same time, top management aims to achieve certain goals that will improve the organizational performance, while conducting the organization towards three institutional purposes (Valero & Figueroa, 2011): (i) providing a useful product or service to society, (ii) adding economic value, and (iii) building the capacity for relative self-preservation over time. In this context, a business simulator is a valuable aid for managing corporate risks and ensuring that the firm arrives when and where it expects, as the simulator helps to design optimal organizational policies.

This chapter discussed the relevance of corporate governing within the context of systems thinking. A simulator may have several uses, but the two main ones are: to support business governance education and to assist organizations in matters of governance and organizational policy design. With such tools, it is possible to design better company policies and to detect in time possible unintended consequences, while selecting sets of policies that optimize the performance of the company.

The simulator presented in this chapter may include additional detail arriving from other areas of the Business Policy Model. This option for future development may enhance its robustness and utility. The Directing Structure may also benefit from the work of Mintzberg (1993) featuring organizational structures, which have been modeled in the form of causal diagrams. Lastly, there are other business areas to consider, from concepts of operations, new product development, I&D, leadership, marketing and sales, etc.

REFERENCES

Anderson, V., & Johnson, L. (1997). *System thinking basics*. Pegasus Communications.

Andrews, K. R. (1981). Corporate-strategy as a vital function of the board. *Harvard Business Review*, *59*(6), 174–184.

Andrews, K. R., & David, D. K. (1971). *The concept of corporate strategy*. Richard D. Irwin.

Calleja, R., & Melé, D. (2017). Valero's "enterprise politics": A model of humanistic management and corporate governance. *Journal of Management Development*, *36*(5), 644–659. doi:10.1108/JMD-12-2015-0187

Checkland, P. (1991). *Soft systems methodology*. Wiley.

Christensen, C. R., Andrews, K. R., Bower, J. L., Hamermesh, R. G., & Porter, M. E. (1973). *Business policy: Text and cases*. Richard D. Irwin.

Fisher, L. M. (2005). *The profet of unintended consequences*. Retrieved from https://www.strategy-business.com/article/05308

Forrester, J. W. (1961). *Industrial dynamics*. Cambridge: Pegasus Communications.

Forrester, J. W. (1968). *Principles of systems*. Cambridge: Pegasus Communications.

Gómez, J. I., & Rocha, H. (2019). Business Policy: Historical Evolution and Epistemological Roots. In A. A. Caldart, J. E. Ricart, & A. A. Carrera (Eds.), *General management in latin and ibero-american organizations: A humanistic perspective*. Routledge.

Gonzàlez-Toruno, M. (2005). La Iniciativa institucional. In J. L. Lucas (Ed.), *Iniciativa, dinero y poder en la empresa mercantil*. Ed. Instituto Internacional San Telmo.

Meadows, D. (2008). *Thinking in systems: A primer*. Chelsea Green Publishing.

Mintzberg, H. (1993). *Structure in fives: Designing effective organizations*. Prentice Hall.

Palácios, J. (2006). Empresas bien configuradas. In A. G. Castro (Ed.), *El perfeccionamiento de la alta dirección*. Ed. Instituto Internacional San Telmo.

Roberts, N., Andersen, D. F., Deal, R. M., Garet, M. S., & Shaffer, W. A. (1983). *Introduction to computer simulation: The system dynamics approach*. Addison-Wesley Publishing Company.

Schwartz, P. (1996). *The art of the long view*. Doubleday.

Senge, P. (1990). *The fifth discipline*. Doubleday.

Sterman, J. (2000). *Business dynamics: Systems thinking and modeling for a complex world*. Irwin McGraw-Hill.

Swenney, L. B. (2001). *When a butterfly sneezes*. Pegasus Communications.

Valero, A., & Figueroa, E. T. (2011). *La empresa de negócios y la alta dirección: Procedimientos politicos de gobierno*. Eunsa.

Valero, A., & Lucas, J. L. (1991). *Política de empresa: El gobierno de la empresa de negocios*. Eunsa.

Warren, K. (2012). *The trouble with strategy: The brutal reality of why business strategy doesn't work and what to do about it*. Createspace Independent Publishing Platform.

APPENDIX 1

Causal diagrams are an important part of the tools associated with systemic thinking and are used in this document, so they deserve some explanation (Forrester, 1961; Sterman, 2000; Meadows, 2008). A causal loop diagram is a model of the important relationships between variables or system parameters. It has some virtues, namely:

- It is a simple way to represent ideas, which sometimes are still confusing at the beginning of any study of a system.
- It allows clear and effective communication with stakeholders about a model or study.

The causal relationship uses '+' and '-' signs to indicate the type (or direction) of influence between two variables. For instance, a causal relationship between two variables A and B with a '+' sign means they change in the same direction (direct effect). That is to say, everything else being equal, when A increases, B tends to increase or when A decreases, B tends to decrease. Similarly, a relationship with a '-' sign means a change in the opposite direction (inverse effect). That is to say, everything else being equal, when A increases, B tends to decrease and when A decreases, B tends to increase.

Combinations of these two types of relationships allow drawing causal diagrams as complex as needed. Particularly important are the feedback loops that may arise in the structure of a system, which potentially can be positive or negative.

It is normal to represent the effect of A over B. However, this representation is incomplete, because the result of B is a new condition in the system which in turn may influence A. In a positive cycle (reinforcement cycle) there is either no negative influence or an even number of causal relationships with a '-' sign. In a negative cycle (balancing cycle) there is an odd number of causal relationships with a '-' sign. It is in the form of positive feedback from the structure of the system that one finds the forces of growth. It is in the structure of negative feedback systems, or targeting systems, that the causes of fluctuation and instability are found (Forrester, 1968, Cap. 1, p. 7).

By itself, a causal diagram does not show the detailed dynamics that emerge from the behavior of a system. This is only possible using a simulator that can be built from a causal diagram using system dynamics, a technique created to simulate complex systems (Forrester, 1961). However, although limited, the causal model can still provide useful information to help focus attention on key relationships. Sterman (2000) provides a good introduction to system dynamics and causal loop diagrams. In developing a causal diagram representative of a system, it is important to subject the problem under consideration to a set of questions (Anderson & Johnson, 1997):

- **Questions that can expose behavior patterns**: Has this behavior happened in the past?
- **Questions for inserting new information in the analysis:** What makes us say that?
- **Questions that lead to a deeper understanding of the problem in question and expose hidden cycles:** What systemic structure may be causing a certain observable behavior?
- **Questions to detect time lag effects:** What effect will time delays have on the system's resources?
- **Questions that seek to expose potential unintended consequences:** What else will happen if the objectives set are met?

APPENDIX 2

The following code contains the mathematical equations of the dynamic model presented in Figure 6.

```
(01) "% Sales margin"=
5
Units: Dmnl
As a percentage %%
(02) ".Power"=
Kp*IF THEN ELSE(Money>=0, Money*accomplished Initiatives, 0)
Units: Initiatives/$
(03) accomplished Initiatives=
"Business (Products, SVCs, Projects)"*(1/"Time to finish
Initiatives [months]"
)
Units: Initiatives/Month
(04) "Business (Products, SVCs, Projects)"= INTEG (
"Initiative(s)"-accomplished Initiatives,
1)
Units: Initiatives
(05) decreasing=
"Initiative(s)"
Units: $/Month
(06) FINAL TIME = 100
Units: Month
The final time for the simulation.
```

```
(07) increasing=
Sales
Units: $/Month
(08) INITIAL TIME = 0
Units: Month
The initial time for the simulation.
(09) "Initiative(s)"=
MAX(0, Money)*".Power"
Units: Initiatives/Month
(10) Kp=
0.6
Units: Dmnl
(11) Money= INTEG (
increasing-decreasing,
2)
Units: $
(12) Sales=
(1+("% Sales margin"/100))*accomplished Initiatives
Units: $
(13) SAVEPER =
TIME STEP
Units: Month [0,?]
The frequency with which output is stored.
(14) TIME STEP = 1
Units: Month [0,?]
The time step for the simulation.
(15) "Time to finish Initiatives [months]"=
3
Units: Month
```

Chapter 10
Systematic Literature Review on Global Strategy:
Mapping Trends and Gaps

Nelson deMatos
ESGHT, University of Algarve, Portugal & Cinturs, Portugal

Miguel Ángel Sánchez Jiménez
Departamento de Marketing y Comunicación, Instituto de Investigación para el Desarrollo Social (INDESS), Universidad de Cádiz, Spain

Célia M. Q. Ramos
https://orcid.org/0000-0002-3413-4897
ESGHT, University of Algarve, Portugal & Cinturs, Portugal

Nuno Baptista
https://orcid.org/0000-0001-7130-0543
Escola Superior de Comunicação Social, Instituto Politécnico de Lisboa, Portugal & NECE, University of Beira Interior, Portugal

João José de Matos Ferreira
https://orcid.org/0000-0002-5928-2474
NECE, Research Center in Business Sciences, University of Beira Interior, Portugal

DOI: 10.4018/978-1-7998-4552-2.ch010

ABSTRACT

The global economy changed the way products and services are exchange and reminded organizations' managers to find new ways to obtain competitive advantage and formulate their strategy in the global market. Thus, this chapter's aim is to perform a systematic literature review to identify the main theoretical topics of global strategy in the past 43 years using bibliometric analysis. The results allowed to identify and cluster five main trends: Cluster 1 – firm performance in the global market; Cluster 2 – power and market space development; Cluster 3 – government regulation, government and regulation; Cluster 4 – economic periods; Cluster 5 – societal changes. Findings also allowed to find potential gaps in global strategy related with the topics of entrepreneurship, competitive strategy, capitalism, transitions, climate change, law, portfolio, financial performance, global sourcing, and global value chain. Conclusions are drawn.

INTRODUCTION

The global economy brought intense pressure for all organizations, from small and medium-sized enterprises (SME) to multinational enterprises (MNE) and at the same time it reshaped every organizations role in the global economy (Woods, 2010) since performance became an ever more competitive factor in the market success. But, the globalization also affected different corporate levels, particularly the managers during the decision-making process, regarding the marketing policies and strategies (Arli, Tjiptono & Winit, 2015; Flores & Aguilera, 2007; Knoerich, 2010; Liang & Gao, 2020; Menon & Menon, 1997).

On one end of the spectrum, with the globalization the market became more open, leading companies to search for strategic alliances or new networks (Liu, Jiang, Zhang, & Zhao, 2013; Veilleux et al., 2012). It also led to firms moving their production to overseas and finding new spaces and places, services (outsourcing), people (i.e., workforces), outside their units (e.g., outsourcing) and eventually news ways to do and create businesses (entrepreneurship) (Ghannad & Andersson, 2012; Liang & Gao, 2020; Linares Navarro et al., 2009; Pearce & Papanastassiou, 1999).

On the other end, globalization boosted market competitiveness, raised the barriers to entry in many markets and showed how culture can play a crucial role in firms strategy (Blom et al., 2008; Dalimunthe, 2016; Jain & Tucker, 1995; Min et al., 2015; Ralston et al., 2008). The implications of globalization extended to firms ethics, corruption, but also to concerns related with climate change, environmental protection and social responsibility (Arli et al., 2015; Beets, 2005; Christian & Gumbus, 2009; Peršič & Peršič, 2016; Pinkse & Kolk, 2012). In this environment, even innovation was approached differently by organizations, as a driving factor for successful strategies and performance (Carmona-Lavado, Gopalakrishnan & Zhang, 2020; Ikeda & Marshall, 2016; Rouen, 2020).

But, despite all these economy shifts, global strategy remains the same at its core, strategizing every organization's governing, either at acquiring, diversifying, restricting, and even abandoning strategic business units or products. The market on the other hand, will continue to require an ever more attention from the academia and practionaires, to the global strategy theory and its subfields research areas, regarding planning, decision-making and implementation of a successful global strategy. The need to maintain a competitive advantage to deal with the global competitive set, increases the importance of framing the global strategy body of knowledge.

For instance, which changes has the market seen in the past decades, regarding consumers' behavior? How did the organizations or economic agents adapted to those changes? which new policies, rules, laws perspectives, trends occurred? Despite previous studies (e.g., Degbey, 2015; Kireeva-Karimova, 2015; Krasniqi, 2013) few studies nevertheless, offered a broad view of how previous research shaped and changed global strategy theory. In this regard, this paper seeks to answer two questions: What are the main developments within global strategy construct? What are the main trends and gaps in the past four decades?

Thus, to achieve this aim a systematic literature review will be made to identify the main theoretical topics of global strategy in the past 43 years using bibliometric analysis. The bibliometric analysis will permit to identify the evolution of the construct throughout the years, and will provide a more comprehensive, robust understanding of the construct, instead of a focus in just a part and not on whole scientific phenomena. Researchers and practitioners, will also be able to explore new and emerging trends and have access to a useful review of seminal papers, enabling them to be more informed and consequently better prepared to formulate their strategy at the global level.

METHODOLOGY

The methodologic approach was dependent on the large number of articles on global strategy that needed to be analyzed. Therefore, a systematic literature review, frequent in the academia (Maritz, De Wall, & Verhoeven, 2011; Schmeisser, 2013), was performed since it assured a systematic methodology and defined procedures allowing to obtain results which are reliable and reproducible. Another decision made, was to use online database sources for identifying and retrieving the most relevant literature/papers. In the same regard, a software tool to provide better understanding and visualization of the data collected on what is already known (main trends), but also on potential gaps to be explored was also employed.

In this context, the Scopus database was selected, since it generally provides in "the Social Sciences and Humanities a higher citation count than ISI" (Harzing, 2011, p. 225). The software tool used was Vosviewer v1.6.4 (Barlow et al., 2017; Blanco-Mesa et al., 2017) which relies on the techniques, visualization of similarities (VOS) and multidimensional scaling, to generate bibliometric maps. Although other popular techniques are used for bibliometric mapping, such as Pajek (Mrvar and Batagelj, 2016; Nooy et al., 2011) or even SPSS (Saz-Gil, Almaguer-Kalixto, & Gómez-Quintero, 2016; Yudhya, 2016), these were disregarded since Vosviewer enables a better exploration and visualization of the data outputs by the researchers (Eck & Waltman, 2014).

The Systematic Literature Review was conducted on the 2nd of February 2017, using Scopus database and the search terms defined were "global strategy". Other alternatives were considered, but to prevent bias in generating other search results with wider scope, only these two keywords were used. An initial result of 93,701 documents (articles, conference papers, articles in press, book chapters) in total were found. To reduce the number of documents, and consistency of the data to be analysed (ranging from book review to conference proceedings) a few steps were taken in the search refinement. Thus, it was only considered: a) articles, b) in the subject areas of Business, Management and Accounting, Social Sciences, c) in English language. A total of 1947 documents (articles), from 1974 to 2017, were used as initial sample. The next step considered the download of all information of the articles to a reference manager (Mendeley) for an initial screening to verify duplication of articles or even the exclusion of those not within the study's objective. In the end, 1900 articles were validated for analysis. Eck and Waltman's (2014) recommendations, regarding the number of occurrences (minimum 10), and selection (60%) of the number of terms retrieved (583), were employed during the software procedures. Also, to prevent deviation in the data, fractional counting was considered preferable over full counting as posited by several authors (Perianes-Rodriguez, Waltman & van Eck, 2016).

RESULTS AND DISCUSSION

Overview of the Body of Knowledge Main Contributors

The first key output generated from the research, figure 1, was the number of documents printed, 1974 to 2017. In this regard, 2014, proved to be the best year so far, with 202 articles published. The first milestones were reached in the end of the 80's (1989 with 14 articles) and in the 90's with more than the double of articles printed when compared with the previous decade (1999 with 36 articles). After 2009, the number of article addressing global strategy constantly surpassed the one hundred, with 115 (2009), 147 (2010), 124 (2011), 154 (2012), 176 (2013), 202 (2014), 175 (2015) and 178 (2016). Even, 2017 has the potential to reach the past figures, or even surpass it, since only 1/12 of the year has gone by and 19 articles were already in press.

Figure 1.

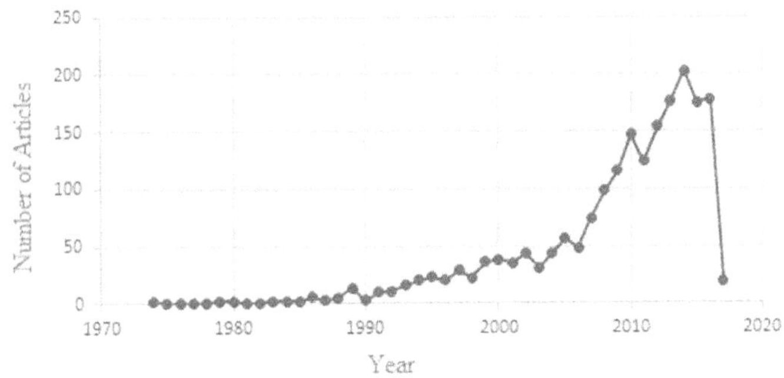

Another output generated from an analysis of the sample of articles was to identify the source that contributed the most for the publishing of articles about the topic "global strategy". As figure 2 shows, Long Range Planning was the first with 78 articles published, followed by International Marketing Review (66), Globalizations and Journal of International Business Studies (55) in *ex-aequo* as the top three.

Figure 2.

The distribution of articles per country/territory (Figure 3) was also assessed, United States (628 articles), United Kingdom (292), Australia (145) and Canada (110) are leading the field and the number of publication about Global Strategy. The remaining countries identified in figure 3, France and Germany (75), China (71), Netherlands (62), India and Spain (57), Italy and South Africa (55-57) also contributed immensely for body of knowledge.

Figure 3.

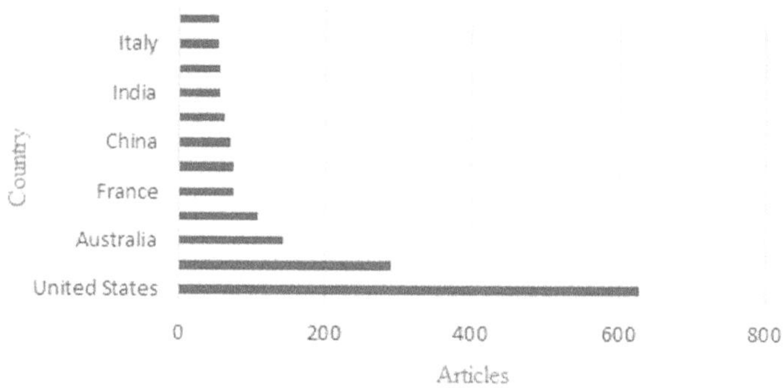

Another analysis performed addressed the most prolific and impacting authors about global strategy. In this regard, the most published were S. Tamer Cavusgil with 10 articles (addressing mainly the topics of *firm performance*, *innovation* and *corporate venture*), and David A. Griffith with 8 articles (addressing the topics of *trends in the retailing, social capital, implications of strategic fit and product performance, incidents and response strategies, convergence effects, reciprocity*). They were both followed closely by M. Kotabe, Y. Luo, A. M. Rugman and M. Harvey with 6 articles. Another analysis performed, was not on the quantity of articles, but instead on their impact in the academia, therefore the sample was assessed regarding the number of citations on Scopus.

The findings confirmed the importance (1497 citations) of Woodruff's (1997) work, on ways to achieve and retain a competitive advantage by keeping an outward orientation toward customers. He addressed the implications and presented a framework based on "…customer value, customer value learning, and the related skills that managers will need to create and implement superior customer value strategies" (Woodruff, 1997, p.139). The second most impacting work, with 746 citations, focused on born-global firms, highlighting "… the critical role of innovative culture, as well as knowledge and capabilities, in this unique breed of international, entrepreneurial firm… [and found] … that despite the scarce resources typical of young firms […] born-global firms leverage a distinctive mix of orientations and strategies that allow them to succeed in diverse international markets" (Knight & Cavusgil, 2004, p.124). The third most cited article (718) was Luo and Tung's (2007) research on the internationalization of emerging market multinational corporations. They assessed the disadvantages of multinational corporations in the global market, and their aggressive and risk-taking measures to overcome their competitive weaknesses. Other authors, such as Etzkowitz, Webster, Gebhardt, and Terra's (2000) interest for the future of universities as entrepreneurial paradigm (662 citations), Adger's (2003) social capital on climate change (627 citations), and Mathews (2006) focus on multinationals as the new players in 21st century (573 citations), were also found.

3.2. Bibliometric Mapping Trends

Next, the research topics regarding trends and gaps were identified using Vosviewer software that provides improved graphical representation and simplicity in comprehending and visualizing constructed bibliometric networks (van Eck & Waltman, 2010, p. 536). In the label view (figure 4), items are identified by labels and circles (or nodes), and their importance is represented by the (larger) size of the label/circle.

Figure 4.

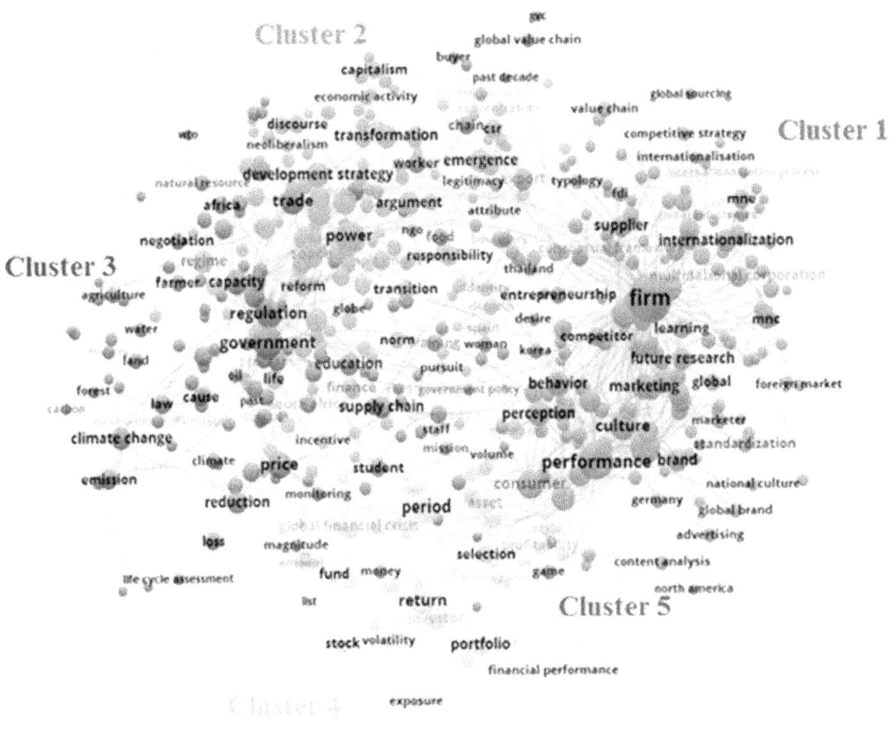

The different colours represent clusters, and the closer the clusters are to each other the stronger the networks between the fields of research. Per the figure 4, the nodes (circle) and networks (colored lines) show a clear pattern, in which **5 main clusters** are identified., in red, green, blue, yellow and purple. These areas identified and outlined in the figure, demonstrate visually the greater dimension of the red cluster from the other four, i.e., size, followed by the green, blue, yellow and finally purple (as emergent topics and cluster). To have a better understanding of the trends and gaps among the clusters these will be explored individually, including a brief discussion stressing some of the studies topics.

Cluster 1: Firm Performance in the Global Market

In this 1st cluster (in figure 4), red color, the most found topics were the terms *firm* (395 occurrences), followed by *performance* (222), *manager* (167), *consumer* (111) and *culture* (99). The interest shown by previous researchers in the item *Firm* extended from performance (Lahiri & Kedia, 2009) to the various levels, national (Choi & Kawk, 2015), international and global (Ferraris et al., 2016). The same concerns were presented when researchers seeked to gain more insights into the managerial responsibilities, at global level (Bartlett & Ghoshal, 1992), but also evaluating and distinguishing the style, gender (Pioquinto, 2016) and flexibility (Galindo & Limjuco, 2016) for example. Moreover, other topics found were customer's perceptions on the market place, considering them as global consumers (Alden et al., 1999) or focusing on their attitudes (Chaar & Lee, 2012), the influence of age (Omelchenko et al., 2016; Rahman, 2012), the relation with ethnocentrism (Jin et al., 2015) in specific economic times (Kreckova et al., 2012), plataforms (Parsons, 2013) or channels (like social media) (Rippé et al., 2015). Culture was also not ignored, and the impact of culture at within the national boundaries (Ralston et al., 2008) or across various cultures (Anakwe et al., 2000; Harrison-Hill, 2015) were investigated.

Cluster 2: Power and Market Space Development

In cluster 2, in green color, the hot topics/occurrences were: *power* (119), *space* (85), *development strategy* (76), *transformation* (70) as the most frequent. Researchers considered the importance of power in politics (Veebel & Kulu, 2014), from the private sector (Petkoski et al., 2009) like firms (Tokatli, 2013), corporations (Brinkman & Brinkman, 2002) their relationships (Cheng, 2016), asymmetries (Neilson, 2014) but also the role and growing influence of the power of the public (Samper, 2016) through public policies more customer focused (Morash & Lynch, 2002). Space or location, where economic (Patel-Campillo, 2010) competition but also social (Heidenreich, 2012) impacts occurred, were pursued as important topics by researchers. But spatial distribution, in urban spaces (Barroso et al., 2014), geographies (Sheppard, 2002), technologies (Zaheer & Manrakhan, 2001) and industries (Saz-Gil et al., 2016) were also not neglected. In this cluster, topics related to development strategies by companies and transnational corporations that transform structurally (Aryeetey & Moyo, 2012; Pavlínek, 2003) using innovation (Frolova & Tokar, 2014), outsourcing (Bagot, 2013) in countries (e.g. Latin America) were found (Sanchez, 2003).

Cluster 3: Government Regulation

Cluster 3, in Blue color, allowed to identify *government* (156 occurrences), *regulation* (108), *price* (96) and *trade* (93). The governments' decisions to increase the effectiveness (Williams & Martinez, 2012) are important, among which is defining and implementing innovative government (Rios-Morales & Brennan, 2009) programs, with consequences to education (Mok, 2005) policies, businesses (Lu & Lazonick, 2001) and tourism (Stoykova, 2009), for example. Other topics considered, regulation over pollution and ecological protection (Ji et al., 2014), governance strategies regarding the transforming global market and global chains (Patel-Campillo, 2010). Results also demonstrated price to be a hot topic among which, price strategies used by multinationals on global economy (example: food price) (Guariso et al., 2014), price-sensitive (Hu & Motwani, 2014), low price emphasis (Rosenbloom, 1994), price-quality products (Brouthers et al., 2000), raw materials procurement and fluctuating prices (Arnold et al., 2009) are some of the directions previous researchers followed. On trade, the new and more demanding global market required for better policies (Pangestu et al., 2015) and also an assessment of international and intra-group trade exchanges (Lopes, 2008) and networks (Leitão Marques, 2003), because of the impact on organizations' competitiveness (Montalbano & Nenci, 2014). The implications of managerial practices, negotiations between parties (ElgstrÖm, 2007) and free trade were also among the most prominent topics in this cluster.

Cluster 4: Economic Periods

The cluster 4, yellow color, groups the topics *period* (149 occurrences), *return* (91 occurrences), *asset* (75), *global financial crisis* (73), *investor* (71) and *portfolio* (65). The economic progression and resulting changes in the world, shifted the economic global order (Dobson, 2012), reshaped business strategies to counter competition's growth (Amendolagine et al., 2014) including the educational institutions role (Motitswe, 2014) throughout several periods. The global financial crisis intensified and investors' fears regarding their returns (Vandermerwe, 1989, 1997), and asscts (Blitz & Van Vliet, 2008; Niederle & Grisa, 2008) urged them to find the best practices and investment decision regarding portfolio (Choudhury & Naidu, 2009; Lukasevicius & Lapinskaite, 2014).

Cluster 5: Societal Changes

In the last cluster (5) identified, in purple color, *education* (54), *worker* (42), and *entrepreneurship* (31) were the most prominent. These topics reflect also that along with the economic changes, social also occurred, for instance in education environment of the higher institutions (Abdina et al., 2015) at global level (Sun et al., 2014) in the new era of education 2.0 (Hua, 2015; Kerekes & Nemeslaki, 2009). Workers, faced similar challenges and threats (Balezentis and Balezentis, 2011) to transnational, intra and inter-movement of workers (Bieler et al., 2014), rights (Egels-Zandén & Hyllman, 2007), unions power and influence (Bieler et al., 2014), gender equality (Pearson & Kusakabe, 2012) as a way to respond to the global and local market changes. Entrepreneurship, was also an important topic for researchers, from its evolving domains (Carlsson et al., 2013), behaviors and determinants (Yu, 2000), skills (Smith & Paton, 2010) and academic programs (Rae & Woodier-Harris, 2013).

Figure 5.

Overall, considering all keywords as the figure 5 – *Most frequent keywords* shows, by using a word cloud generator, from the sample retrieved from the Scopus data: *firm, studies, world, global* along with *marketing, strategies and economics* have been overall at the core of the main topics researched in the past 4 decades.

3.3. Bibliometric Mapping Time Series

Moreover, an analysis of the networks among the topics over a decade (period of 2004-2014), in figure 6, in which the colors represent distinctive times, i.e., corresponding to the dark blue color is the year 2004-2006, light blue (2007-2008), light green (2009), yellow (2010-2011), orange/red (2012-2014). Overall, light blue is the most dominant color and research topics it recognizes reached the peak *(time)* by 2007 and 2008, for example, firm.

Figure 6.

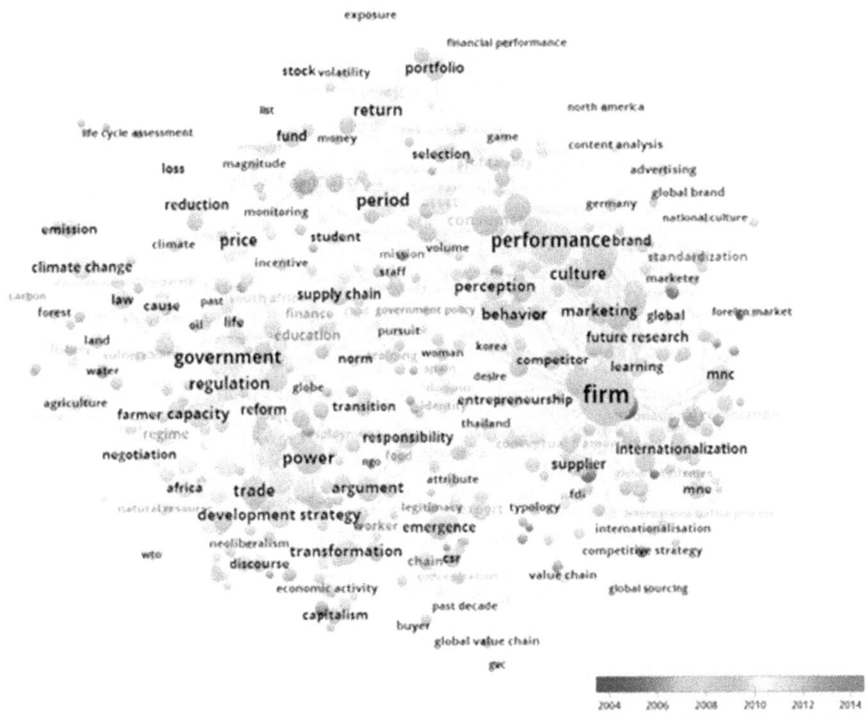

A more detailed view of the map in figure 6, confirms once again the dominance of blue color (2004-2008). It also shows in 2004-2006 that *competitive strategy*, followed by *mission* as the oldest topics identified in dark blue (Li et al., 2005; Luo & Zhao, 2004; Maddy & Stilwell, 2005; Stephan, 2005; Tsai, 2005). In light blue color (2007-2008), other topics like *firm, responsibility, competitor, marketing and advertising* identified (Andersson & Evangelista, 2006; Connolly & Prothero, 2008; Du et al., 2008; Peng & Delios, 2006). The light green (2009) shows *performance, power, development strategy* and *transformation behavior* (La et al., 2009; Prayag, 2009; Schilke et al., 2009). Yellow identifies *period, return, price, government* and *regulation* in the following years, 2010-2011 (West, 2011), followed by orange color 2012-2014, with the topics *supply chain and global value chain* (Gunasekaran & Yang, 2014).

3.4. Bibliometric Mapping Gaps

To identify previous hot topics in the academia and potential gaps, the density map provided in figure 7, shows "an overview of the general structure of a map [...] draw[s] attention to the most important areas" (Van Eck & Waltman, 2010:529), these important or hot areas are represented in red color, followed by the less important, yellow and green. From the density map, three main clusters are identified in the hot areas or red areas, these are in the cluster 1 – *firm performance in the global market* and cluster 2 - *power and market space development* and cluster 3 – *government regulation* position, as previously seen in figure 5.

In the first cluster area, the hottest and most trendy research topics were by their highlight (size and in bold) *firm* and *performance*. This finding demonstrates the constant search from the academia in past decades to improve and attain better insights into achieving better performance in their organizations (firm, multinational corporations, multinational enterprises...). The second hottest areas are located between cluster two and three with four main topics stressed, *government, regulation, pow*er and *trade*. The developments of the society and economy within the global market era broke boundaries, but also required for new ones to be established to face the growing power of organizations to maintain a fair trade, but on the other hand new powers arose, such as the public.

In the yellow areas, within clusters 1, 2 and 3, not so trendy topics such as *internationalization, supplier, competitor, mnc, period, price, supply chain*, and *development strategy* to name a few can be found. Similar results can be seen on yellow areas of clusters 4 and 5 (that do not evidence hot topics) with *period, return, emergence and csr* (corporate social responsibility). These topics address difficulties researchers and managers with responsibilities for the global strategy had to respond. It also covers, time periods of great economic and social importance

Figure 7.

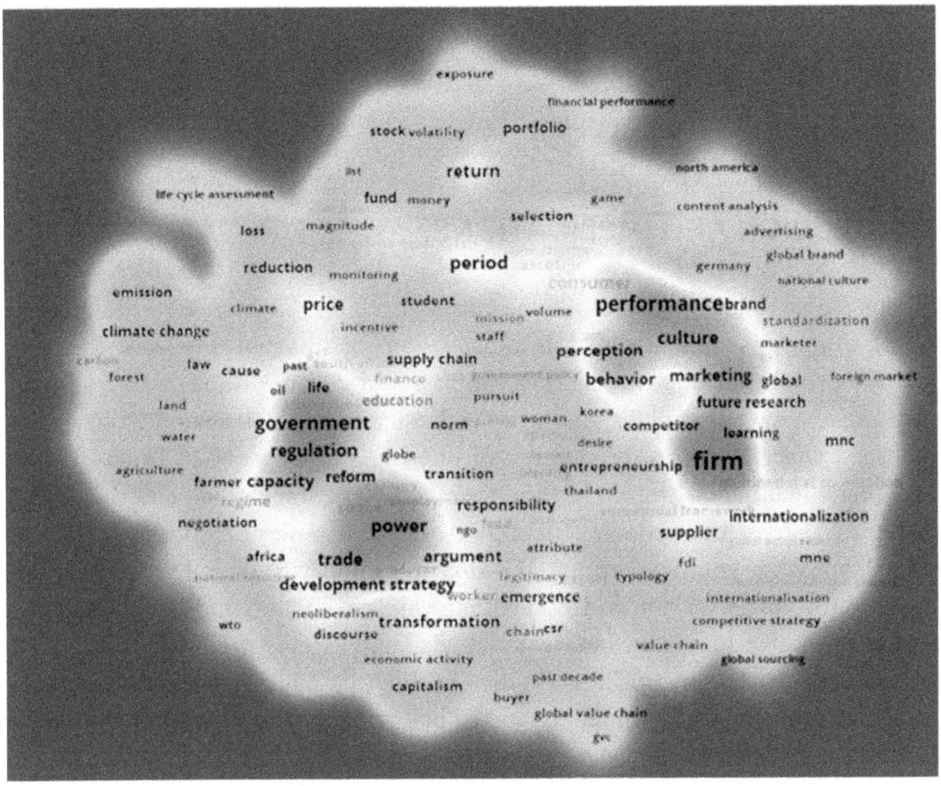

to the development of strategies, in which *price, suppliers, competitors* and *social responsibility* among other topics, were important to overcome risks and threats for the future of their organizations and businesses, but also society. Contrary to the most important areas, in red and yellow (Van Eck & Waltman, 2010), the green and blue area have not been the major focus of the academia, and consequently can be used as future research by authors (without neglecting the previous areas red and yellow own gaps).

In this regard, in the green areas, located in all 5 clusters, potential areas of interest in which gaps can be further investigated are for instance related to *climate change, emission, water, land, global brand, reduction, climate, law* and *entrepreneurship*. The environment and climate change constitute like other topics in the past, an additional test for the academia to respond, in the same way the expansion and proliferation of global brands or even new forms of doing businesses and risks taking in the form of entrepreneurship. In the light blue, more potential areas of research can be found in the 5 clusters, since they have not been widely researched previously: *global sourcing, global value chain, exposure, natural resource and financial performance*. In addition, the complex task and ability required for organizations to compete in the global market required better understanding of global sourcing strategies, and the role of organizations and their subsidiaries position in the valued-added chain and exploitation of natural resources to foster economic and financial developments.

CONCLUSION AND IMPLICATIONS

The main goal of this study was attained through a bibliometric review of the *main global strategy* themes or research topics using for this end, the most frequent keywords employed by researchers in the past four decades through a systematic literature review. The conclusions drawn is that the topic "global strategy" remains important and relevant as the number of published articles shows from 1974 to 2017 (early February). Moreover, to answer the first goal regarding how the global strategy construct evolved, the findings demonstrated the predominant role of English-speaking world regarding; a) *Authors,* with Cavusgil, and Griffith as the most prolific, and Woodruff's (1997) with the highest citation impact, b) *Journals,* with Long Range Planning, International Marketing Review, Globalizations and Journal of International Business Studies leading the number of publications, c) *Countries of publication,* United States, United Kingdom and Australia, in which the interest for the topic was shown since early stages.

Results also demonstrated through mapping time series, in which networks between the different items and areas of knowledge are possible to distinguished by periods, the 2004-2014 as the most prolific so far. In fact, specially between 2007-2008, the most dominant cluster 1 – *firm performance in the global market*, reached its peak regarding its most important research topic *firm*. Currently, this topic remains relevant with Bandiera, Prat, Hansen and Sadun (2020), Ballal and Bapat (2020) among other, continuing to address firm's performance within various contexts.

The research provided an overview of the global strategy construct throughout a time span of 43 years, and answer the second research goal, which research trends and gaps can be identified? Through the bibliometric visualization software, the trends and potential research gaps can be identified, using for this purpose the density map to visualize the hot and "cold" areas. In the study, the most researched topics and gaps identified, were grouped into 5 clusters: Cluster 1 – Firm performance in the global market, Cluster 2 – Power and market space development, Cluster 3 – Government regulation; Cluster 4 – Economic periods; Cluster 5 – Societal changes.

All in all, the global strategy construct still requires further attention from the academia, since not much neighbourhood, networks were found among some items or topics identified in the density map. One of such examples, is the two red clusters that show two big areas separated (left and right) without any link between the two. The industry and market in the present environment, in which MNE and other firms often require extensive strategic management at the global level to respond to local and transnational partnerships and global integrations (Jennex, 2020; Hansen, 2020) will provide the opportunity to establish links between the concepts.

The study's literature review allowed to verify the complexity of the construct and to testify the robustness of the body of knowledge with many different perspectives, ideas, concepts and utterly, understandings of the global strategy body of knowledge. The findings are expected to help the practionaires to adopt better managerial decisions and strategies by considering the topics, trends and gaps identified in his study. Consequently, an increase of their corporations, companies or overall organizations competitiveness and success.

Limitations and Future Research

The limitations of this systematic literature review include the scope of study which ranged from 1974 to 2017. The search terms sought to be comprehensive to encompass a wider number of studies, but despite this fact, it remains that the study is systematic review a process which includes filtering, screening and consequently decisions. As such, papers were removed and others were not included in the search step, for the reason of the language was not English. The review was also limited to online databases, excluding potential paper on non-digital databases which might be able to be included in the paper.

Also, the simplicity of color scheme in density map, neglected the potential of studying the most signaled or hottest areas and relationships. The Scopus database gives one unit to each author, university or country involved in the paper, without distinguishing whether it was one or more authors in the study. Therefore, this may bring some deviations in the analysis. However, the study considers some figures with fractional counting to partially solve these limitations. Based on the limitations and findings, the study suggests the following topics for future research.

Future studies should include concepts linked to firm performance in the global market, to this end, researchers have to apply and develop new methods to assess firms' performance. Technology (e.g., machine learning) provides various tools to measure more efficiently firms at the national and global level (e.g., new economies or old economies). In addition, there is yet much to investigate regarding firms' employees (e.g., CEO, immigrant workers) and their performance impact on firm's success. Moreover, employee's interactions and relationships along with the style of management and type of firm (family, SME, MNE) are also relevant topics. Customers' perception of firms' behaviours (e.g., ethical, on social media) during the different economic times and in the various cultural contexts deserves to be explored due to the firms' goal of establishing strong customer-firm relationships.

Regarding *power and market space development,* the power some firms (e.g., SME, MNE) have in the market, and how their asymmetries shape the development of markets (emerging, maturing) requests further development. In addition, the transformation of markets due to *government regulation* to respond to climate change, pollution, education policies, cost efficiency, energy needs, and market competitiveness demonstrates that firms and managers' have to incorporate more variables in their market strategy. In the same way, *economic periods* driven by petrol, financial or health crisis (e.g., covid-19) will change and shape the world market and society. The *Societal changes* leading to firms searching for more sustainable ways of production and eco-friendly policies, implies costs to companies and society at large that need to be explored. In the same way with emergence of corporate social responsibility firms are required to be more self-regulated and socially accountable, at what cost? The global market and the distinct value chains will continue to transform the firms and the space they operate at a greater speed, leading to more asymmetries and power struggles that remind managers of the need to improve their local and global strategies.

ACKNOWLEDGMENT

This paper is financed by National Funds provided by FCT- Foundation for Science and Technology through project UIDB/04020/2020.

REFERENCES

Abdina, A. K., Abdildina, H. S., Gappasova, A. G., Kakimzhanova, M. K., Ni Valerievich, D., & Sadykova, T. M.Seifullin Kazakh Agro Technical University. (2015). Foreign students' social adaptation to the education environment of a higher educational institution: By the example of S. Seifullin Kazakh Agro Technical University. *Mediterranean Journal of Social Sciences*, *6*(5), 184–194. doi:10.5901/mjss.2015.v6n5p184

Adger, W. N. (2003). Social capital, collective action, and adaptation to climate change. *Economic Geography*, *79*(4), 387–404. doi:10.1111/j.1944-8287.2003.tb00220.x

Alden, D. L., Steenkamp, J.-B. E. M., & Batra, R. (1999). Brand positioning through advertising in Asia, North America, and Europe: The role of global consumer culture. *Journal of Marketing, 63*(1), 75–87. doi:10.1177/002224299906300106

Amendolagine, V., Capolupo, R., & Ferri, G. (2014). Innovativeness, offshoring and black economy decisions. Evidence from Italian manufacturing firms. *International Business Review, 23*(6), 1153–1166. doi:10.1016/j.ibusrev.2014.03.011

Anakwe, U. P., Igbaria, M., & Anandarajan, M. (2000). Management practices across cultures: Role of support in technology usage. *Journal of International Business Studies, 31*(4), 653–666. doi:10.1057/palgrave.jibs.8490927

Andersson, S., & Evangelista, F. (2006). The entrepreneur in the Born Global firm in Australia and Sweden. *Journal of Small Business and Enterprise Development, 13*(4), 642–659. doi:10.1108/14626000610705796

Arli, D., Tjiptono, F., & Winit, W. (2015). Consumer ethics among young consumers in developing countries: A cross national study. *Social Responsibility Journal, 11*(3), 449–466. doi:10.1108/SRJ-05-2013-0059

Arnold, J., Minner, S., & Eidam, B. (2009). Raw material procurement with fluctuating prices. *International Journal of Production Economics, 121*(2), 353–364. doi:10.1016/j.ijpe.2007.02.038

Aryeetey, E., & Moyo, N. (2012). Industrialisation for structural transformation in Africa: Appropriate roles for the state. *Journal of African Economies, 21*(2), 55–85. doi:10.1093/jae/ejr043

Bagot, G. F. (2013). Outsourcing an industry: A new paradigm and strategy for national economic development- the new form of old Colonialism! *International Journal of Business Research, 13*(4), 5–18. doi:10.18374/IJBR-13-4.1

Balezentis, A., & Balezentis, T. (2011). Framework of strategic management model for strategy Europe 2020: Diachronic analysis and proposed guidelines. *The Engineering Economist, 22*(3), 271–282.

Ballal, J. M., & Bapat, V. (2020). Socioemotional Wealth and Its Effect on Family Firm Performance. In J. M. Palma-Ruiz, I. Barros-Contreras, & L. Gnan (Eds.), *Handbook of research on the strategic management of family businesses* (pp. 201–227). IGI Global. doi:10.4018/978-1-7998-2269-1.ch010

Bandiera, O., Prat, A., Hansen, S., & Sadun, R. (2020). Ceo behavior and firm performance. *Journal of Political Economy, 128*(4).

Barlow, P., McKee, M., Basu, S., & Stuckler, D. (2017). The health impact of trade and investment agreements: A quantitative systematic review and network co-citation analysis. *Globalization and Health, 13*(1), 1–9. doi:10.118612992-017-0240-x PMID:28274238

Barroso, I. C., González-Romero, G., & Lara, P. L. (2014). The crisis and territorial development in Andalusian cities. *Revista de Estudios Regionales, 100*, 47–82.

Bartlett, C. A., & Ghoshal, S. (1992). What is a global manager? *Harvard Business Review, 70*(5), 124–132. PMID:10121314

Beets, S. D. (2005). Understanding the demand-side issues of international corruption. *Journal of Business Ethics, 57*(1), 65–81. doi:10.100710551-004-3824-3

Bieler, A., Hilary, J., & Lindberg, I. (2014). Trade unions, 'free trade', and the problem of transnational solidarity: An introduction. *Globalizations, 11*(1), 1–9. doi:10.1080/14747731.2014.860319

Blanco-Mesa, F., Merigó, J. M., & Gil-Lafuente, A. M. (2017). Fuzzy decision making: A bibliometric-based review. *Journal of Intelligent & Fuzzy Systems, 32*(2), 2033–2050. doi:10.3233/JIFS-161640

Blitz, D. C., & Van Vliet, P. (2008). Global tactical cross-asset allocation: Applying value and momentum across asset classes. *Journal of Portfolio Management, 35*(1), 23–38. doi:10.3905/JPM.2008.35.1.23

Blom, R., Melin, H., Sarno, A., & Sarno, I. (2008). Managerial threats and prospects in Russian firms: The case of St. Petersburg 1999-2005. *World Review of Entrepreneurship, Management and Sustainable Development, 4*(2–3), 169–181. doi:10.1504/WREMSD.2008.018223

Brinkman, R. L., & Brinkman, J. E. (2002). Corporate power and the globalization process. *International Journal of Social Economics, 29*(9), 730–752. doi:10.1108/03068290210442739

Brouthers, L. E., Werner, S., & Matulich, E. (2000). The influence of triad nations' environments on price-quality product strategies and MNC performance. *Journal of International Business Studies, 31*(1), 39–62. doi:10.1057/palgrave.jibs.8490899

Carlsson, B., Braunerhjelm, P., McKelvey, M., Olofsson, C., Persson, L., & Ylinenpää, H. (2013). The evolving domain of entrepreneurship research. *Small Business Economics, 41*(4), 913–930. doi:10.100711187-013-9503-y

Carmona-Lavado, A., Gopalakrishnan, S., & Zhang, H. (2020). Product radicalness and firm performance in B2B marketing: A moderated mediation model. *Industrial Marketing Management*, *85*, 58–68. doi:10.1016/j.indmarman.2019.08.013

Chaar, B. B., & Lee, J. (2012). Role of socioeconomic status on consumers' attitudes towards DTCA of prescription medicines in Australia. *Journal of Business Ethics*, *105*(4), 447–460. doi:10.100710551-011-0977-8

Cheng, J. Y. S. (2016). Xi Jinping's 'new model of major power relationships' for Sino-American relations. *Journal of Comparative Asian Development*, *15*(2), 226–254. doi:10.1080/15339114.2016.1203342

Choi, S. B., & Kawk, Y. M. (2015). Corporate social responsibility and financial constraints: Evidence from Korean firms. *Global Business and Finance Review*, *20*(2), 15–26. doi:10.17549/gbfr.2015.20.2.15

Choudhury, A. H., & Naidu, G. N. (2009). A new selection strategy for portfolio diversification in the European Union. *Academy of Accounting and Financial Studies Journal*, *13*(3), 79–92.

Christian, V., & Gumbus, A. (2009). Shades of gray: Applying professional codes of ethics to workplace dilemmas. *Organizational Management Journal*, *6*(3), 178–199. doi:10.1057/omj.2009.22

Connolly, J., & Prothero, A. (2008). Green consumption: Life-politics, risk and contradictions. *Journal of Consumer Culture*, *8*(1), 117–145. doi:10.1177/1469540507086422

De Nooy, W., Mrvar, A., & Batagelj, V. (2011). *Exploratory social network analysis with pajek*. Cambridge University Press. doi:10.1017/CBO9780511996368

Degbey, W. Y. (2015). Customer retention: A source of value for serial acquirers. *Industrial Marketing Management*, *46*, 11–23. doi:10.1016/j.indmarman.2015.01.002

Dobson, H. (2012). Japan's response to the changing global order: The case of a 'Gaggle of Gs'. *International Relations of the Asia-Pacific*, *12*(2), 229–257. doi:10.1093/irap/lcr023

Du, L., Hou, J., & Huang, Y. (2008). Mechanisms of power and action for cause-related marketing: Perspectives of enterprise and non-profit organizations. *Baltic Journal of Management*, *3*(1), 92–104. doi:10.1108/17465260810844284

Eck, N.J. Van & Waltman, L. (2014). *Visualizing bibliometric networks, measuring scholarly impact: Methods and practice*. doi:10.1007/978-3-319-10377-8_13

Egels-Zandén, N., & Hyllman, P. (2007). Evaluating strategies for negotiating workers' rights in transnational corporations: The effects of codes of conduct and global agreements on workplace democracy. *Journal of Business Ethics*, *76*(2), 207–223. doi:10.100710551-006-9269-0

Elgström, O. (2007). Outsiders' perceptions of the European union in international trade negotiations. *Journal of Common Market Studies*, *45*(4), 949–967. doi:10.1111/j.1468-5965.2007.00755.x

Etzkowitz, H., Webster, A., Gebhardt, C., & Terra, B. R. C. (2000). The future of the university and the university of the future: Evolution of ivory tower to entrepreneurial paradigm. *Research Policy*, *29*(2), 313–330. doi:10.1016/S0048-7333(99)00069-4

Ferraris, A., Bresciani, S., & Del Giudice, M. (2016). International diversification and firm performance: A four-stage model. *EuroMed Journal of Business*, *11*(3), 362–375. doi:10.1108/EMJB-10-2015-0048

Flores, R. G., & Aguilera, R. V. (2007). Globalization and location choice: An analysis of US multinational firms in 1980 and 2000. *Journal of International Business Studies*, *38*(7), 1187–1210. doi:10.1057/palgrave.jibs.8400307

Frolova, T., & Tokar, V. (2014). The European Union TNCs' investment strategies of innovation development. *Economic Annals-XXI*, *5–6*, 13–16.

Galindo, M. Q., & Limjuco, R. P. (2016). Awareness on ASEAN 2015 integration, managerial flexibility and school preparedness for transnational students: Basis for a cross-cultural adaptation program. *International Journal of Applied Business and Economic Research*, *14*(2), 1171–1196.

Ghannad, N., & Andersson, S. (2012). The influence of the entrepreneur's background on the behaviour and development of born globals' internationalisation processes. *International Journal of Entrepreneurship and Small Business*, *15*(2), 136–153. doi:10.1504/IJESB.2012.045201

Guariso, A., Squicciarini, M. P., & Swinnen, J. (2014). Food price shocks and the political economy of global agricultural and development policy. *Applied Economic Perspectives and Policy*, *36*(3), 387–415. doi:10.1093/aepp/ppu020

Hansen, M. W. (2020). Toward a strategic management perspective on local content in African extractives: MNC procurement strategies between local responsiveness and global integration. *Africa Journal of Management*, *6*(1), 1–19. doi:10.1080/23322373.2020.1717283

Harrison-Hill, T. (2015). How far is a long way? Contrasting two cultures' perspectives of travel distance. *Qualitative Research in Organizations and Management, 13*(3), 3–17.

Harzing, A. W. (2011). *The publish or perish book: Your guide to effective and responsible citation analysis*. Tamar Software Research Publisher.

Heidenreich, M. (2012). The social embeddedness of multinational companies: A literature review. *Socio-economic Review, 10*(3), 549–579. doi:10.1093er/mws010

Hu, X. & Motwani, J.G. (2014). Minimizing downside risks for global sourcing under price-sensitive stochastic demand, exchange rate uncertainties, and supplier capacity constraints. *International Journal of Production Economics, 147*(B), 398–409.

Hua, T. (2015). Strategy to internationalise China's customs management education system. *World Customs Journal, 9*(1), 109–114.

Ikeda, K., & Marshall, A. (2016). How successful organizations drive innovation. *Strategy and Leadership, 44*(3), 9–19. doi:10.1108/SL-04-2016-0029

Jain, S. C., & Tucker, L. R. (1995). The influence of culture on strategic constructs in the process of globalization: An empirical study of North American and Japanese MNCs. *International Business Review, 4*(1), 19–37. doi:10.1016/0969-5931(94)00029-L

Jennex, M. E. (2020). Towards Understanding and Implementing Knowledge Management Strategy. In M. E. Jennex (Ed.), *Current Issues and Trends in Knowledge Management, Discovery, and Transfer* (pp. 103–125). IGI Global. doi:10.4018/978-1-7998-2189-2.ch005

Ji, G., Gunasekaran, A., & Yang, G. (2014). Constructing sustainable supply chain under double environmental medium regulations. *International Journal of Production Economics, 147*, 211–219. doi:10.1016/j.ijpe.2013.04.012

Ji, G., Gunasekaran, A. & Yang, G. (2014). Constructing sustainable supply chain under double environmental medium regulations. *International Journal of Production Economics, 147*(B), 211–219.

Jin, Z., Lynch, R., Attia, S., Chansarkar, B., Gülsoy, T., Lapoule, P., Liu, X., Newburry, W., Nooraini, M. S., Parente, R., Purani, K., & Ungerer, M. (2015). The relationship between consumer ethnocentrism, cosmopolitanism and product country image among younger generation consumers: The moderating role of country development status. *International Business Review, 24*(3), 380–393. doi:10.1016/j.ibusrev.2014.08.010

Kerekes, S., & Nemeslaki, A. (2009). Education 2.0: Exploring the challenges of Corvinus University in the long tail economy of global higher education. *Society and Economy*, *31*(1), 125–146. doi:10.1556/SocEc.31.2009.1.8

Kireeva-Karimova, A. (2015). Institutional challenges and economic agents forming a competitive market environment. *Mediterranean Journal of Social Sciences*, *6*(1S3), 211–216.

Knight, G. A., & Cavusgil, S. T. (2004). Innovation, organizational capabilities, and the born-global firm. *Journal of International Business Studies*, *35*(2), 124–141. doi:10.1057/palgrave.jibs.8400071

Knoerich, J. (2010). Gaining from the global ambitions of emerging economy enterprises: An analysis of the decision to sell a German firm to a Chinese acquirer. *Journal of International Management*, *16*(2), 177–191. doi:10.1016/j.intman.2010.03.008

Krasniqi, A. (2013). Legislative changes for economic development on regional basis, the possibilities or conditions for the integration of the West Balkan Countries in the European union - Kosovo case. *Journal of Advanced Research in Law and Economics*, *4*(2), 121–127.

Kreckova, Z., Odehnalova, J., & Reardon, J. (2012). Consumer ethnocentricity within the environment of economic crisis. *The Engineering Economist*, *23*(3), 271–281.

La, V., Patterson, P., & Styles, C. (2009). Client-perceived performance and value in professional B2B services: An international perspective. *Journal of International Business Studies*, *40*(2), 274–300. doi:10.1057/palgrave.jibs.8400406

Lahiri, S., & Kedia, B. L. (2009). The effects of internal resources and partnership quality on firm performance: An examination of Indian BPO providers. *Journal of International Management*, *15*(2), 209–224. doi:10.1016/j.intman.2008.09.002

Leitão Marques, M. M. (2003). From international trade to intra-group trade and exchanges between members of cooperation associations. The poly-local firm and the networks. *Revue Internationale de Droit Economique*, *17*(3–4), 411–441. doi:10.3917/ride.173.0411

Li, S., Tallman, S. B., & Ferreira, M. P. (2005). Developing the eclectic paradigm as a model of global strategy: An application to the impact of the Sep. 11 terrorist attacks on MNE performance levels. *Journal of International Management*, *11*(4), 479–496. doi:10.1016/j.intman.2005.09.006

Liang, X., & Gao, Y. (2020). Marketing performance measurement systems and firm performance: Are marketing capabilities the missing links? *European Journal of Marketing*, *54*(4), 885–907. doi:10.1108/EJM-05-2018-0302

Linares Navarro, E., Pla Barber, J., & Puig Blanco, F. (2009). The strategy of international outsourcing in spain: An approximation to the traditional manufacturing industries. *Investigaciones Europeas de Dirección y Economía de la Empresa*, *15*(3), 55–67. doi:10.1016/S1135-2523(12)60100-2

Liu, H., Jiang, X., Zhang, J., & Zhao, X. (2013). Strategic flexibility and international venturing by emerging market firms: The moderating effects of institutional and relational factors. *Journal of International Marketing*, *21*(2), 79–98. doi:10.1509/jim.12.0047

Lopes, T. S. (2008). Markets, knowledge and trade in brands. *Global Business and Economics Review*, *10*(4), 449–466. doi:10.1504/GBER.2008.020595

Lu, Q., & Lazonick, W. (2001). The organization of innovation in a transitional economy: Business and government in Chinese electronic publishing. *Research Policy*, *30*(1), 55–77. doi:10.1016/S0048-7333(99)00082-7

Lukasevicius, A., & Lapinskaite, I. (2014). Strategy of sustainable development in investment portfolio case. *European Research Studies Journal*, *17*(4), 3–18. doi:10.35808/ersj/429

Luo, Y., & Tung, R. L. (2007). International expansion of emerging market enterprises: A springboard perspective. *Journal of International Business Studies*, *38*(4), 481–498. doi:10.1057/palgrave.jibs.8400275

Luo, Y., & Zhao, H. (2004). Corporate link and competitive strategy in multinational enterprises: A perspective from subsidiaries seeking host market penetration. *Journal of International Management*, *10*(1), 77–105. doi:10.1016/j.intman.2003.12.006

Maddy, D. J., & Stilwell, J. A. (2005). Roads scholar tours: A marketing tool for building strong campus/community relationships. *Journal of Extension*, *43*(6), 291–295.

Maritz, A., De Wall, A., & Verhoeven, B. (2011). Entrepreneurial and innovative marketing: A systematic review of the literature. *Innovative Marketing*, *7*(4), 28–37.

Mathews, J. A. (2006). Dragon multinationals: New players in 21st century globalization. *Asia Pacific Journal of Management*, *23*(1), 5–27. doi:10.100710490-006-6113-0

Menon, A., & Menon, A. (1997). Enviropreneurial marketing strategy: The emergence of corporate environmentalism as market strategy. *Journal of Marketing*, *61*(1), 51–67. doi:10.1177/002224299706100105

Min, B. S., Cashel-Cordo, P., & Rhim, J. C. (2015). Corporate leverage strategy in an emerging market. *Global Business and Finance Review*, *20*(2), 35–48. doi:10.17549/gbfr.2015.20.2.35

Mok, K. H. (2005). Fostering entrepreneurship: Changing role of government and higher education governance in Hong Kong. *Research Policy*, *34*(4), 537–554. doi:10.1016/j.respol.2005.03.003

Montalbano, P., & Nenci, S. (2014). The trade competitiveness of southern emerging economies: A multidimensional approach through cluster analysis. *World Economy*, *37*(6), 783–810. doi:10.1111/twec.12195

Morash, E. A., & Lynch, D. F. (2002). Public policy and global supply chain capabilities and performance: A resource-based view. *Journal of International Marketing*, *10*(1), 25–51. doi:10.1509/jimk.10.1.25.19529

Motitswe, J. (2014). The role of institute level support teams on addressing barriers to learning and provide support in schools. Are they functional? *Mediterranean Journal of Social Sciences*, *5*(8), 259–264. doi:10.5901/mjss.2014.v5n8p259

Mrvar, A., & Batagelj, V. (2016). Analysis and visualization of large networks with program package Pajek. *Complex Adaptive Systems Modeling*, *4*(1), 1–6. doi:10.118640294-016-0017-8

Neilson, J. (2014). Value chains, neoliberalism and development practice: The Indonesian experience. *Review of International Political Economy*, *21*(1), 38–69. doi:10.1080/09692290.2013.809782

Niederle, P. A., & Grisa, C. (2008). Livelihoods diversification and access to actors and assets: A framework about the local development dynamics of family farm. *Cuadernos de Desarrollo Rural*, *5*(61), 41–69.

Omelchenko, E., Andreeva, Y., Arif, E., & Polyakov, S. (2016). Where do time and all of the money go? Consumer strategies of urban youth in modern Russia. *Economia e Sociologia*, *9*(4), 176–190. doi:10.14254/2071-789X.2016/9-4/11

Pangestu, M., Rahardja, S., & Ing, L. Y. (2015). Fifty years of trade policy in indonesia: New world trade, old treatments. *Bulletin of Indonesian Economic Studies*, *51*(2), 239–261. doi:10.1080/00074918.2015.1061915

Parsons, A. (2013). Using social media to reach consumers: A content analysis of official facebook pages. *Academy of Marketing Studies Journal*, *17*(2), 27–36.

Patel-Campillo, A. (2010). Rival commodity chains: Agency and regulation in the US and colombian cut flower agro-industries. *Review of International Political Economy*, *17*(1), 75–102. doi:10.1080/09692290903296094

Pavlínek, P. (2003). Transformation of the Czech automotive components industry through foreign direct investment. *Eurasian Geography and Economics*, *44*(3), 184–209. doi:10.2747/1538-7216.44.3.184

Pearce, R., & Papanastassiou, M. (1999). Overseas RandD and the strategic evolution of MNE: Evidence from laboratories in the UK. *Research Policy*, *28*(1), 23–41. doi:10.1016/S0048-7333(98)00104-8

Pearson, R., & Kusakabe, K. (2012). Who cares? Gender, reproduction, and care chains of Burmese migrant workers in Thailand. *Feminist Economics*, *18*(2), 149–175. doi:10.1080/13545701.2012.691206

Peng, M. W., & Delios, A. (2006). What determines the scope of the firm over time and around the world? An Asia Pacific perspective. *Asia Pacific Journal of Management*, *23*(4), 385–405. doi:10.100710490-006-9021-4

Perianes-Rodriguez, A., Waltman, L., & Van Eck, N. J. (2016). Constructing bibliometric networks: A comparison between full and fractional counting. *Journal of Informetrics*, *10*(4), 1178–1195. doi:10.1016/j.joi.2016.10.006

Petkoski, D., Warren, D. E., & Laufer, W. S. (2009). Collective strategies in fighting corruption: Some intuitions and counter intuitions. *Journal of Business Ethics*, *88*(4), 815–822. doi:10.100710551-009-0321-8

Pinkse, J., & Kolk, A. (2012). Multinational enterprises and climate change: Exploring institutional failures and embeddedness. *Journal of International Business Studies*, *43*(3), 332–341. doi:10.1057/jibs.2011.56

Pioquinto, M. A. J. G. (2016). Management styles of women managers: Its effect on job performance as prime mover to the ASEAN economic community (AEC) integration. *Global Business and Finance Review*, *21*(2), 47–64. doi:10.17549/gbfr.2016.21.2.47

Prayag, G. (2009). Tourists' evaluations of destination image, satisfaction, and future behavioral intentions-the case of mauritius. *Journal of Travel & Tourism Marketing*, *26*(8), 836–853. doi:10.1080/10548400903358729

Rae, D., & Woodier-Harris, N. R. (2013). How does enterprise and entrepreneurship education influence postgraduate students' career intentions in the New Era economy? *Education + Training*, *55*(8–9), 926–948. doi:10.1108/ET-07-2013-0095

Rahman, M. S. (2012). Young consumer's perception on foreign made fast moving consumer goods: The role of religiosity, spirituality and animosity. *International Journal of Business and Management Science*, *5*(2), 103–118.

Ralston, D. A., Holt, D. H., Terpstra, R. H., & Kai-Cheng, Y. (2008). The impact of national culture and economic ideology on managerial work values: A study of the United States, Russia, Japan, and China. *Journal of International Business Studies*, *39*(1), 8–26. doi:10.1057/palgrave.jibs.8400330

Rios-Morales, R., & Brennan, L. (2009). Ireland's innovative governmental policies promoting internationalisation. *Research in International Business and Finance*, *23*(2), 157–168. doi:10.1016/j.ribaf.2008.03.012

Rippé, C. B., Weisfeld-Spolter, S., Yurova, Y., & Sussan, F. (2015). Is there a global multichannel consumer? *International Marketing Review*, *32*(3–4), 329–349. doi:10.1108/IMR-10-2013-0225

Rosenbloom, B., & Dupuis, M. (1994). Low price, low cost, high service: A new paradigm for global retailing? *International Review of Retail, Distribution and Consumer Research*, *4*(2), 149–158. doi:10.1080/09593969400000013

Rouen, E. (2020). Rethinking measurement of pay disparity and its relation to firm performance. *The Accounting Review*, *95*(1), 343–378. doi:10.2308/accr-52440

Sanchez, O. (2003). Globalization as a development strategy in Latin America? *World Development*, *31*(12), 1977–1995. doi:10.1016/j.worlddev.2003.09.002

Saz-Gil, I., Almaguer-Kalixto, P., & Gómez-Quintero, J. D. (2016). Social capital and networks: Analysis of the third sector in rural contexts. *CIRIEC - Espana. C.I.R.I.E.C. España*, *86*(1), 123–154.

Schilke, O., Reimann, M., & Thomas, J. S. (2009). When does international marketing standardization matter to firm performance? *Journal of International Marketing*, *17*(4), 24–46. doi:10.1509/jimk.17.4.24

Schmeisser, B. A. (2013). Systematic review of literature on offshoring of value chain activities. *Journal of International Management*, *19*(4), 390–406. doi:10.1016/j.intman.2013.03.011

Sheppard, E. (2002). The spaces and times of globalization: Place, scale, networks, and positionality. *Economic Geography*, *78*(3), 307–330. doi:10.2307/4140812

Smith, A., & Paton, R. A. (2010). An entrepreneurship toolkit for intensive skills development. *International Journal of Entrepreneurship and Small Business*, *9*(2), 162–176. doi:10.1504/IJESB.2010.030618

Stephan, M. (2005). Diversification strategy of global media conglomerates: A comment. *Journal of Media Economics*, *18*(2), 85–103. doi:10.120715327736me1802_1

Stoykova, B. (2009). Contemporary tendencies in development of sacred tourism in Bulgaria. *International Review on Public and Nonprofit Marketing*, *6*(1), 1–9. doi:10.100712208-008-0020-7

Sun, J., Tamaki, K., Yeh, S., & Takiuti, N. (2014). A study of global manufacturing education and training for Chinese company manager. *Industrial Engineering and Management Systems*, *13*(3), 252–257. doi:10.7232/iems.2014.13.3.252

Tokatli, N. (2013). Doing a Gucci: The transformation of an Italian fashion firm into a global powerhouse in a 'Los Angeles-izing' World. *Journal of Economic Geography*, *13*(2), 239–255. doi:10.1093/jeg/lbs050

Tsai, S.-P. (2005). Integrated marketing as management of holistic consumer experience. *Business Horizons*, *48*(5), 431–441. doi:10.1016/j.bushor.2005.02.005

van Eck, N. J., & Waltman, L. (2010). Software survey: VOSviewer, a computer program for bibliometric mapping. *Scientometrics*, *84*(2), 523–538. doi:10.100711192-009-0146-3 PMID:20585380

van Eck, N. J., & Waltman, L. (2010). Software survey: VOSviewer, a computer program for bibliometric mapping. *Scientometrics*, *84*(2), 523–538. doi:10.100711192-009-0146-3 PMID:20585380

Vandermerwe, S. (1989). Strategies for a pan European market. *Long Range Planning*, *22*(3), 45–53. doi:10.1016/0024-6301(89)90006-X

Vandermerwe, S. (1997). Increasing returns: Competing for customers in the global market. *Journal of World Business*, *32*(4), 333–350. doi:10.1016/S1090-9516(97)90016-X

Veebel, V., & Kulu, L. (2014). Against the political expectations and theoretical models: How to implement austerity and not to lose political power. *Baltic Journal of Economics*, *14*(1–2), 2–16. doi:10.1080/1406099X.2014.991140

Veilleux, S., Haskell, N., & Pons, F. (2012). Going global: How smaller enterprises benefit from strategic alliances. *The Journal of Business Strategy*, *33*(5), 22–31. doi:10.1108/02756661211282768

West, J. (2011). The OECD and Asia: Worlds apart in today's globalization? *Revista de Economía Mundial, 28*, 67–92.

Williams, C., & Martinez, C. A. (2012). Government effectiveness, the global financial crisis, and multinational enterprise internationalization. *Journal of International Marketing, 20*(3), 65–78. doi:10.1509/jim.12.0078

Woodruff, R. B. (1997). Customer value: The next source for competitive advantage. *Journal of the Academy of Marketing Science, 25*(2), 139–153. doi:10.1007/BF02894350

Woods, N. (2010). Global Governance after the financial crisis: A new multilateralism or the last gasp of the great powers? *Global Policy, 1*(1), 51–63. doi:10.1111/j.1758-5899.2009.0013.x

Yu, T. F.-L. (2000). Hong Kong's entrepreneurship: Behaviours and determinants. *Entrepreneurship and Regional Development, 12*(3), 179–194. doi:10.1080/089856200413455

Yudhya, T. B. (2016). Analysis of green marketing strategies on consumer purchase intention studies on The Body Shop Bandung Indonesia. *International Journal of Applied Business and Economic Research, 14*(2), 1027–1040.

Zaheer, S., & Manrakhan, S. (2001). Concentration and dispersion in global industries: Remote electronic access and the location of economic activities. *Journal of International Business Studies, 32*(4), 667–686. doi:10.1057/palgrave.jibs.8490989

Chapter 11
Improved Global Competitiveness on the Basis of New Business Models Influenced by Dynamic Strategic Thinking

Drago Dubrovski
https://orcid.org/0000-0001-9753-9552
International School for Social and Business Studies, Celje, Slovenia

ABSTRACT

In modern business, dynamic changes in the environment (macro trends) provoke changes within the company. Companies can protect themselves from latent, acute crises. In addition, companies can navigate a turbulent environment while ensuring organizational existence and development. Organizational forms and characteristics, as well as business models to maintain or increase existence and create competitive advantages in the global market, are increasingly sought in a more creative manner. These actions are based on dynamic strategic thinking. Revolutionary methods are often required for the creation and adaptation of competitive business models. The data from companies that face a current crisis show a gap between the need to change business models and the introduction of adapted business models to achieve the desired level of competitiveness.

DOI: 10.4018/978-1-7998-4552-2.ch011

INTRODUCTION

Increasing intensity and dynamics of events and developments, within both the organization and its environment, result in difficulties and complexities in competitiveness. Consequently, it impacts the existence and development of the organization. Over the last 20 years, the business environment has become a highly turbulent field. Rapid and substantial changes are obstacles to achieving organizational goals (McCarthy, Serban, & Rouse, 2016). This has impacted the theory and practice of modern leadership and management.

In the past, managers relied on general managerial approaches with a certain level of predictability and order. This presumption, which is based on Newtonian science as the basis of scientific management, stimulates simplifications. It thrives in regulated conditions. However, simplifications are no longer useful due to changing conditions.

Both nonlinearity (nonproportionality) of events and cause and effect relationships (and their dynamic, complex, and unsure nature) make it difficult for managers to plan their long-term development. It is hard to predict monthly or yearly changes in the environment. However, said changes can alter the circumstances or position in which the business processes are evolving. If short- and long-term plans for the strategic developmental direction, when prepared based on the circumstances in which business processes were carried out in a certain environment and period, should fail to suffice or be directly useful, the vision of the company becomes even more important.

As events in the environment become increasingly intense, less linear, and less predicted or predictable, it is important to monitor the events and adapt the company (active vs. reactive or evolutionary vs. revolutionary) to said changes, especially if the company is involved in international relations. One example includes marketers who can no longer rely on the traditional presupposition that a positive starting point or market result will automatically cause the best financial outcomes. Another example is significant investments in promotions that will not bring about corresponding sales. A final example is the launching of a product that does not automatically mean larger company income. However, this puts management in a position of constant vigilance and readiness to implement change. A passive approach cannot be successful. This holds true for developed systems and processes of monitoring the development of the environment. It also applies to their introduction into the organization and adaptation to perceived changes.

Due to their exhausted content and rigidity, many methods and techniques related to macroeconomic prediction have become useless and counterproductive. The current developmental discontinuities are completely different than the period of relatively stable conditions. This is the basis for the Newtonian mechanistic conceptualizations of the function of economic principles, which states that there is a clearly defined cause for every consequence. This is particularly true for the period following 2007, when the multifaceted consequences of the global economic and financial crisis (development discontinuities) became obvious.

Modern, high-quality strategic management is increasingly important for a successful and efficient company. Strategic decisions involve a broad spectrum of operating opportunities. These must be adopted under increasingly precarious circumstances that require constant managerial attention and activity. The key task of strategic management is to create a business model with which an organization can ensure its existence and competitive development. This is one of the fundamental objectives of the organization.

The development of information and communication technology (ICT) may bring about the false idea that managerial decisions can be replaced by ready-made technological solutions. Any progress in the field of ICT will support managerial decisions. However, it cannot replace subjective managerial judgments and decisions, regardless of the degree of sophistication of the technological solutions. It is dangerous to rely on strategic decisions being adopted "outside" of the strategic managerial judgment or use this as an excuse for decisions.

Increased complexity of strategic management is also influenced by modified tasks, authorizations, and responsibilities of managers. Due to modern characteristics of business processes, this includes both management of the organizational unit (i.e., company, business system, sector, or department) and the process of planning, coordinating, managing, and controlling business transactions. Through strategic partnerships, capital connections, manufacturing cooperation, and outsourcing, said processes take place within the organizational unit and other companies. As a consequence, instead of worrying about the success of "their own" company (organizational unit), management begins worrying about the success of business transactions outside of the company. The success of the company (i.e., enterprise, legal person) they manage is, therefore, based on outside transactions.

In this case, management must oversee relationships with stakeholders that operate in other countries or political, economic, and social environments to manage both transactions and the company. This requires new competencies. Only a global manager with a global mindset, cultural adaptability, multicultural values, cultural intelligence, an ability to learn, and global managerial competencies can master such management (Ernst, 2008).

DYNAMIC AND TURBULENT (GLOBAL) ENVIRONMENT

Globalization is a multidimensional process consisting of economic, political, legal, and cultural components. It involves countries, organizations, and individuals. In business terms, globalization is a state of international trade, investment, and financial and human flow. It is increasingly joined by more regions, countries, and companies, as well as products, services, technologies, knowledge, information, and capital. This forms a global market with specific local characteristics.

The globalization of international business (global internationalization) blurs borders between countries and regional areas, altering the traditional definition of the geographic origin of a product (service). Therefore, the dimensions of competitive processes are also changing. Today, globalization is an inevitable point of view for organizations to consider, regardless of their level of internationalization, market appearance, or the economic or noneconomic field in which they operate. As competition intensifies in all (global) markets, local (national, regional) competitiveness does not suffice for trade (import) opportunities related to survival and development. Globalization requires global competitiveness.

If we presuppose that changes in global or local environments occur increasingly often and faster, while also being less predictable, what are the rules or recipes that managers should follow to prevent a latent or acute crisis from developing in the company? How do we achieve this while also allowing the company to continue existing as they rapidly develop? Due to the specific nature of each case (company), there is no such thing as a generally applicable recipe. This is why, considering the modern turn of events, the business practice constantly develops new approaches to guarantee success and thrive in a turbulent, complex, and chaotic global environment. These approaches, however, are based on the necessity and constant nature of the three-stage approach:

1. Monitor events and changes in the environment
2. Transfer current and future characteristics of the environment into the company
3. Implement changes in the functioning of the company based on said transfer

This is the only way for the company to react to the tumultuous nature of the environment in which business conditions may be prosperous one day and hostile the next. However, a three-stage approach cannot be a temporary or occasional task. It should represent a constant behavior of the management. Research shows that managers who succeed in more tumultuous environments can better understand how to shape an organization (i.e., management, culture, structures, managerial behavior) that will be successful in such an environment. Internal-oriented managers functioning in the framework of the "closed" mindset are, on average, less successful (Underwood,

2002). Managers who run their companies in a demanding and open competitive environment are faster in the development of successful strategic approaches. This type of manager is more successful than managers in monopolistic or state-owned companies that are not facing (global) competition.

Globalization also affect the development of management in theory and practice because they dictate significant changes to current and future competences. Due to the intense, comprehensive, radical, and dynamic changes, organizations and management boards are required to establish creative and innovative management development solutions. They must ensure their company's continued existence and development, considering international business relationships as an important factor.

Changes in the modern and global business environment are dynamic, tumultuous, and unpredictable. A company must permanently adapt by preparing and implementing both active and reactive (evolutionary and revolutionary) changes. This dynamic, unpredictable "hypercompetition" environment requires flexible, innovative, and creative organizations that quickly adapt to the amended rules of the competitive arena.

Technological development allows for accelerated globalization. Its development is also a consequence of globalization. Technological development refers to both the development of technology as a set of scientific methods and applied knowledge. By means of a combination of three actors, it enables the construction of products from raw materials in an organized, economically rational, and socially eligible manner. Technology management includes the development of technology, its introduction and use in the fields of economics or management, the oversight of innovation processes in research and development, the introduction of new technologies and prototypes, production, and other activities in the organization (Bavec, 2001).

Technological development continues to bring new technologies. This, in turn, shortens the product lifecycle and tightens international competitiveness. Companies are forced to deliver better, more innovative, cheaper, and faster products. Such development is expensive and risky. Due to these demands, it can no longer be sustained using funds from one source (the company).

Modern society, which has evolved from industrial to digital, faces far more risk. Globalization results in a faster, simpler flow of products, services, technologies, people, and information. Thus, the degree of interdependence and level of risk is increasingly high. People and institutions are becoming more vulnerable to unpleasant and dangerous events. Modern features of technological development introduce us to the fact that the technological complexity of the production process is also linked to the size of enterprises, whether stand-alone or connected. It serves as grounds to form high-quality human resource (HR) and technological development centers. These, however, are formed using more international resources.

From the global economy and business point of view, technological development has accelerated the internationalization of companies and activities through global networks. This significantly impacts the following fields:

- ICT
- International logistics
- Shift of production toward service technology

In the context of technological development, the process of the internationalization and globalization of business and companies has been greatly influenced (with reciprocal influence) by advances in ICT. It has produced several valuable innovations over the last 40 years, including the Internet, laptops, mobile phones, and e-mail. At the same time, it provides important support for an organization's business operations, decision making, and building of competitive advantage.

E-business defines the business processes that take place via electronic networks using ICT (i.e., e-stores, e-marketing, e-commerce). These are designed as global by default (e-highway). As such, it provides a means for the direct entry of small companies into global markets or international distribution channels. In some segments, especially the service sector, it changes conventional business models (i.e., retail trade, tourism), competitive factors (i.e., transaction cost, response time, price), banking and other financial transactions, the exchange of external trade documents, information distribution, and analytical comparability. Global e-commerce enables transactions between global buyers and retailers in business-to-business (B2B), business-to-consumer (B2C), consumer-to-consumer (C2C), business-to-government (B2G), and other directions. Digital trade (e-commerce) increased by almost 50% in 2016 as compared to 2012. In B2B commerce, the value of digital commerce is six times that of B2C (WTO, 2018).

Key challenges faced by today's organizations include learning economies and companies, knowledge management, global competitiveness, contemporary organizational paradigms, information and telecommunication technologies, e-business, the multicultural environment and social responsibility, interorganizational organization, Industry 4.0, green information technology, big data analytics, autonomous robots and systems, horizontal and vertical system integration with new standards, Internet security, the industrial Internet of things (IoT), the use of clouds, and simulation modeling. New discoveries and technologies exploit the power of digitization and information technology in combination with knowledge management. New methods of value building derive from digital transformation as a fundamental change in the overall business environment. This occurs due to the introduction of new technologies and business models. In this context Wirtz (2019) has developed "four-forces model" of digital business, consisting of convergence and technology, customer empowerment, digitalization and innovation dynamic and market complexity.

Digital break and the transformation of the business sphere, which impact changes to business models on the levels of systems, structures, activities, and processes (Verhoef & Bijmolt, 2019), constitute one of the world's megatrends. It is comprised of the following actions (Schaeffer & Sovie, 2019):

- Transformation of core activities through digitization and the integration of development engineering, production, and service support for a product to achieve a new level of efficiency
- Companies focusing on business experience and results by creating hyperpersonalized values for supply and market management distinction
- Creating a new business ecosystem by connecting with relevant partners to acquire innovations and capabilities
- Innovative reconstruction or building of new business models by discovering revenue sources for creating greater value
- Employee training in handling digital technology (digital-ready workforce) through the acquisition and training of the next generation of talented HR
- Running smart centers for investment balancing and distributing funds between the core activity and introduced activities

Logistics (the process of planning, implementing, and monitoring the effective flow of goods, services, and information) is a specific area of technological development that has provided for the implementation of both technical and physical aspects of the development of globalization. It also changes the business models. Logistics consists of delivering the right product in the right way (quantity and quality) to the right place and in time. Thanks to the ability to detect the location of almost everything ("death of distance"), the world has become a "smaller geographical area" in various aspects. This is also a consequence of the speed at which events occur and cause an effect (Liesch, Steen, Knight, & Czinkota, 2008). Logistics, which is part of the global supply chain, is a network of organizations involved in upstream and downstream links in various processes and activities that produce value in the form of products and services in the hands of the consumer (Mangan, Lalwani, Butcher, & Javadpour, 2012).

Turning production into a service industry changes the direction of the exchange of products and services, investments, information, knowledge, and capital. It decreases mass production through more differentiated, specialized offerings. In 2019, software and solutions (40%), electronics (30%), mechanical parts (20%), and digital components (10%) represented the largest source of product value. However, in the future, the largest source of value will be digital components (70%), software solutions (20%), mechanical parts (5%), and electronics (5%). Users no longer aspire to own a product. Instead, they want access to the product, which leads to the use of the product as a service (Schaeffer & Sovie, 2019). Such user preferences require major changes in operating models, product innovation processes, platforms, and culture.

This is a complete revision of the product. No industry is immune to the penetration of digital technology (e.g., cloud, artificial intelligence, 5G network robotics, etc.). DT directly affects and changes over 75% of industries, replacing mass supply with personal experience, proven examples, and context-specific services (Schaeffer & Sovie, 2019).

Considering the previously discussed contemporary developments, it can be stated that companies, based on the old principles of independent operation and self-sufficiency, will not be able to secure the necessary global competitiveness to further their existence and development. It is necessary to adapt to a rapidly changing environment, identifying new ways to ensure the efficiency and success of operations. This can be achieved by improving and consolidating existing business models or developing new models with the characteristics of modern management and the current global environment.

DYNAMIC STRATEGIC THINKING AND KNOWLEDGE MANAGEMENT

Learning organizations differ from classical ones in systematic problem solving, the systematic search for acquisition and testing of new knowledge in practice, learning from past successes, mistakes, and foreign experience, and effective knowledge transfer within the company. When it comes to the systematic search for and use of knowledge in an organization, such an organization operates according to the principles of knowledge management. They act in accordance with the optimal use of available resources based on the knowledge of internal or external individuals, groups, or entities (Lussier, 2017). In turn, they improve management practice. A learning organization is, therefore, linked to knowledge management because the latter is key to the learning organization. The data leads to information. This information adds data to a specific concept, leading to knowledge and understanding. Experience leads to wisdom. The latter two lead to better decisions and outcomes (Hunter, 2016).

Knowledge management is realized through individual stages or processes (Devi, Chong, & Lin, 2007; cf. Dermol, 2013):

- **Creation and Discovery of Knowledge:** The organization consciously searches for and defines knowledge and its internal and external sources, creating it through discovery (i.e., employees develop ways of working or new ways are acquired from the external environment)
- **Knowledge Acquisition:** New knowledge is identified as relevant and valuable for current and future needs, presented in a reasonable way that can be easily accessed, drawn from, and shared
- **Knowledge Selection and Organization:** New knowledge is shackled and organized through filtering for the identification and cross-application of useful dimensions of knowledge for various products and services
- **Saving and Storage of Knowledge:** Codified knowledge is kept in a reasonable form, allowing access to other people from the organization (database management and data warehousing technologies also help in this process)
- **Distribution and Transfer of Knowledge:** Knowledge is personalized and distributed in a useful form that meets specific user needs, as well as articulated in a common language using tools that are understandable to all users
- **Use of Knowledge:** Knowledge is applied in new situations where users can learn and generate new knowledge (analysis and critical evaluation must be included in the learning process to generate new patterns for future use)

Hunter (2016) compared the understanding and use of knowledge in (learning) organizations to a diamond. For example, it always seems different depending on the angle. Furthermore, knowledge management in different organizations can never be the same. According to the author, diamond and knowledge management comprise the following seven "planes" (processes): (1) assessment of information and knowledge; (2) collection and acquisition of knowledge; (3) retention and updating of knowledge; (4) acquiring knowledge; (5) combination and creation of knowledge; (6) distribution of knowledge; and (7) sharing of knowledge.

To adopt the concept of knowledge management, an organization needs the following (Gouillart & Kelly, 1994):

- **Knowledge-Based Architecture:** For generating and expanding systematic knowledge and adapting it to the required skills
- **Knowledge-Based Management Process:** Formal methodology for collecting, integrating, and distributing knowledge
- **Technical Architecture:** A computer-aided approach to obtaining knowledge

From a practical point of view, the concept of a continuously learning company that has adopted knowledge management means that all employees are educated and trained (acquiring and creating knowledge) on an ongoing (daily) basis in formal and informal ways. This knowledge is then shared with other employees (selecting, retaining, and spreading knowledge). Finally, the company develops strategic activities on the basis of knowledge acquired and responses to changes in the environment (use of knowledge). Such a desired behavior of the organization, as well as its parts and participants, does not arise by itself. It requires complete mobilization, creation, and integration of all available knowledge.

The content of modern strategic management is inherently linked to the management of the learning organization. It is based on the adopted concept and processes of knowledge management acquired and processed using dynamic strategic thinking under modern business conditions.

RETAINING AND IMPROVING COMPETITIVENESS THROUGH NEW OR IMPROVED BUSINESS MODELS

Strategic management literature and practice indicate that companies achieve competitive advantages based on established and implemented business models (Verhoef & Bijmolt, 2019). Competition is defined by the business conduct of cosuppliers (corespondents) in the market or by market competition between multiple providers (multiple solicitors). Therefore, it is perceived as the endeavour of two or more persons or companies to achieve the same numerically limited goal in the same or a similar field. Competition is a constant struggle between companies to achieve a comparative advantage in assets that will bring a competitive market position for certain market segments and, consequently, above-average financial success (Hunt, 2000). The competitive advantage of a company is often defined as a unique and lasting advantage that the company achieves with respect to other companies in the industry. It is shown, on the outside, as a long-term advantage in the market. However, it has already been mentioned that the possibilities for achieving permanent competitive advantages in today's dynamic environment are very limited. Such occurrences are often an exception. Instead, periods of occasional (temporary) advantages arise. However, these do not ensure long-term success.

Ensuring the overall competitiveness of products or services offered in the global market is more complex than in the case of local areas. Competitiveness is intertwined and interdependent with its own factors of product competitiveness (price and sales conditions, quality, availability in time and space, marketing activities dedicated to the product), as well as from the competitiveness factors of the national economy (country of origin) and the enterprise itself (corporate branding, involvement in broader business systems and networks, lobbying). Strategic cooperation and integration or strategic partnerships that bring about the concentration and integration of industries are some of the modern ways of maintaining and increasing competitiveness in a global market environment. Increasing competition in all respects requires more thorough cooperation between the company and its suppliers, the company and its customers, the company and its competitors, and the providers of certain functions.

Numerous business models that represent the basic framework of adopting decisions in individual past situations are no longer useful or are useful to a lesser extent. This is due to limitations and unreal presuppositions on which these models are based. In current business circumstances, past (archaic) management models, approaches, styles, and competencies (skills, knowledge, capabilities) do not suffice. Innovative models have to be developed. This can take place through dynamic strategic thinking.

Innovation not only means the development of new products and services or the relevant modification of existing ones. It is also the development of research methods, sophisticated marketing approaches, management models, a strengthened value chain, and, in general, all nonmaterial components that are part of the supply package. In many industries, competitiveness can no longer be guaranteed by applying traditional production and service programs although they may be attractive in terms of affordability.

The fourth industrial revolution, known as Industry 4.0, has four effects on various industries (Schwab, 2016):

1. Modified customer expectations
2. Improvement of products based on available data, resulting in improved asset productivity and partnerships as businesses become aware of the importance of new forms of collaboration
3. Transformation of operating models into new digital models

The business model defines the way in which an organization with a unique combination of programs (i.e., products, services, knowledge, capital, information, technologies for targeted participants), sales conditions, distribution channels, and market communication, as well as a unique combination of assets in a competitive environment, creates value in their business processes (benefit) for customers. This achieves its own fundamental goal and indirect goals of the participants in the organization.

The business model shows how a certain company satisfies the special needs of a costumer on the target market on a certain place and at a certain time (Chernev, 2017). Each business model includes core assets and core competencies (Wirtz, 2019) and core strategy to achieve the basic objective. A business model reveals how the company adds its own contribution to the value of the final product (service) throughout the entire chain of adding value to input materials and initial services. A company is being paid for successfully selling its products and services. Therefore, it generates income (after cost deduction), which is another component of the business model termed the "profit formula" (Johnson, 2018).

A business model contains numerous options at the core levels of the company's functioning. These options shape a special practice and behavior of the company. The latter are generally invisible and are rarely expressed in an explicit manner. Therefore, we are often unaware of the model.

Although there are no best business models, there is a decision on the selection of possibilities suitable for a particular environment (Birkinshaw & Goddard, 2009). Every idea is not yet a business model. Out of 3,000 ideas, 300 are developed into a project idea. Of these, 125 are developed into a smaller project. Nine become a development project. Seven are developed into a product available on the market. Only one becomes a commercial success (Wildemann, 2017). Over time, business models become more resistant to change (Christensen, Bartman, & van Bever, 2016).

As described in previous chapters, (also) due to the impact of globalization and accelerated technological development, with an emphasis on ICT, companies must start thinking about new business models. This is a challenge for strategic management. According to Wildemann (2017), the new business model is based on:

1. **Customer Needs and Innovations:** Specialized solutions, high quality, flexible/ modular offering
2. **Distinction from the Competition:** Close relationship with clients, partners, the best solution on the market or the best price-service relation
3. **Key Assets/Core Competencies:** Technological know-how, long-term knowledge of customers, system and process know-how
4. **Value-Creating Architecture:** Concentration on core capacities, intelligent networking, smart organization

The interest of researchers proves a growth in relation to construction, maintenance, and amendment of business models. According to a 2009 study, 70% of companies are trying to create innovative business models and 98% are modifying existing models (Casadesus-Masanell & Ricart, 2011). According to Wildemann (2017), new business models mostly come from product and program development (57%), technology development (25%), market (15%), and large leaps (turns). The implementation of a new model consists of the following demanding phases (Johnson, 2010):

- Creation (1-3 years)
- Acceleration (2-5 years)
- Transfer (1-3 years)

The level of failure in modifying existing business models is extremely high (up to 70%). The holistic (helicopter) condition is needed to plan the change (Hendrickx, 2015).

EVOLUTIONARY VS. REVOLUTIONARY INTRODUCTION OF BUSINESS MODELS

The introduction of new business models and the changing of existing ones to ensure competitiveness of supply on the global market may take place by means of evolutionary or revolutionary change (Dubrovski, 2018). In terms of quantity, the former is more common. The latter is more common in terms of size and complexity (Burke, 2002). Methods of evolutionary change consist of all related measures that, on a day-to-day basis, lead to change within the mission and vision of the company, long-term goals, and core strategies. This ensures a consistent and gradually increasing level of performance and operating efficiency. This may apply to regular strategic operation or achieve specific objectives based on a project approach. Methods of revolutionary change, however, include restructuring (emphasis on the comprehensive change of structures) and reengineering (emphasis on comprehensive changes in processes).

There are several differences between revolutionary change methods and evolutionary attainment of change. Revolutionary methods are used less often. They are comprehensive and aimed at achieving broader goals. Furthermore, revolutionary methods are conducted with greater intensity and in a shorter time period. They are riskier and require sacrifices. These sacrifices may relate to material assets (the sale of fixed assets and investments or “family silverware,” withdrawal from capital and business associations, the sale of objects affecting the social standard, reduction of funds for nonbusiness purposes, the sale of real estate and leaseback) and intangible assets (employee dismissal, replacement and departure of experts, sale of patents or trademarks, loss of information resources, disruption of business networks or connections with customers). Due to these sacrifices, revolutionary change methods are not pleasant. Instead, they cause of fear, uncertainty, distress, and stress.

The relationship between revolutionary and evolutionary methods can reflect in the dilemma of whether the undertaking should implement gradual changes planned in the context of the objectives or whether the company should follow flexibility to respond to unintentional changes by changing internal structures. Often, the solution will be a combination of methods, in which planning serves as the premise of development on top of which flexible strategies must be implemented (Wildemann, 2004). As a rule, evolutionary change is achieved over a longer period of time as compared to revolutionary change when comparing the situation at the beginning and end of a period in which the employees (and external environment) do not perceive the changes as drastic, dramatic, or unpleasant and the sacrifices are not noticeable or are not present due to the planned operation. Both types of changes affect the following three levels: (1) individual; (2) group; and (3) organizational.

Regardless of the type of method used for achieving change, the aim of both (evolutionary and revolutionary) is the same: achieving a renewal that leads to a higher stage of development. The reconstruction of the company or organization is based on new models, processes, systems, strategies, programs, and structures. This ensures the company's improved efficiency (ratio between results and inputs, which is indicated in the productivity of the work assets and the work, as well as the economy of materials) and the success of the company's operations (ratio between the results and the set goals, which is indicated in the profitability, marketability and flexibility), as well the achievement of a higher level of development.

Business models can be introduced and modified through either evolutionary or revolutionary methods. These require different approaches. As a rule, revolutionary methods of changing of the business model will be required when the company: (1) faces a significant backlog as compared to the competition; (2) faces an acute crisis or is threatened by a crisis in the near future; (3) does not keep up with technological and general changes; and/or (4) has set an aggressive development policy. Revolutionary methods of changing business models require sacrifice. On the whole, they are more expensive and significantly riskier. In the cases described, there is simply no alternative.

EMPIRICAL EVIDENCE OF CHANGING THE BUSINESS MODEL: COMPANIES IN CRISIS

The following section is based on findings from theoretical discussions in this chapter, prior empirical studies in this field (Dubrovski, 2010, 2016), and the author's many years of strategic management and restructuring consultancy practice. A review of the information found several issues related to companies facing an acute crisis in Slovenia that attempted to solve that crisis through an insolvency procedure of compulsory arrangement (in-court restructuring, debtor in possession proceedings).

- The companies paid surprisingly little attention to changing ineffective business models (that led to the acute crisis). They did not introduce new

strategies, structures, processes, and/or systems, although this is the most important area of renewal (ensuring further existence and development).
- In most cases, the companies attempted to solve the acute crisis through forms of financial restructuring. Therefore, they were dealing with the consequences rather than the causes of the crisis. This brought on the need for financial disburdening.
- The companies were implementing short-term, superficial measures. Yet the deep extent of the crisis was encroaching on several areas. Among the prepared measures, those most emphasized included legal aspects (this is expected with regard of the type of sample) and financial perspective (as part of the broader economic perspective).

Meanwhile, unexpectedly little attention is paid to other aspects, especially traditional. As a break with previous practice and the start of a new organizational lifecycle, the formation of new foundations will build up the core capabilities of the organization and its competitiveness. Another example is the introduction of a new managerial ideology and approaches. In this case, they were studied considering radical change and the introduction of new business models.

For companies facing an acute crisis and/or bankruptcy, it is fair to assume that the source of their problems is uncompetitive supply and an inadequate or outdated business model. The model may have previously secured existence and development. However, due to radical changes in the global environment, it is no longer viable. It is true that financial restructuring is the main step in solving problems in the insolvency process. However, this cannot, in the medium term, eliminate the crisis if the business models do not guarantee global competitiveness of the supply or company.

If bankruptcy is a method of solving a crisis, then a compulsory arrangement is a method of recovery where creditors play the key roll. Creditors of a company in trouble will not accept the company's proposal (worsening the status of their claims) if they cannot see radical changes in business practice of the debtor. Therefore, it would be expected that new strategies, structures, processes, and systems are presented in a standard company in the frame of a new business model to replace previous ineffective business.

Regarding assessment of interventions and cause of crisis, management gets trapped in cognitive preconceptions that tint their view of the world. A well-prepared and executed compulsory arrangement is a necessary, but insufficient, condition for achieving drastic change and ensuring the redevelopment of a company. An insolvency procedure is a process, not a solution (Miller, 2008). It gives a company time and access to new ways of financing for recovery and renewal when new business models must be created based on dynamic strategic thinking and knowledge management to achieve the desired level of global competitiveness.

CONCLUSION

Due to globalization and general and technological advances, global competitiveness can no longer be guaranteed through outdated business models (although they once enabled satisfactory performance and generated development-oriented cash flow). In the face of intense, large-scale, radical, and dynamic changes, the management of a company needs to find development solutions that will ensure its continued existence and development. In doing so, the organization can protect itself from possible or acute crises in a turbulent environment.

The key task of strategic management is to create a business model that consists of a unique combination of programs (i.e., products, services, knowledge, capital, ICT for the target participants), sales conditions, distribution channels, and market communication. In addition, it must create value (benefit) for target customers by applying a unique combination of assets in a competitive environment. This will allow the company to achieve its fundamental goal and, indirectly, the goals of the organization's participants.

Innovative means, based on dynamic strategic thinking, are aimed at looking for organizational forms and features. It seeks business models to maintain or increase existing competitive advantages in today's global market. In addition, it creates improved business models that can be modified through revolutionary or evolutionary methods and are based on digital transformation and knowledge management. The models are derived from a philosophical framework of strategic dynamic thinking. Various studies (in this case, studies of companies in trouble) suggest that there is still a gap between the declared need to introduce and improve existing business models and the actual change in business practice.

REFERENCES

Bavec, C. (2001). Management tehnologije. In Management v evropskem okolju. Zbornik 1. strokovnega posveta, Bernardin. Koper: Visoka šola za management.

Birkinshaw, J., & Goddard, J. (2009). What is your management model? *MIT Sloan Management Review*, *50*(2), 81–90.

Burke, W. W. (2002). *Organization change, theory and practice*. Sage.

Casadesus-Masanell, R., & Ricart, J. E. (2011). How to design a winning business model. *Harvard Business Review*, *89*(1-2), 101–107.

Chernev, A. (2017). *The business model: How to develop new products, create market value and make the competition irrelevant.* Cerebellum Press.

Christensen, C. M., Bartman, T., & van Bever, D. (2016). The hard truth about business model innovation. *MIT Sloan Management Review*, *58*(1), 30–40.

Dermol, V. (2013). *Učenje in ustvarjanje znanja v podjetju.* Celje: Mednarodna fakulteta za družbene in poslovne študije.

Devi, R. S., Chong, S. C., & Lin, B. (2007). Organisational culture and KM processes from the perspective of an institution of higher learning. *International Journal of Management Education*, *1*(1-2), 57–67.

Dubrovski, D. (2010). Pomembnost ugotavljanja pravilnih vzrokov za nastanek podjetniške krize. *Management*, *5*(1), 37–52.

Dubrovski, D. (2016). Handling corporate crises based on the correct analysis of its causes. *Journal of Financial Risk Management*, *5*(04), 264–280. doi:10.4236/jfrm.2016.54024

Dubrovski, D. (2018). *Management in organizacija. Celje.* International School of Social and Business Studies.

Ernst, C. (2008). The global manager's work. In C. Wankel (Ed.), 21st century management. A reference handbook. Los Angeles, CA: Sage Publications.

Gouillart, F. J., & Kelly, J. N. (1995). *Transforming the organization.* McGraw-Hill.

Hendrickx, H. H. M. (2015). Business architect: A critical role in enterprise transformation. *Journal of Enterprise Transformation*, *5*(1), 1–29. doi:10.1080/19488289.2014.893933

Hunt, S. D. (2000). *A general theory of competition.* Sage.

Hunter, B. N. (2016). *The power of KM.* Spirit Rising Productions.

Johnson, M. W. (2010). *Seizing the white space.* Harvard Business Press.

Johnson, M. W. (2018). *Reinvent your business model.* Harvard Business Review Press.

Liesch, P. W., Steen, J., Knight, G. A., & Czinkota, M. R. (2008). Internationally managing in the face of terrorism-induced uncertainty. In C. Wankel (Ed.), 21st century management. A reference handbook. Los Angeles, CA: Sage Publications. doi:10.4135/9781412954006.n20

Lussier, R. N. (2017). *Management fundamentals: Concepts, applications, and skill development*. Sage Publications, Inc.

Mangan, J., Lalwani, C., Butcher, T., & Javadpour, R. (2012). *Global logistics & supply chain management*. John Wiley & Sons.

McCarthy, N., Serban, N., & Rouse, W. (2016). A multidimensional apporach to understanding the value deficiencies that drive enterprise transformation. *Journal of Enterprise Transformation*, *6*(1), 1–22. doi:10.1080/19488289.2016.1191563

Miller, S. (2008). *The turnaround kid*. HarperCollins.

Schaeffer, E., & Sovie, D. (2019). *Reinventing the product. How to transform your business and create value in the digital age*. Kogan Page.

Schwab, K. (2016). *Četrta industrijska revolucija*. Geneva, Switzerland: World Economic Forum.

Underwood, J. (2002). *Complexity and paradox*. Capstone.

Verhoef, P. C., & Bijmolt, T. H. A. (2019). Marketing perspectives on digital business models: A framework and overview of the special issue. *International Journal of Research in Marketing*, *36*(3), 341–349. doi:10.1016/j.ijresmar.2019.08.001

Wildemann, H. (2004). *Sanierungsstrategien*. TCW Transfer-Centrum.

Wildemann, H. (2017). *Neue Geschaftsmodelle in der Industrie 4.0*. TCW Transfer-Centrum.

Wirtz, B. W. (2019). *Digital business models*. Springer Nature. doi:10.1007/978-3-030-13005-3

World Trade Organization (WTO). (2018). *World Trade statistical review 2018*. WTO.

Compilation of References

Aaboen, L., Dubois, A., & Lind, F. (2012). Capturing processes in longitudinal multiple case studies. *Industrial Marketing Management*, *41*(2), 235–246. doi:10.1016/j.indmarman.2012.01.009

Abdina, A. K., Abdildina, H. S., Gappasova, A. G., Kakimzhanova, M. K., Ni Valerievich, D., & Sadykova, T. M.Seifullin Kazakh Agro Technical University. (2015). Foreign students' social adaptation to the education environment of a higher educational institution: By the example of S. Seifullin Kazakh Agro Technical University. *Mediterranean Journal of Social Sciences*, *6*(5), 184–194. doi:10.5901/mjss.2015.v6n5p184

Ackerman, F., & Mirza, S. (2001). Waste in the inner city: Asset or assault? *Local Environment*, *6*(2), 113–120. doi:10.1080/13549830120052764

Addo, P., Guegan, D., & Hassani, B. (2018). *Credit risk analysis using machine and deep learning models*. Risks. doi:10.3390/risks6020038

Adger, W. N. (2003). Social capital, collective action, and adaptation to climate change. *Economic Geography*, *79*(4), 387–404. doi:10.1111/j.1944-8287.2003.tb00220.x

Adler, N., Friedman, L., & Sinuany-Stern, Z. (2002). Review of ranking methods in the Data Envelopment Analysis context. *European Journal of Operational Research*, *140*(2), 249–265. doi:10.1016/S0377-2217(02)00068-1

Afuah, A., & Tucci, C. L. (2002). Internet business models and strategies: Text and cases. New York: McGraw-Hill.

Aigner, D., Lovell, C. A. K., & Schmidt, P. (1977). Formulation and estimation of stochastic frontier production function models. *Journal of Econometrics*, *6*(1), 21–37. doi:10.1016/0304-4076(77)90052-5

Aiken, L. S., & West, S. G. (1991). *Multiple regression: testing and interpreting interactions*. Sage Publications.

Al-Debei, M., El-Haddadeh, R., & Avison, D. (2008). Defining the business model in the new world of digital business. In *Proceedings of the Fourteenth Americas Conference on Information Systems* (pp.1-11). Toronto, Canada: Association for Information Systems

Alden, D. L., Steenkamp, J.-B. E. M., & Batra, R. (1999). Brand positioning through advertising in Asia, North America, and Europe: The role of global consumer culture. *Journal of Marketing*, *63*(1), 75–87. doi:10.1177/002224299906300106

Allouche, J., Amann, B., Jaussaud, J., & Kurashina, T. (2008). The Impact of Family Control on the Performance and Financial Characteristics of Family Versus Nonfamily Businesses in Japan: A Matched-Pair Investigation. *Family Business Review*, *21*(4), 315–329. doi:10.1177/08944865080210040104

Almeida, F., & Monteiro, J. (2017). Approaches and Principles for UX Web Experiences. *Journal of Information Technology and Web Engineering*, *12*(2), 49–65. doi:10.4018/IJITWE.2017040103

Alt, R., & Zimmermann, H.-D. (2001). Introduction to special section: Business models. *Electronic Markets*, *1*(11), 3–9.

Alves, G. M., Sousa, B. M., & Machado, A. (2020). The Role of Digital Marketing and Online Relationship Quality in Social Tourism. In J. Santos & Ó. Silva (Eds.), *Digital Marketing Strategies for Tourism, Hospitality, and Airline Industries* (pp. 49–70). IGI Global. doi:10.4018/978-1-5225-9783-4.ch003

Amendolagine, V., Capolupo, R., & Ferri, G. (2014). Innovativeness, offshoring and black economy decisions. Evidence from Italian manufacturing firms. *International Business Review*, *23*(6), 1153–1166. doi:10.1016/j.ibusrev.2014.03.011

Amran, A., Lee, S. P., & Devi, S. S. (2014). The influence of governance structure and strategic corporate social responsibility toward sustainability reporting quality. *Business Strategy and the Environment*, *23*(4), 217–235. doi:10.1002/bse.1767

Anagnostopoulos, I. (2018). Fintech and regtech: Impact on regulators and banks. *Journal of Economics and Business*, *100*, 7–25. doi:10.1016/j.jeconbus.2018.07.003

Anakwe, U. P., Igbaria, M., & Anandarajan, M. (2000). Management practices across cultures: Role of support in technology usage. *Journal of International Business Studies*, *31*(4), 653–666. doi:10.1057/palgrave.jibs.8490927

Anderson, R. C., & Reeb, D. M. (2003). Founding-family ownership and firm performance: Evidence from the S&P 500. *The Journal of Finance*, *58*(3), 1301–1329. doi:10.1111/1540-6261.00567

Anderson, V., & Johnson, L. (1997). *System thinking basics*. Pegasus Communications.

Andersson, S., & Evangelista, F. (2006). The entrepreneur in the Born Global firm in Australia and Sweden. *Journal of Small Business and Enterprise Development*, *13*(4), 642–659. doi:10.1108/14626000610705796

Andrade, P. (2019). *Can Innovation be a sustainable competitive advantage for a bank?* ISCTE-IUL.

Andrews, K. R. (1981). Corporate-strategy as a vital function of the board. *Harvard Business Review*, *59*(6), 174–184.

Andrews, K. R., & David, D. K. (1971). *The concept of corporate strategy*. Richard D. Irwin.

Anstine, J. (2000). Consumers' willingness to pay for recycled content in plastic kitchen garbage bags: A hedonic price approach. *Applied Economics Letters*, *7*(1), 35–39. doi:10.1080/135048500352068

APA. (2018). *APA stress in America™ survey: Generation Z stressed about issues in the news but least likely to vote*. Retrieved from https://www.apa.org/news/press/releases/2018/10/generation-z-stressed

Arli, D., Tjiptono, F., & Winit, W. (2015). Consumer ethics among young consumers in developing countries: A cross national study. *Social Responsibility Journal*, *11*(3), 449–466. doi:10.1108/SRJ-05-2013-0059

Arnold, J., Minner, S., & Eidam, B. (2009). Raw material procurement with fluctuating prices. *International Journal of Production Economics*, *121*(2), 353–364. doi:10.1016/j.ijpe.2007.02.038

Artz, K. W., Norman, P. M., Hatfield, D. E., & Cardinal, L. B. (2010). A longitudinal study of the impact of R&D, patents, and product innovation on firm performance. *Journal of Product Innovation Management*, *27*(5), 725–740. doi:10.1111/j.1540-5885.2010.00747.x

Aryeetey, E., & Moyo, N. (2012). Industrialisation for structural transformation in Africa: Appropriate roles for the state. *Journal of African Economies*, *21*(2), 55–85. doi:10.1093/jae/ejr043

Arzubiaga, U., Kotlar, J., De Massis, A., Maseda, A., & Iturralde, T. (2018). Entrepreneurial orientation and innovation in family SMEs: Unveiling the (actual) impact of the Board of Directors. *Journal of Business Venturing*, *33*(4), 455–469. doi:10.1016/j.jbusvent.2018.03.002

Ashta, A., & Biot-Paquerot, G. (2018). FinTech evolution: Strategic value management issues in a fast changing industry. *Strategic Change*, *27*(4), 301–311. doi:10.1002/jsc.2203

Ashwin, A. S., Krishnan, R. T., & George, R. (2015). Family firms in India: Family involvement, innovation and agency and stewardship behaviors. *Asia Pacific Journal of Management*, *32*(4), 869–900. doi:10.100710490-015-9440-1

Auvinen, T., Sajasalo, P., Sintonen, T., Pekkala, K., Takala, T., & Luoma-aho, V. (2019). Evolution of strategy narration and leadership work in the digital era. *Leadership*, *15*(2), 205–225. doi:10.1177/1742715019826426

Baden-Fuller, C., & Haefliger, S. (2013). Business models and technological innovation. *Long Range Planning*, *46*(6), 419–426. doi:10.1016/j.lrp.2013.08.023

Bagot, G. F. (2013). Outsourcing an industry: A new paradigm and strategy for national economic development- the new form of old Colonialism! *International Journal of Business Research*, *13*(4), 5–18. doi:10.18374/IJBR-13-4.1

Balezentis, A., & Balezentis, T. (2011). Framework of strategic management model for strategy Europe 2020: Diachronic analysis and proposed guidelines. *The Engineering Economist*, *22*(3), 271–282.

Ballal, J. M., & Bapat, V. (2020). Socioemotional Wealth and Its Effect on Family Firm Performance. In J. M. Palma-Ruiz, I. Barros-Contreras, & L. Gnan (Eds.), *Handbook of research on the strategic management of family businesses* (pp. 201–227). IGI Global. doi:10.4018/978-1-7998-2269-1.ch010

Bandara, R., Fernando, M., & Akter, S. (2017). The privacy paradox in the data-driven marketplace: The role of knowledge deficiency and psychological distance. *Procedia Computer Science, 121*, 562–567. doi:10.1016/j.procs.2017.11.074

Bandiera, O., Prat, A., Hansen, S., & Sadun, R. (2020). Ceo behavior and firm performance. *Journal of Political Economy, 128*(4).

Banker, R., Charnes, A., & Cooper, W. (1984). Some models for estimating technical and scale inefficiencies in data envelopment analysis. *Management Science, 30*(9), 1078–1098. doi:10.1287/mnsc.30.9.1078

Banker, R., Cooper, W., Seiford, L., Thrall, R., & Zhu, J. (2004b). Returns to scale in different DEA models. *European Journal of Operational Research, 154*(2), 345–362. doi:10.1016/S0377-2217(03)00174-7

Banker, R., Janakiraman, S., & Natarajan, R. (2004a). Analysis of trends in technical and allocative efficiency: An application to Texas public school districts. *European Journal of Operational Research, 154*(2), 477–491. doi:10.1016/S0377-2217(03)00183-8

Bantouna, A., Poulios, G., Tsagkaris, K., & Demestichas, P. (2014). Network load predictions based on big data and the utilization of self-organizing maps. *Journal of Network and Systems Management, 22*(2), 150–173. doi:10.100710922-013-9285-1

Barlow, P., McKee, M., Basu, S., & Stuckler, D. (2017). The health impact of trade and investment agreements: A quantitative systematic review and network co-citation analysis. *Globalization and Health, 13*(1), 1–9. doi:10.118612992-017-0240-x PMID:28274238

Barney, J. (1991). Firm Resources and Sustained Competitive Advantage. *Journal of Management, 17*(1), 99–120. doi:10.1177/014920639101700108

Baron, R. M., & Kenny, D. A. (1986). The moderator–mediator variable distinction in social psychological research: Conceptual, strategic and statistical considerations. *Journal of Personality and Social Psychology, 51*(6), 1173–1182. doi:10.1037/0022-3514.51.6.1173 PMID:3806354

Barroso, I. C., González-Romero, G., & Lara, P. L. (2014). The crisis and territorial development in Andalusian cities. *Revista de Estudios Regionales, 100*, 47–82.

Bartlett, C. A., & Ghoshal, S. (1992). What is a global manager? *Harvard Business Review, 70*(5), 124–132. PMID:10121314

Basco, R. (2013). The family's effect on family firm performance: A model testing the demographic and essence approaches. *Journal of Family Business Strategy, 4*(1), 42–66. doi:10.1016/j.jfbs.2012.12.003

Bavec, C. (2001). Management tehnologije. In Management v evropskem okolju. Zbornik 1. strokovnega posveta, Bernardin. Koper: Visoka šola za management.

Beets, S. D. (2005). Understanding the demand-side issues of international corruption. *Journal of Business Ethics*, *57*(1), 65–81. doi:10.100710551-004-3824-3

Belanche, D., Casaló, L., & Flavián, C. (2019). Artificial Intelligence in FinTech: Understanding robo-advisors adoption among customers. *Industrial Management & Data Systems*, *119*(7), 1411–1430. Advance online publication. doi:10.1108/IMDS-08-2018-0368

Belz, F. M., & Peattie, K. (2009). Sustainability marketing: A global perspective. Academic Press.

Berrone, P., Cruz, C., & Gómez-Mejía, L. R. (2012). Socioemotional Wealth in Family Firms: Theoretical Dimensions, Assessment Approaches, and Agenda for Future Research. *Family Business Review*, *25*(3), 258–279. doi:10.1177/0894486511435355

Berrone, P., Cruz, C., Gómez-Mejía, L. R., & Larraza-Kintana, M. (2010). Socioemotional Wealth and Corporate Responses to Institutional Pressures: Do Family-Controlled Firms Pollute Less? *Administrative Science Quarterly*, *55*(1), 82–113. doi:10.2189/asqu.2010.55.1.82

Berthon, P., Pitt, L., Parent, M., & Berthon, J.-P. (2009). Aesthetics and ephemerality: Observing and preserving the luxury brand. *California Management Review*, *55*(1), 45–66. doi:10.1525/cmr.2009.52.1.45

Bertrand, M., & Schoar, A. (2006). The role of family in family firms. *The Journal of Economic Perspectives*, *20*(2), 73–96. doi:10.1257/jep.20.2.73

Bieler, A., Hilary, J., & Lindberg, I. (2014). Trade unions, 'free trade', and the problem of transnational solidarity: An introduction. *Globalizations*, *11*(1), 1–9. doi:10.1080/14747731.2014.860319

Bienhaus, F., & Haddud, A. (2018). Procurement 4.0: Factors influencing the digitisation of procurement and supply chains. *Business Process Management Journal*, *24*(4), 965–984. doi:10.1108/BPMJ-06-2017-0139

Bird, R., & McHugh, A. (1977). Financial ratios – an empirical study. *Journal of Business Finance & Accounting*, *4*(1), 29–45. doi:10.1111/j.1468-5957.1977.tb00159.x

Birkinshaw, J., & Goddard, J. (2009). What is your management model? *MIT Sloan Management Review*, *50*(2), 81–90.

Blanco-Mesa, F., Merigó, J. M., & Gil-Lafuente, A. M. (2017). Fuzzy decision making: A bibliometric-based review. *Journal of Intelligent & Fuzzy Systems*, *32*(2), 2033–2050. doi:10.3233/JIFS-161640

Blitz, D. C., & Van Vliet, P. (2008). Global tactical cross-asset allocation: Applying value and momentum across asset classes. *Journal of Portfolio Management*, *35*(1), 23–38. doi:10.3905/JPM.2008.35.1.23

Block, J. H., Miller, D., Jaskiewicz, P., & Spiegel, F. (2013). Economic and Technological Importance of Innovations in Large Family and Founder Firms: An Analysis of Patent Data. *Family Business Review*, *26*(2), 180–199. doi:10.1177/0894486513477454

Blom, R., Melin, H., Sarno, A., & Sarno, I. (2008). Managerial threats and prospects in Russian firms: The case of St. Petersburg 1999-2005. *World Review of Entrepreneurship, Management and Sustainable Development*, *4*(2–3), 169–181. doi:10.1504/WREMSD.2008.018223

Blomsma, F., & Brennan, G. (2017). The emergence of circular economy: A new framing around prolonging resource productivity. *Journal of Industrial Ecology*, *21*(3), 603–614. doi:10.1111/jiec.12603

Bodislav, D., Bran, F., & Popescu, L. (2018). The business-automated data economy model, 2018 early update. *Quality - Access to Success*, 80-84.

Bömer, M., & Maxin, H. (2018). Why fintechs cooperate with banks—evidence from germany. *Zeitschrift fur die gesamte Versicherungswissenschaft*, 359-386. doi:10.100712297-018-0421-6

Boschma, J., & Groen, I. (2010). *Generatie Einstein*. AW Bruna Uitgevers.

Boussofiane, A., Dyson, R., & Thanassoulis, E. (1991). Applied Data Envelopment Analysis. *European Journal of Operational Research*, *52*(1), 1–15. doi:10.1016/0377-2217(91)90331-O

Braz, R. G. F., Scavarda, L. F., & Martins, R. A. (2011). Reviewing and improving performance measurement systems: An action research. *International Journal of Production Economics*, *133*(2), 751–760. doi:10.1016/j.ijpe.2011.06.003

Brinkman, R. L., & Brinkman, J. E. (2002). Corporate power and the globalization process. *International Journal of Social Economics*, *29*(9), 730–752. doi:10.1108/03068290210442739

Brochado, A. (2018a). Snapshot da Indústria das Criptomoedas. Caderno do Mercado de Valores Mobiliários, 83-108.

Brochado, A. (2018b). Snapshot das Initial Coin Offerings (ICOs). Cadernos do Mercado de Valores Mobiliários, 53-76.

Brouthers, L. E., Werner, S., & Matulich, E. (2000). The influence of triad nations' environments on price-quality product strategies and MNC performance. *Journal of International Business Studies*, *31*(1), 39–62. doi:10.1057/palgrave.jibs.8490899

Brown, D. P. (2015). Garbage: How population, landmass and development interact with culture in the production of waste. *Resources, Conservation and Recycling*, *98*, 41–54. doi:10.1016/j.resconrec.2015.02.012

Brown, M. G. (1996). *Keeping Score: Using the Right Metrics to Drive World-Class Performance*. Productivity Press Inc.

Brown, S. L., & Eisenhardt, K. M. (1998). *Competing on the Edge*. Harvard Business School Press.

Brown, T., Boon, E., & Pitt, L. (2017). Seeking funding in order to sell: Crowdfunding as a marketing tool. *Business Horizons*, *60*(2), 189–195. doi:10.1016/j.bushor.2016.11.004

Bruijl, G. H. T. (2018). *The Relevance of Porter's Five Forces in Today's Innovative and Changing Business Environment*. Available online at SSRN: https://ssrn.com/abstract=3192207

Brundtland, G. H. (1987). *Our common future: The world commission on environment and development*. Oxford University Press.

Bughin, J., Hazan, E., Ramaswamy, S., Chui, M., Allas, T., Dahlstrom, P., Henke, N., & Trench, M. (2017). *Artificial intelligence the next digital frontier*. McKinsey Global Institute, Discussion Paper. Retrieved from https://www.mckinsey.com/~/media/McKinsey/Industries/Advanced%20Electronics/Our%20Insights/How%20artificial%20intelligence%20can%20deliver%20real%20value%20to%20companies/MGI-Artificial-Intelligence-Discussion-paper.ashx

Bughin, J., Deakin, J., & O'Beirne, B. (2019). Digital transformation: Improving the odds. *The McKinsey Quarterly*.

Burke, W. W. (2002). *Organization change, theory and practice*. Sage.

Burnard, K., & Bhamra, R. (2011). Organisational resilience: Development of a conceptual framework for organisational responses. *International Journal of Production Research*, *49*(18), 5581–5599. doi:10.1080/00207543.2011.563827

Calleja, R., & Melé, D. (2017). Valero's "enterprise politics": A model of humanistic management and corporate governance. *Journal of Management Development*, *36*(5), 644–659. doi:10.1108/JMD-12-2015-0187

Camagni, R., & Capello, R. (2013). Regional Innovation Patters and the EU Regional Policy Reform: Toward Smart Innovation Policies. *Growth and Change*, *44*(2), 355–389. doi:10.1111/grow.12012

Caniëls, M. C. J., & Baaten, S. M. J. (2019). How a learning-oriented organizational climate is linked to different proactive behaviors: The role of employee resilience. *Social Indicators Research*, *143*(2), 561–577. doi:10.100711205-018-1996-y

Caniëls, M. C. J., & Gelderman, C. J. (2007). Power and interdependence in buyer supplier relationships: A purchasing portfolio approach. *Industrial Marketing Management*, *36*(2), 219–229. doi:10.1016/j.indmarman.2005.08.012

Carlsson, B., Braunerhjelm, P., McKelvey, M., Olofsson, C., Persson, L., & Ylinenpää, H. (2013). The evolving domain of entrepreneurship research. *Small Business Economics*, *41*(4), 913–930. doi:10.100711187-013-9503-y

Carmona-Lavado, A., Gopalakrishnan, S., & Zhang, H. (2020). Product radicalness and firm performance in B2B marketing: A moderated mediation model. *Industrial Marketing Management*, *85*, 58–68. doi:10.1016/j.indmarman.2019.08.013

Carney, M. (2005). Corporate Governance and Competitive Advantage in Family-Controlled Firms. *Entrepreneurship Theory and Practice*, *29*(3), 249–265. doi:10.1111/j.1540-6520.2005.00081.x

Carney, M., Van Essen, M., Gedajlovic, E. R., & Heugens, P. P. M. A. R. (2015). What do we know about private family firms? A meta-analytical review. *Entrepreneurship Theory and Practice*, *39*(3), 513–544. doi:10.1111/etap.12054

Casadesus-Masanell, R., & Ricart, J. E. (2011). How to design a winning business model. *Harvard Business Review*, *89*(1-2), 101–107.

Casadesus-Masanell, R., & Zhu, F. (2013). Business model innovation and competitive imitation: The case of sponsor-based business models. *Strategic Management Journal*, *34*(4), 464–482. doi:10.1002mj.2022

Castellani, V., Sala, S., & Mirabella, N. (2015). Beyond the throwaway society: A life cycle-based assessment of the environmental benefit of reuse. *Integrated Environmental Assessment and Management*, *11*(3), 373–382. doi:10.1002/ieam.1614 PMID:25557152

Castro, C. (2018). *Crise ajudou negócio do KuantoKusta*. Retrieved from https://www.dinheirovivo.pt/empresas/mub-cargo-uber-das-mercadorias-chega-a-espanha-este-ano/

Catry, B. (2003). The great pretenders: The magic of luxury goods. *Business Strategy Review*, *14*(3), 10–17. doi:10.1111/1467-8616.00267

Chaar, B. B., & Lee, J. (2012). Role of socioeconomic status on consumers' attitudes towards DTCA of prescription medicines in Australia. *Journal of Business Ethics*, *105*(4), 447–460. doi:10.100710551-011-0977-8

Chang, S.-C., & Wang, C.-F. (2007). The effect of product diversification strategies on the relationship between international diversification and firm performance. *Journal of World Business*, *42*(1), 61–79. doi:10.1016/j.jwb.2006.11.002

Charnes, A., Cooper, W. W., & Rhodes, E. (1978). Measuring the efficiency of decision-making units. *European Journal of Operational Research*, *2*(6), 429–444. doi:10.1016/0377-2217(78)90138-8

Checkland, P. (1991). *Soft systems methodology*. Wiley.

Cheng, G., & Mevis, D. (2018). What happened to profitability? Shocks, challenges and perspectives for euro area banks. *European Journal of Finance*, 1–25. doi:10.1080/1351847X.2018.1470994

Cheng, J. Y. S. (2016). Xi Jinping's 'new model of major power relationships' for Sino-American relations. *Journal of Comparative Asian Development*, *15*(2), 226–254. doi:10.1080/15339114.2016.1203342

Chenhall, R. H., & Langfield-Smith, K. (2007). Multiple perspectives of performance measures. *European Management Journal*, *25*(4), 266–282. doi:10.1016/j.emj.2007.06.001

Chen, Y. (2018). Blockchain tokens and the potential democratization of entrepreneurship and innovation. *Business Horizons*, *61*(4), 567–575. doi:10.1016/j.bushor.2018.03.006

Chernev, A. (2017). *The business model: How to develop new products, create market value and make the competition irrelevant*. Cerebellum Press.

Chesbrough, H. (2007). Business model innovation: It's not just about technology anymore. *Strategy and Leadership*, *35*(6), 12–17. doi:10.1108/10878570710833714

Chesbrough, H. (2010). Business model innovation: Opportunities and barriers. *Long Range Planning*, *43*(2-3), 354–363. doi:10.1016/j.lrp.2009.07.010

Chiorazzo, V., D'Apice, V., DeYoung, R., & Morelli, P. (2018). Is the traditional banking model a survivor? *Journal of Banking & Finance*, *97*, 238–256. doi:10.1016/j.jbankfin.2018.10.008

Chirico, F., Sirmon, D. G., Sciascia, S., & Mazzola, P. (2011). Resource orchestration in family firms: Investigating how entrepreneurial orientation, generational involvement, and participative strategy affect performance. *Strategic Entrepreneurship Journal*, *5*(4), 307–326. doi:10.1002ej.121

Choi, S. B., & Kawk, Y. M. (2015). Corporate social responsibility and financial constraints: Evidence from Korean firms. *Global Business and Finance Review*, *20*(2), 15–26. doi:10.17549/gbfr.2015.20.2.15

Choong, K. (2013). Has this large number of performance measurement publications contributed to its better understanding? A systematic review for research and applications. *International Journal of Production Research*, 1–24.

Choudhury, A. H., & Naidu, G. N. (2009). A new selection strategy for portfolio diversification in the European Union. *Academy of Accounting and Financial Studies Journal*, *13*(3), 79–92.

Chrisman, J. J., Chua, J. H., & Kellermanns, F. (2009). Priorities, Resource Stocks, and Performance in Family and Nonfamily Firms. *Entrepreneurship Theory and Practice*, *33*(3), 739–760. doi:10.1111/j.1540-6520.2009.00324.x

Chrisman, J. J., Chua, J. H., Pearson, A. W., & Barnett, T. (2012). Family Involvement, Family Influence, and Family-Centered Non-Economic Goals in Small Firms. *Entrepreneurship Theory and Practice*, *36*(2), 267–293. doi:10.1111/j.1540-6520.2010.00407.x

Chrisman, J. J., & Patel, P. C. (2012). Variations in R&D investments of family and nonfamily firms: Behavioral agency and myopic loss aversion perspectives. *Academy of Management Journal*, *55*(4), 976–997. doi:10.5465/amj.2011.0211

Christensen, C. M. (1997). *The Innovation's Dilemma*. Harvard Business School Press.

Christensen, C. M. (2006). The ongoing process of building a theory of disruption. *Journal of Product Innovation Management*, *23*(1), 39–55. doi:10.1111/j.1540-5885.2005.00180.x

Christensen, C. M., Bartman, T., & van Bever, D. (2016). The hard truth about business model innovation. *MIT Sloan Management Review*, *58*(1), 30–40.

Christensen, C. R., Andrews, K. R., Bower, J. L., Hamermesh, R. G., & Porter, M. E. (1973). *Business policy: Text and cases*. Richard D. Irwin.

Christian, V., & Gumbus, A. (2009). Shades of gray: Applying professional codes of ethics to workplace dilemmas. *Organizational Management Journal*, *6*(3), 178–199. doi:10.1057/omj.2009.22

Chua, J. H., Chrisman, J. J., & Sharma, P. (1999). Defining the family business by behavior. *Entrepreneurship Theory and Practice*, *23*(4), 19–39. doi:10.1177/104225879902300402

Chu, S. C., & Kamal, S. (2011). An investigation of social media usage, brand consciousness, and purchase intention towards luxury products among Millennials. In S. Okazaki (Ed.), *Advances in advertising research* (Vol. 2, pp. 179–190). Gabler. doi:10.1007/978-3-8349-6854-8_12

Coelli, T. J., Rao, D. S. P., O'Donnell, C. J., & Battese, G. E. (2005). *An Introduction to Efficiency and Productivity Analysis* (2nd ed.). Springer.

Coetzee, J. (2018). *Strategic implications of fintech on South African retail banks*. South African Journal of Economic and Management Sciences., doi:10.4102ajems.v21i1.2455

Cohen, J., Cohen, P., West, S. G., & Aiken, L. (2003). *Applied Multiple Regression / Correlation Analysis for the Behavioral Sciences* (3rd ed.). Lawrence Erlbaum Associates.

Coin Dance. (2019, October 25). *Coin Dance*. Retrieved from https://coin.dance/

Connolly, J., & Prothero, A. (2003). Sustainable consumption: Consumption, consumers and the commodity discourse. *Consumption Markets & Culture*, *6*(4), 275–291. doi:10.1080/1025386032000168311

Connolly, J., & Prothero, A. (2008). Green consumption: Life-politics, risk and contradictions. *Journal of Consumer Culture*, *8*(1), 117–145. doi:10.1177/1469540507086422

Costa-Climent, R., & Martínez-Climent, C. (2018). Sustainable profitability of ethical and conventional banking. *Contemporary Economics*, 519-530. doi:10.5709/ce.1897-9254.294

Crainer, S. (2013). Squaring the circle. *Business Strategy Review*, *24*(4), 13–19. doi:10.1111/j.1467-8616.2013.00988.x

Crofts, K., & Bisman, J. (2010). Interrogating accountability: An illustration of the use of Leximancer software for qualitative data analysis. *Qualitative Research in Accounting & Management*, *7*(2), 180–207. doi:10.1108/11766091011050859

Cross, K. F., & Lynch, R. L. (1988). The SMART way to define and sustain success. *National Productivity Review*, *9*(1), 23–33. doi:10.1002/npr.4040080105

Cruz, C. C., Gómez-Mejía, L. R., & Becerra, M. (2010). Perceptions of benevolence and the design of agency contracts: CEO-TMT relationships in family firms. *Academy of Management Journal*, *53*(1), 69–89. doi:10.5465/amj.2010.48036975

Cruz, C., & Nordqvist, M. (2012). Entrepreneurial orientation in family firms: A generational perspective. *Small Business Economics, 38*(1), 33–49. doi:10.100711187-010-9265-8

Cumming, D., Meoli, M., & Vismara, S. (2019). Does equity crowdfunding democratize entrepreneurial finance? *Small Business Economics*. Advance online publication. doi:10.100711187-019-00188-z

Cunningham, J. A., Mangematin, V., O'Kane, C., & O'Reilly, P. (2016). At the frontiers of scientific advancement: The factors that influence scientists to become or choose to become publicly funded principal investigators. *The Journal of Technology Transfer, 41*(4), 778–797. doi:10.100710961-015-9400-4

Cusumano, M. A., Gawer, A. A., & Yoffie, D.B. (2019). The Business of Platforms: Strategy in the Age of Digital Competition, Innovation, and Power. HarperCollins.

D'Aveni, R. (1994). *Hypercompetition*. Free Press.

Dabab, M., & Weber, C. (2018). Business intelligence and data analytics as a driver of dynamic capability strategic approach. *PICMET 2018 - Portland International Conference on Management of Engineering and Technology: Managing Technological Entrepreneurship: The Engine for Economic Growth, Proceedings*, 1–9. 10.23919/PICMET.2018.8481750

Dahles, H., & Susilowati, T. P. (2015). Business resilience in times of growth and crisis. *Annals of Tourism Research, 51*, 34–50. doi:10.1016/j.annals.2015.01.002

Dalziell, E. P., & McManus, S. T. (2004). *Resilience, vulnerability, and adaptive Capacity: Implications for system performance*. Paper presented at the International Forum for Engineering Decision Making (IFED), Stoos, Switzerland.

Dawson, J. F. (2014). Moderation in management research: What, why, when and how. *Journal of Business and Psychology, 29*(1), 1–19. doi:10.100710869-013-9308-7

Daya, P. (2014). Diversity and inclusion in an emerging market context. *Equality, Diversity and Inclusion, 33*(3), 293–308. doi:10.1108/EDI-10-2012-0087

De Massis, A., Kotlar, J., Mazzola, P., Minola, T., & Sciascia, S. (2018). Conflicting Selves: Family Owners' Multiple Goals and Self-Control Agency Problems in Private Firms. *Entrepreneurship Theory and Practice, 42*(3), 362–389. doi:10.1111/etap.12257

De Nooy, W., Mrvar, A., & Batagelj, V. (2011). *Exploratory social network analysis with pajek*. Cambridge University Press. doi:10.1017/CBO9780511996368

Degbey, W. Y. (2015). Customer retention: A source of value for serial acquirers. *Industrial Marketing Management, 46*, 11–23. doi:10.1016/j.indmarman.2015.01.002

DeGhetto, K., Gray, J. R., & Kiggundu, M. N. (2016). The African Union's Agenda 2063: Aspirations, challenges, and opportunities for management research. *Africa Journal of Management, 2*(1), 93–116. doi:10.1080/23322373.2015.1127090

Deitel, H., & Deitel, P. (2004). The complete e-business and e-commerce programming training course. New Jersey: Prentice Hall.

Dell'Atti, S., Trotta, A., Iannuzzi, A. P., & Demaria, F. (2017). *Corporate Social Responsibility Engagement as a Determinant of Bank Reputation: An Empirical Analysis*. doi:10.1002/csr.1430

Deloitte. (2017). Beyond fintech: Eight forces that are shifting the competitive landscape. *Beyond fintech: Eight forces that are shifting the competitive landscape.*

Deloitte. (2019). *Global powers of luxury goods 2019. Bridging the gap between the old and the new*. Retrieved from https://www2.deloitte.com/global/en/pages/consumer-business/articles/gx-cb-global-powers-of-luxury-goods.html

Dermol, V. (2013). *Učenje in ustvarjanje znanja v podjetju*. Celje: Mednarodna fakulteta za družbene in poslovne študije.

Desai, K. R., V, M., V, V., & Jayakumar, K. (2019). Fintech Innovations and Its Impact on the Profitability of Selected Banks. *International Journal of Business and Management Invention*, 41-45.

Devi, R. S., Chong, S. C., & Lin, B. (2007). Organisational culture and KM processes from the perspective of an institution of higher learning. *International Journal of Management Education*, *1*(1-2), 57–67.

Diéguez-Soto, J., Duréndez, A., García-Pérez-de-Lema, D., & Ruiz-Palomo, D. (2016a). Technological, management, and persistent innovation in small and medium family firms: The influence of professionalism. *Canadian Journal of Administrative Sciences*, *33*(4), 332–346. doi:10.1002/cjas.1404

Diéguez-Soto, J., Garrido-Moreno, A., & Manzaneque, M. (2018). Unravelling the link between process innovation inputs and outputs: The moderating role of family management. *Journal of Family Business Strategy*, *9*(2), 114–127. doi:10.1016/j.jfbs.2017.11.007

Diéguez-Soto, J., & López-Delgado, P. (2019). Does Family and Lone Founder Involvement Lead to Similar Indebtedness? *Journal of Small Business Management*, *57*(4), 1531–1558. doi:10.1111/jsbm.12422

Diéguez-Soto, J., Manzaneque, M., González-García, V., & Galache-Laza, T. (2019). A study of the moderating influence of R&D intensity on the family management-firm performance relationship: Evidence from Spanish private manufacturing firms. *BRQ Business Research Quarterly*, *22*(2), 105–118. doi:10.1016/j.brq.2018.08.007

Diéguez-Soto, J., Manzaneque, M., & Rojo-Ramírez, A. A. (2016b). Technological Innovation Inputs, Outputs and Performance: The Moderating Role of Family Involvement in Management. *Family Business Review*, *29*(3), 327–346. doi:10.1177/0894486516646917

Dobson, H. (2012). Japan's response to the changing global order: The case of a 'Gaggle of Gs'. *International Relations of the Asia-Pacific*, *12*(2), 229–257. doi:10.1093/irap/lcr023

Döderlein, D. (2018). What is the optimal mix between banks and fintechs in the payments architecture? *Journal of Payments Strategy and Systems*, 122-129.

Dolati Neghabadi, P., Evrard Samuel, K., & Espinouse, M. L. (2019). Systematic literature review on city logistics: Overview, classification and analysis. *International Journal of Production Research, 57*(3), 865–887. doi:10.1080/00207543.2018.1489153

Dombrowski, U., & Fochler, S. (2018). Servitization as a key driver for Digital Transformation of manufacturing companies' Spare Parts Service. *Proceedings of the 2018 IEEE International Conference on Service Operations and Logistics, and Informatics*, 291–296. 10.1109/SOLI.2018.8476713

Dosi, G. (1982). Technological paradigms and technological trajectories. A suggested interpretation of the determinants and directions of technical change. *Research Policy, 11*(3), 147–162. doi:10.1016/0048-7333(82)90016-6

Douglas, M. (1966). *Purity and danger*. Routledge & Kegan.

Drackner, M. (2005). What is waste? To whom? An anthropological perspective on garbage. *Waste Management & Research, 23*(3), 175–181. doi:10.1177/0734242X05054325 PMID:15988938

Drasch, B., Schweizer, A., & Urbach, N. (2018). Integrating the 'Troublemakers': A taxonomy for cooperation between banks and fintechs. *Journal of Economics and Business, 100*, 26–42. doi:10.1016/j.jeconbus.2018.04.002

Dubois, A., & Araujo, L. (2007). Case research in purchasing and supply management: Opportunities and challenges. *Journal of Purchasing and Supply Management, 13*(3), 170–181. doi:10.1016/j.pursup.2007.09.002

Dubrovski, D. (2010). Pomembnost ugotavljanja pravilnih vzrokov za nastanek podjetniške krize. *Management, 5*(1), 37–52.

Dubrovski, D. (2016). Handling corporate crises based on the correct analysis of its causes. *Journal of Financial Risk Management, 5*(04), 264–280. doi:10.4236/jfrm.2016.54024

Dubrovski, D. (2018). *Management in organizacija. Celje*. International School of Social and Business Studies.

Duchek, S. (2014). Growth in the face of crisis: the role of organizational resilience capabilities. In *Academy of management proceedings* (Vol. 1, p. 13487). Academy of Management. doi:10.5465/ambpp.2014.225

Ducq, Y. M. S. R., & Vallespir, B. (2019a). A state of the art and comparison of approaches for performance measurement systems definition and design. *International Journal of Production Research, 57*(15-16), 5026–5046. doi:10.1080/00207543.2018.1506178

Ducq, Y. M. S. R., & Vallespir, B. (2019b). General enterprise performance measurement architecture. *International Journal of Production Research*. Advance online publication. doi:10.1080/00207543.2019.1692158

Du, L., Hou, J., & Huang, Y. (2008). Mechanisms of power and action for cause-related marketing: Perspectives of enterprise and non-profit organizations. *Baltic Journal of Management*, *3*(1), 92–104. doi:10.1108/17465260810844284

Dyer, W. G. (2006). Examining the "Family Effect" on Firm Performance. *Family Business Review*, *19*(4), 253–273. doi:10.1111/j.1741-6248.2006.00074.x

Eck, N.J. Van & Waltman, L. (2014). *Visualizing bibliometric networks, measuring scholarly impact: Methods and practice*. doi:10.1007/978-3-319-10377-8_13

Edwards, C. (2007). Sony's Surprising PS3 Price Cut. *Bloomberg*. Retrieved from: https://www.bloomberg.com/news/articles/2007-07-09/sonys-surprising-ps3-price-cutbusinessweek-business-news-stock-market-and-financial-advice

Egels-Zandén, N., & Hyllman, P. (2007). Evaluating strategies for negotiating workers' rights in transnational corporations: The effects of codes of conduct and global agreements on workplace democracy. *Journal of Business Ethics*, *76*(2), 207–223. doi:10.100710551-006-9269-0

Eisenhardt, K. M., & Martin, J. A. (2000). Dynamic capabilities: What are they? *Strategic Management Journal*, *21*(10-11), 1105–1121. doi:10.1002/1097-0266(200010/11)21:10/11<1105::AID-SMJ133>3.0.CO;2-E

Elgström, O. (2007). Outsiders' perceptions of the European union in international trade negotiations. *Journal of Common Market Studies*, *45*(4), 949–967. doi:10.1111/j.1468-5965.2007.00755.x

Ernst, C. (2008). The global manager's work. In C. Wankel (Ed.), 21st century management. A reference handbook. Los Angeles, CA: Sage Publications.

Esperança, P., & Matias, F. (2005). *Finanças Empresariais*. Publicações Dom Quixote.

Etzkowitz, H., Webster, A., Gebhardt, C., & Terra, B. R. C. (2000). The future of the university and the university of the future: Evolution of ivory tower to entrepreneurial paradigm. *Research Policy*, *29*(2), 313–330. doi:10.1016/S0048-7333(99)00069-4

European Parliament and the Council of the European Union. (2008). Council directive 2008/98/EC on waste and repealing certain directives. *Official Journal* L312/3. Retrieved from https://eur-lex.europa.eu/legal-content/EN/TXT/?uri=celex%3A32008L0098

Everett, S. (2012). Production places or consumption spaces? The place-making agency of food tourism in Ireland and Scotland. *Tourism Geographies*, *14*(4), 535–554. doi:10.1080/14616688.2012.647321

EY. (2014). *Winning through customer experience*. EY Global Consumer Banking Survey.

EY. (2017). *Unleashing the potential of FinTech in banking*. Author.

EY. (2018). *FinTech ecosystem playbook*. Author.

Eyring, M. J., Johnson, M. W., & Nair, H. (2010). New business models in emerging markets. *Harvard Business Review*, *89*(1-2), 88–95.

Farrell, M. J. (1957). The measurement of productive efficiency. *Journal of the Royal Statistical Society. Series A (General)*, *120*(3), 253–290. doi:10.2307/2343100

Fernandes, T., & Remelhe, P. (2016). How to engage customers in co-creation: Customers' motivations for collaborative innovation. *Journal of Strategic Marketing*, *24*(3-4), 311–326. doi:10.1080/0965254X.2015.1095220

Ferraris, A., Bresciani, S., & Del Giudice, M. (2016). International diversification and firm performance: A four-stage model. *EuroMed Journal of Business*, *11*(3), 362–375. doi:10.1108/EMJB-10-2015-0048

Ferreira, L., & Sousa, B. B. (2020). Understanding the Role of Social Networks in Consumer Behavior in Tourism. In C. Ramos, C. Almeida, & P. Fernandes (Eds.), *Handbook of Research on Social Media Applications for the Tourism and Hospitality Sector* (pp. 367–384). IGI Global. doi:10.4018/978-1-7998-1947-9.ch021

Ferreira, M. P., Serra, F. A. R., & Reis, N. R. (2011). On the adaptation of the firm's strategies to the international business environment: A knowledge-based and evolutionary perspective. *European Journal of International Management*, *5*(6), 633–655. doi:10.1504/EJIM.2011.042735

Figge, F., Young, W., & Barkemeyer, R. (2014). Sufficiency or efficiency to achieve lower resource consumption and emissions? The role of the rebound effect. *Journal of Cleaner Production*, *69*, 216–224. doi:10.1016/j.jclepro.2014.01.031

Fischbacher-Smith, D., & Smith, L. (2015). Navigating the 'dark waters of globalisation': Global markets, inequalities and the spatial dynamics of risk. *Risk Management*, *17*(3), 179–203. doi:10.1057/rm.2015.12

Fisher, L. M. (2005). *The profet of unintended consequences*. Retrieved from https://www.strategy-business.com/article/05308

Fitzgerald, L., Johnston, R., Brignall, S., Silvestro, R., & Voss, C. (1991). *Performance Measurement in Service Business*. CIMA.

Flores, R. G., & Aguilera, R. V. (2007). Globalization and location choice: An analysis of US multinational firms in 1980 and 2000. *Journal of International Business Studies*, *38*(7), 1187–1210. doi:10.1057/palgrave.jibs.8400307

Forrester, J. W. (1961). *Industrial dynamics*. Cambridge: Pegasus Communications.

Forrester, J. W. (1968). *Principles of systems*. Cambridge: Pegasus Communications.

Foster, R. (1986). *Innovation: The Attacker's Advantage*. Summit Books. doi:10.1007/978-3-322-83742-4

Freivogel, C. (2016, June 29). *The social side of Fintech*. Retrieved September 2019, 22, from SwissBanking: https://www.swissbanking.org/en/services/insight/2.16/the-social-side-of-fintech

Frias, A., & Freire, E. (2019). Financial shielding that Bitcoin grants to capitals in the world. *Investment Management and Financial Innovations*, 49-61. doi:10.21511/imfi.16(3).2019.06

Frolova, T., & Tokar, V. (2014). The European Union TNCs' investment strategies of innovation development. *Economic Annals-XXI*, *5–6*, 13–16.

Fuller, D. A. (1999). *Sustainable marketing: Managerial-ecological issues*. Sage Publications.

Galimova, M., Gileva, T., Mukhanova, N., & Krasnuk, L. (2019). Selecting the path of the digital transformation of business-models for industrial enterprises. *IOP Conference Series. Materials Science and Engineering*, *497*(1), 012071. Advance online publication. doi:10.1088/1757-899X/497/1/012071

Galindo, M. Q., & Limjuco, R. P. (2016). Awareness on ASEAN 2015 integration, managerial flexibility and school preparedness for transnational students: Basis for a cross-cultural adaptation program. *International Journal of Applied Business and Economic Research*, *14*(2), 1171–1196.

Gal, M. S., & Elkin-Koren, N. (2017). Algorithmic consumers. *Harvard Journal of Law & Technology*, *30*, 1–45.

Gardyn, R. (2002). Defining luxury: Oh, the good life. *American Demographics*. Retrieved from http://findarticles.com/p/articles/mi_m4021/is_2002_Nov_1/ai_93089467/?tag=content;col1

Gedajlovic, E., Lubatkin, M. H., & Schulze, W. S. (2004). Crossing the threshold from founder management to professional management: A governance perspective. *Journal of Management Studies*, *41*(5), 899–912. doi:10.1111/j.1467-6486.2004.00459.x

Ghannad, N., & Andersson, S. (2012). The influence of the entrepreneur's background on the behaviour and development of born globals' internationalisation processes. *International Journal of Entrepreneurship and Small Business*, *15*(2), 136–153. doi:10.1504/IJESB.2012.045201

Ghisellini, P., Cialani, C., & Ulgiati, S. (2016). A review on circular economy: The expected transition to a balanced interplay on environmental and economic systems. *Journal of Cleaner Production*, *114*, 11–32. doi:10.1016/j.jclepro.2015.09.007

Girish, R. (2018). *Why are businesses shifting to mobile apps in 2018*. Retrieved from https://www.fingent.com/blog/businesses-shifting-mobile-apps-2018

Gohary, E. E. (2019). The impact of financial technology on facilitating e-government services in Egypt. *Journal of Distribution Science*, 51-59. doi:10.15722/JDS.17.5.201905.51

Goldhill, O. (2013). Sony reignites console price war with Microsoft. *The Telegraph*. Retrieved from: https://www.telegraph.co.uk/technology/video-games/10112334/E3-2013-Sony-reignites-console-price-war-with-Microsoft.html

Gölzer, P., & Fritzsche, A. (2017). Data-driven operations management: Organisational implications of the digital transformation in industrial practice. *Production Planning and Control*, *28*(16), 1332–1343. doi:10.1080/09537287.2017.1375148

Gomber, P., Kauffman, R. J., Parker, C., & Weber, B. W. (2018). On the Fintech Revolution: Interpreting the Forces of Innovation, Disruption, and Transformation in Financial Services. *Journal of Management Information Systems, 35*(1), 220–265. doi:10.1080/07421222.2018.1440766

Gómez, J. I., & Rocha, H. (2019). Business Policy: Historical Evolution and Epistemological Roots. In A. A. Caldart, J. E. Ricart, & A. A. Carrera (Eds.), *General management in latin and ibero-american organizations: A humanistic perspective*. Routledge.

Gómez-Mejía, L. R., Campbell, J. T., Martin, G., Hoskisson, R. E., Makri, M., & Sirmon, D. G. (2014). Socioemotional Wealth as a Mixed Gamble: Revisiting Family Firm R&D Investments With the Behavioral Agency Model. *Entrepreneurship Theory and Practice, 38*(6), 1351–1374.

Gómez-Mejía, L. R., Cruz, C., Berrone, P., & De Castro, J. (2011). The Bind that Ties: Socioemotional Wealth Preservation in Family Firms. *The Academy of Management Annals, 5*(1), 653–707. doi:10.5465/19416520.2011.593320

Gómez-Mejía, L. R., Haynes, K. T., Núñez-Nickel, M., Jacobson, K. J. L., & Moyano-Fuentes, J. (2007). Socioemotional Wealth and Business Risks in Family-controlled Firms: Evidence from Spanish Olive Oil Mills. *Administrative Science Quarterly, 52*(1), 106–137. doi:10.2189/asqu.52.1.106

Gómez-Mejía, L. R., Makri, M., & Larraza-Kintana, M. (2010). Diversification Decisions in Family-Controlled Firms. *Journal of Management Studies, 47*(2), 223–252. doi:10.1111/j.1467-6486.2009.00889.x

Gómez-Mejía, L. R., Núñez-Nickel, M., & Gutierrez, I. (2001). The role of family ties in agency contracts. *Academy of Management Journal, 44*(1), 81–95.

Gómez-Mejía, L. R., Patel, P. C., & Zellweger, T. M. (2018). In the Horns of the Dilemma: Socioemotional Wealth, Financial Wealth, and Acquisitions in Family Firms. *Journal of Management, 44*(4), 1369–1397. doi:10.1177/0149206315614375

Gonzalez, L. (2019). Blockchain, herding and trust in peer-to-peer lending. *Managerial Finance*, MF-09-2018-0423. Advance online publication. doi:10.1108/MF-09-2018-0423

González, M., Guzmán, A., Pombo, C., & Trujillo, M. A. (2013). Family firms and debt: Risk aversion versus risk of losing control. *Journal of Business Research, 66*(11), 2308–2320. doi:10.1016/j.jbusres.2012.03.014

Gonzàlez-Toruno, M. (2005). La Iniciativa institucional. In J. L. Lucas (Ed.), *Iniciativa, dinero y poder en la empresa mercantil*. Ed. Instituto Internacional San Telmo.

Google. (2019, October 25). *Google Trends*. Retrieved from https://trends.google.com/

Gordon, R., Carrigan, M., & Hastings, G. (2011). A framework for sustainable marketing. *Marketing Theory, 11*(2), 143–163. doi:10.1177/1470593111403218

Gottardo, P., & Moisello, A. M. (2015). The impact of socioemotional wealth on family firms' financial performance. *Problems and Perspectives in Management, 13*(1), 67–77.

Gouillart, F. J., & Kelly, J. N. (1995). *Transforming the organization.* McGraw-Hill.

Granata, G., & Scozzese, G. (2017). The Influence of Virtual Communities in Marketing Decision. *International Business Research, 10*(12), 191–196. doi:10.5539/ibr.v10n12p191

Grant, R. M. (1991). The resource based theory of competitive advantage: Implications for strategy formulation. *California Management Review, 33*(3), 114–135. doi:10.2307/41166664

Gries, T., & Naudé, W. (2010). Entrepreneurship and structural economic transformation. *Small Business Economics, 34*(1), 13–29. doi:10.100711187-009-9192-8

Guariso, A., Squicciarini, M. P., & Swinnen, J. (2014). Food price shocks and the political economy of global agricultural and development policy. *Applied Economic Perspectives and Policy, 36*(3), 387–415. doi:10.1093/aepp/ppu020

Guide, V. D., & Wassenhove, L. N. (2009). The evolution of closed-loop supply chain research. *Operations Research, 57*(1), 10–18. doi:10.1287/opre.1080.0628

Gujarati, D., & Porter, D. (2008). Basic econometrics (5th ed.). Boston: McGraw-Hill Education.

Gupta, G., & Bose, I. (2018, June). Strategic learning for digital market pioneering: Examining the transformation of Wishberry's crowdfunding model. *Technological Forecasting and Social Change, 146*, 865–876. doi:10.1016/j.techfore.2018.06.020

Gupta, N. (2018). *Driving Digital Strategy: a Guide to Reimagining your Business*. Harvard Business Review Press.

Hair, J. F., Black, B., Babin, B., & Anderson, R. E. (2010). *Multivariate data analysis* (6th ed.). Prentice Hall.

Hamel, G., & Välikangas, L. (2003). The quest for resilience. *Harvard Business Review, 81*(9), 52–63. PMID:12964393

Hansen, M. W. (2020). Toward a strategic management perspective on local content in African extractives: MNC procurement strategies between local responsiveness and global integration. *Africa Journal of Management, 6*(1), 1–19. doi:10.1080/23322373.2020.1717283

Harland, L., Harrison, W., Jones, J. R., & Reiter-Palmon, R. (2005). Leadership behaviors and subordinate resilience. *Journal of Leadership & Organizational Studies, 11*(2), 2–14. doi:10.1177/107179190501100202

Harrigan, K. R. (1983). A Framework for Looking at Vertical Integration. *The Journal of Business Strategy, 3*(3), 30–37. doi:10.1108/eb038975

Harrison, J. & Wicks, A. (2013). Stakeholder theory, value and firm performance. *Business Ethics Quarterly, 23*(1).

Harrison-Hill, T. (2015). How far is a long way? Contrasting two cultures' perspectives of travel distance. *Qualitative Research in Organizations and Management, 13*(3), 3–17.

Hart, S. L. (1995). A natural resource-based view of the firm. *Academy of Management Review*, *20*(4), 986–1014. doi:10.5465/amr.1995.9512280033

Harvey, J., & Branco-Illodo, I. (2019). Why Cryptocurrencies Want Privacy: A Review of Political Motivations and Branding Expressed in "Privacy Coin" Whitepapers. *Journal of Political Marketing*, 1–30. Advance online publication. doi:10.1080/15377857.2019.1652223

Harzing, A. W. (2011). *The publish or perish book: Your guide to effective and responsible citation analysis*. Tamar Software Research Publisher.

Hassani, H., Huang, X., & Silva, E. (2018). Banking with blockchain-ed big data. *Journal of Management Analytics*, 256-275. doi:10.1080/23270012.2018.1528900

Heidenreich, M. (2012). The social embeddedness of multinational companies: A literature review. *Socio-economic Review*, *10*(3), 549–579. doi:10.1093er/mws010

Heine, K. (2012). The concept of luxury brands. *Luxury Brand Management*, *1*, 2193–1208.

Hendrickx, H. H. M. (2015). Business architect: A critical role in enterprise transformation. *Journal of Enterprise Transformation*, *5*(1), 1–29. doi:10.1080/19488289.2014.893933

Herbane, B. (2019). Rethinking organizational resilience and strategic renewal in SMEs. *Entrepreneurship and Regional Development*, *31*(5–6), 476–495. doi:10.1080/08985626.2018.1541594

Hill, J., & Lee, H. (2012). Young Generation Y consumers' perceptions of sustainability in the apparel industry. *Journal of Fashion Marketing and Management*, *16*(4), 477–491. doi:10.1108/13612021211265863

Hill, R. (2018). Theory of marketplace morality and impoverished consumers. *Marketing Theory*, *18*(3), 411–420. doi:10.1177/1470593117753983

Hoegen, A., Steininger, D., & Veit, D. (2018). How do investors decide? An interdisciplinary review of decision-making in crowdfunding. *Electronic Markets*, *28*(3), 339–365. doi:10.100712525-017-0269-y

Hollis, S. (2018). *How Wish grew to over $1 billion in revenue by inverting Amazon's strategy*. Retrieved from https://jilt.com/blog/wish-growth/

Horrigan, J. (1965). Some empirical bases of financial ratio analysis. *The Accounting Review*, 558–568.

Hoskisson, R. E., Eden, L., Lau, C. M., & Wright, M. (2000). Strategy in emerging economies. *Academy of Management Journal*, *43*(3), 249–267.

Hrustek, L., Tomicic Furjan, M., & Pihir, I. (2019). Influence of Digital Transformation Drivers on Business Model creation. *2019 42nd International Convention on Information and Communication Technology, Electronics and Microelectronics*, 1304–1308. 10.23919/MIPRO.2019.8756666

Hu, X. & Motwani, J.G. (2014). Minimizing downside risks for global sourcing under price-sensitive stochastic demand, exchange rate uncertainties, and supplier capacity constraints. *International Journal of Production Economics, 147*(B), 398–409.

Hua, T. (2015). Strategy to internationalise China's customs management education system. *World Customs Journal, 9*(1), 109–114.

Hunter, B. N. (2016). *The power of KM*. Spirit Rising Productions.

Hunt, S. D. (2000). *A general theory of competition*. Sage.

Iansiti, M. (1998). *Technology Integration*. Harvard Business School Press.

Ikeda, K., & Marshall, A. (2016). How successful organizations drive innovation. *Strategy and Leadership, 44*(3), 9–19. doi:10.1108/SL-04-2016-0029

Iman, N. (2019). Traditional banks against fintech startups: A field investigation of a regional bank in Indonesia. *Banks and Bank Systems*, 20-33. doi:10.21511/bbs.14(3).2019.03

Islam, T. (2019). *Cost per click: the most used model of online advertising*. Retrieved from https://charpotra.blogspot.com/2019/04/cost-per-click-most-used-model-of.html

Jain, S. C., & Tucker, L. R. (1995). The influence of culture on strategic constructs in the process of globalization: An empirical study of North American and Japanese MNCs. *International Business Review, 4*(1), 19–37. doi:10.1016/0969-5931(94)00029-L

Jain, V., Vatsa, R., & Jagani, K. (2014). Exploring generation Z's purchase behavior towards luxury apparel: A conceptual framework. *Romanian Journal of Marketing, 2*(Apr-Jun), 18–29.

Jakšič, M., & Marinč, M. (2019). Relationship banking and information technology: The role of artificial intelligence and FinTech. *Risk Management*. Advance online publication. doi:10.105741283-018-0039-y

Jamrog, J. J., McCann, J. E. III, Lee, J. M., Morrison, C. L., Selsky, J. W., & Vickers, M. (2006). *Agility and resilience in the face of continuous change: A global study of current trends and future possibilities 2006-2016*. American Management Association.

Janssen, C., Vanhamme, J., Lindgreen, A., & Lefebvre, C. (2014). The Catch-22 of responsible luxury: Effects of luxury product characteristics on consumers' perception of fit with corporate social responsibility. *Journal of Business Ethics, 119*(1), 45–57. doi:10.100710551-013-1621-6

Japparova, I., & Rupeika-Apoga, R. (2017). Banking business models of the digital future: The case of Latvia. *European Research Studies Journal*, 864-878.

Jennex, M. E. (2020). Towards Understanding and Implementing Knowledge Management Strategy. In M. E. Jennex (Ed.), *Current Issues and Trends in Knowledge Management, Discovery, and Transfer* (pp. 103–125). IGI Global. doi:10.4018/978-1-7998-2189-2.ch005

Ji, G., Gunasekaran, A. & Yang, G. (2014). Constructing sustainable supply chain under double environmental medium regulations. *International Journal of Production Economics, 147*(B), 211–219.

Ji, G., Gunasekaran, A., & Yang, G. (2014). Constructing sustainable supply chain under double environmental medium regulations. *International Journal of Production Economics*, *147*, 211–219. doi:10.1016/j.ijpe.2013.04.012

Jin, Z., Lynch, R., Attia, S., Chansarkar, B., Gülsoy, T., Lapoule, P., Liu, X., Newburry, W., Nooraini, M. S., Parente, R., Purani, K., & Ungerer, M. (2015). The relationship between consumer ethnocentrism, cosmopolitanism and product country image among younger generation consumers: The moderating role of country development status. *International Business Review*, *24*(3), 380–393. doi:10.1016/j.ibusrev.2014.08.010

JN. (2019). *KuantoKusta investe três milhões de euros para alargar plataforma de venda "online"*. Retrieved from https://www.jn.pt/inovacao/interior/kuantokusta-investe-tres-milhoes-de-euros-para-alargar-plataforma-de-venda-online-10615695.html

Johnson, M. W. (2010). *Seizing the white space*. Harvard Business Press.

Johnson, M. W. (2018). *Reinvent your business model*. Harvard Business Review Press.

Johnson, M. W., Christensen, C. M., & Kagermann, H. (2008). Reinventing your business model. *Harvard Business Review*, *86*(12), 57–68.

Jones, P., Clarke-Hill, C., Comfort, D., & Hillier, D. (2008). Marketing and sustainability. *Marketing Intelligence & Planning*, *26*(2), 123–13. doi:10.1108/02634500810860584

Joseph Pine, B. II, & Gilmore, H., J. (. (2014). A leader's guide to innovation in the experience economy. *Strategy and Leadership*, *42*(1), 24–29. doi:10.1108/SL-09-2013-0073

Jung, D., Dorner, V., Weinhardt, C., & Pusmaz, H. (2018). Designing a robo-advisor for risk-averse, low-budget consumers. *Electronic Markets*, *28*(3), 367–380. doi:10.100712525-017-0279-9

Kanchanapibul, M., Lacka, E., Wang, X., & Chan, H. K. (2014). An empirical investigation of green purchase behaviour among the young generation. *Journal of Cleaner Production*, *66*, 528–536. doi:10.1016/j.jclepro.2013.10.062

Kaplan, R., & Norton, D. (1992). The balanced scorecard-measures that drive performance. *Harvard Business Review*, *70*(1), 71–79. PMID:10119714

Kaplan, R., & Norton, D. (1996). *The balanced scorecard: Translating strategy into action*. Harvard Business Review Press.

Kapustina, I., Pereverzeva, T., Stepanova, T., & Rusu, I. (2019). Convergence of institutes of retail traditional and digital economy. *IOP Conference Series. Materials Science and Engineering*, *497*(1), 012120. Advance online publication. doi:10.1088/1757-899X/497/1/012120

Karakaya, F., & Stahl, M. (2009). After market entry barriers in e-commerce markets. *Journal of Electronic Commerce Research, 10*(3), 130–143.

Kauffman, S. (1995). *At Home in the Universe*. Oxford University Press.

Kaz, K. (2019). Building resilience into the organization. In R. Schmidpeter, N. Capaldi, S. Idowu, & A. Stürenberg Herrera (Eds.), *International dimensions of sustainable management. CSR, sustainability, ethics & governance: Latest perspectives from corporate governance, responsible finance and CSR* (pp. 69–85). Springer. doi:10.1007/978-3-030-04819-8_5

Keegan, D. P., Eiler, R. G. & Jones, C. (1989, June). Are your performance measures obsolete? *Management Accounting*, 45-50.

Kelly, D., & Amburgey, T. L. (1991). Organizational inertia and momentum: A dynamic model of strategic change. *Academy of Management Journal, 34*(3), 591–612.

Kemper, J. A., & Ballantine, P. W. (2019). What do we mean by sustainability marketing? *Journal of Marketing Management, 35*(3/4), 277–309. doi:10.1080/0267257X.2019.1573845

Kerekes, S., & Nemeslaki, A. (2009). Education 2.0: Exploring the challenges of Corvinus University in the long tail economy of global higher education. *Society and Economy, 31*(1), 125–146. doi:10.1556/SocEc.31.2009.1.8

Kettunen, P., & Laanti, M. (2017). Future software organizations – agile goals and roles. *European Journal of Futures Research, 5*(1), 1–15. doi:10.100740309-017-0123-7

Khanna, S., & Martins, H. (2018). *Six digital growth strategies for banks*. McKinsey Insights.

Khanna, T., & Palepu, K. G. (2010). *Winning in emerging markets: A road map for strategy and execution*. Harvard Business Press.

Kilbourne, W. E. (1998). Green marketing: A theoretical perspective. *Journal of Marketing Management, 14*(6), 641–655. doi:10.1362/026725798784867743

Kilbourne, W. E., & Carlson, L. (2008). The dominant social paradigm, consumption and environmental attitudes: Can macromarketing education help? *Journal of Macromarketing, 28*(2), 106–121. doi:10.1177/0276146708314586

Kim, B. (2013). Responsive web design, discoverability, and mobile challenge. *Library Technology Reports, 49*(6), 29–39.

Kim, K., & Hann, I. (2019). Crowdfunding and the democratization of access to capital-an illusion? Evidence from housing prices. *Information Systems Research, 30*(1), 276–290. doi:10.1287/isre.2018.0802

Kim, W. C., & Mauborgne, R. (2005). *Blue Ocean Strategy: How to Create Uncontested Market Space and Make Competition Irrelevant*. Harvard Business School Publishing.

Kim, W. C., & Mauborgne, R. (2017). *Blue ocean shift: Beyond competing - proven steps to inspire confidence and seize new growth*. Macmillan.

Kim, Y., & Gao, F. Y. (2013). Does family involvement increase business performance? Family-longevity goals' moderating role in Chinese family firms. *Journal of Business Research, 66*(2), 265–274. doi:10.1016/j.jbusres.2012.08.018

Kireeva-Karimova, A. (2015). Institutional challenges and economic agents forming a competitive market environment. *Mediterranean Journal of Social Sciences, 6*(1S3), 211–216.

Knight, G. A., & Cavusgil, S. T. (2004). Innovation, organizational capabilities, and the born-global firm. *Journal of International Business Studies, 35*(2), 124–141. doi:10.1057/palgrave.jibs.8400071

Knoerich, J. (2010). Gaining from the global ambitions of emerging economy enterprises: An analysis of the decision to sell a German firm to a Chinese acquirer. *Journal of International Management, 16*(2), 177–191. doi:10.1016/j.intman.2010.03.008

Kotarba, M. (2018). Digital transformation of business models. *Foundations of Management, 10*(1), 123–142. doi:10.2478/fman-2018-0011

Kotey, B. (2005). Are performance differences between family and non-family SMEs uniform across all firm sizes? *International Journal of Entrepreneurial Behaviour & Research, 11*(6), 394–421. doi:10.1108/13552550510625168

Kotlar, J., De Massis, A., Fang, H., & Frattini, F. (2014a). Strategic reference points in family firms. *Small Business Economics, 43*(3), 597–619. doi:10.100711187-014-9556-6

Kotlar, J., De Massis, A., Frattini, F., & Kammerlander, N. (2020). Motivation Gaps and Implementation Traps: The Paradoxical and Time-Varying Effects of Family Ownership on Firm Absorptive Capacity. *Journal of Product Innovation Management, 37*(1), 2–25. doi:10.1111/jpim.12503

Kotlar, J., Fang, H., De Massis, A., & Frattini, F. (2014b). Profitability Goals, Control Goals, and the R&D Investment Decisions of Family and Nonfamily Firms. *Journal of Product Innovation Management, 31*(6), 1128–1145. doi:10.1111/jpim.12165

Kotler, P. (2011). Reinventing marketing to manage the environmental imperative. *Journal of Marketing, 75*(4), 132–135. doi:10.1509/jmkg.75.4.132

Kotler, P., & Triasde Bes, F. (2003). *Lateral Marketing: New Techniques for Finding Breakthrough Ideas*. John Wiley & Sons.

Kotter, J. P. (1979). Managing External Dependence. *Academy of Management Review, 4*(1), 87–92. doi:10.5465/amr.1979.4289188

Kotter, J. P. (1996). *Leading Change*. Harvard Business School Press.

Kovanen, A. (2019). Competing with bitcoin - some policy considerations for issuing digitalized legal tenders. *International Journal of Financial Research*, 1-16. doi:10.5430/ijfr.v10n4p1

Kovoor-Misra, S., Zammuto, R. F., & Mitroff, I. I. (2000). Crisis preparation in organizations: Prescription versus reality. *Technological Forecasting and Social Change*, *63*(1), 43–62. doi:10.1016/S0040-1625(99)00049-9

Kozlova, N., Jacobsen, B., Golovkina, S., & Kupriyanova, M. (2019). Russian-German investment relations in the context of digital transformation of the state and financial sector of the economy. *IOP Conference Series. Materials Science and Engineering*, *497*(1), 012122. Advance online publication. doi:10.1088/1757-899X/497/1/012122

KPMG. (2019). *Regulation and supervision of fintech: Ever-expanding expectations*. KPMG.

KPMG. (2019a). *The Pulse of Fintech. Biannual global analysis of investment in fintech*. KPMG.

Krasniqi, A. (2013). Legislative changes for economic development on regional basis, the possibilities or conditions for the integration of the West Balkan Countries in the European union - Kosovo case. *Journal of Advanced Research in Law and Economics*, *4*(2), 121–127.

Kreckova, Z., Odehnalova, J., & Reardon, J. (2012). Consumer ethnocentricity within the environment of economic crisis. *The Engineering Economist*, *23*(3), 271–281.

Kreidych, I., Roshchyna, N., & Kazak, O. (2018). The application of monetary incentive policy in current economic conditions. *Baltic Journal of Economic Studies*, 129-139. doi:10.30525/2256-0742/2018-4-5-129-139

Kshetri, N. (2017). Blockchain's roles in strengthening cybersecurity and. *Telecommunications Policy*, 1–12. doi:10.1016/j.telpol.2017.09.003

Kupp, M., & Lange, K. (2012, May 20). Dearth of orders gave birth to Medneo. *Financial Times*.

La Porta, R., Lopez-De-Silanes, F., & Shleifer, A. (1999). Corporate Ownership Around the World. *The Journal of Finance*, *54*(2), 471–517. doi:10.1111/0022-1082.00115

Lacity, M. C., & Willcocks, L. P. (2001). *Global information technology outsourcing*. Wiley. doi:10.1108/17538290810857457

Lahiri, S., & Kedia, B. L. (2009). The effects of internal resources and partnership quality on firm performance: An examination of Indian BPO providers. *Journal of International Management*, *15*(2), 209–224. doi:10.1016/j.intman.2008.09.002

Lammers, T., Tomidei, L., & Regattieri, A. (2018). What Causes Companies to Transform Digitally? *Portland International Conference on Management of Engineering and Technology*, 1–8.

Landau, C., Karna, A., & Sailer, M. (2016). Business model adaptation for emerging markets: A case study of a German automobile manufacturer in India. *R & D Management*, *46*(3), 480–503. doi:10.1111/radm.12201

Larios-Hernández, G. (2017). Blockchain entrepreneurship opportunity in the practices of the unbanked. *Business Horizons*, *60*(6), 865–874. doi:10.1016/j.bushor.2017.07.012

Laudon, K., & Traver, C. (2018). *E-Commerce* (14th ed.). London: Pearson.

La, V., Patterson, P., & Styles, C. (2009). Client-perceived performance and value in professional B2B services: An international perspective. *Journal of International Business Studies*, *40*(2), 274–300. doi:10.1057/palgrave.jibs.8400406

Lavrinenko, A., & Shmatko, N. (2019). Twenty-first century skills in finance: prospects for a profound job transformation. *Foresight and STI Governance*, 42-51. doi:10.17323/2500-2597.2019.2.42.51

Le Breton-Miller, I., Miller, D., & Lester, R. H. (2011). Stewardship or agency? A social embeddedness reconciliation of conduct and performance in public family businesses. *Organization Science*, *22*(3), 704–721. doi:10.1287/orsc.1100.0541

Lebas, M., & Euske, K. (2011). A conceptual and operational delineation of performance. In A. Neely (Ed.), *Business performance measurement - Unifying theories and integrating practice* (2nd ed., pp. 125–139). Cambridge University Press.

Leitão Marques, M. M. (2003). From international trade to intra-group trade and exchanges between members of cooperation associations. The poly-local firm and the networks. *Revue Internationale de Droit Economique*, *17*(3–4), 411–441. doi:10.3917/ride.173.0411

Lengnick-Hall, C. A., & Beck, T. E. (2016). Resilience capacity and strategic agility: Prerequisites for thriving in a dynamic environment. In Ch. P. Nemeth, E. Hollnagel, & S. Dekker (Eds.), Resilience engineering perspectives, Vol. 2: Preparation and restoration (pp. 39-69). Surrey, UK: Ashgate Publishing Limited.

Lengnick-Hall, C. A., Beck, T. E., & Lengnick-Hall, M. L. (2011). Developing a capacity for organizational resilience through strategic human resource management. *Human Resource Management Review*, *21*(3), 243–255. doi:10.1016/j.hrmr.2010.07.001

Leta, F., Mello, J., Gomes, E., & Meza, L. (2005). Métodos de melhora de ordenação em DEA aplicados à avaliação estática de tornos mecânicos. *Investigação Operacional*, *25*, 229–242.

Lev, B., & Sunder, S. (1979). Methodological issues in the use of financial ratios. *Journal of Accounting and Economics*, *1*(3), 187–210. doi:10.1016/0165-4101(79)90007-7

Levstek, A., Hovelja, T., & Pucihar, A. (2018). IT Governance Mechanisms and Contingency Factors: Towards an Adaptive IT Governance Model. *Organizacija*, *51*(4), 286–310. doi:10.2478/orga-2018-0024

Liang, X., & Gao, Y. (2020). Marketing performance measurement systems and firm performance: Are marketing capabilities the missing links? *European Journal of Marketing*, *54*(4), 885–907. doi:10.1108/EJM-05-2018-0302

Lieberman, M. B., & Asaba, S. (2006). Why Do Firms Imitate Each Other. *Academy of Management Review*, *31*(2), 366–385. doi:10.5465/amr.2006.20208686

Liesch, P. W., Steen, J., Knight, G. A., & Czinkota, M. R. (2008). Internationally managing in the face of terrorism-induced uncertainty. In C. Wankel (Ed.), 21st century management. A reference handbook. Los Angeles, CA: Sage Publications. doi:10.4135/9781412954006.n20

Lim, J., Davis, A., Tang, A. R., Shannon, C. N., & Bonfield, C. M. (2019). Caregiver stress in children with craniosynostosis: A systematic literature review. *Child's Nervous System*, *35*(2), 217–225. doi:10.100700381-018-3959-7 PMID:30155782

Lim, W. M. (2016). A blueprint for sustainability marketing: Defining its conceptual boundaries for progress. *Marketing Theory*, *16*(2), 232–249. doi:10.1177/1470593115609796

Linares Navarro, E., Pla Barber, J., & Puig Blanco, F. (2009). The strategy of international outsourcing in spain: An approximation to the traditional manufacturing industries. *Investigaciones Europeas de Dirección y Economía de la Empresa*, *15*(3), 55–67. doi:10.1016/S1135-2523(12)60100-2

Li, S., Tallman, S. B., & Ferreira, M. P. (2005). Developing the eclectic paradigm as a model of global strategy: An application to the impact of the Sep. 11 terrorist attacks on MNE performance levels. *Journal of International Management*, *11*(4), 479–496. doi:10.1016/j.intman.2005.09.006

Liu, D., Chen, S., & Chou, T. (2011). Resource fit in digital transformation: Lessons learned from the CBC Bank global e-banking project. *Management Decision*, *49*(10), 1728–1742. doi:10.1108/00251741111183852

Liu, H., Jiang, X., Zhang, J., & Zhao, X. (2013). Strategic flexibility and international venturing by emerging market firms: The moderating effects of institutional and relational factors. *Journal of International Marketing*, *21*(2), 79–98. doi:10.1509/jim.12.0047

Loebbecke, C., & Picot, A. (2015). Reflections on societal and business model transformation arising from digitization and big data analytics: A research agenda. *The Journal of Strategic Information Systems*, *24*(3), 149–157. doi:10.1016/j.jsis.2015.08.002

Lopes, T. S. (2008). Markets, knowledge and trade in brands. *Global Business and Economics Review*, *10*(4), 449–466. doi:10.1504/GBER.2008.020595

López-Delgado, P., & Diéguez-Soto, J. (2015). Lone founders, types of private family businesses and firm performance. *Journal of Family Business Strategy*, *6*(2), 73–85. doi:10.1016/j.jfbs.2014.11.001

Lubatkin, M. H., Schulze, W. S., Ling, Y., & Dino, R. N. (2005). The effects of parental altruism on the governance of family-managed firms. *Journal of Organizational Behavior*, *26*(3), 313–330. doi:10.1002/job.307

Lukasevicius, A., & Lapinskaite, I. (2014). Strategy of sustainable development in investment portfolio case. *European Research Studies Journal*, *17*(4), 3–18. doi:10.35808/ersj/429

Luo, Y., & Tung, R. L. (2007). International expansion of emerging market enterprises: A springboard perspective. *Journal of International Business Studies*, *38*(4), 481–498. doi:10.1057/palgrave.jibs.8400275

Luo, Y., & Zhao, H. (2004). Corporate link and competitive strategy in multinational enterprises: A perspective from subsidiaries seeking host market penetration. *Journal of International Management*, *10*(1), 77–105. doi:10.1016/j.intman.2003.12.006

Lu, Q., & Lazonick, W. (2001). The organization of innovation in a transitional economy: Business and government in Chinese electronic publishing. *Research Policy*, *30*(1), 55–77. doi:10.1016/S0048-7333(99)00082-7

Lussier, R. N. (2017). *Management fundamentals: Concepts, applications, and skill development.* Sage Publications, Inc.

Lustgarten, S. H. (1975). The Impact of Buyer Concentration in Manufacturing Industries. *The Review of Economics and Statistics*, *57*(2), 125–132. doi:10.2307/1923993

Luttrell, W. (2009). Qualitative educational research. Abingdon-on-Thames: Routledge.

Luxury Institute. (2019). *'State of The Luxury Industry' survey shows wealthy shoppers around the world crave emotional and human connections with luxury brands.* Retrieved from https://www.globenewswire.com/news-release/2019/01/22/1703335/0/en/Luxury-Institute-s-State-Of-The-Luxury-Industry-Survey-Shows-Wealthy-Shoppers-Around-The-World-Crave-Emotional-and-Human-Connections-With-Luxury-Brands.html

MacArthur, E. (2013). *Towards a circular economy. Economic and business rationale for an accelerated transition* (Vol. 1). Ellen McArthur Foundation. Retrieved from https://www.ellenmacarthurfoundation.org/assets/downloads/publications/Ellen-MacArthur-Foundation-Towards-the-Circular-Economy-vol.1.pdf

Maddy, D. J., & Stilwell, J. A. (2005). Roads scholar tours: A marketing tool for building strong campus/community relationships. *Journal of Extension*, *43*(6), 291–295.

Magee, B. (2016). Evaluating data driven practices in sales environments: User engagement and sales results. *Journal of Decision Systems*, *25*(sup1), 622–631. doi:10.1080/12460125.2016.1192084

Magnier, L., Mugge, R., & Schoormans, J. (2019). Turning ocean garbage into products: Consumers' evaluations of products made of recycled ocean plastic. *Journal of Cleaner Production*, *215*, 84–98. doi:10.1016/j.jclepro.2018.12.246

Mahadevan, B. (2000). Business models for internet based e-commerce: An anatomy. *California Management Review*, *42*(4), 55–69. doi:10.2307/41166053

Maisam, S., & Mahsa, R. D. (2016). Positive word of mouth marketing: Explaining the roles of value congruity and brand love. *Journal of Competitiveness*, *8*(1), 19–37. doi:10.7441/joc.2016.01.02

Mallak, L. (1998). Putting organizational resilience to work. *Industrial Management (Des Plaines)*, *40*(6), 8–13.

Mangan, J., Lalwani, C., Butcher, T., & Javadpour, R. (2012). *Global logistics & supply chain management.* John Wiley & Sons.

Mangematin, V., Sapsed, J., & Schüßler, E. (2014). Disassembly and reassembly: An introduction to the Special Issue on digital technology and creative industries. *Technological Forecasting and Social Change*, *83*(1), 1–9. doi:10.1016/j.techfore.2014.01.002

Maritz, A., De Wall, A., & Verhoeven, B. (2011). Entrepreneurial and innovative marketing: A systematic review of the literature. *Innovative Marketing*, *7*(4), 28–37.

Martínez-Alonso, R., Martínez-Romero, M. J., & Rojo-Ramírez, A. A. (2018). Technological innovation and Socioemotional wealth in family firm research: Literature review and proposal of a conceptual framework. *Management Research: The Journal of the Iberoamerican Academy of Management*, *16*(3), 270–301. doi:10.1108/MRJIAM-01-2018-0803

Martínez-Alonso, R., Martínez-Romero, M. J., & Rojo-Ramírez, A. A. (2019). Examining the Impact of Innovation Forms on Sustainable Economic Performance: The Influence of Family Management. *Sustainability*, *11*(21), 6132. doi:10.3390u11216132

Martínez-Alonso, R., Martínez-Romero, M. J., & Rojo-Ramírez, A. A. (2020). The impact of technological innovation efficiency on firm growth: The moderating role of family involvement in management. *European Journal of Innovation Management*, *23*(1), 134–155. doi:10.1108/EJIM-09-2018-0210

Martínez-Romero, M. J. (2018). *Financial performance and value creation in privately held family businesses: the influence of socioemotional wealth* (Doctoral thesis). Almería.

Martínez-Romero, M. J., Martínez-Alonso, R., & Casado-Belmonte, M. P. (2020a). The influence of socioemotional wealth on firm financial performance: Evidence from small and medium privately held family businesses. *International Journal of Entrepreneurship and Small Business*, *40*(1), 7–31. doi:10.1504/IJESB.2020.106930

Martínez-Romero, M. J., Martínez-Alonso, R., Casado-Belmonte, M. P., & Diéguez-Soto, J. (2019) (Forthcoming). Family management and firm performance – The interaction effect of technological innovation efficiency. In *Intrapreneurship and Sustainable Human Capital: Digital Transformation through Dynamic Competences*. Springer.

Martínez-Romero, M. J., Martínez-Alonso, R., Rojo-Ramírez, A. A., & Diéguez-Soto, J. (2020b). Understanding Family Firm Profitability Heterogeneity. Differences Within Family Managed Firms and the Interaction Effect of Innovative Effort. In C. Camison & T. González-Cruz (Eds.), *Competitiveness, Organizational Management, and Governance in Family Firms* (pp. 305–329). IGI Global. doi:10.4018/978-1-7998-1655-3.ch013

Martínez-Romero, M. J., & Rojo-Ramírez, A. A. (2016). SEW: Looking for a definition and controversial issues. *European Journal of Family Business*, *6*(1), 1–9. doi:10.1016/j.ejfb.2015.09.001

Martínez-Romero, M. J., & Rojo-Ramírez, A. A. (2017). Socioemotional wealth's implications in the calculus of the minimum rate of return required by family businesses' owners. *Review of Managerial Science*, *11*(1), 95–118. doi:10.100711846-015-0181-9

Martin, G., & Gómez-Mejía, L. R. (2016). The relationship between socioemotional and financial wealth: Re-visiting family firm decision making. *Management Research: The Journal of the Iberoamerican Academy of Management*, *14*(3), 234–243. doi:10.1108/MRJIAM-02-2016-0638

Martins, A. (2001). *O Método dos Rácios no Sector Bancário em Portugal - Avaliação da normalidade e da proporcionalidade* (Unpublished master's thesis). Faculdade de Economia, Universidade do Algarve.

Mathews, J. A. (2006). Dragon multinationals: New players in 21st century globalization. *Asia Pacific Journal of Management*, *23*(1), 5–27. doi:10.100710490-006-6113-0

Mazzi, C. (2011). Family business and financial performance: Current state of knowledge and future research challenges. *Journal of Family Business Strategy*, *2*(3), 166–181. doi:10.1016/j.jfbs.2011.07.001

McCarthy, N., Serban, N., & Rouse, W. (2016). A multidimensional apporach to understanding the value deficiencies that drive enterprise transformation. *Journal of Enterprise Transformation*, *6*(1), 1–22. doi:10.1080/19488289.2016.1191563

McKinsey&Company. (2018). *New rules for an old game: Banks in the changing world of financial intermediation*. McKinsey Global Banking Annual Review.

McLeay, S. (1986). The ratio of means, the means of ratios and other benchmarks: An examination of characteristic financial ratios in the French Corporate Sector. *Journal of the French Finance Association*, *7*(1), 75–93.

Meadows, D. (2008). *Thinking in systems: A primer*. Chelsea Green Publishing.

Meena, S. D., Sriram, M., & Sundaram, N. (2017). Digital financial inclusion is a need of the hour: An investigation amongst bank account holders in Vellore district of Tamil Nadu, India. *International Journal of Applied Business and Economic Research*, 1-6.

Meeusen, W., & van den Broeck, J. (1977). Efficiency Estimation from Cobb-Douglas Production Functions with Composed Error. *International Economic Review*, *18*(2), 435–444. doi:10.2307/2525757

Mehar, M., Shier, C., Giambattista, A., Gong, E., Fletcher, G., Sanayhie, R., Kim, H. M., & Laskowski, M. (2019). Understanding a revolutionary and flawed grand experiment in blockchain: The DAO attack. *Journal of Cases on Information Technology*, *21*(1), 19–32. doi:10.4018/JCIT.2019010102

Melnyk, S. A., Bititci, U., Platts, K., Tobias, J., & Andersen, B. (2014). Is performance measurement and management fit for the future? *Management Accounting Research*, *25*(2), 173–186. doi:10.1016/j.mar.2013.07.007

Memili, E., & Dibrell, C. (2019). *The Palgrave Handbook of Heterogeneity among Family Firms* (E. Memili & C. Dibrell, Eds.). doi:10.1007/978-3-319-77676-7

Menon, A., & Menon, A. (1997). Enviropreneurial marketing strategy: The emergence of corporate environmentalism as market strategy. *Journal of Marketing*, *61*(1), 51–67. doi:10.1177/002224299706100105

Merriam, S. (2015). Qualitative research: A guide to design and implementation. New Jersey: John Wiley & Sons.

Meyer, M. (2011). Finding performance: the new discipline in management. In A. Neely (Ed.), *Business performance measurement - unifying theories and integrating practice* (2nd ed., pp. 113–124). Cambridge University Press.

Meza, L., & Lins, M. (2002). Review of methods for increasing discrimination in Data Envelopment Analysis. *Annals of Operations Research, 116*(1/4), 225–242. doi:10.1023/A:1021340616758

Michaud, C., & Llerena, D. (2011). Green consumer behaviour: An experimental analysis of willingness to pay for remanufactured products. *Business Strategy and the Environment, 20*(6), 408–420.

Micheler, E., & Whaley, A. (2019). Regulatory Technology: Replacing Law with Computer Code. *European Business Organization Law Review*. Advance online publication. doi:10.100740804-019-00151-1

Michiels, A., Voordeckers, W., Lybaert, N., & Steijvers, T. (2014). Dividends and family governance practices in private family firms. *Small Business Economics, 44*(2), 299–314. doi:10.100711187-014-9594-0

Miller, D. (1992). Environmental fit versus internal fit. *Organization Science, 3*(2), 159–178. doi:10.1287/orsc.3.2.159

Miller, D., & Le-Breton-Miller, I. (2005). *Managing for the Long Run: Lessons in Competitive Advantage from Great Family Businesses*. Harvard Business School Press.

Miller, S. (2008). *The turnaround kid*. HarperCollins.

Mills, J. (2014). Qualitative methodology. Thousand Oaks, CA: Sage Publications.

Min, B. S., Cashel-Cordo, P., & Rhim, J. C. (2015). Corporate leverage strategy in an emerging market. *Global Business and Finance Review, 20*(2), 35–48. doi:10.17549/gbfr.2015.20.2.35

Min, H. (2019). Blockchain technology for enhancing supply chain resilience. *Business Horizons, 62*(1), 35–45. doi:10.1016/j.bushor.2018.08.012

Minichilli, A., Corbetta, G., & MacMillan, I. C. (2010). Top management teams in family-controlled companies: "Familiness", "faultlines", and their impact on financial performance. *Journal of Management Studies, 47*(2), 205–222. doi:10.1111/j.1467-6486.2009.00888.x

Mintzberg, H. (1993). *Structure in fives: Designing effective organizations*. Prentice Hall.

Miralles-Marcelo, J. L., Miralles-Quirós, M. M., & Lisboa, I. (2014). The impact of family control on firm performance: Evidence from Portugal and Spain. *Journal of Family Business Strategy, 5*(2), 156–168. doi:10.1016/j.jfbs.2014.03.002

Mitchell, R. W., Wooliscroft, B., & Higham, J. (2010). Sustainable market orientations: A new approach to managing marketing strategy. *Journal of Macromarketing*, *30*(2), 160–170. doi:10.1177/0276146710361928

Modigliani, F., & Miller, M. (1958). The cost of capital, corporation finance and the theory of investment. *The American Economic Review*, *48*(3), 261–297.

Mok, K. H. (2005). Fostering entrepreneurship: Changing role of government and higher education governance in Hong Kong. *Research Policy*, *34*(4), 537–554. doi:10.1016/j.respol.2005.03.003

Montalbano, P., & Nenci, S. (2014). The trade competitiveness of southern emerging economies: A multidimensional approach through cluster analysis. *World Economy*, *37*(6), 783–810. doi:10.1111/twec.12195

Morash, E. A., & Lynch, D. F. (2002). Public policy and global supply chain capabilities and performance: A resource-based view. *Journal of International Marketing*, *10*(1), 25–51. doi:10.1509/jimk.10.1.25.19529

Morris, M., Schindehutte, M., & Allen, J. (2005). The entrepreneur's business model: Toward a unified perspective. *Journal of Business Research*, *58*(6), 726–735. doi:10.1016/j.jbusres.2003.11.001

Motitswe, J. (2014). The role of institute level support teams on addressing barriers to learning and provide support in schools. Are they functional? *Mediterranean Journal of Social Sciences*, *5*(8), 259–264. doi:10.5901/mjss.2014.v5n8p259

Mrvar, A., & Batagelj, V. (2016). Analysis and visualization of large networks with program package Pajek. *Complex Adaptive Systems Modeling*, *4*(1), 1–6. doi:10.118640294-016-0017-8

Muñoz-Bullón, F., & Sanchez-Bueno, M. J. (2011). Is there new evidence to show that product and international diversification influence SMEs' performance? *EuroMed Journal of Business*, *6*(1), 63–76. doi:10.1108/14502191111130316

Naz, F. (2014). Word of mouth and its impact on marketing. *International Journal of Scientific and Research Publications*, *4*(1), 1–4.

Neely, A. D., & Adams, C. (2001). Perspectives on performance: The performance prism. *Journal of Cost Management*, *15*(1), 7–15.

Neely, A., Adams, C., & Crowe, P. (2001). The performance prism in practice. *Measuring Business Excellence*, *5*(2), 6–13. doi:10.1108/13683040110385142

Neely, A., Gregory, M., & Platts, K. (2005). Performance measurement system design: A literature review and research agenda. *International Journal of Operations & Production Management*, *25*(12), 1228–1263.

Neely, A., Kennerley, M., & Adams, C. (2007). Performance measurement frameworks: a review. In A. Neely (Ed.), *Business Performance Measurement – Unifying theories and integrating practice* (2nd ed., pp. 143–162). Cambridge University Press. doi:10.1017/CBO9780511488481.010

Neilson, J. (2014). Value chains, neoliberalism and development practice: The Indonesian experience. *Review of International Political Economy*, *21*(1), 38–69. doi:10.1080/09692290.2013.809782

Neubaum, D. O., Kammerlander, N., & Brigham, K. H. (2019). Capturing Family Firm Heterogeneity: How Taxonomies and Typologies Can Help the Field Move Forward. *Family Business Review*, *32*(2), 106–130. doi:10.1177/0894486519848512

Neves, J. C., & Lourenço, S. (2009). Using data envelopment analysis to select strategies that improve the performance of hotel companies. *International Journal of Contemporary Hospitality Management*, *21*(6), 698–712. doi:10.1108/09596110910975963

Nia, A., & Zaichhkowsky, J. L. (2000). Do counterfeits devalue the ownership of luxury brands? *Journal of Product and Brand Management*, *9*(7), 485–497. doi:10.1108/10610420010351402

Niederle, P. A., & Grisa, C. (2008). Livelihoods diversification and access to actors and assets: A framework about the local development dynamics of family farm. *Cuadernos de Desarrollo Rural*, *5*(61), 41–69.

Nieto, M. J., Santamaria, L., & Fernandez, Z. (2015). Understanding the Innovation Behavior of Family Firms. *Journal of Small Business Management*, *53*(2), 382–399. doi:10.1111/jsbm.12075

Nigam, N., Mbarek, S., & Benetti, C. (2019). Can crowdfunding promote innovation in the wine industry? *International Journal of Entrepreneurship and Small Business*, *36*(3), 335–354. doi:10.1504/IJESB.2019.097741

Nudurupati, S. S., Bititci, U. S., Kumar, V., & Chan, F. T. S. (2011). State of the art literature review on performance measurement. *Computers & Industrial Engineering*, *60*(2), 279–290. doi:10.1016/j.cie.2010.11.010

O'Boyle, E. H., Pollack, J. M., & Rutherford, M. W. (2012). Exploring the relation between family involvement and firms' financial performance: A meta-analysis of main and moderator effects. *Journal of Business Venturing*, *27*(1), 1–18. doi:10.1016/j.jbusvent.2011.09.002

O'Reilly, C., & Tushman, M. (2004). The Ambidextrous Organization. *Harvard Business Review*, *82*(4), 74–81. PMID:15077368

Omelchenko, E., Andreeva, Y., Arif, E., & Polyakov, S. (2016). Where do time and all of the money go? Consumer strategies of urban youth in modern Russia. *Economia e Sociologia*, *9*(4), 176–190. doi:10.14254/2071-789X.2016/9-4/11

Organization for Economic Cooperation Development. (2013). *Municipal waste in OECD Factbook*. Paris: OECD Publishing. Retrieved from https://www.oecd-ilibrary.org/economics/oecd-factbook-2013/municipal-waste_factbook-2013-71-en

Osterwalder, A. (2004). *The business model ontology a proposition in a design science approach* (Unpublished doctoral dissertation). Faculté des Hautes Études Commerciales, Université de Lausanne, Lausanne, Switzerland.

Osterwalder, A., & Pigneur, Y. (2002). An e-business model ontology for modeling e-business [paper presentation]. *15th Bled Electronic Commerce Conference*. Retrieved from: http://citeseerx.ist.psu.edu/viewdoc/download?doi=10.1.1.16.633&rep=rep1&type=pdf

Osterwalder, A., & Pigneur, Y. (2010). Business model generation. New Jersey: John Wiley & Sons.

Ow, T., Spaid, B., Wood, C., & Ba, S. (2018). Trust and experience in online auctions. *Journal of Organizational Computing and Electronic Commerce*, *28*(4), 294–314. doi:10.1080/10919392.2018.1517478

Palácios, J. (2006). Empresas bien configuradas. In A. G. Castro (Ed.), *El perfeccionamiento de la alta dirección*. Ed. Instituto Internacional San Telmo.

Palmatier, R. W., Houston, M. B., & Hulland, J. (2018). *Review articles: purpose, process, and structure*. Academic Press.

Pangestu, M., Rahardja, S., & Ing, L. Y. (2015). Fifty years of trade policy in indonesia: New world trade, old treatments. *Bulletin of Indonesian Economic Studies*, *51*(2), 239–261. doi:10.1080/00074918.2015.1061915

Park, M., & Yoo, J. (2018). Benefits of mass customized products: Moderating role of product involvement and fashion innovativeness. *Heliyon*, *4*(2), e00537. doi:10.1016/j.heliyon.2018.e00537 PMID:29560452

Parsons, A. (2013). Using social media to reach consumers: A content analysis of official facebook pages. *Academy of Marketing Studies Journal*, *17*(2), 27–36.

Passi, L. (2018). An open banking ecosystem to survive the revised payment services directive: Connecting international banks and fintechs with the CBI globe platform. *Journal of Payments Strategy and Systems*, 335-345.

Patel-Campillo, A. (2010). Rival commodity chains: Agency and regulation in the US and colombian cut flower agro-industries. *Review of International Political Economy*, *17*(1), 75–102. doi:10.1080/09692290903296094

Patel, P. C., & Fiet, J. O. (2011). Knowledge combination and the potential advantages of family firms in searching for opportunities. *Entrepreneurship Theory and Practice*, *35*(6), 1179–1197. doi:10.1111/j.1540-6520.2011.00497.x

Patton, M. Q. (2002). *Qualitative research and evaluation methods* (3rd ed.). Sage Publishing.

Pavlínek, P. (2003). Transformation of the Czech automotive components industry through foreign direct investment. *Eurasian Geography and Economics*, *44*(3), 184–209. doi:10.2747/1538-7216.44.3.184

Pearce, J., & Robinson, R. (2014). Strategic management. New York: McGraw-Hill Education.

Pearce, R., & Papanastassiou, M. (1999). Overseas RandD and the strategic evolution of MNE: Evidence from laboratories in the UK. *Research Policy*, *28*(1), 23–41. doi:10.1016/S0048-7333(98)00104-8

Pearson, R., & Kusakabe, K. (2012). Who cares? Gender, reproduction, and care chains of Burmese migrant workers in Thailand. *Feminist Economics*, *18*(2), 149–175. doi:10.1080/13545701.2012.691206

Peattie, K. (2001). Towards sustainability: The third age of green marketing. *The Marketing Review*, *2*(2), 129–146. doi:10.1362/1469347012569869

Peattie, K., & Peattie, S. (2009). Social marketing: A pathway to consumption reduction? *Journal of Business Research*, *62*(2), 260–268. doi:10.1016/j.jbusres.2008.01.033

Peng, M. W., & Delios, A. (2006). What determines the scope of the firm over time and around the world? An Asia Pacific perspective. *Asia Pacific Journal of Management*, *23*(4), 385–405. doi:10.100710490-006-9021-4

Penrose, E. (1959). The Theory of the Growth of the Firm. Oxford University Press.

Pérez-González, F. (2006). Inherited control and firm performance. *The American Economic Review*, *96*(5), 1159–1588. doi:10.1257/aer.96.5.1559

Perianes-Rodriguez, A., Waltman, L., & Van Eck, N. J. (2016). Constructing bibliometric networks: A comparison between full and fractional counting. *Journal of Informetrics*, *10*(4), 1178–1195. doi:10.1016/j.joi.2016.10.006

Petkoski, D., Warren, D. E., & Laufer, W. S. (2009). Collective strategies in fighting corruption: Some intuitions and counter intuitions. *Journal of Business Ethics*, *88*(4), 815–822. doi:10.100710551-009-0321-8

Petrovic, O., Kittl, C., & Tekstenc, R. D. (2001). Developing business models for e-business. *Proceedings of the International Conference on Electronic Commerce.*

Pfeffer, J. (1972). Interorganizational Influence and Managerial Attitudes. *Academy of Management Journal*, *15*(3), 317–330. doi: 10.2307/254856

Piera, C., Roberto, C., Giuseppe, C., & Teresa, M. (2014). E-procurement and e-supply chain: Features and development of e-collaboration. *IERI Procedia*, *6*, 8–14. doi:10.1016/j.ieri.2014.03.003

Pinkse, J., & Kolk, A. (2012). Multinational enterprises and climate change: Exploring institutional failures and embeddedness. *Journal of International Business Studies*, *43*(3), 332–341. doi:10.1057/jibs.2011.56

Pioquinto, M. A. J. G. (2016). Management styles of women managers: Its effect on job performance as prime mover to the ASEAN economic community (AEC) integration. *Global Business and Finance Review*, *21*(2), 47–64. doi:10.17549/gbfr.2016.21.2.47

Polonsky, M. J. (2011). Transformative green marketing: Impediments and opportunities. *Journal of Business Research, 64*(12), 1311–1319. doi:10.1016/j.jbusres.2011.01.016

Porter, M. (1985). *Competitive Advantage: Creating and Sustaining Superior Performance*. Free Press.

Porter, M. (1990). *The Competitive Advantage of Nations*. Macmillan. doi:10.1007/978-1-349-11336-1

Porter, M. E. (1980). *Competitive strategy*. Free Press.

Porter, M. E. (1996). What is strategy? *Harvard Business Review, 74*(6), 61–78. PMID:10158475

Porter, M. E., & Heppelmann, J. E. (2014). How Smart, Connected Products Are Transforming Competition. *Harvard Business Review, 92*, 64–88.

Porter, M., & Kramer, M. (2011). Creating Shared Value. *Harvard Business Review, 89*(1/2), 62–77.

Prahalad, C. K., & Hamel, G. (1994). *Competing for the Future*. Harvard Business School Press.

Prakash, K., Reddy, P., & Vasaswi, K. (2019). Equity crowdfunding in Europe - A new financial phenomenon for Gen-Z entrepreneurs. *International Journal of Recent Technology and Engineering*, 1944-1948.

Prayag, G. (2009). Tourists' evaluations of destination image, satisfaction, and future behavioral intentions-the case of mauritius. *Journal of Travel & Tourism Marketing, 26*(8), 836–853. doi:10.1080/10548400903358729

Prayag, G., Spector, S., Orchiston, C., & Chowdhury, M. (2019). Psychological resilience, organizational resilience and life satisfaction in tourism firms: Insights from the Canterbury earthquakes. *Current Issues in Tourism, 1*(18), 1–18.

Procházka, D. (2018). Accounting for bitcoin and other cryptocurrencies under IFRS: A comparison and assessment of competing models. *International Journal of Digital Accounting Research*, 161-188. doi:10.4192/1577-8517-v18_7

Prothero, A., McDonagh, P., & Dobscha, S. (2010). Is green the new black? Reflections on a green commodity discourse. *Journal of Macromarketing, 30*(2), 147–159. doi:10.1177/0276146710361922

PWC. (2016). *Blurred lines: How FinTech is shaping Financial Services*. Global FinTech Report.

PWC. (2019). *Crossing the lines: How fintech is propelling FS and TMT companies out of their lanes*. Global Fintech Report.

Queirós, A., Faria, D., & Almeida, F. (2017). Strengths and limitations of qualitative and quantitative research methods. *European Journal of Education Studies, 3*(9), 369–387.

Radman, G., & Belin, A. (2017). Competitiveness in technology and innovation: How to keep on? *International Journal of Digital Technology & Economy, 2*(1), 45–56.

Rae, D., & Woodier-Harris, N. R. (2013). How does enterprise and entrepreneurship education influence postgraduate students' career intentions in the New Era economy? *Education + Training*, *55*(8–9), 926–948. doi:10.1108/ET-07-2013-0095

Rahman, M. S. (2012). Young consumer's perception on foreign made fast moving consumer goods: The role of religiosity, spirituality and animosity. *International Journal of Business and Management Science*, *5*(2), 103–118.

Ralston, D. A., Holt, D. H., Terpstra, R. H., & Kai-Cheng, Y. (2008). The impact of national culture and economic ideology on managerial work values: A study of the United States, Russia, Japan, and China. *Journal of International Business Studies*, *39*(1), 8–26. doi:10.1057/palgrave.jibs.8400330

Ranta, V., Aarikka-Stenroos, L., & Mäkinen, S. J. (2018). Creating value in the circular economy: A structured multiple-case analysis of business models. *Journal of Cleaner Production*, *201*, 988–1000. doi:10.1016/j.jclepro.2018.08.072

Rappa, M. (2004). The utility business model and the future of computing services. *IBM Systems Journal*, *43*(1), 32–42. doi:10.1147j.431.0032

Rappaport, A. (1998). *Creating Shareholder Value – a guide for managers and investors* (2nd ed.). Free Press.

Rauchs, M., Blandin, A., Bear, K., & McKeon, S. (2019). *2nd Global Enterprise Blockchain Benchmarking Study*. Cambridge Centre for Alternative Finance. doi:10.2139srn.3461765

Rau, S. B., Schneider-Siebke, V., & Gunther, C. (2019). Family Firm Values Explaining Family Firm Heterogeneity. *Family Business Review*, *32*(2), 195–215. doi:10.1177/0894486519846670

Rios-Morales, R., & Brennan, L. (2009). Ireland's innovative governmental policies promoting internationalisation. *Research in International Business and Finance*, *23*(2), 157–168. doi:10.1016/j.ribaf.2008.03.012

Rippé, C. B., Weisfeld-Spolter, S., Yurova, Y., & Sussan, F. (2015). Is there a global multichannel consumer? *International Marketing Review*, *32*(3–4), 329–349. doi:10.1108/IMR-10-2013-0225

Rivkin, J. W. (2000). Imitation of Complex Strategies. *Management Science*, *46*(6), 824–844. doi:10.1287/mnsc.46.6.824.11940

Roberts, N., Andersen, D. F., Deal, R. M., Garet, M. S., & Shaffer, W. A. (1983). *Introduction to computer simulation: The system dynamics approach*. Addison-Wesley Publishing Company.

Rojo-Ramírez, A. A., & Martínez-Romero, M. J. (2018). Required and obtained equity returns in privately held businesses: The impact of family nature—evidence before and after the global economic crisis. *Review of Managerial Science*, *12*(3), 771–801. doi:10.100711846-017-0230-7

Roland Berger. (2018, August). The digitalization race: Can financial service providers hack the pace? Third European Retail Banking Survey - Findings and recommendations. *Focus.* Retrieved September 21, 2019, from https://www.rolandberger.com/publications/publication_pdf/roland_berger_retail_banking_survey_en.pdf

Romanova, I., Grima, S., Spiter, J., & Kudinska, M. (2018). The payment services Directive II and competitiveness: The perspective of European fintech companies. *European Research Studies Journal*, 3-22.

Rosenbloom, B., & Dupuis, M. (1994). Low price, low cost, high service: A new paradigm for global retailing? *International Review of Retail, Distribution and Consumer Research*, *4*(2), 149–158. doi:10.1080/09593969400000013

Rouen, E. (2020). Rethinking measurement of pay disparity and its relation to firm performance. *The Accounting Review*, *95*(1), 343–378. doi:10.2308/accr-52440

Rutherford, M. W., Kuratko, D. F., & Holt, D. T. (2008). Examining the Link and Performance: Can the F-PEC Untangle the Family Business Theory Jungle? *Entrepreneurial Theory and Practice*, *32*(6), 1089–1110. doi:10.1111/j.1540-6520.2008.00275.x

Sahid, A., Maleh, Y., & Belaissaoui, M. (2017). An agile framework for ITS management in organizations. A case study based on DevOps. *ACM International Conference Proceeding Series.* 10.1145/3167486.3167556

Sanchez, O. (2003). Globalization as a development strategy in Latin America? *World Development*, *31*(12), 1977–1995. doi:10.1016/j.worlddev.2003.09.002

Sanders, T. I. (1998). *Strategic thinking and the new science: planning in the midst of chaos, complexity, and change.* Free Press.

Saz-Gil, I., Almaguer-Kalixto, P., & Gómez-Quintero, J. D. (2016). Social capital and networks: Analysis of the third sector in rural contexts. *CIRIEC - Espana. C.I.R.I.E.C. España*, *86*(1), 123–154.

Schaeffer, E., & Sovie, D. (2019). *Reinventing the product. How to transform your business and create value in the digital age.* Kogan Page.

Schepers, J., Voordeckers, W., Steijvers, T., & Laveren, E. (2014). The entrepreneurial orientation–performance relationship in private family firms: The moderating role of socioemotional wealth. *Small Business Economics*, *43*(1), 39–55. doi:10.100711187-013-9533-5

Schepinin, V., & Bataev, A. (2019). Digitalization of financial sphere: Challenger banks efficiency estimation. *IOP Conference Series. Materials Science and Engineering*, *497*(1), 012051. Advance online publication. doi:10.1088/1757-899X/497/1/012051

Schilke, O., Reimann, M., & Thomas, J. S. (2009). When does international marketing standardization matter to firm performance? *Journal of International Marketing*, *17*(4), 24–46. doi:10.1509/jimk.17.4.24

Schindler, S., & Demaria, F. (2019). Garbage is gold: Waste-based commodity frontiers, modes of valorization and ecological distribution conflicts. *Capitalism, Nature, Socialism*, 1–8. doi:10.1080/10455752.2019.1694553

Schizas, E., McKain, G., Zhang, B., Ganbold, A., Kumar, P., Hussain, H., & Yerolemou, N. (2019). *The Global RegTech Industry Benchmark Report*. Cambridge Center for Alternative Finance. doi:10.2139srn.3560811

Schmeisser, B. A. (2013). Systematic review of literature on offshoring of value chain activities. *Journal of International Management*, *19*(4), 390–406. doi:10.1016/j.intman.2013.03.011

Schor, J. B. (1998). *The overspent American: Why we want what we don't need*. Harper Perennial.

Schramm, W. (1971). *Notes on case studies of instructional media projects*. Institute for Communication Research. Retrieved from https://files.eric.ed.gov/fulltext/ED092145.pdf

Schueffel, P. (2016). *Taming the Beast: A Scientific Definition of Fintech*. SSRN., doi:10.2139srn.3097312

Schulze, W. S., Lubatkin, M. H., Dino, R. N., & Buchholtz, A. K. (2001). Agency relationships in family firms: Theory and Evidence. *Organization Science*, *12*(2), 99–116. doi:10.1287/orsc.12.2.99.10114

Schumpeter, J. A. (1942). *Capitalism, Socialism, and Democracy*. Harper.

Schwab, K. (2016). *Četrta industrijska revolucija*. Geneva, Switzerland: World Economic Forum.

Schwartz, P. (1996). *The art of the long view*. Doubleday.

Sciascia, S., & Mazzola, P. (2008). Family Involvement in Ownership and Management: Exploring Nonlinear Effects on Performance. *Family Business Review*, *21*(4), 331–345. doi:10.1177/08944865080210040105

Sciascia, S., Mazzola, P., & Kellermanns, F. W. (2014). Family management and profitability in private family-owned firms: Introducing generational stage and the socioemotional wealth perspective. *Journal of Family Business Strategy*, *5*(2), 131–137. doi:10.1016/j.jfbs.2014.03.001

Scott, R. (2003). *Organizations: Rational, Natural and Open Systems* (5th ed.). Prentice Hall.

Semenyuta, O., Andreeva, A., Sichev, R., & Filippov, Y. (2019). Digital technologies in lending small and medium-size enterprises in Russia. International Journal of Economics and Business Administration, 40-52.

Senge, P. (1990). *The fifth discipline*. Doubleday.

Sfenrianto, S., Wijaya, T., & Wang, G. (2018). Assessing the buyer trust and satisfaction factors in the e-marketplace. *Journal of Theoretical and Applied Electronic Commerce Research*, *13*(2), 43–57. doi:10.4067/S0718-18762018000200105

Shafer, S. M., Smith, H. J., & Linder, J. C. (2005). The power of business models. *Business Horizons*, *48*(3), 199–207. doi:10.1016/j.bushor.2004.10.014

Sharma, P., & Carney, M. (2012). Value Creation and Performance in Private Family Firms: Measurement and Methodological Issues. *Family Business Review*, *25*(3), 233–242. doi:10.1177/0894486512457295

Sheppard, E. (2002). The spaces and times of globalization: Place, scale, networks, and positionality. *Economic Geography*, *78*(3), 307–330. doi:10.2307/4140812

Shoniregun, C. A. (2004). Classification and taxonomy of TEISMEs. *ACM International Conference Proceeding Series*, *60*, 196–200. 10.1145/1052220.1052245

Sicard, M.-C. (2003). *Luxe, mensonges & marketing - Mais que font les marques de luxe?* (3rd ed.). Pearson Education.

Sigo, M., Selvam, M., Balasundram, M., Kannaiah, D., Kathiravan, C., & Vadivel, T. (2018). Big data analytics-application of artificial neural network in forecasting stock price trends in India. Academy of Accounting and Financial Studies Journal, 1-13.

Silverstein, M. J., & Fiske, N. (2003). Luxury for the masses. *Harvard Business Review*, *81*(4), 48–57. PMID:12687919

Sirmon, D. G., Arregle, J.-L., Hitt, M., & Webb, J. W. (2008). The role of family influence in firms' strategic response to competitive threat of imitation. *Entrepreneurship Theory and Practice*, *32*(6), 979–998. doi:10.1111/j.1540-6520.2008.00267.x

Sloboda, L., Dunas, N., & Limański, A. (2018). Contemporary challenges and risks of retail banking development in Ukraine. *Banks and Bank Systems*, *13*(1), 88–97. doi:10.21511/bbs.13(1).2018.09

Slowak, A. P., & Regenfelder, M. (2017). Creating value, not wasting resources: Sustainable innovation strategies. *Innovation (Abingdon)*, *30*(4), 455–475. doi:10.1080/13511610.2016.1192990

Smith, A., & Paton, R. A. (2010). An entrepreneurship toolkit for intensive skills development. *International Journal of Entrepreneurship and Small Business*, *9*(2), 162–176. doi:10.1504/IJESB.2010.030618

Smith, W. K., Binns, A., & Tushman, M. L. (2010). Complex business models: Managing strategic paradoxes simultaneously. *Long Range Planning*, *43*(2-3), 448–461. doi:10.1016/j.lrp.2009.12.003

Spyromitrosa, E., & Tsintzos, P. (2019). Credit expansion in a monetary policy game: Implications of the valuation haircut framework. Finance Research Letters, 125-129. doi:10.1016/j.frl.2018.04.012

Stähler, P. (2002). Business models as a unit of analysis for strategizing. In *Proceedings of the International Workshop on Business Models* (vol. 45, no. 7, pp. 2990-2995). University of Lausanne.

Statista Research Department. (2011). *Video game consoles: global market share 2006-2010.* Retrieved from: https://www.statista.com/statistics/272048/global-market-shares-of-game-consoles/

Staw, B. M., Sandelands, L. E., & Dutton, J. E. (1981). Threat Rigidity Effects in Organizational Behavior: A Multilevel Analysis. *Administrative Science Quarterly*, *26*(4), 501–524. doi:10.2307/2392337

Steier, L. (2001). Family Firms, Plural Forms of Governance, and the Evolving Role of Trust. *Family Business Review*, *14*(4), 353–367. doi:10.1111/j.1741-6248.2001.00353.x

Stephan, M. (2005). Diversification strategy of global media conglomerates: A comment. *Journal of Media Economics*, *18*(2), 85–103. doi:10.120715327736me1802_1

Sterman, J. (2000). *Business dynamics: Systems thinking and modeling for a complex world.* Irwin McGraw-Hill.

Stewart, H., & Jürjens, J. (2018). Data security and consumer trust in FinTech innovation in Germany. *Information and Computer Security*, 109-128. doi:10.1108/ICS-06-2017-0039

Stewart, A., & Hitt, M. A. (2012). Why Can't a Family Business Be More Like a Nonfamily Business?: Modes of Professionalization in Family Firms. *Family Business Review*, *25*(1), 58–86. doi:10.1177/0894486511421665

Stockmans, A., Lybaert, N., & Voordeckers, W. (2010). Socioemotional Wealth and Earnings Management in Private Family Firms. *Family Business Review*, *23*(3), 280–294. doi:10.1177/0894486510374457

Stoltz, P. G. (2004). Building resilience for uncertain times. *Leader to Leader*, *2004*(31), 16–20. doi:10.1002/ltl.58

Storvang, P., Haug, A., & Nguyen, B. (2019). Stimulating consumer community creation through a co-design approach. *International Journal of Market Research.*

Stoykova, B. (2009). Contemporary tendencies in development of sacred tourism in Bulgaria. *International Review on Public and Nonprofit Marketing*, *6*(1), 1–9. doi:10.100712208-008-0020-7

Stuart, T. (2009). *Waste: Uncovering the global food scandal.* Penguin Books.

Su, B., Heshmati, A., Geng, Y., & Yu, X. (2013). A review of the circular economy in China: Moving from rhetoric to implementation. *Journal of Cleaner Production*, *42*, 215–227. doi:10.1016/j.jclepro.2012.11.020

Suess-Reyes, J. (2014). Family governance - Literature review and the development of a conceptual model. *Journal of Family Business Strategy*, *5*(2), 138–155. doi:10.1016/j.jfbs.2014.02.001

Sun Tzu. (1963). The Art of War (S. B. Griffith, Trans.). Oxford University Press. (Original work: roughly 5th century BC)

Sung, H., & Lee, J. (2011). Environmental management portfolio of Korean fashion brands. *Journal of Global Fashion Marketing*, *2*(1), 44–54. doi:10.1080/20932685.2011.10593082

Sun, J., Tamaki, K., Yeh, S., & Takiuti, N. (2014). A study of global manufacturing education and training for Chinese company manager. *Industrial Engineering and Management Systems*, *13*(3), 252–257. doi:10.7232/iems.2014.13.3.252

Sutcliffe, K. M., & Vogus, T. J. (2003). Organizing for resilience. In K. S. Cameron, J. E. Dutton, & R. E. Quinn (Eds.), *Positive organizational scholarship: Foundations of a new discipline* (pp. 94–110). Berrett-Koehler.

Swenney, L. B. (2001). *When a butterfly sneezes*. Pegasus Communications.

Teece, D. (2010). Business models, business strategy and innovation. *Long Range Planning*, *43*(2-3), 172–194. doi:10.1016/j.lrp.2009.07.003

Teece, D. J. (2012). Dynamic capabilities: Routines versus entrepreneurial action. *Journal of Management Studies*, *49*(8), 1395–1401. doi:10.1111/j.1467-6486.2012.01080.x

Teece, D. J., Pisano, G., & Shuen, A. (1997). Dynamic capabilities and strategic management. *Strategic Management Journal*, *18*(7), 509–533. doi:10.1002/(SICI)1097-0266(199708)18:7<509::AID-SMJ882>3.0.CO;2-Z

Tezza, R., Bornia, A. C., & Vey, I. H. (2010). Sistemas de medição de desempenho: Uma revisão e classificação da literatura. *Gestão & Produção*, *17*(1), 75–93. doi:10.1590/S0104-530X2010000100007

Thanassoulis, E. (2003). *Introduction to the Theory and Application of Data Envelopment Analysis: a foundation text with integrated software* (2nd ed.). Kluwer Academic Publishers.

Thomas, C. (2005). Poverty, development, and hunger. In J. Baylis, S. Smith, & P. Owens (Eds.), *The Globalization of World Politics: An Introduction to International Relations* (3rd ed., pp. 559–581). Oxford University Press.

Tikkinen-Piri, C., Rohunen, A., & Markkula, J. (2018). EU general data protection regulation: Changes and implications for personal data collecting companies. *Computer Law & Security Review*, *34*(1), 134–153. doi:10.1016/j.clsr.2017.05.015

Timmers, P. (1998). Business models for electronic markets. *Electronic Markets*, *8*(2), 3–8. doi:10.1080/10196789800000016

Tiwary, A. (2016). Know online advertising: All information about online advertising at one place. Bloomington: Partridge India.

Tokatli, N. (2013). Doing a Gucci: The transformation of an Italian fashion firm into a global powerhouse in a 'Los Angeles-izing' World. *Journal of Economic Geography*, *13*(2), 239–255. doi:10.1093/jeg/lbs050

Trigueiros, D. (1995). Accounting identities and the distribution of ratios. *The British Accounting Review, 27*(2), 109–126. doi:10.1006/bare.1994.0006

Trigueiros, D. (1997). Non-proportionality in ratios: An alternative approach. *The British Accounting Review, 29*(3), 213–230. doi:10.1006/bare.1996.0042

Truong, Y., McColl, R., & Kitchen, P. J. (2008). New luxury brand positioning and the emergence of masstige brands. *Journal of Brand Management, 16*(5/6), 375–382.

Trusov, M., Bucklin, R., & Pauwels, K. (2009). Effects of word-of-mouth versus traditional marketing: Findings from an internet social networking site. *Journal of Marketing, 73*(5), 90–102. doi:10.1509/jmkg.73.5.90

Tsai, S.-P. (2005). Integrated marketing as management of holistic consumer experience. *Business Horizons, 48*(5), 431–441. doi:10.1016/j.bushor.2005.02.005

Tully, S., & Caplin, J. (2008). Look who pays for the bailout. Meet the Henrys (high earners, not rich yet). *Fortune International, 158*(8), 50.

Turban, E., Outland, J., King, D., Lee, J. K., Liang, T.-P., & Turban, D. C. (2018). Electronic commerce 2018: A managerial and social networks perspective (9th ed.). New York: Springer. doi:10.1007/978-3-319-58715-8

Tushman, M., & O'Reilly, C. A. (1997). *Winning through innovation: A practical guide to leading organizational change and renewal.* Harvard Business School Press. doi:10.1108/eb054591

Tussyadiah, I. P., & Pesonen, J. (2018). Drivers and barriers of peer-to-peer accommodation stay–an exploratory study with American and Finnish travellers. *Current Issues in Tourism, 21*(6), 703–720. doi:10.1080/13683500.2016.1141180

Tybout, A. M., & Calkins, T. (Eds.). (2019). *Kellogg on Branding in a Hyper-Connected World.* John Wiley & Sons.

U.S. Department of Commerce. (2010). *Measuring Green Economy Report.* Retrieved from https://www.commerce.gov/news/reports/2010/04/measuring-green-economy

Underwood, J. (2002). *Complexity and paradox.* Capstone.

United Nations Environment Programme (UNEP), Division of Technology, Industry and Economics, United Nations Global Compact (UNGC), & Utopies. (2005). *Talk the walk: Advancing sustainable lifestyles through marketing and communications.* Retrieved form http://wedocs.unep.org/handle/20.500.11822/8399

University of Cambridge. (2018). *The 3rd Asia Pacific Region Alternative Finance Industry Report.* Cambridge Centre for Alternative Finance.

University of Cambridge. (2018). *The Future of Finance is Emerging: New Hubs, New Landscapes.* Global Fintech Hub Report.

University of Cambridge. (2018a). *Reaching New Heights*. The 3rd Americas Alternative Finance Industry Report.

Urbinati, A., Franzo, S., De Massis, A., & Frattini. (2017). Innovation in Family Firms: A Review of Prior Studies and a Framework for Future Research. In A. Brem & E. Viardot (Eds.), *Revolution of Innovation Management* (pp. 213–246). London: Palgrave Macmillan. doi:10.1057/978-1-349-95123-9_8

Urbinati, A., Chiaroni, D., & Chiesa, V. (2017). Towards a new taxonomy of circular economy business models. *Journal of Cleaner Production*, *168*, 487–498. doi:10.1016/j.jclepro.2017.09.047

Valdani, E., & Arbore, A. (2013). *Competitive Strategies: Managing the Present*. Imagining the Future. doi:10.1057/9780230354586

Valero, A., & Figueroa, E. T. (2011). *La empresa de negócios y la alta dirección: Procedimientos politicos de gobierno*. Eunsa.

Valero, A., & Lucas, J. L. (1991). *Política de empresa: El gobierno de la empresa de negocios*. Eunsa.

Van Alstyne, M. W., Parker, G. G., & Choudary, S. P. (2016). Pipelines, Platforms, and the New Rules of Strategy. *Harvard Business Review*, *94*(4), 54–62.

Van Dam, Y. K., & Apeldoorn, P. A. (1996). Sustainable marketing. *Journal of Macromarketing*, *6*(2), 45–56. doi:10.1177/027614679601600204

van Eck, N. J., & Waltman, L. (2010). Software survey: VOSviewer, a computer program for bibliometric mapping. *Scientometrics*, *84*(2), 523–538. doi:10.100711192-009-0146-3 PMID:20585380

Vandekerkhof, P., Steijvers, T., Hendriks, W., & Voordeckers, W. (2018). Socio-Emotional Wealth Separation and Decision-Making Quality in Family Firm TMTs: The Moderating Role of Psychological Safety. *Journal of Management Studies*, *55*(4), 648–676. doi:10.1111/joms.12277

Vandermerwe, S. (1989). Strategies for a pan European market. *Long Range Planning*, *22*(3), 45–53. doi:10.1016/0024-6301(89)90006-X

Vandermerwe, S. (1997). Increasing returns: Competing for customers in the global market. *Journal of World Business*, *32*(4), 333–350. doi:10.1016/S1090-9516(97)90016-X

Varey, R. J. (2011). A sustainable society logic for marketing. *Social Business*, *1*(1), 69–83. doi:10.1362/204440811X570563

Veebel, V., & Kulu, L. (2014). Against the political expectations and theoretical models: How to implement austerity and not to lose political power. *Baltic Journal of Economics*, *14*(1–2), 2–16. doi:10.1080/1406099X.2014.991140

Veilleux, S., Haskell, N., & Pons, F. (2012). Going global: How smaller enterprises benefit from strategic alliances. *The Journal of Business Strategy*, *33*(5), 22–31. doi:10.1108/02756661211282768

Verhoef, P. C., & Bijmolt, T. H. A. (2019). Marketing perspectives on digital business models: A framework and overview of the special issue. *International Journal of Research in Marketing*, *36*(3), 341–349. doi:10.1016/j.ijresmar.2019.08.001

Vico, G. (1976). *La Scienza Nuova e altri scritti*. UTET. (Original work: 1725, 1730, 1744)

Villalonga, B., & Amit, R. (2006). How do family ownership, control and management affect firm value? *Journal of Financial Economics*, *80*(2), 385–417. doi:10.1016/j.jfineco.2004.12.005

Vives, X. (2017). *The Impact of Fintech on Banking*. European Economy.

Voelk, T. (2018, Mar. 6). Porsche Positions Itself Against Tesla, on the Road and Beside It. *The New York Times*.

Voorveld, H., van Noort, G., Muntinga, D., & Bronner, F. (2018). Engagement with social media and social media advertising: The differentiating role of platform type. *Journal of Advertising*, *47*(1), 38–54. doi:10.1080/00913367.2017.1405754

Wallin, J., Parida, V., & Isaksson, O. (2015). Understanding product-service system innovation capabilities development for manufacturing companies. *Journal of Manufacturing Technology Management*, *26*(5), 763–787. doi:10.1108/JMTM-05-2013-0055

Warren, K. (2012). *The trouble with strategy: The brutal reality of why business strategy doesn't work and what to do about it*. Createspace Independent Publishing Platform.

Waters, R. (2007). Microsoft raises ante in price wars. *Financial Times*. Retrieved from: https://amp.ft.com/content/caf2b046-450f-11dc-82f5-0000779fd2ac

Weick, K. E. (1993). The collapse of sensemaking in organizations. *Administrative Science Quarterly*, *38*(4), 628–652. doi:10.2307/2393339

Weick, K. E., & Sutcliffe, K. M. (2001). *Managing the unexpected: Assuring high performance in an age of complexity*. Jossey-Bass.

Weill, P., & Vitale, M. R. (2001). *Place to space: migrating to e-business models*. Boston: Harvard Business Press.

West, J. (2011). The OECD and Asia: Worlds apart in today's globalization? *Revista de Economía Mundial*, *28*, 67–92.

Whittington, G. (1980). Some basic properties of accounting ratios. *Journal of Business Finance & Accounting*, *7*(2), 219–232. doi:10.1111/j.1468-5957.1980.tb00738.x

Wildemann, H. (2004). *Sanierungsstrategien*. TCW Transfer-Centrum.

Wildemann, H. (2017). *Neue Geschaftsmodelle in der Industrie 4.0*. TCW Transfer-Centrum.

Williams, C., & Martinez, C. A. (2012). Government effectiveness, the global financial crisis, and multinational enterprise internationalization. *Journal of International Marketing*, *20*(3), 65–78. doi:10.1509/jim.12.0078

Wirtz, B. W. (2019). *Digital business models*. Springer Nature. doi:10.1007/978-3-030-13005-3

Wolf, C., & Redford, D. (2019). *Fostering entrepreneurship for innovation in African Banks' subsidiaries*. Africa Journal of Management. doi:10.1080/23322373.2019.1649558

Woodruff, R. B. (1997). Customer value: The next source for competitive advantage. *Journal of the Academy of Marketing Science, 25*(2), 139–153. doi:10.1007/BF02894350

Woods, N. (2010). Global Governance after the financial crisis: A new multilateralism or the last gasp of the great powers? *Global Policy, 1*(1), 51–63. doi:10.1111/j.1758-5899.2009.0013.x

World Commission on Environment and Development. (1987). *Our common future*. Oxford University Press.

World Trade Organization (WTO). (2018). *World Trade statistical review 2018*. WTO.

Woudstra, U., Berghout, E., Tan, C.-W., Eekeren, P. v., & Dedene, G. (2017). *Resource Complementarity and IT Economies of Scale: Mechanisms and Empirical Evidence*. doi:10.1080/10580530.2017.1288527

Xu, D., & Meyer, K. E. (2013). Linking theory and context: 'Strategy research in emerging economies' after Wright et al. (2005). *Journal of Management Studies, 50*(7), 1322-1346.

Yasav, S. (2015). The impact of digital technology on consumer purchase behavior. *Journal of Financial Perspectives, 3*(3), 1–13.

Yeniaras, V., Sener, P., & Unver, S. (2017). Is market learning the missing link between family involvement – firm performance relationship? A resource-based perspective. *The International Entrepreneurship and Management Journal, 13*(2), 575–604. doi:10.100711365-016-0417-4

Yin, R. K. (2009). Case study research: Design and methods (4th ed.). Thousand Oaks, CA: Sage Publications.

Yin, R. K. (2009). *Case study research: Design and Methods* (4th ed.). Sage Publications.

Yin, R. K. (2018). *Case study research and applications: Design and methods* (6th ed.). Sage Publications.

Yoon, K., & Jun, J. (2019). Liability And Antifraud Investment In Fintech Retail Payment Services. *Contemporary Economic Policy, 191-194*. Advance online publication. doi:10.1111/coep.12281

Young, D., & O'Byrne, S. (2001). *EVA and Value-Based Management: a practical guide to implementation*. Mc-Graw Hill.

Yudhya, T. B. (2016). Analysis of green marketing strategies on consumer purchase intention studies on The Body Shop Bandung Indonesia. *International Journal of Applied Business and Economic Research, 14*(2), 1027–1040.

Yu, T. F.-L. (2000). Hong Kong's entrepreneurship: Behaviours and determinants. *Entrepreneurship and Regional Development, 12*(3), 179–194. doi:10.1080/089856200413455

Zaheer, S., & Manrakhan, S. (2001). Concentration and dispersion in global industries: Remote electronic access and the location of economic activities. *Journal of International Business Studies*, *32*(4), 667–686. doi:10.1057/palgrave.jibs.8490989

Zalan, T., & Toufaily, E. (2017). The promise of fintech in emerging markets: Not as disruptive. *Contemporary Economics*, 415-430. doi:10.5709/ce.1897-9254.253

Zattoni, A., Gnan, L., & Huse, M. (2015). Does Family Involvement Influence Firm Performance? Exploring the Mediating Effects of Board Processes and Tasks. *Journal of Management*, *41*(4), 1214–1243. doi:10.1177/0149206312463936

Zellweger, T. M., Eddleston, K. A., & Kellermanns, F. W. (2010). Exploring the concept of familiness: Introducing family firm identity. *Journal of Family Business Strategy*, *1*(1), 54–63. doi:10.1016/j.jfbs.2009.12.003

Zellweger, T. M., Nason, R. S., Nordqvist, M., & Brush, C. G. (2013). Why do family firms strive for nonfinancial goals? An organizational identity perspective. *Entrepreneurship Theory and Practice*, *37*(2), 229–248. doi:10.1111/j.1540-6520.2011.00466.x

Ziegler, T., Shneor, R., Wenzlaff, K., Odorović, A., Johanson, D., Hao, R., & Ryll, L. (2019). Shifting Paradigms. The 4th European Alternative Finance Benchmarking Report.

Zilber, S., Silveira, F., Carvalho, L., & Imbrizi, A. (2016). Crowd funding as an alternative for new ventures funding in emerging countries. *International Business Management*, 575-584. doi:10.3923/ibm.2016.575.584

Zimmermann, A., Schmidt, R., Sandkuhl, K., Wißotzki, M., Jugel, D., & Möhring, M. (2015). Digital enterprise architecture-transformation for the internet of things. *Proceedings of the 2015 IEEE 19th International Enterprise Distributed Object Computing Conference Workshops and Demonstrations*, 130–138. 10.1109/EDOCW.2015.16

Zoroja, J., & Bach, M. (2016). Editorial: Impact of information and communication technology to the competitiveness of European countries - Cluster Analysis Approach. *Journal of Theoretical and Applied Electronic Commerce Research*, *11*(1), 1–10. doi:10.4067/S0718-18762016000100001

Zott, C., & Amit, R. (2010). Business model design: An activity system perspective. *Long Range Planning*, *43*(2-3), 216–226. doi:10.1016/j.lrp.2009.07.004

About the Contributors

Georgette Andraz is a senior lecturer of strategic management and entrepreneurship at the School of Management, Hospitality and Tourism of the University of the Algarve. She holds a Master in Economic and Business Administration Sciences from the Faculty of Economics, University of the Algarve and a PhD in Management Sciences from the University of Évora. Her main research interest include Strategy and Performance and Entrepreneurship. She is a member of CEFAGE - Research Center of the University of Évora, has authored, and coauthored various national and international scientific publications. Orcid 0000-0001-5553-7620

Helder M. Brito Carrasqueira is a professor at the University of the Algarve - School of Management, Hospitality and Tourism (ESGHT), in the Department of Economics, where he teaches Portuguese and European Economics, International Economics, International Marketing, and Internationalization of Tourism Companies. He holds a PhD in Economics (FEUAlg) and a Master in International Economics (ISEG/UL). He was Dean of ESGHT and President of the Scientific Council, as well as the Head of the Evaluation and Quality Office at the University of the Algarve. He has authored and co-authored twenty book chapters, fourteen indexed journal articles, and he is a member of the scientific board of three journals. He was a member of the scientific committee of eleven international conferences and has participated in five projects (two of which as project coordinator). Helder M. Brito Carrasqueira has supervised twenty-eight postgraduate and undergraduate dissertations, has made eighteen conference presentations and has been an invited speaker in more than thirty academic events. He is a CiTUR researcher (ORCID-0000-0001-6907-6175).

Rosaria Pereira has a PhD in tourism from the Faculty of Economics of the University of the Algarve and is Associate Professor at the School of Management, Hospitality and Tourism of the University of Algarve. She is a member of the Research Centre for Tourism, Sustainability and Well-being (CinTurs). Her research interests are related to tourism, tourist marketing, branding, and destinations branding and personality. She has published articles in international journals such as International Journal of Culture, Tourism and Hospitality Research, Journal of Destinations Marketing and Management and Journal of Quality Assurance in Tourism and Hospitality, among others, as well as some book chapters. She also belongs to the Scientific Commission of the journal Tourism & Management Studies, participates in international conferences in the area of tourist and tourism marketing and has been invited several times to participate in scientific committees of international conferences on tourism (ORCID: 0000-0002-2335-5694).

Rita Baleiro holds a PhD and a Masters in English and Portuguese Studies from the New University of Lisbon, and a first degree in Modern Languages and Literatures – Portuguese and English – also from the New University of Lisbon. She is a senior lecturer of English for Specific Purposes and Portuguese Language and Culture at the School of Management, Hospitality and Tourism of the University of the Algarve. She is a member of CiTUR (Centre for Research, Development and Innovation in Tourism), and she collaborates with Atlas das Paisagens Literárias de Portugal Continental and with CETAPS (Centre for English, Translations and Anglo-Portuguese Studies), based at Universidade Nova de Lisboa. She has been co-chief-editor of Dos Algarves: A Multidisciplinary e-Journal since 2007. Her research interests include literature studies, academic writing and the intersections between literature and tourism. She has authored and co-authored various national and international scientific publications (ORCID 0000-0002-3188-5150).

* * *

Pedro B. Água has over 26 years of experience across several industries and technological domains, from subsea Oil and Gas business to naval systems. Pedro worked closely with multicultural and heterogeneous groups in a diverse array of organizational settings. Currently, he lectures at the Portuguesa Naval Academy and is the Navy Research Center special advisor for Innovation. He is also a Senior Teaching Fellow at AESE Business School, where he teaches Business Policy. He is recognized for his research on Business Policy and Systems Thinking. His research interests cover Innovation Models, Defense Industrial Strategy, Business Policy, Corporate Governance, Systems Thinking and Decision Making. Pedro holds a Ph.D. in Engineering and Management from the Lisbon University and an Executive MBA by IESE Business School/AESE Business School.

Fernando Luís Almeida has a PhD in Computer Science Engineering from Faculty of Engineering of University of Porto (FEUP). He also holds an MSc in Innovation and Entrepreneurship and an MSc in Informatics Engineering from FEUP. He has around 10 years of teaching experience at higher education levels in the field of computer science and management. He has also worked for 15 years in several positions as software engineer and project manager for large organizations and research centers like Critical Software, CICA/SEF, INESC TEC and ISR Porto. His current research areas include innovation policies, entrepreneurship, software development and decision support systems.

Noelia Araújo-Vila is PhD in Tourism Management and Planning and Bachelor in Business Administration and Management. Since 2007 she collaborates in the coordination tasks of the University Master in Tourism Management and Planning and teaches as professor in the Departments of Business Organization and Marketing and Financial Economics and Accounting (University of Vigo). She participates in various research projects linked to the tourism and business sector. She is a member of the research group of the University of Vigo Emitur (Marketing and Tourism). She holds a Master in Management and Management of SMEs with a prize for the best business project.

Alessandro Arbore is Professor of Practice and Faculty Deputy of Marketing and Sales at SDA Bocconi School of Management. Former Director of the Executive Master in Marketing and Sales, author of several publications, his research activities focus on market strategies, innovation, and customer value management. He earned a Degree in Business Administration from Bocconi University, Ph.D. and Master from the George Washington University. He was Visiting at the Wharton Business School, University of Pennsylvania. His wide professional activity ranges from B2B to B2C companies.

Arthur Araújo is a PhD in tourism studies by the University of Aveiro and currently teaches at Lusófona do Porto University. He has published works mainly in film tourism, slum tourists' motivations and destination imagery. Recent publications have appeared in Annals of Tourism Research, Journal of Travel and Tourism Marketing and British Food Journal. In the industry, Arthur has experiences in Brazil and Spain, in areas such as tourism accessibility, inbound tourism statistics and educational tourism.

Nuno Baptista received his MsC in International Management from the University of Liverpool, England. He has a solid professional background in Financial Management having assumed the position of Financial Director in several companies in the hospitality and food distribution businesses. He is a invited Professor of Economics at Escola Superior de Comunicação Social from the Instituto Politécnico de Lisboa, Portugal.

Ana Brochado is a professor at the ISCTE-IUL and a researcher at DINAMIA'CET. She served as the Vice Dean for administrative affairs and Vice Dean for faculty for five years. She worked for more than one decade as Senior Economist for the Portuguese Competition Authority and the Securities Commission. She joined the Strategic Board of Compete2020. She has a Bachelor of Science in Economics, a Master of Science in Quantitative Methods and a Doctor of Management. Her main research interest is Fintech. She has authored or co-authored over 60 publications in top international journals. Her research received over 1100 citations.

Cristina Calvo-Porral is PhD Professor at the Business Department at the University of La Coruña (Spain). She is graduated in Management and Business Administration in ICADE (Comillas Pontificial University, Madrid) and also graduated in Marketing and Market Research in the same centre. She has numerous academic publications on the Marketing field.

José Campino is a PhD in Management applicant at ISCTE-IUL Business School with a career in banking. His research interests are on strategy, banking, fintech and related fields. He has a Bachelor of Science in Political Science and International Relations by Nova University of Lisbon and a Master of Science in International Management by ISCTE-IUL Business School. Professionally, he performed several roles in an international bank and also has experience in consulting.

Julio Diéguez-Soto is an Associate Professor of Finance and Accounting at the University of Málaga (Spain). He is the Director of the Finance and Accounting Department and the Academic Director of Firm Feasibility Chair. His main research interests include Performance, Capital Structure, Innovation, Professionalization and MCS in Family Firms. He has published his latest research findings in International journals such as Small Business Economics, Journal of Small Business Management, Family Business Review, Journal of Family Business Strategy, Business Research Quarterly, Review of Managerial Science, Canadian Journal of Administrative Sciences, Innovation: Organization and Management, Journal of Scientific and Industrial Research, and Review of Business Management, among others.

Drago Dubrovski took his doctorate degree in Economics, from the Business Faculty in Maribor (Slovenia), field International Business. He is a part-time Associate Professor at Faculty of Management Koper and International School for Social and Business Studies Celje and managing director in a private management consulting company, which focuses on restructuring projects and crisis management. He worked also as sales manager in international industrial company and was also a crisis manager in several Slovenian companies. He is verified expert of Slovene

Economists' Association and judicial expert; he is a member of several Supervisory Boards and has a licence for managing insolvency proceedings. His research interests are in crisis management and corporate renewal, strategic alliances, mergers and acquisitions, and international business. He gives regular lectures at several Slovene faculties. He is author of 8 books and 80 articles from the above-mentioned fields.

João Ferreira (PhD in Management) is Associate Professor at University of Beira Interior and Coordinator of research Unit NECE. He is author of some books and he published in several international journals. Research interests are: Stategy and Entrepreneurship.

Ronnie Figueiredo is Assistant Professor at the Universidade Europeia, Lisbon, Portugal. He holds a PhD in Management from the Federal Fluminense University (UFF), Brazil and Post-Doc in Management & Economics from the University of Beira Interior (UBI), Portugal. Currently, he is the researcher affiliated at Research Unit for Business Sciences (NECE/UBI/FCT). He´s the author of Spinner Innovation Model (SIM), published in indexed international journals. He has edited or co-edited books on strategic management, knowledge management & innovation management and published papers in international journals, including Journal of the Knowledge Economy, Business Process Management Journal, International Journal of Social Ecology and Sustainable Development, Journal of Family Business Management and Journal of Global Information Management. He is an expert in qualitative research developing studies focus on SMEs (Small to Medium Enterprises) applying the Spinner Innovation Model.

Rubén Martínez-Alonso is a Junior Researcher at the University of Almería, Spain. He collaborates with the Santander Family Business Chair at this University. His research interests include family firm research focusing on technological innovation and emotional considerations. He has published his latest research findings in international journals such as European Journal of Innovation Management, International Journal of Entrepreneurship and Small Business and, Management Research: Journal of the Iberoamerican Academy of Management.

María J. Martínez-Romero is an Assistant Professor of Accounting and Finance in the Economics and Business Department at the University of Almería, Spain. She collaborates with the Santander Family Business Chair at this University. Her primary research interests include family firm research focusing on emotional, innovative, finance and corporate governance aspects. She has published her latest research findings in international journals such as Small Business Economics, Review of Managerial Science, European Journal of Innovation Management, International

Journal of Entrepreneurship and Small Business, Management Research: Journal of the Iberoamerican Academy of Management.

Ana Martins is a lecturer in the School of Management, Hospitality and Tourism at the University of the Algarve, where she teaches, since 1996, curricular units in the area of Corporate Finance. She received her PhD in Business and Economics Science - specialty in Management from the Faculty of Economics of the University of the Algarve in 2013. She has participated as author and moderator in several national and international scientific meetings and has scientific publications at the national level in the area of Corporate Finance. Ana Martins has been a reviewer of scientific articles in this area. Her current research interests include business valuation, performance and DEA (data envelopment analysis) applied to the banking industry.

Fernanda Matias is professor in the School of Management, Hospitality and Tourism at the University of the Algarve, where she teaches, since 1988, curricular units in the area of Corporate Finance. She received her PhD in Finance from ISCTE – University Institute of Lisbon in 2001. She was vice-rector of the University of Algarve for eight years. She has participated as author and moderator in several national and international scientific meetings and has scientific publications in the area of Corporate Finance. Fernanda is the co-author of two books, Corporate Finance and Financial Mathematics. Her research interests are in the areas of corporate governance, strategy, financial management and entrepreneurship.

Nelson Matos is a marketing Professor at School of Hospitality, Management and Tourism, where he teaches several courses in the field of Marketing and Tourism. He holds a PhD in Tourism from UALG and is a member of CINTURS. He has performed several management functions related to marketing in the hotel and service industry and has participated in several business projects, as a consultant and marketing trainer. His main research interests are in the areas of Marketing (namely brands and consumer behavior), tourism (namely destinations and tourist experience), and Management (Strategy). He is the author of publications in Journals, books and other scientific publications.

André Vilares Morgado is currently Associate Professor of Marketing at AESE Business School. He has authored several prize winning case studies, while continuing his research studies in the field of industrial marketing and regular work with companies in sales, business development and training projects. André is a guest speaker at events and has published in prestigious publications and journals featuring various marketing subjects. He combines his teaching profile with an extensive professional and business background of more than 10 years dedicated to the fast pace telecommunications industry. During his professional life André had the chance to occupy highly visible roles such as Strategic Marketing Manager working on a global scale at Nokia Siemens Networks. André holds a Ph.D in Management awarded by the University of Lisbon, and an Executive MBA by IESE Business School/AESE Business School. He also holds a B.Sc in Marketing Management by IPAM - The Marketing School. He is a recognized active influencer by bridging and maintaining regular contact between the Industry and academia. He has done several consulting, conferences or "in company" programs for companies like: everis, Pfizer, BASF, Colt Telecom, Axians, among others. He is also a fellow member of the Industrial Marketing and Purchasing Group and a 'endorser' of the Community for Responsible Research in Business & Management.

Célia M. Q. Ramos graduated in Computer Engineering from the University of Coimbra, obtained her Master in Electrical and Computers Engineering from the Higher Technical Institute, Lisbon University, and the PhD in Econometrics in the University of the Algarve (UALG), Faculty of Economics, Portugal. She is Adjunct Professor at School for Management, Hospitality and Tourism, also in the UALG, where she lectures computer science. Areas of research and special interest include conception and development of information systems, tourism information systems, big data, etourism, econometric modeling and panel-data models. Célia Ramos has published in the fields of information systems and tourism, namely, she has authored a book, book chapters, conference papers and journal articles. At the level of applied research, she has participated in several funded projects.

Sandra Rebelo is a lecturer in the School of Management, Hospitality and Tourism at the University of the Algarve, where she teaches, since 1997, curricular units in the area of Corporate Finance. She received her PhD in Management - specialty in Finance and Accounting from the Faculty of Economics of the University of the Algarve in 2017 and is a member of CITUR Algarve. She has scientific publications in the area of Corporate Finance namely, she has authored a book, book chapters, conference papers and journal articles. Her current research interests include capital structure, performance and DEA (data envelopment analysis) applied to the hotel industry (ORCID 0000-0002-8943-9794).

Alfonso A. Rojo-Ramírez is a Full Professor of Accounting and Finance in the Department of Economics and Business at the University of Almería, Spain. He is also the director of the Santander Family Business Chair at this university since 2009. He headed the Department of Business Management and is a member of the Valuation Committee of the Spanish Association of Accounting and Business Administration. He has published his latest research findings in international journals such as Small Business Economics, Family Business Review, Review of Managerial Science, European Journal of Innovation Management, and Management Research: Journal of the Iberoamerican Academy of Management.

João Roque has a BSc. in Computer Science for Management from Higher Polytechnic Institute of Gaya (ISPGaya). He works in the computer industry field, where he is responsible for the modeling and development of new applications for Web platforms. His current research areas include software engineering, human interaction and Web applications.

Álvaro Rosa, assistant professor at ISCTE-IUL and researcher at BRU-ISCTE. His research interests are strategy, data science and related fields.

Miguel Ángel Sánchez Jiménez is a Professor and Researcher at the Department of Marketing and Communication, University of Cádiz (Spain). PhD in Marketing and Communication. Coordinator of the module of tourism marketing strategies in the Master's Degree Program in Tourism at the University of Cádiz and member of the Research Institute for Sustainable Social Development (INDESS). Research activity oriented to tourism and new digital technologies in marketing and communication. Author of several publications in indexed journals, books and participation in research congresses.

José Duarte Santos received his PhD in Management from the University of Vigo, Spain. He is also Master of Marketing and has a Bachelor degree in Business Sciences. Additionally, he obtained the title Specialist in Marketing and Advertising in accordance with Portuguese Decree-Law No. 206/August 31, 2009. Between 1987 and 2002, he has played various roles in sales, marketing, and management of companies in the information technologies sector. From 2003, he has performed functions of management and marketing consultant. Since 1999, he has been a professor in higher education in Portugal in the field of management and marketing. He is currently a professor at the Instituto Superior Politécnico Gaya (ISPGaya) and at the Instituto Superior de Contabilidade e Administração do Porto (ISCAP). He is also research at the Centre for Organisational and Social Studies of Polytechnic of Porto (CEOS.PP). His current research areas include, social media marketing, social customer relationship management and social selling.

Jorge Simões is a teacher at a Polytechnic Institute, a higher learning institution, in Portugal. He has a PhD on Gamification of Education. He is currently performing research on e-learning, social networks, game-based learning and gamification.

Raquel Reis Soares is Dean of the School of Business and Social Sciences and Assistant Professor at the Universidade Europeia, Lisbon, Portugal. She holds a PhD in Business and Management Studies - specialization in Marketing and Strategy from the Faculty of Economics, University of Porto, Portugal. Currently, she is integrated researcher at UNIDCOM-IADE, Design and Communication Research Unit, collaborator researcher at Cinturs – Research Centre for Tourism, Sustainability and Well-being and researcher at Universidade Europeia, Business and Law Research Unit. She integrates different editorial and scientific committees of international journals and conferences and published in indexed international journals. Her research interests include services marketing, social media marketing, consumer behavior and business models.

Diego R. Toubes is PhD in Economic and Business Sciences. He is an Associate professor of Strategic Management in the Faculty of Administration and Tourism of Ourense, at the University de Vigo (Spain). He is a member of the research group Emitur of the University of Vigo. His research interests include risk management and organizational resilience. He has published academic papers and collaborations in the fields of entrepreneurship, risk perception and crisis communication in tourism.

Index

V

W

www.ingramcontent.com/pod-product-compliance
Lightning Source LLC
LaVergne TN
LVHW081346300926
849161LV00008B/2078
* 9 7 8 1 7 9 9 8 4 5 5 2 2 *